Surprise!

You may be reading the wrong way!

It's true: In keeping with the original Japanese comic format, this book reads from right to left—so action, sound effects and word balloons are completely reversed. This preserves the orientation of the original artwork—plus, it's fun! Check out the diagram shown here to get the hang of things, and then turn to the other side of the book to get started!

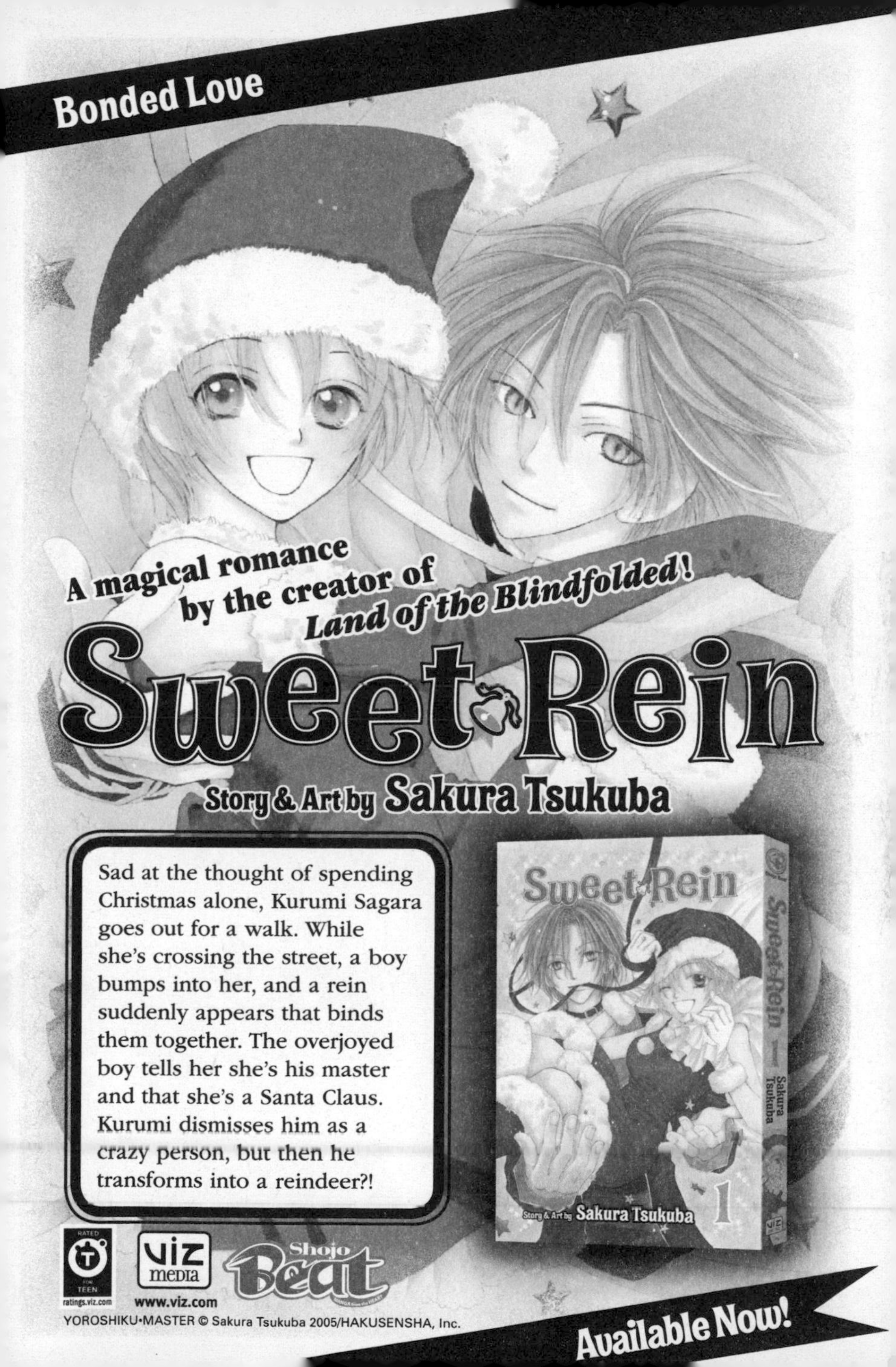

Bonded Love
A magical romance by the creator of Land of the Blindfolded!
Sweet Rein
Story & Art by Sakura Tsukuba
Sad at the thought of spending Christmas alone, Kurumi Sagara goes out for a walk. While she's crossing the street, a boy bumps into her, and a rein suddenly appears that binds them together. The overjoyed boy tells her she's his master and that she's a Santa Claus. Kurumi dismisses him as a crazy person, but then he transforms into a reindeer?!
Sweet Rein
Story & Art by Sakura Tsukuba
1
RATED T FOR TEEN
ratings.viz.com
VIZ media
www.viz.com
Shojo Beat
YOROSHIKU•MASTER © Sakura Tsukuba 2005/HAKUSENSHA, Inc.
Available Now!

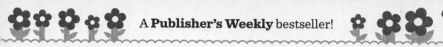

Don't Hide What's Inside
OTOMEN
by AYA KANNO
Despite his tough jock exterior, Asuka Masamune harbors a secret love for sewing, shojo manga, and all things girly. But when he finds himself drawn to his domestically inept classmate Ryo, his carefully crafted persona is put to the test. Can Asuka ever show his true self to anyone, much less to the girl he's falling for?
Find out in the Otomen manga—buy yours today!
Shojo Beat Manga
OTOMEN
OTOMEN 1 Aya Kanno
Aya Kanno
1
Shojo Beat
www.shojobeat.com
Available at your local bookstore or comic store.
OTOMEN © Aya Kanno 2006/HAKUSENSHA, Inc.
RATED T FOR TEEN
ratings.viz.com
VIZ MEDIA
www.viz.com

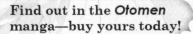

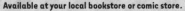

THE HEIRESS AND THE CHAUFFEUR
Vol. 1
Shojo Beat Edition

STORY AND ART BY
KEIKO ISHIHARA

English Translation & Adaptation/pinkie-chan
Touch-Up Art & Lettering/Rina Mapa
Design/Yukiko Whitley
Editor/Amy Yu

Ojosama no Untenshu by Keiko Ishihara
© Keiko Ishihara 2011
All rights reserved.
First published in Japan in 2011 by HAKUSENSHA, Inc., Tokyo.
English language translation rights arranged
with HAKUSENSHA, Inc., Tokyo.

Printed in the U.S.A.

Published by VIZ Media, LLC
P.O. Box 77010
San Francisco, CA 94107

10 9 8 7 6 5 4 3 2 1
First printing, May 2016

www.viz.com   www.shojobeat.com

PARENTAL ADVISORY
THE HEIRESS AND THE CHAUFFEUR is rated T
for Teen and is recommended for ages 13 and up.
This volume contains suggestive themes.
ratings.viz.com

Shojo Beat

The Heiress and the Chauffeur

1

Story & Art by
Keiko Ishihara

The Heiress and the Chauffeur

1

CONTENTS

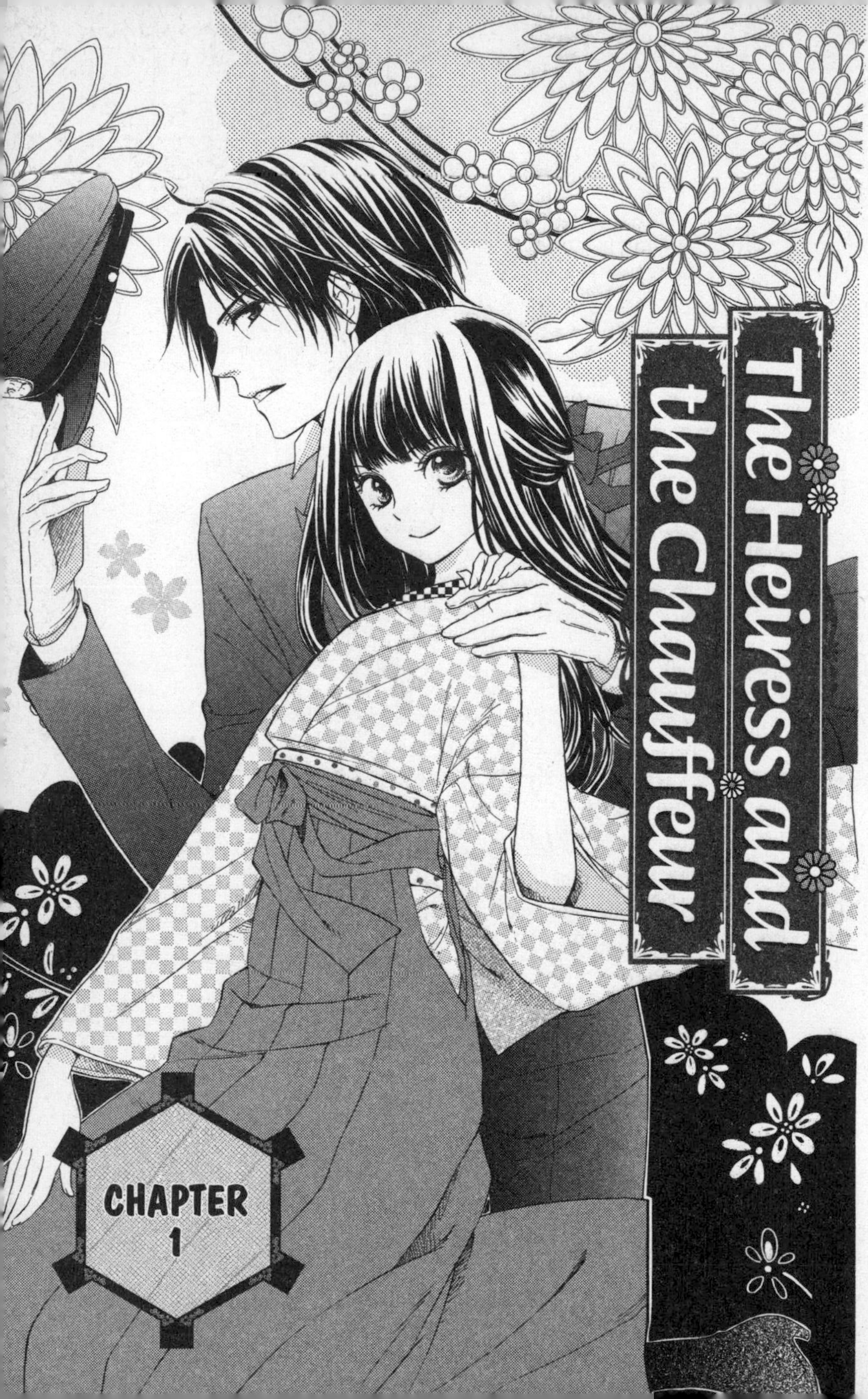
The Heiress and the Chauffeur
CHAPTER 1

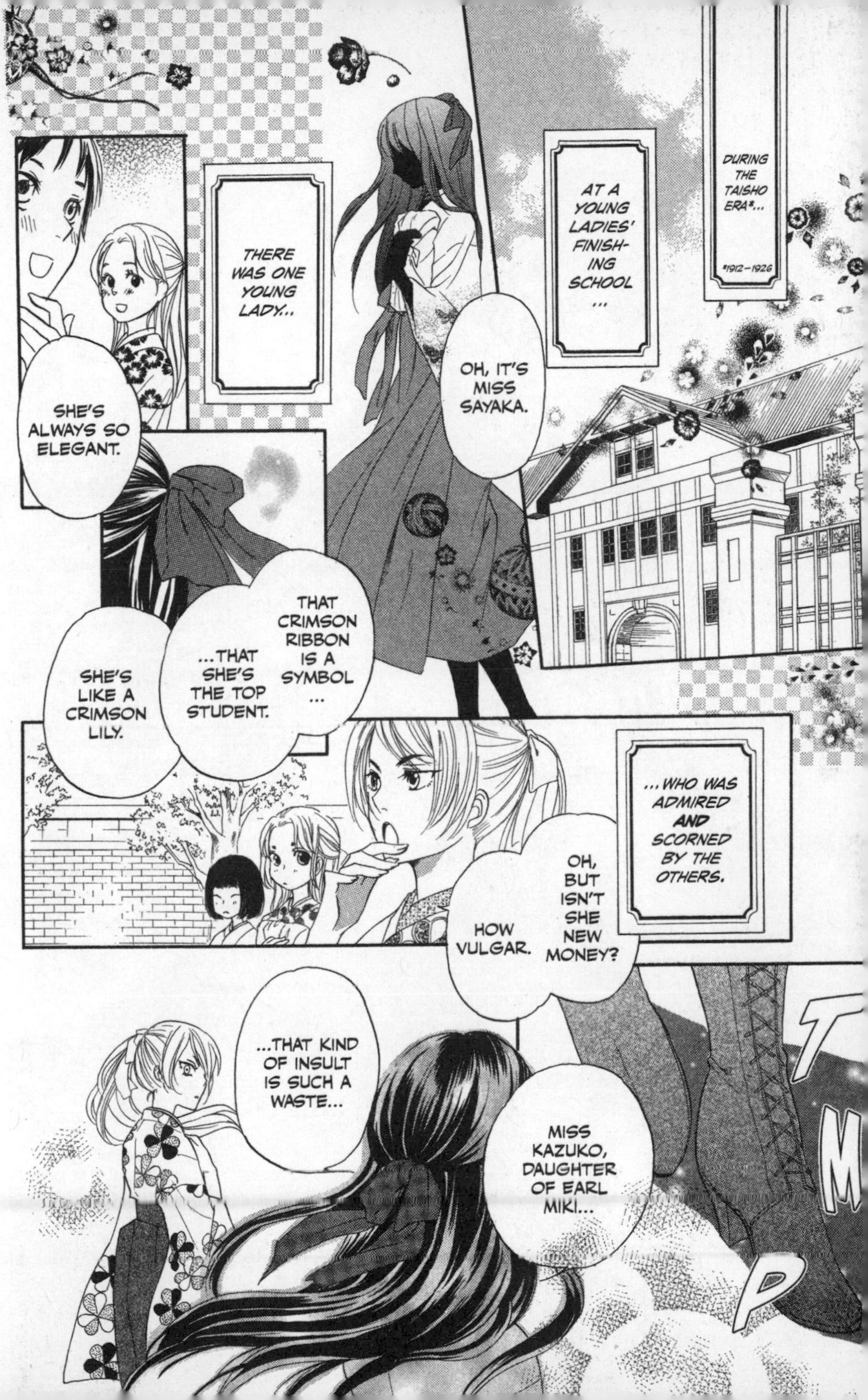
DURING THE TAISHO ERA*...
*1912–1926
AT A YOUNG LADIES' FINISHING SCHOOL ...
THERE WAS ONE YOUNG LADY...
OH, IT'S MISS SAYAKA.
SHE'S ALWAYS SO ELEGANT.
THAT CRIMSON RIBBON IS A SYMBOL ...
...THAT SHE'S THE TOP STUDENT.
SHE'S LIKE A CRIMSON LILY.
...WHO WAS ADMIRED AND SCORNED BY THE OTHERS.
OH, BUT ISN'T SHE NEW MONEY?
HOW VULGAR.
TMP
MISS KAZUKO, DAUGHTER OF EARL MIKI...
...THAT KIND OF INSULT IS SUCH A WASTE...

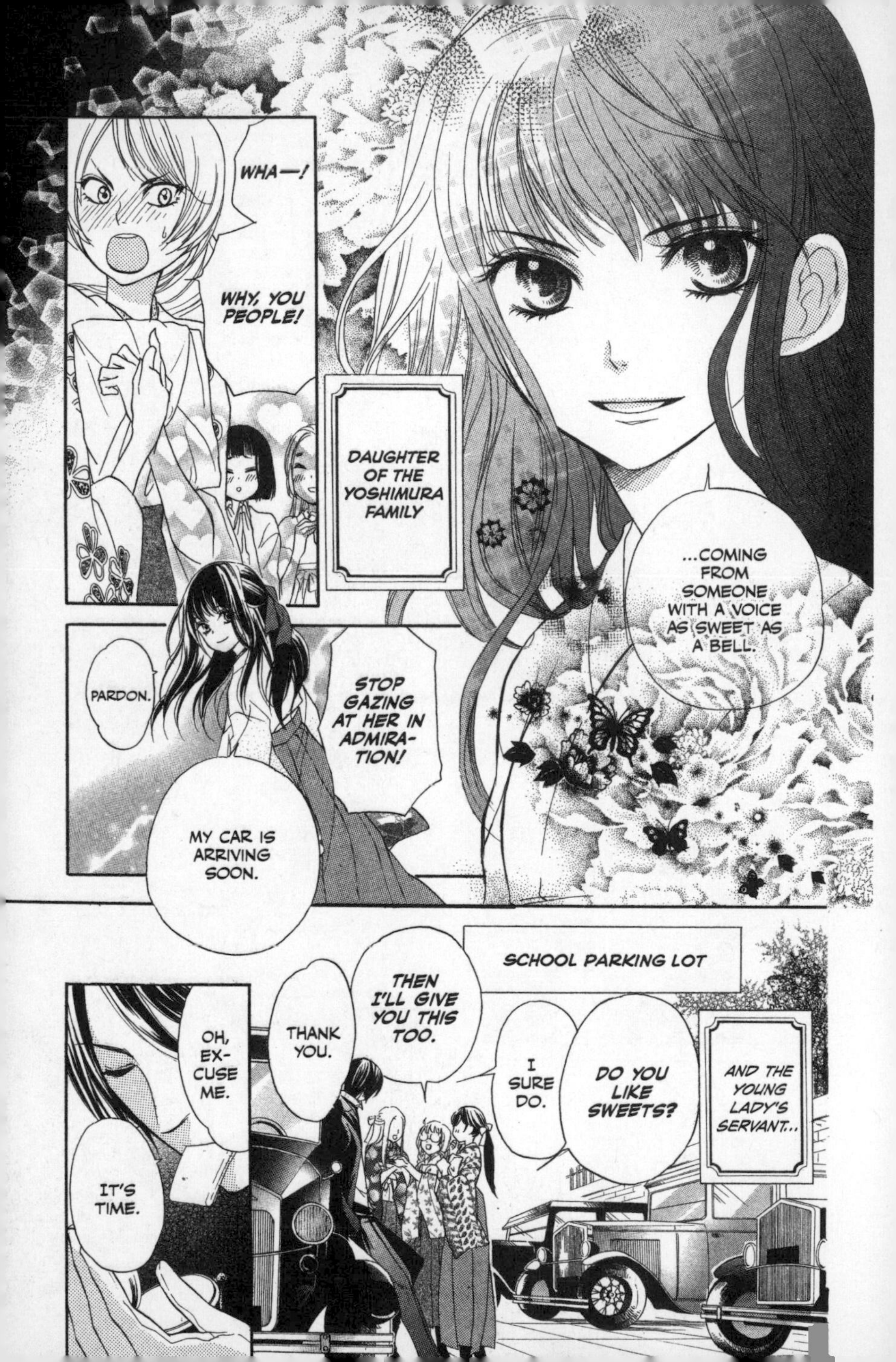
...COMING FROM SOMEONE WITH A VOICE AS SWEET AS A BELL.
DAUGHTER OF THE YOSHIMURA FAMILY
WHA—!
WHY, YOU PEOPLE!
STOP GAZING AT HER IN ADMIRA-TION!
PARDON.
MY CAR IS ARRIVING SOON.
SCHOOL PARKING LOT
AND THE YOUNG LADY'S SERVANT...
DO YOU LIKE SWEETS?
I SURE DO.
THEN I'LL GIVE YOU THIS TOO.
THANK YOU.
OH, EX-CUSE ME.
IT'S TIME.

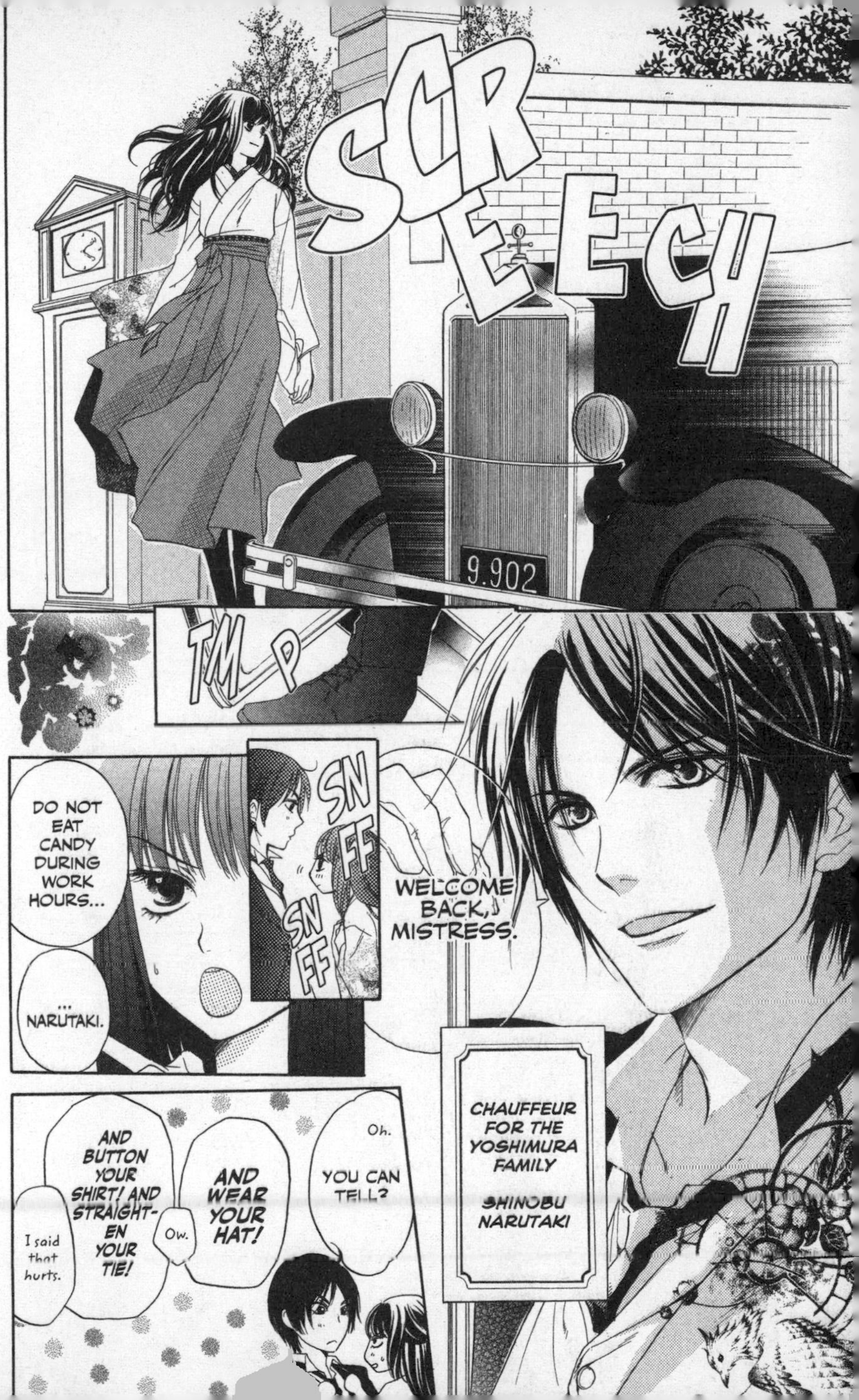
SCREECH
WELCOME BACK, MISTRESS.
CHAUFFEUR FOR THE YOSHIMURA FAMILY
SHINOBU NARUTAKI
TMP
SNIFF
SNIFF
DO NOT EAT CANDY DURING WORK HOURS...
...NARUTAKI.
Oh.
YOU CAN TELL?
AND WEAR YOUR HAT!
AND BUTTON YOUR SHIRT! AND STRAIGHTEN YOUR TIE!
Ow.
I said that hurts.

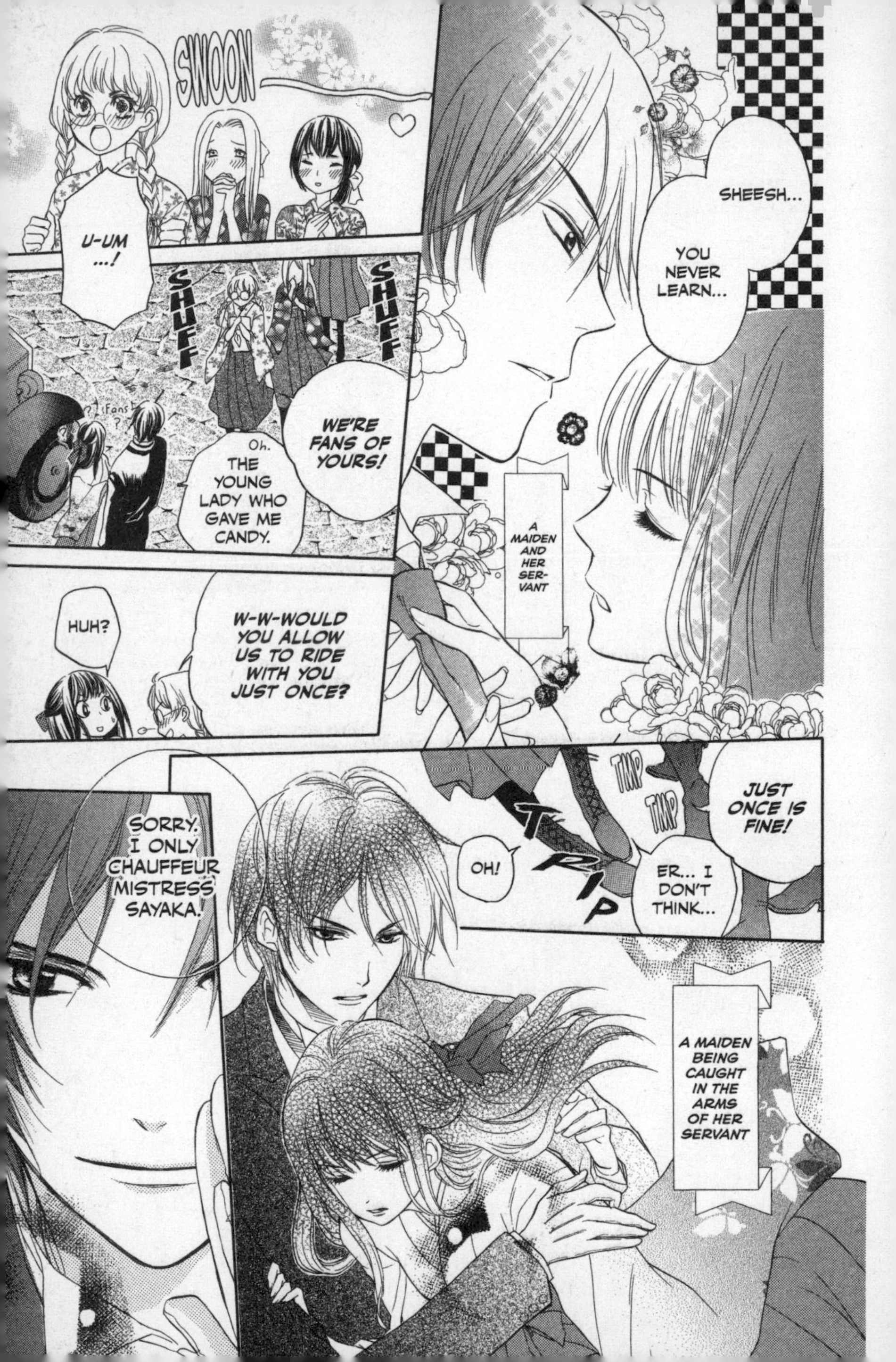

SHEESH...
YOU NEVER LEARN...
A MAIDEN AND HER SER-VANT
SWOON
U-UM ...!
SHUFF
SHUFF
WE'RE FANS OF YOURS!
Oh. THE YOUNG LADY WHO GAVE ME CANDY.
Fans?
W-W-WOULD YOU ALLOW US TO RIDE WITH YOU JUST ONCE?
HUH?
JUST ONCE IS FINE!
TMP
TMP
ER... I DON'T THINK...
TRIP
OH!
A MAIDEN BEING CAUGHT IN THE ARMS OF HER SERVANT
SORRY. I ONLY CHAUFFEUR MISTRESS SAYAKA!

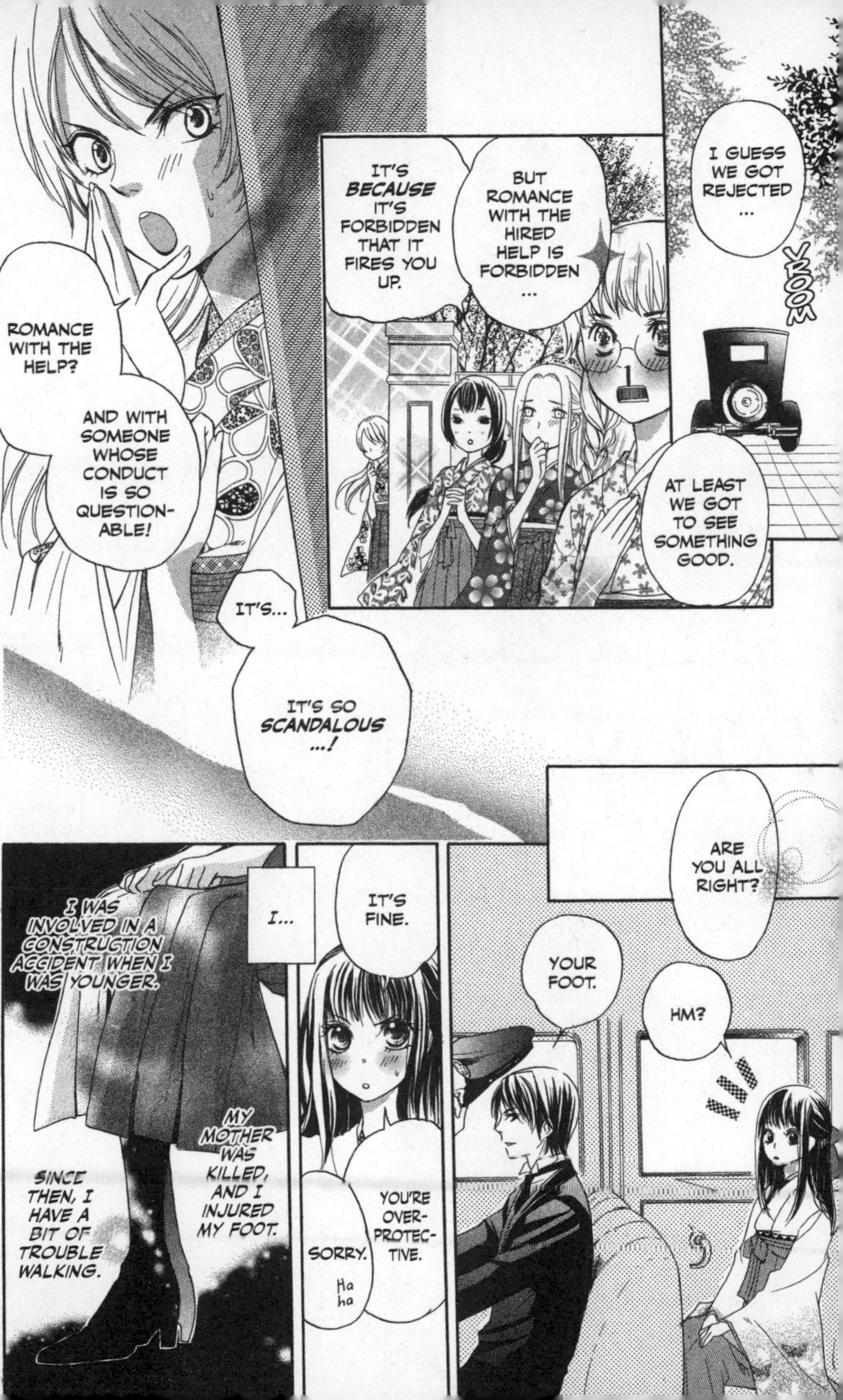
I GUESS WE GOT REJECTED...
VROOM
AT LEAST WE GOT TO SEE SOMETHING GOOD.
BUT ROMANCE WITH THE HIRED HELP IS FORBIDDEN...
IT'S BECAUSE IT'S FORBIDDEN THAT IT FIRES YOU UP.
ROMANCE WITH THE HELP?
AND WITH SOMEONE WHOSE CONDUCT IS SO QUESTIONABLE!
IT'S...
IT'S SO SCANDALOUS...!
ARE YOU ALL RIGHT?
HM?
YOUR FOOT.
IT'S FINE.
I...
YOU'RE OVER-PROTECTIVE.
SORRY.
Ha ha
I WAS INVOLVED IN A CONSTRUCTION ACCIDENT WHEN I WAS YOUNGER.
MY MOTHER WAS KILLED, AND I INJURED MY FOOT.
SINCE THEN, I HAVE A BIT OF TROUBLE WALKING.

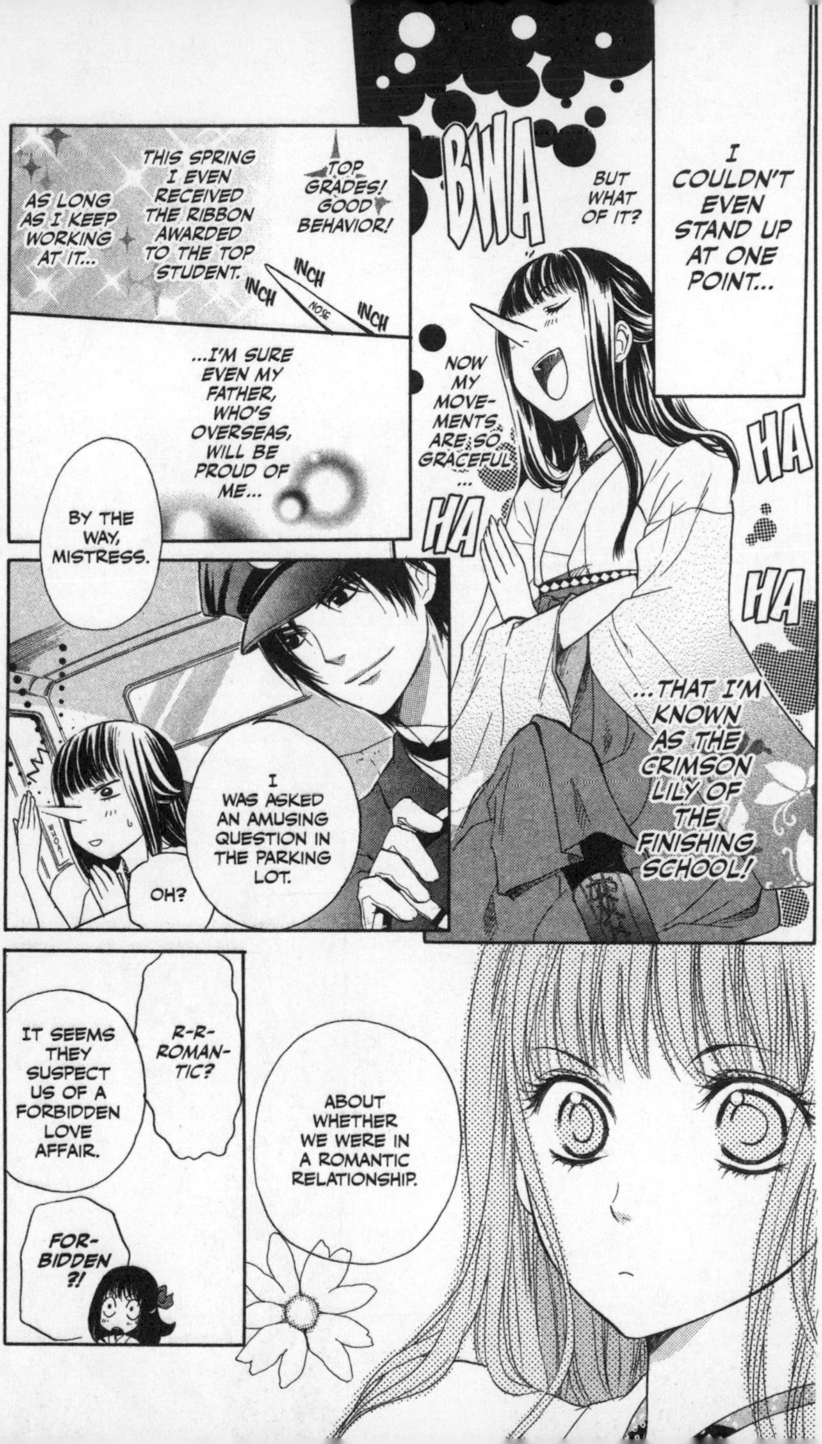
I COULDN'T EVEN STAND UP AT ONE POINT...
BUT WHAT OF IT?
BWA
NOW MY MOVEMENTS ARE SO GRACEFUL...
HA
HA
HA
...THAT I'M KNOWN AS THE CRIMSON LILY OF THE FINISHING SCHOOL!
TOP GRADES! GOOD BEHAVIOR!
THIS SPRING I EVEN RECEIVED THE RIBBON AWARDED TO THE TOP STUDENT.
AS LONG AS I KEEP WORKING AT IT...
INCH
INCH
NOSE
INCH
...I'M SURE EVEN MY FATHER, WHO'S OVERSEAS, WILL BE PROUD OF ME...
BY THE WAY, MISTRESS.
I WAS ASKED AN AMUSING QUESTION IN THE PARKING LOT.
OH?
ABOUT WHETHER WE WERE IN A ROMANTIC RELATIONSHIP.
R-R-ROMAN-TIC?
IT SEEMS THEY SUSPECT US OF A FORBIDDEN LOVE AFFAIR.
FOR-BIDDEN?!

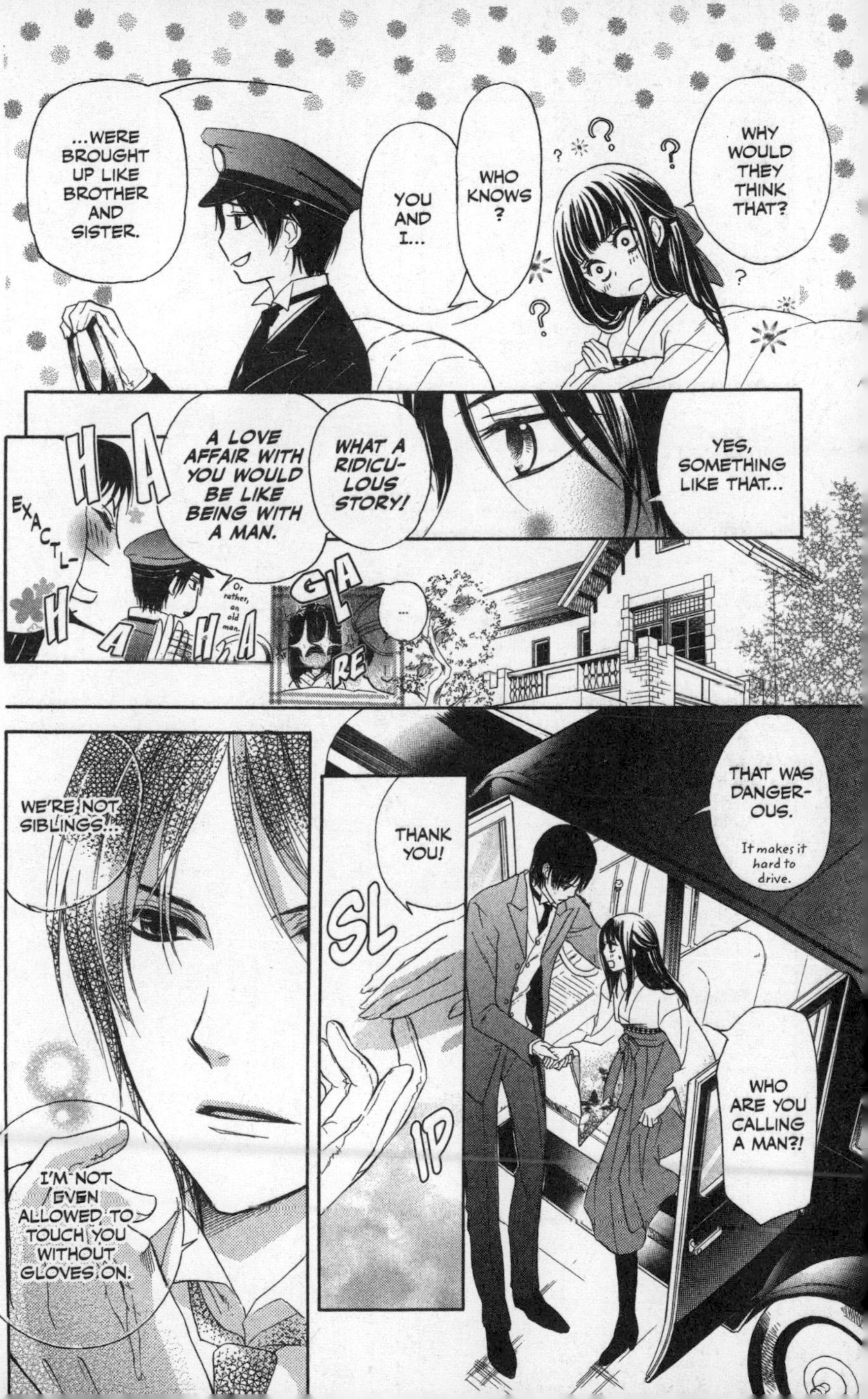
WHY WOULD THEY THINK THAT?
WHO KNOWS?
YOU AND I...
...WERE BROUGHT UP LIKE BROTHER AND SISTER.
YES, SOMETHING LIKE THAT...
WHAT A RIDICULOUS STORY!
A LOVE AFFAIR WITH YOU WOULD BE LIKE BEING WITH A MAN.
...
GLARE
Or rather, an old man.
EXACTL-
HA HA HA HA
THAT WAS DANGEROUS.
It makes it hard to drive.
WHO ARE YOU CALLING A MAN?!
THANK YOU!
SLIP
WE'RE NOT SIBLINGS...
I'M NOT EVEN ALLOWED TO TOUCH YOU WITHOUT GLOVES ON.

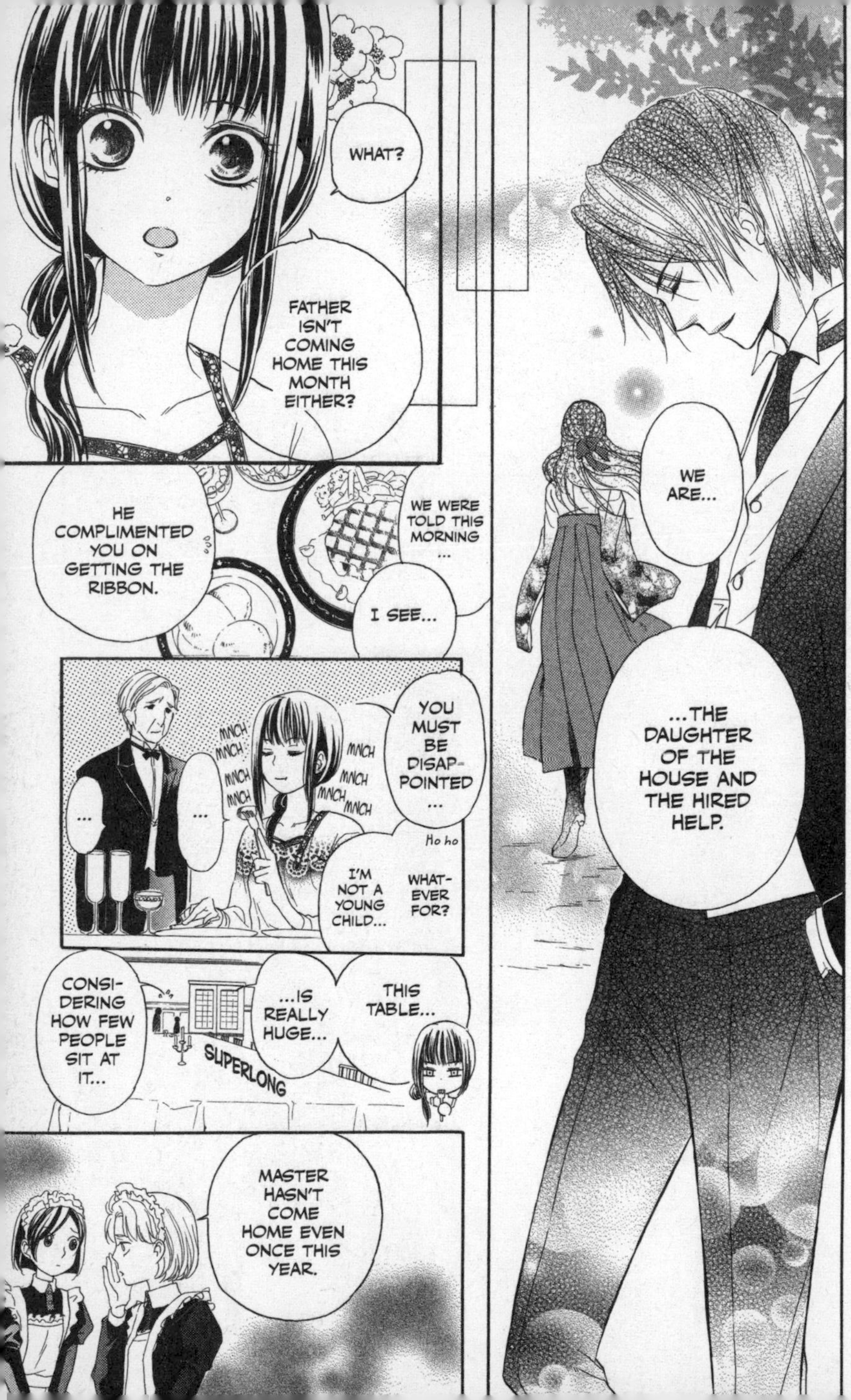
WE ARE...
...THE DAUGHTER OF THE HOUSE AND THE HIRED HELP.
WHAT?
FATHER ISN'T COMING HOME THIS MONTH EITHER?
WE WERE TOLD THIS MORNING ...
HE COMPLIMENTED YOU ON GETTING THE RIBBON.
I SEE...
YOU MUST BE DISAPPOINTED ...
MNCH MNCH MNCH MNCH
MNCH MNCH MNCH MNCH
...
...
Ho ho
WHAT-EVER FOR?
I'M NOT A YOUNG CHILD...
THIS TABLE...
...IS REALLY HUGE...
CONSI-DERING HOW FEW PEOPLE SIT AT IT...
SUPERLONG
MASTER HASN'T COME HOME EVEN ONCE THIS YEAR.

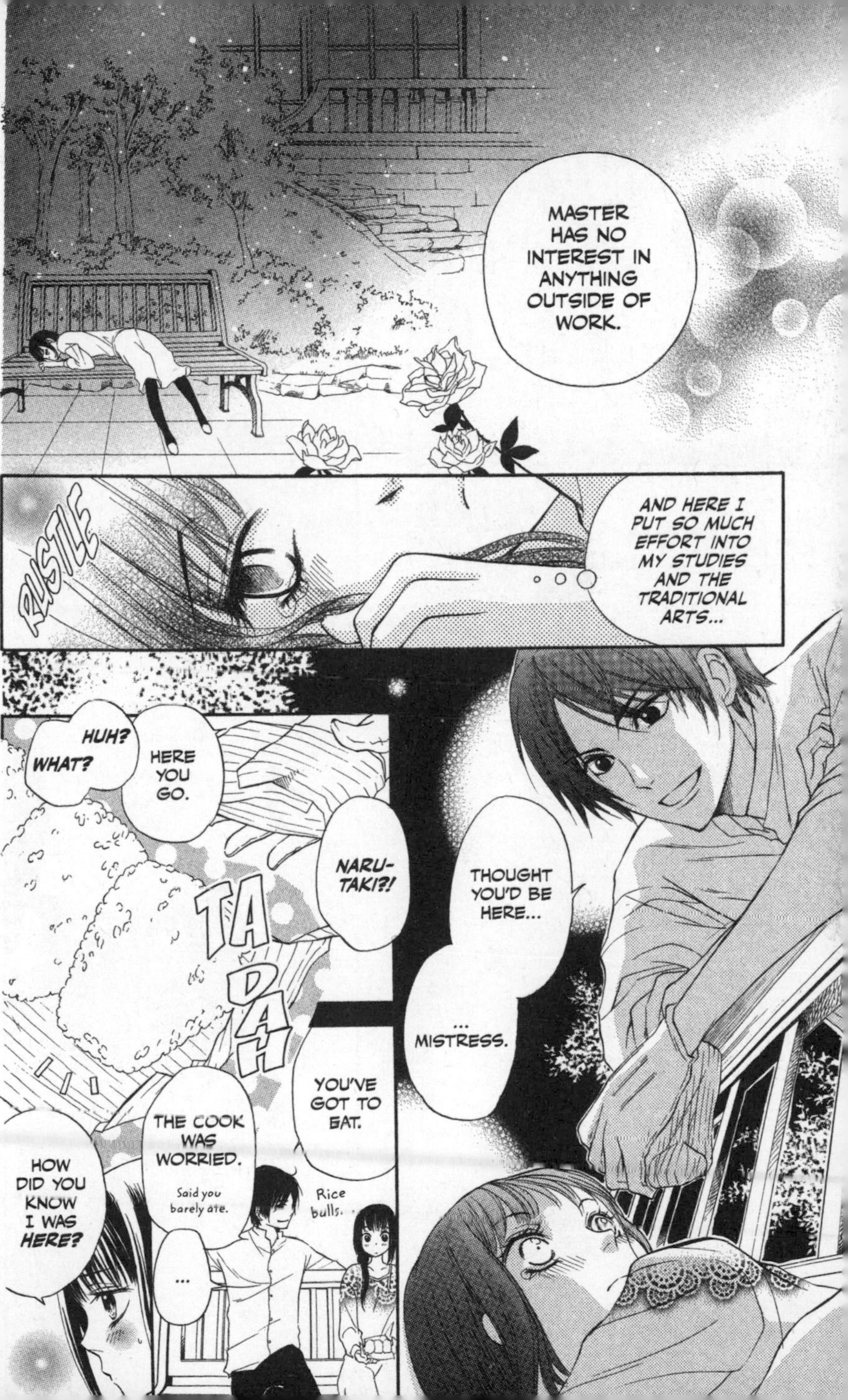
MASTER HAS NO INTEREST IN ANYTHING OUTSIDE OF WORK.
AND HERE I PUT SO MUCH EFFORT INTO MY STUDIES AND THE TRADITIONAL ARTS...
RUSTLE
THOUGHT YOU'D BE HERE...
... MISTRESS.
HERE YOU GO.
HUH? WHAT?
NARU-TAKI?!
TA DAH
YOU'VE GOT TO EAT.
THE COOK WAS WORRIED.
Rice bulls.
Said you barely ate.
HOW DID YOU KNOW I WAS HERE?
...

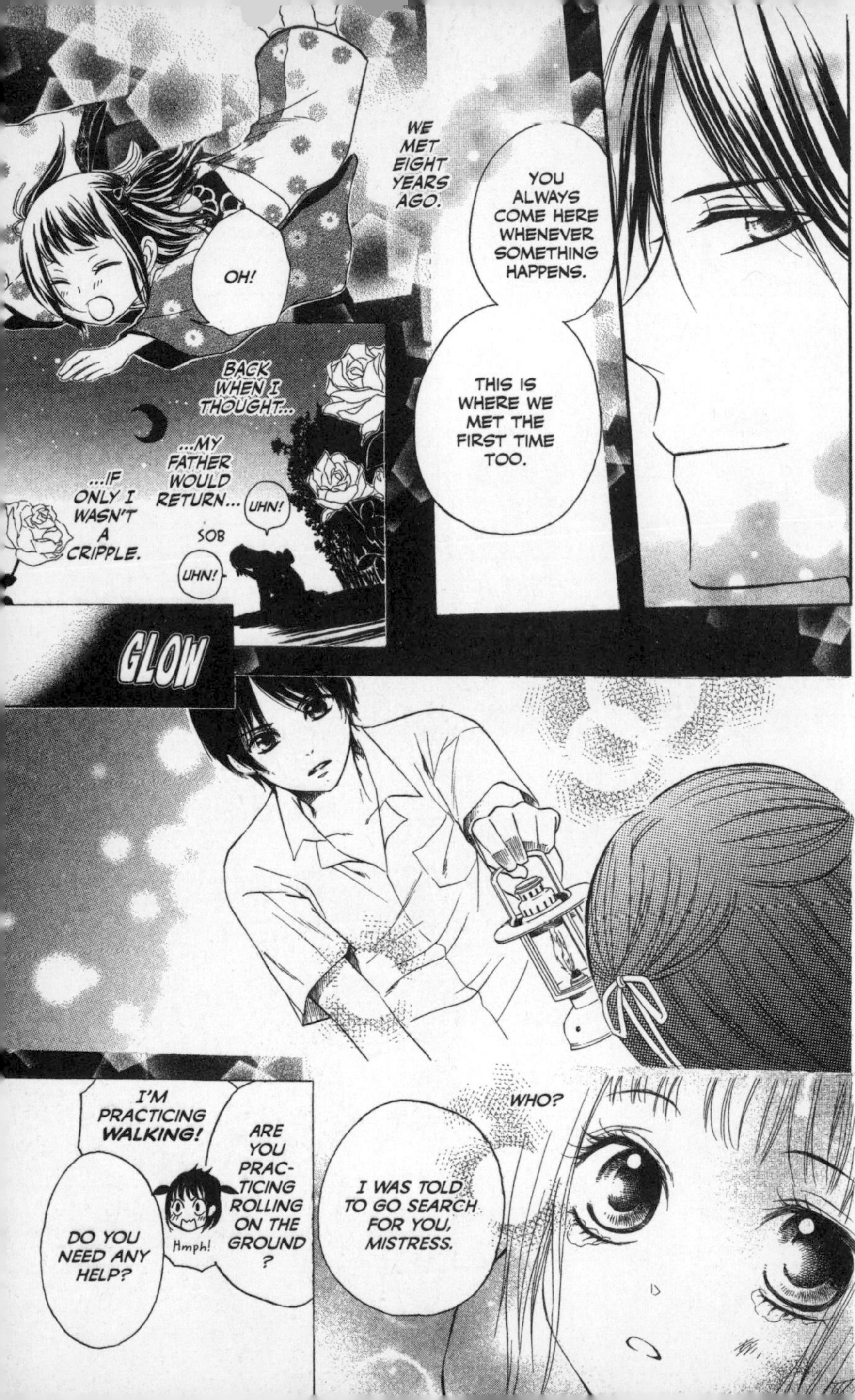
YOU ALWAYS COME HERE WHENEVER SOMETHING HAPPENS.
THIS IS WHERE WE MET THE FIRST TIME TOO.
WE MET EIGHT YEARS AGO.
OH!
BACK WHEN I THOUGHT...
...MY FATHER WOULD RETURN...
...IF ONLY I WASN'T A CRIPPLE.
UHN!
SOB
UHN!
GLOW
WHO?
I WAS TOLD TO GO SEARCH FOR YOU, MISTRESS.
ARE YOU PRACTICING ROLLING ON THE GROUND?
I'M PRACTICING WALKING!
Hmph!
DO YOU NEED ANY HELP?

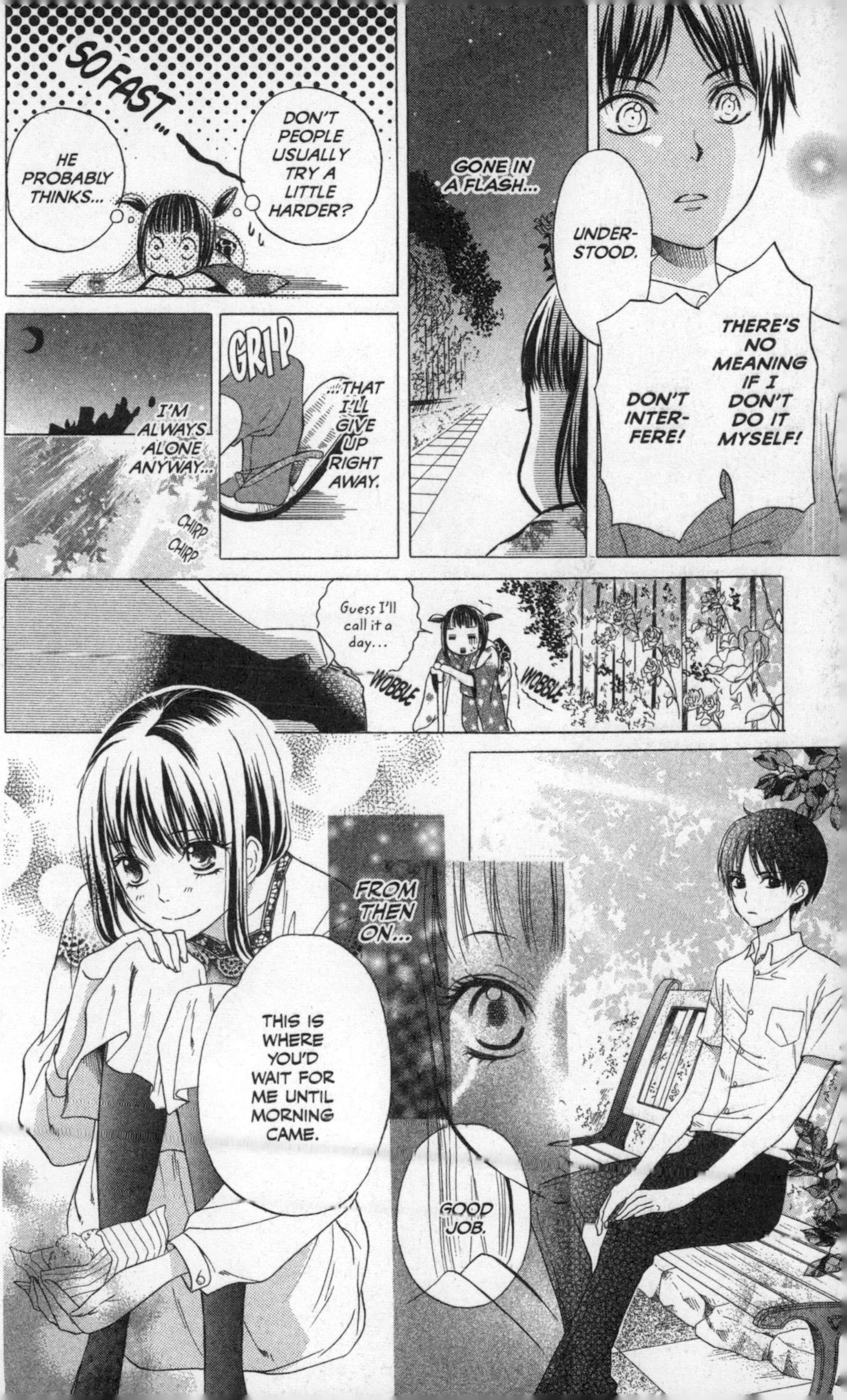
UNDER-STOOD.
THERE'S NO MEANING IF I DON'T DO IT MYSELF!
DON'T INTER-FERE!
GONE IN A FLASH...
SO FAST...
DON'T PEOPLE USUALLY TRY A LITTLE HARDER?
HE PROBABLY THINKS...
GRIP
...THAT I'LL GIVE UP RIGHT AWAY.
I'M ALWAYS ALONE ANYWAY...
CHIRP
CHIRP
WOBBLE
Guess I'll call it a day...
WOBBLE
FROM THEN ON...
GOOD JOB.
THIS IS WHERE YOU'D WAIT FOR ME UNTIL MORNING CAME.

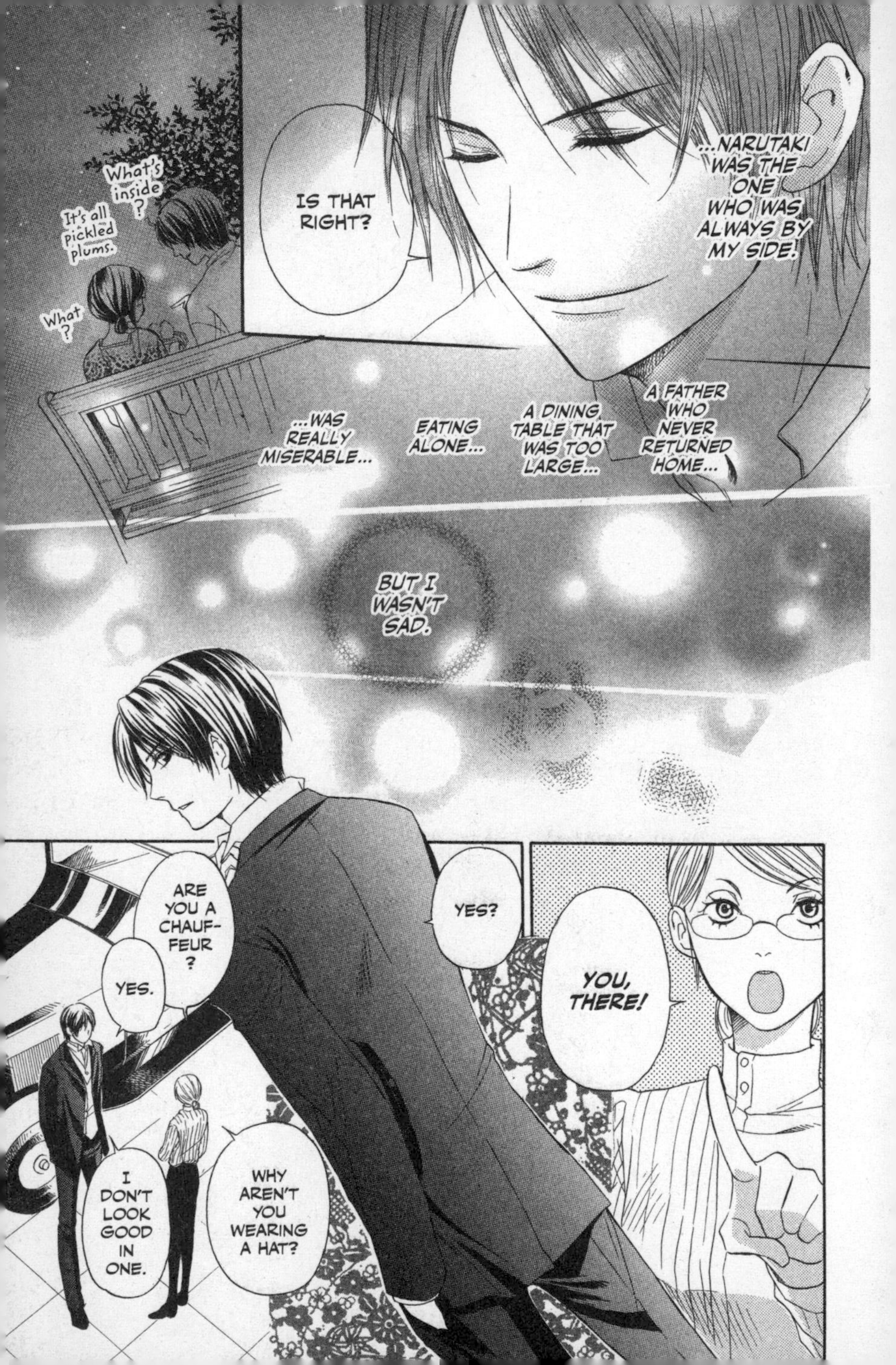
...NARUTAKI WAS THE ONE WHO WAS ALWAYS BY MY SIDE.
IS THAT RIGHT?
What's inside?
It's all pickled plums.
What?
A FATHER WHO NEVER RETURNED HOME...
A DINING TABLE THAT WAS TOO LARGE...
EATING ALONE...
...WAS REALLY MISERABLE...
BUT I WASN'T SAD.
YOU, THERE!
YES?
ARE YOU A CHAUFFEUR?
YES.
WHY AREN'T YOU WEARING A HAT?
I DON'T LOOK GOOD IN ONE.

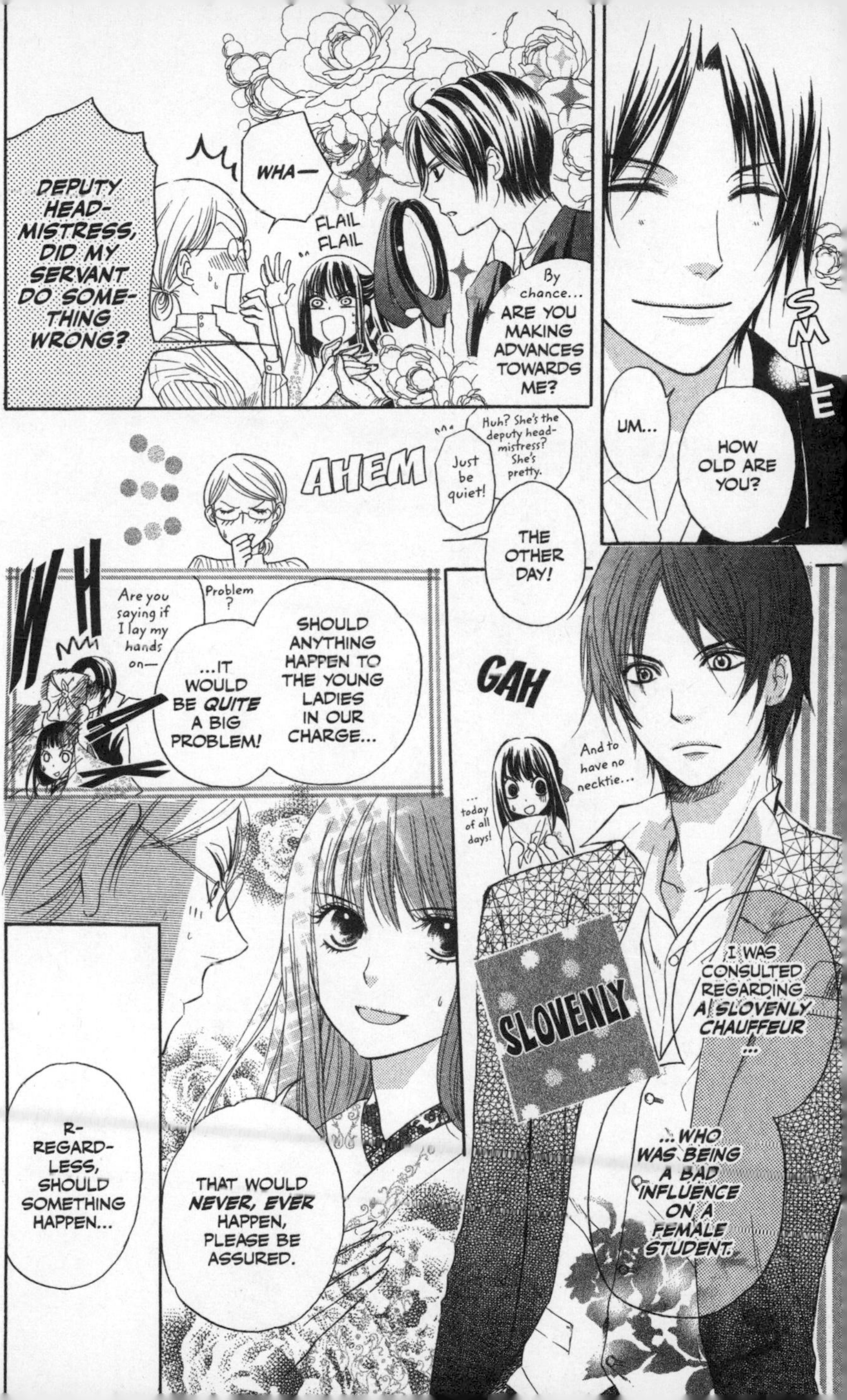
SMILE
UM...
HOW OLD ARE YOU?
By chance... ARE YOU MAKING ADVANCES TOWARDS ME?
WHA—
FLAIL FLAIL
DEPUTY HEADMISTRESS, DID MY SERVANT DO SOMETHING WRONG?
Huh? She's the deputy headmistress? She's pretty.
Just be quiet!
AHEM
THE OTHER DAY!
GAH
And to have no necktie...
...today of all days!
SLOVENLY
I WAS CONSULTED REGARDING A SLOVENLY CHAUFFEUR...
...WHO WAS BEING A BAD INFLUENCE ON A FEMALE STUDENT.
SHOULD ANYTHING HAPPEN TO THE YOUNG LADIES IN OUR CHARGE...
...IT WOULD BE QUITE A BIG PROBLEM!
Problem?
Are you saying if I lay my hands on—
WH
THAT WOULD NEVER, EVER HAPPEN, PLEASE BE ASSURED.
R-REGARDLESS, SHOULD SOMETHING HAPPEN...

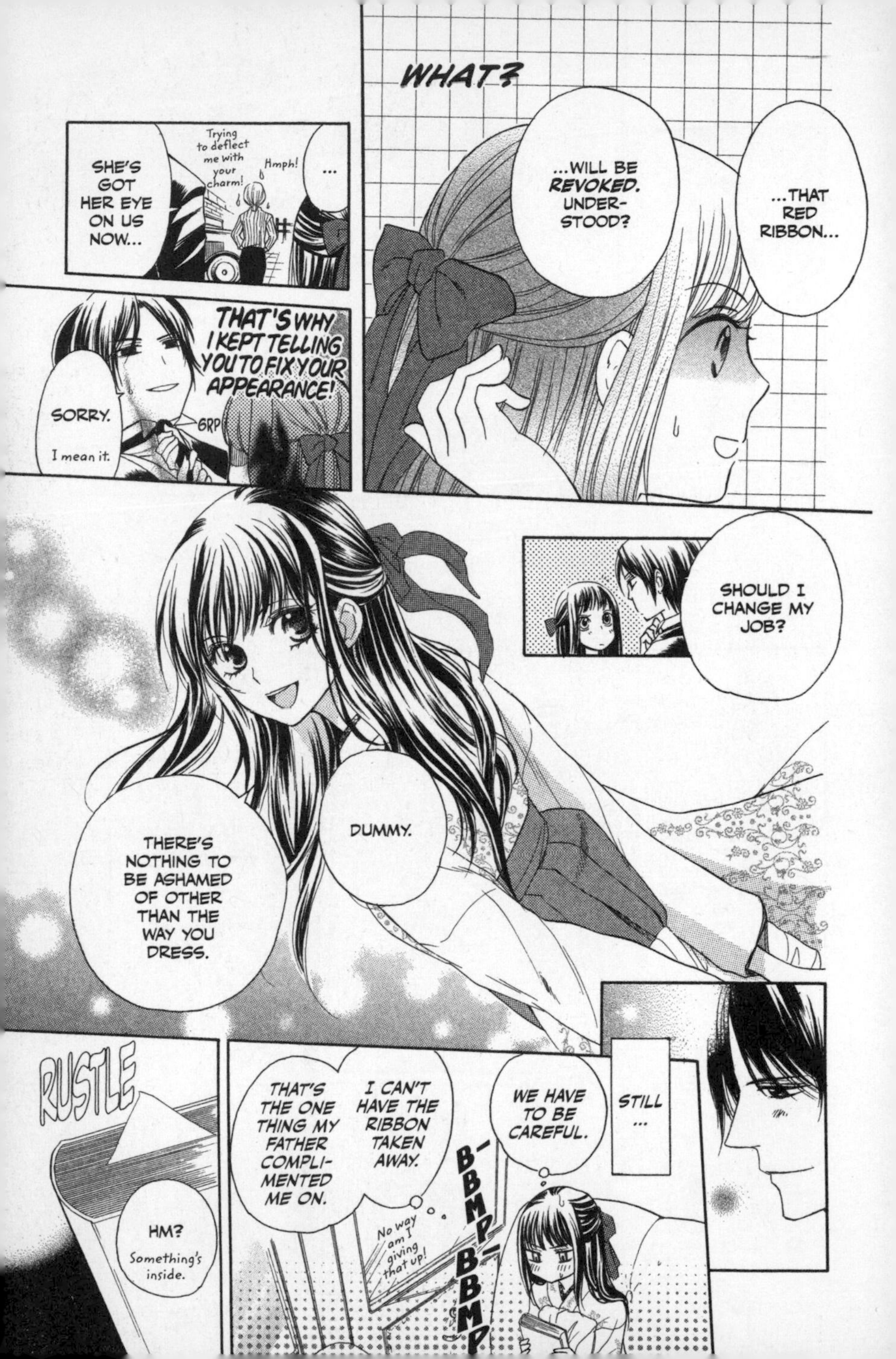
...THAT RED RIBBON...
...WILL BE REVOKED. UNDERSTOOD?
WHAT?
...
Hmph!
Trying to deflect me with your charm!
SHE'S GOT HER EYE ON US NOW...
THAT'S WHY I KEPT TELLING YOU TO FIX YOUR APPEARANCE!
GRP
SORRY.
I mean it.
SHOULD I CHANGE MY JOB?
DUMMY.
THERE'S NOTHING TO BE ASHAMED OF OTHER THAN THE WAY YOU DRESS.
STILL ...
WE HAVE TO BE CAREFUL.
I CAN'T HAVE THE RIBBON TAKEN AWAY.
THAT'S THE ONE THING MY FATHER COMPLIMENTED ME ON.
No way am I giving that up!
BBMP- BBMP- BBMP
RUSTLE
HM?
Something's inside.

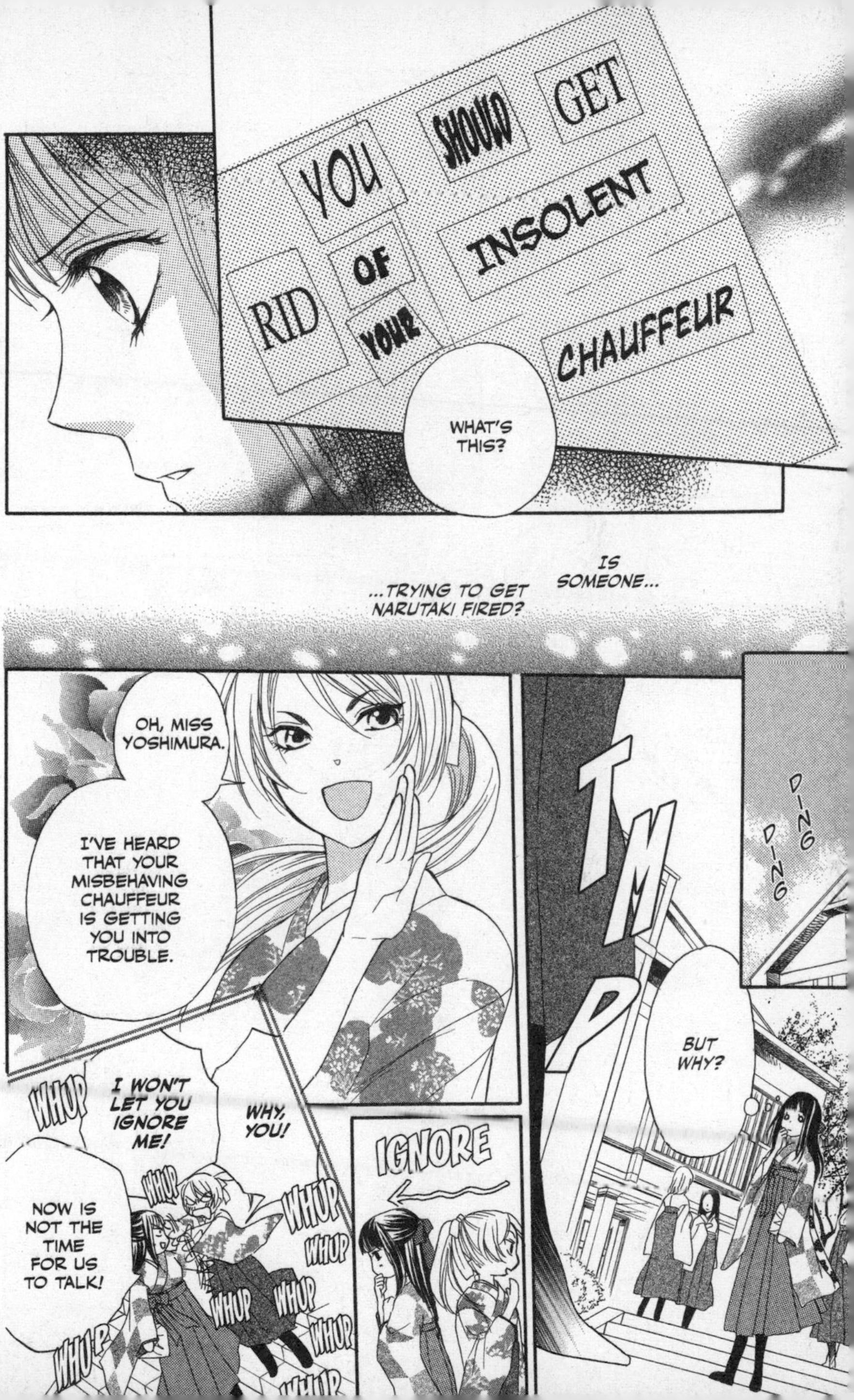
YOU SHOULD GET RID OF YOUR INSOLENT CHAUFFEUR
WHAT'S THIS?
IS SOMEONE...
...TRYING TO GET NARUTAKI FIRED?
DING DING
TMP
BUT WHY?
OH, MISS YOSHIMURA.
I'VE HEARD THAT YOUR MISBEHAVING CHAUFFEUR IS GETTING YOU INTO TROUBLE.
IGNORE
WHY, YOU!
I WON'T LET YOU IGNORE ME!
WHUP
NOW IS NOT THE TIME FOR US TO TALK!
WHUP WHUP WHUP WHUP WHUP WHUP

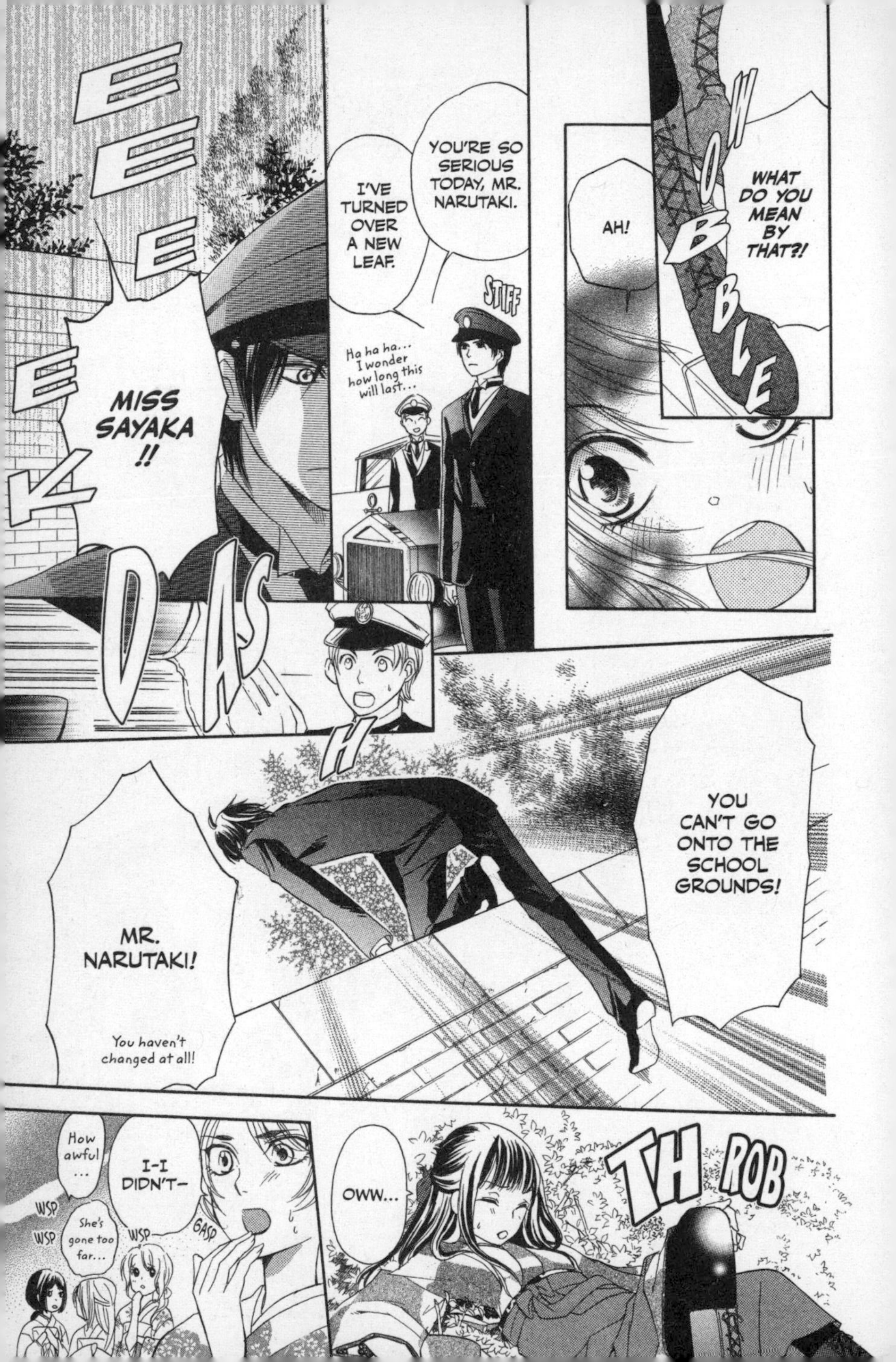
WOBBLE
WHAT DO YOU MEAN BY THAT?!
AH!
YOU'RE SO SERIOUS TODAY, MR. NARUTAKI.
I'VE TURNED OVER A NEW LEAF.
STIFF
Ha ha ha... I wonder how long this will last...
EEEEK
MISS SAYAKA!!
DASH
YOU CAN'T GO ONTO THE SCHOOL GROUNDS!
MR. NARUTAKI!
You haven't changed at all!
THROB
OWW...
I-I DIDN'T-
GASP
How awful...
WSP
WSP
She's gone too far...
WSP

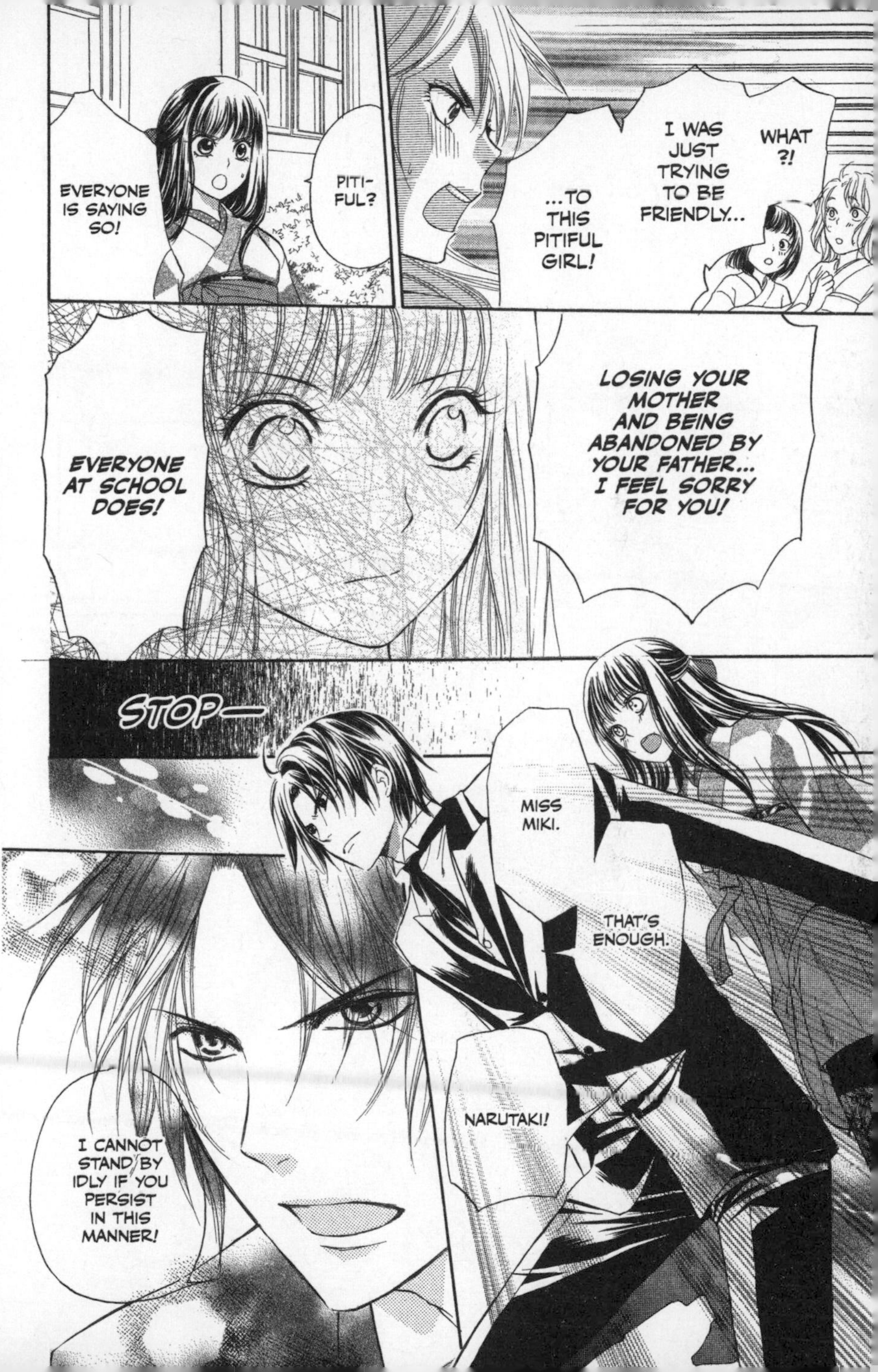
WHAT?!
I WAS JUST TRYING TO BE FRIENDLY...
...TO THIS PITIFUL GIRL!
PITI-FUL?
EVERYONE IS SAYING SO!
LOSING YOUR MOTHER AND BEING ABANDONED BY YOUR FATHER... I FEEL SORRY FOR YOU!
EVERYONE AT SCHOOL DOES!
STOP—
MISS MIKI.
THAT'S ENOUGH.
NARUTAKI!
I CANNOT STAND BY IDLY IF YOU PERSIST IN THIS MANNER!

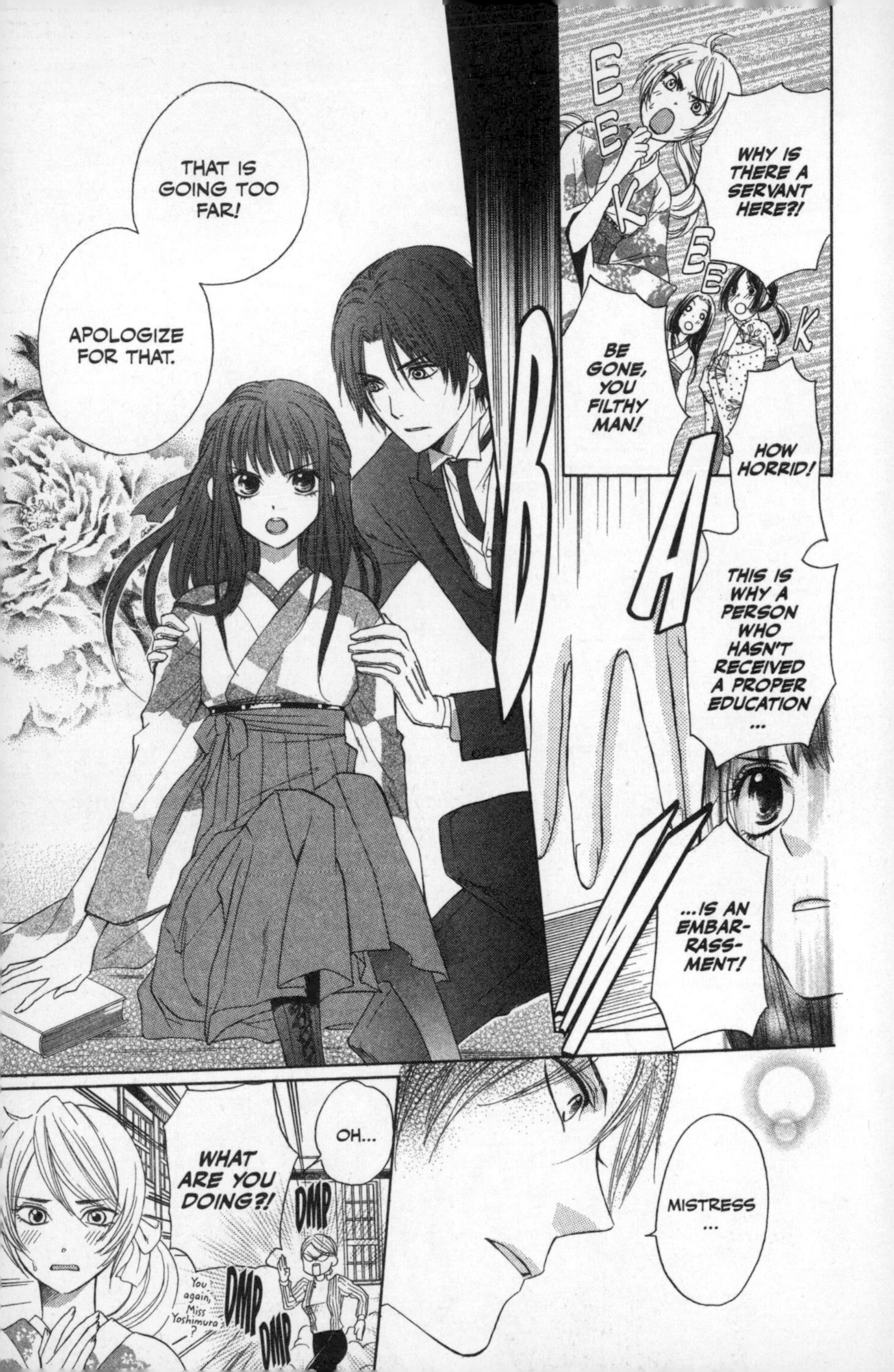
WHY IS THERE A SERVANT HERE?!
EEK
EEEK
BE GONE, YOU FILTHY MAN!
HOW HORRID!
THIS IS WHY A PERSON WHO HASN'T RECEIVED A PROPER EDUCATION...
...IS AN EMBARRASSMENT!
BAM
THAT IS GOING TOO FAR!
APOLOGIZE FOR THAT.
MISTRESS...
OH...
WHAT ARE YOU DOING?!
DMP
DMP
DMP
You again, Miss Yoshimura?

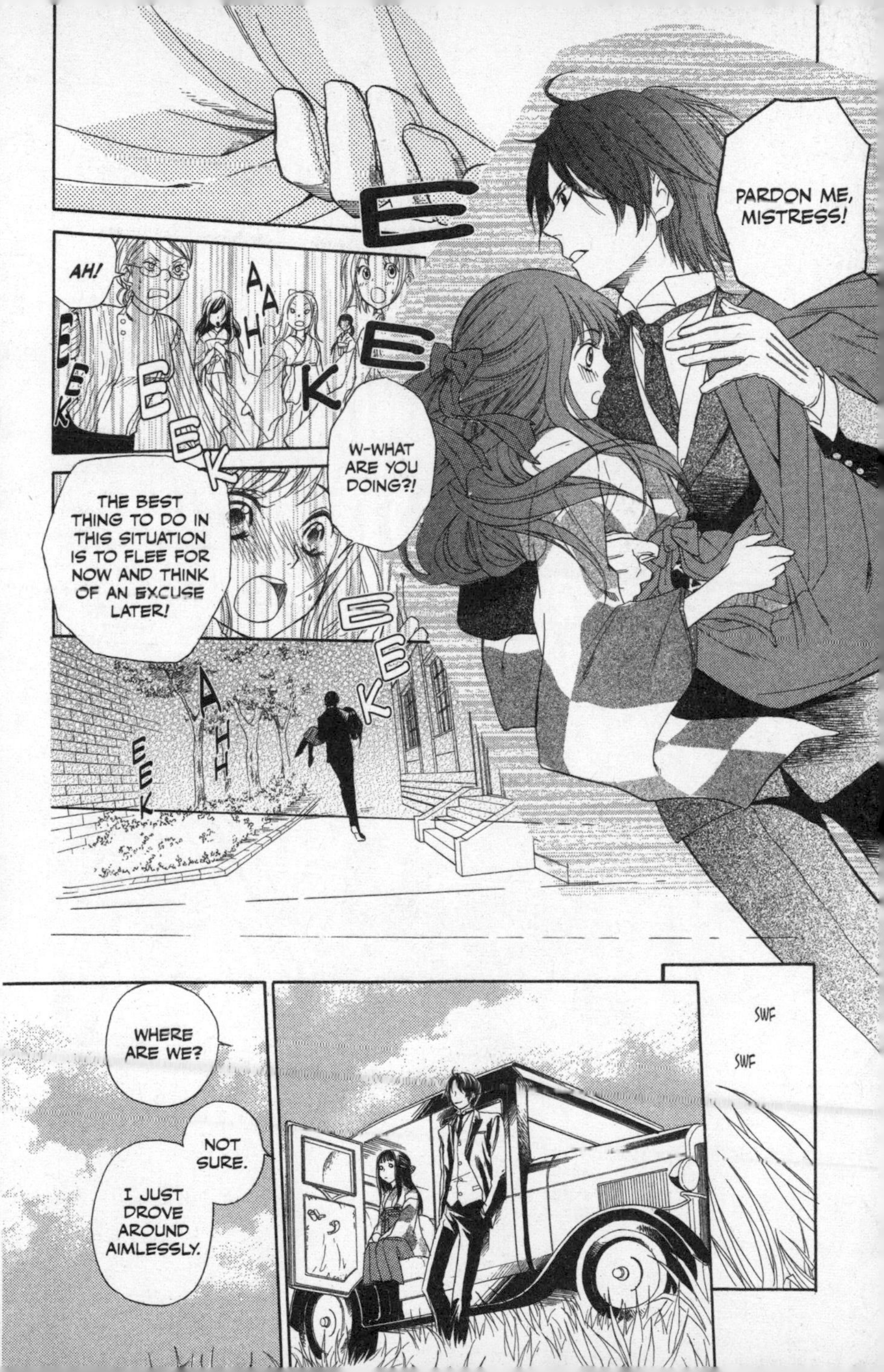
PARDON ME, MISTRESS!
W-WHAT ARE YOU DOING?!
EEK
AH!
AAH
EEK
EEK
THE BEST THING TO DO IN THIS SITUATION IS TO FLEE FOR NOW AND THINK OF AN EXCUSE LATER!
EEK
AHH
EEK
SWF
SWF
WHERE ARE WE?
NOT SURE.
I JUST DROVE AROUND AIMLESSLY.

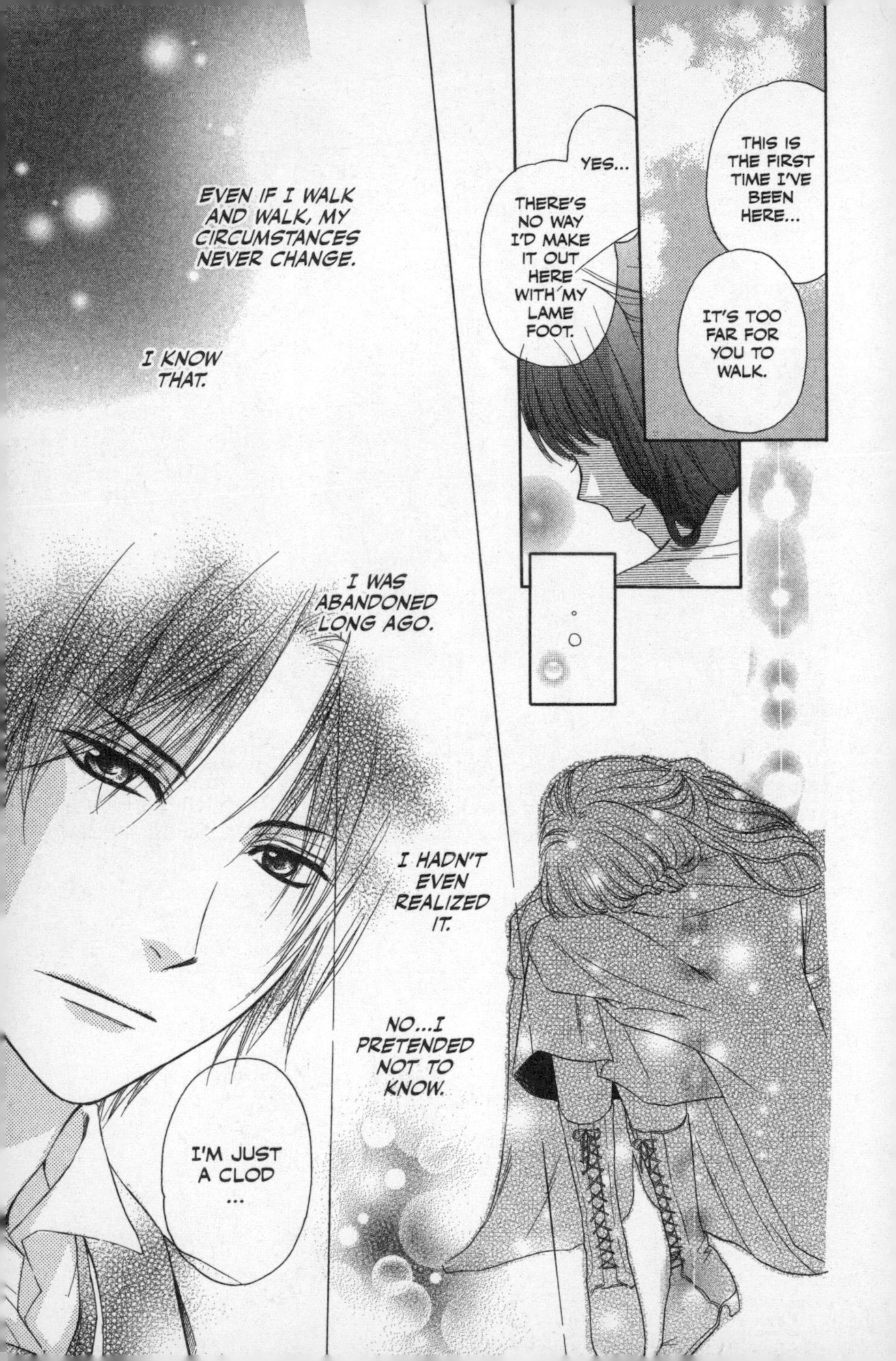
THIS IS THE FIRST TIME I'VE BEEN HERE...
IT'S TOO FAR FOR YOU TO WALK.
YES...
THERE'S NO WAY I'D MAKE IT OUT HERE WITH MY LAME FOOT.
EVEN IF I WALK AND WALK, MY CIRCUMSTANCES NEVER CHANGE.
I KNOW THAT.
I WAS ABANDONED LONG AGO.
I HADN'T EVEN REALIZED IT.
NO...I PRETENDED NOT TO KNOW.
I'M JUST A CLOD ...

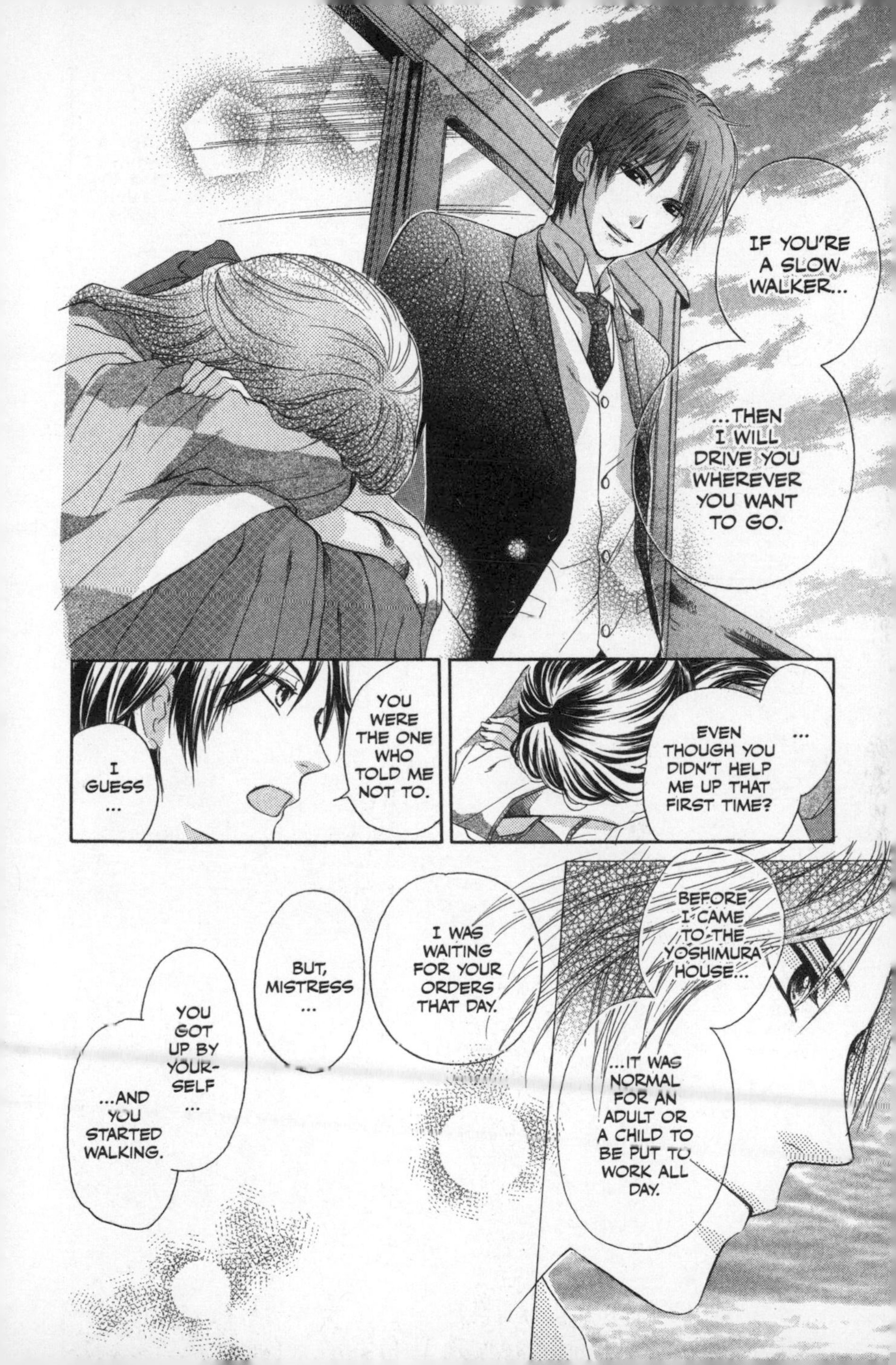
IF YOU'RE A SLOW WALKER...
...THEN I WILL DRIVE YOU WHEREVER YOU WANT TO GO.
...
EVEN THOUGH YOU DIDN'T HELP ME UP THAT FIRST TIME?
YOU WERE THE ONE WHO TOLD ME NOT TO.
I GUESS ...
BEFORE I CAME TO THE YOSHIMURA HOUSE...
...IT WAS NORMAL FOR AN ADULT OR A CHILD TO BE PUT TO WORK ALL DAY.
I WAS WAITING FOR YOUR ORDERS THAT DAY.
BUT, MISTRESS ...
YOU GOT UP BY YOUR-SELF ...
...AND YOU STARTED WALKING.

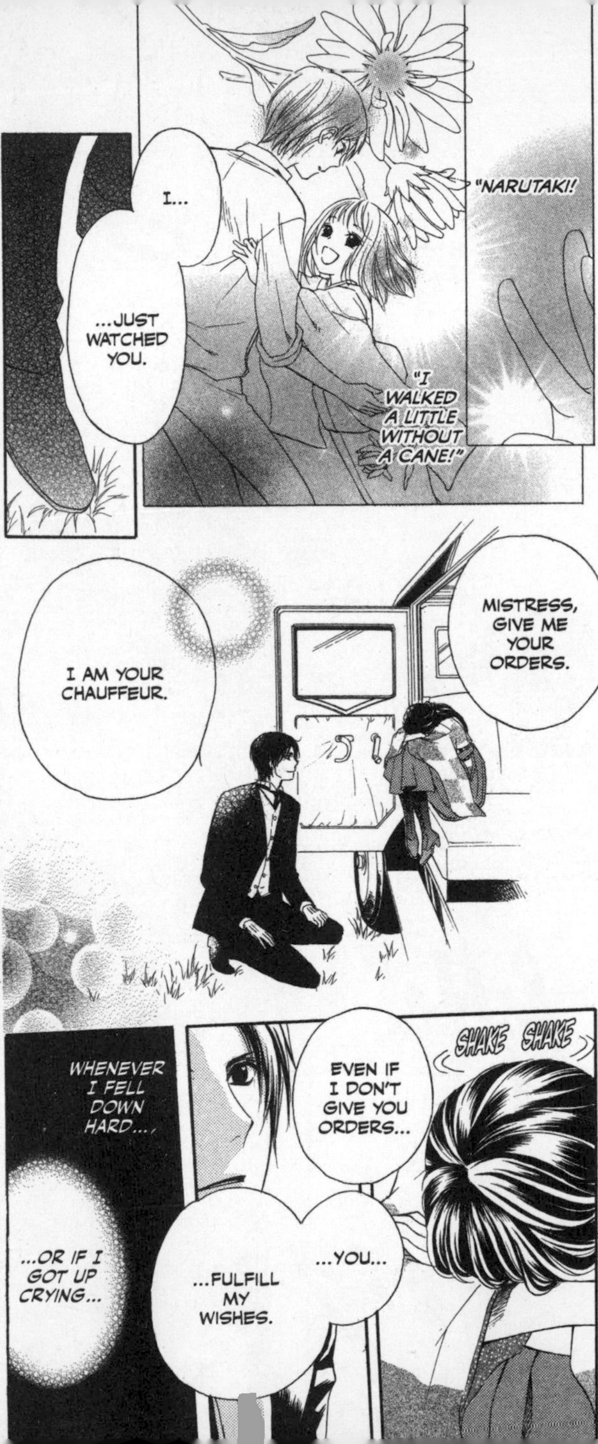
"NARUTAKI!
"I WALKED A LITTLE WITHOUT A CANE!"
I...
...JUST WATCHED YOU.
MISTRESS, GIVE ME YOUR ORDERS.
I AM YOUR CHAUFFEUR.
SHAKE SHAKE
EVEN IF I DON'T GIVE YOU ORDERS...
...YOU...
...FULFILL MY WISHES.
WHENEVER I FELL DOWN HARD...,
...OR IF I GOT UP CRYING...

THE HEIRESS AND THE CHAUFFEUR

Nice to meet you. Thank you very much for picking up my very first comic book.

This story was actually supposed to be a yokai (monster) exorcism story set in the Heian period (794–1185). But at the time, I didn't have a good grasp of the Heian period, and my editor said, "Why don't you set it in the Meiji (1867–1912) or the Taisho era then?" So the time period changed, and the yokai idea went away too. In the end, it became like this.

At first, Narutaki was going to be a butler. But in the Taisho era, it was popular for young ladies to run off with their chauffeurs. "What? That sounds interesting. With a chauffeur, you can go anywhere." So that's why he became a chauffeur.

However, as I was drawing the storyboards...

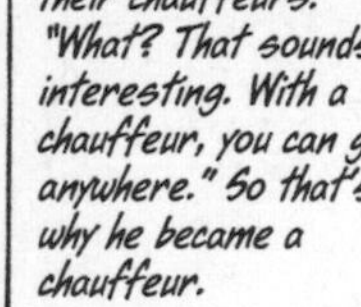
How am I going to draw this car?

I hadn't thought of that.

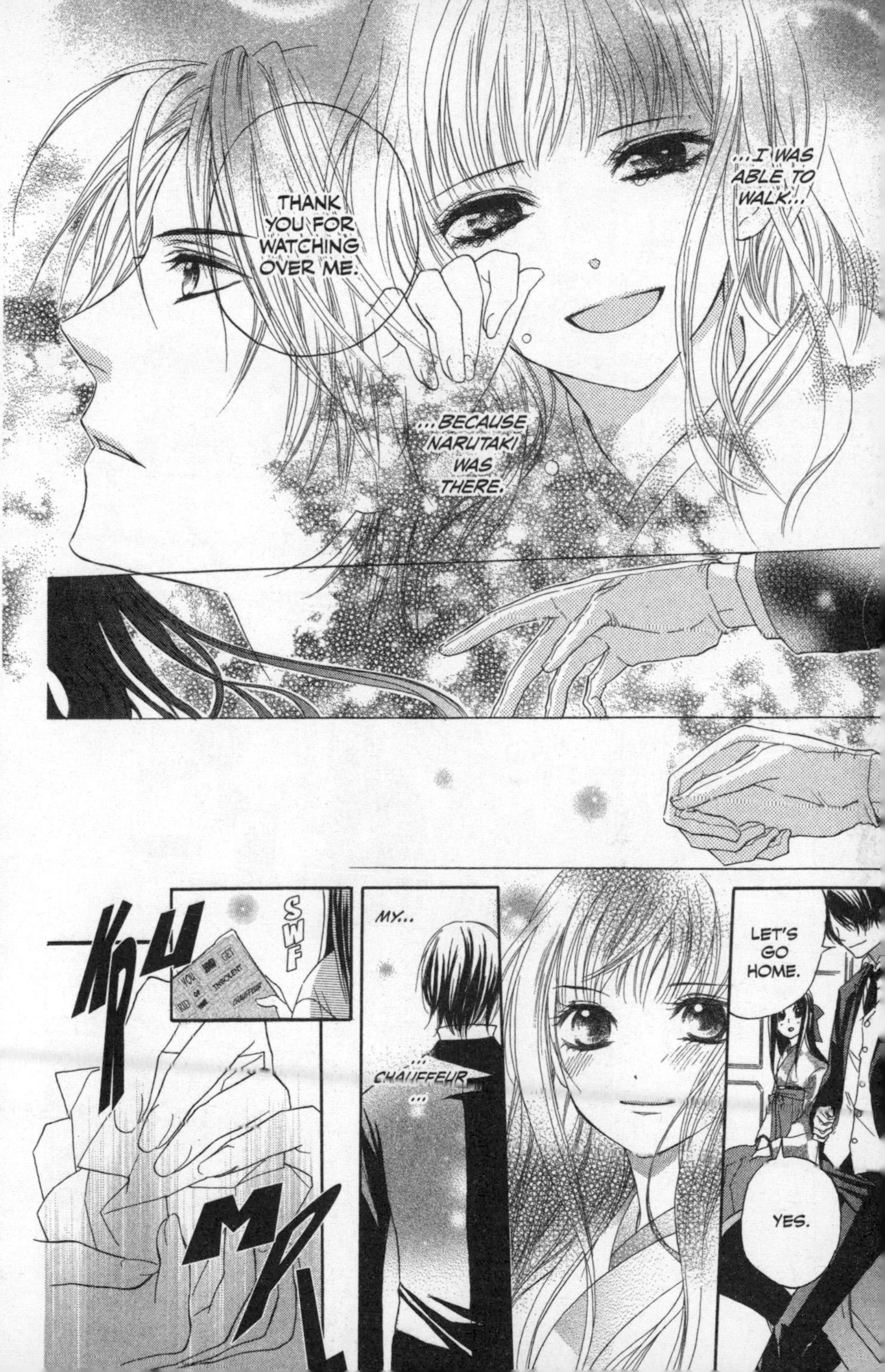
...I WAS ABLE TO WALK...
THANK YOU FOR WATCHING OVER ME.
...BECAUSE NARUTAKI WAS THERE.
LET'S GO HOME.
YES.
MY...
...CHAUFFEUR...
SWF
KRUMPL

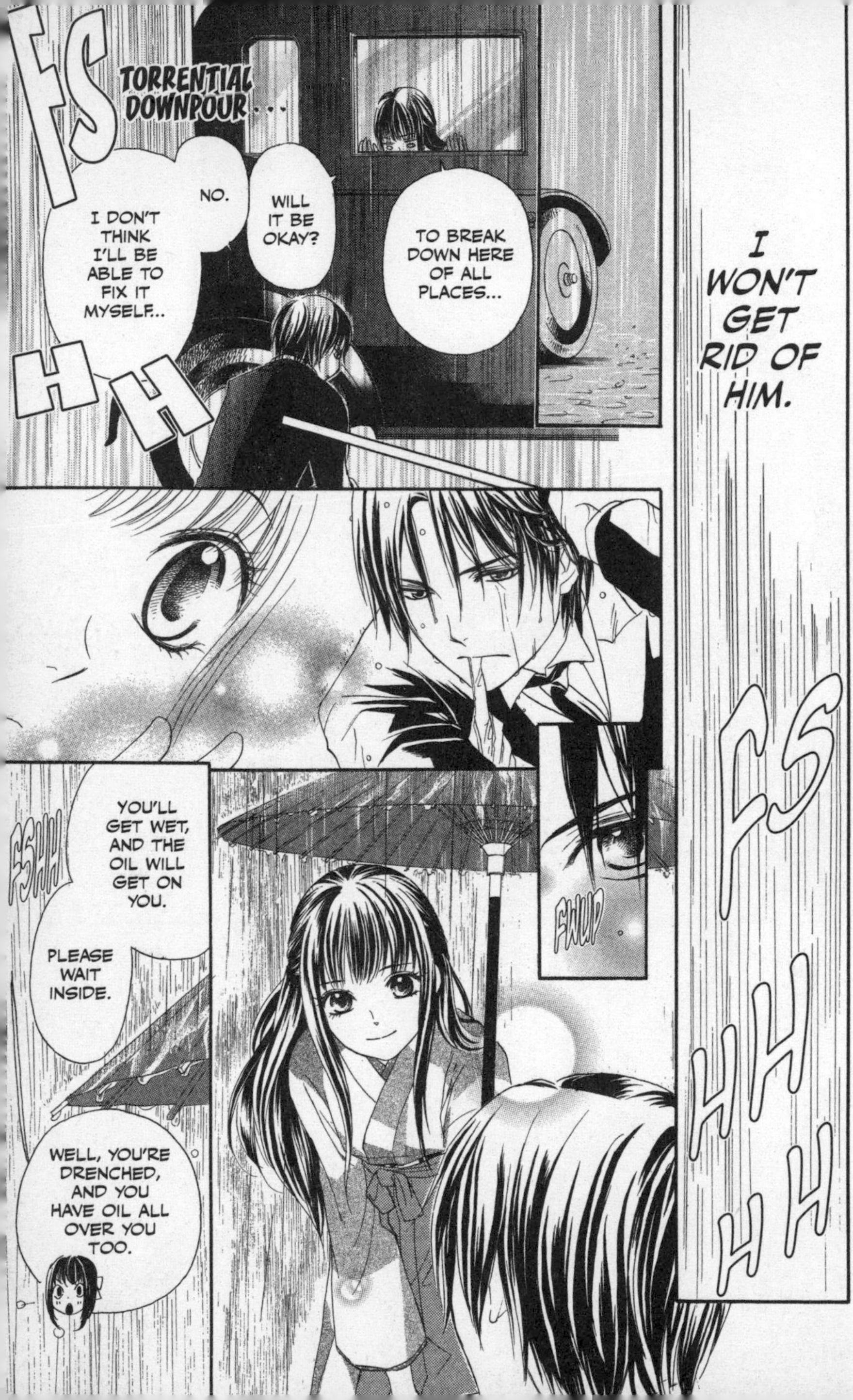
I WON'T GET RID OF HIM.
FSHHHH
FS
TORRENTIAL DOWNPOUR...
TO BREAK DOWN HERE OF ALL PLACES...
WILL IT BE OKAY?
NO.
I DON'T THINK I'LL BE ABLE TO FIX IT MYSELF...
HH
FWUP
YOU'LL GET WET, AND THE OIL WILL GET ON YOU.
PLEASE WAIT INSIDE.
FSHH
WELL, YOU'RE DRENCHED, AND YOU HAVE OIL ALL OVER YOU TOO.

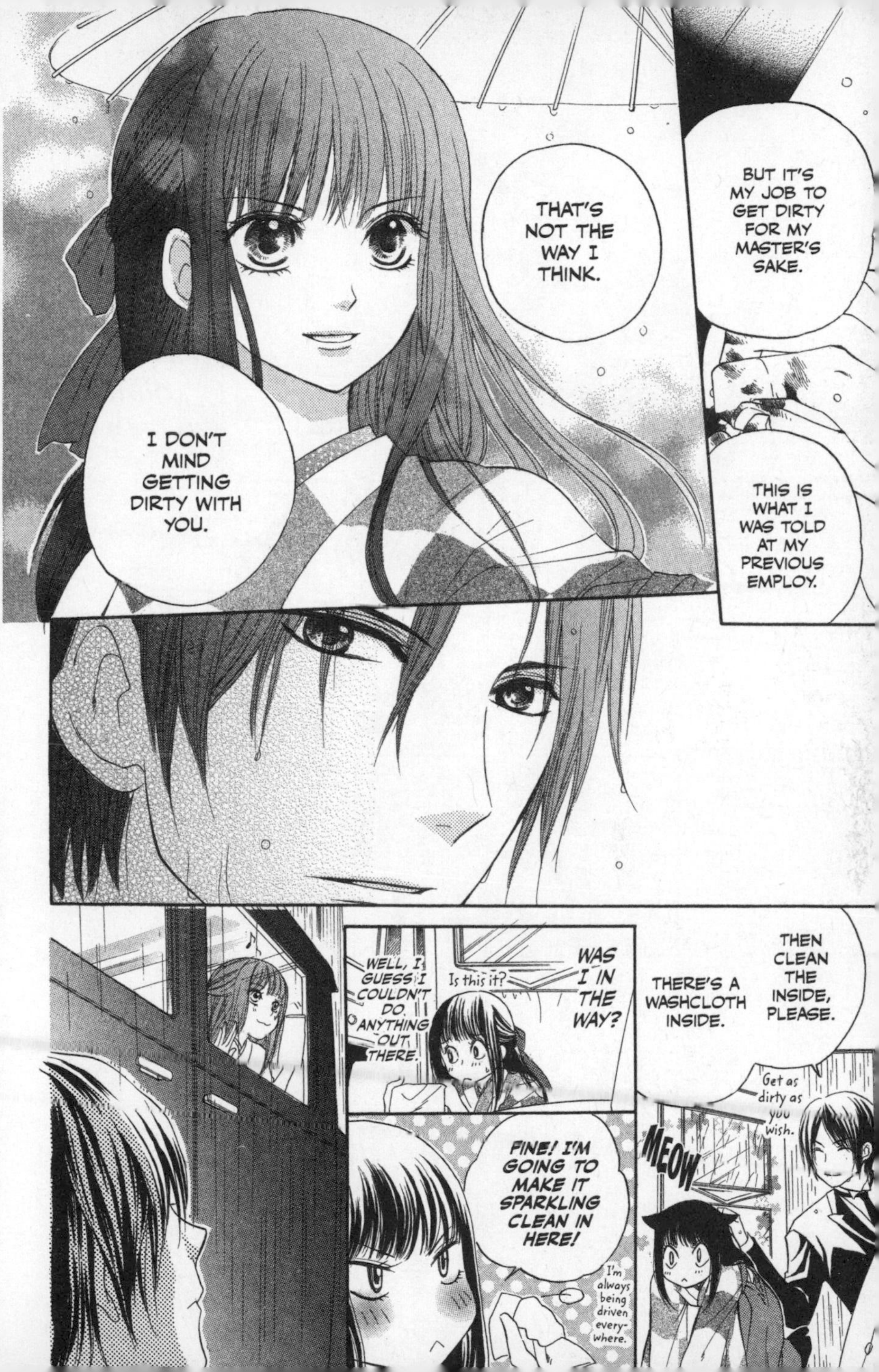
BUT IT'S MY JOB TO GET DIRTY FOR MY MASTER'S SAKE.
THIS IS WHAT I WAS TOLD AT MY PREVIOUS EMPLOY.
THAT'S NOT THE WAY I THINK.
I DON'T MIND GETTING DIRTY WITH YOU.
THEN CLEAN THE INSIDE, PLEASE.
THERE'S A WASHCLOTH INSIDE.
Get as dirty as you wish.
MEOW
WAS I IN THE WAY?
Is this it?
WELL, I GUESS I COULDN'T DO ANYTHING OUT THERE.
FINE! I'M GOING TO MAKE IT SPARKLING CLEAN IN HERE!
I'm always being driven every-where.

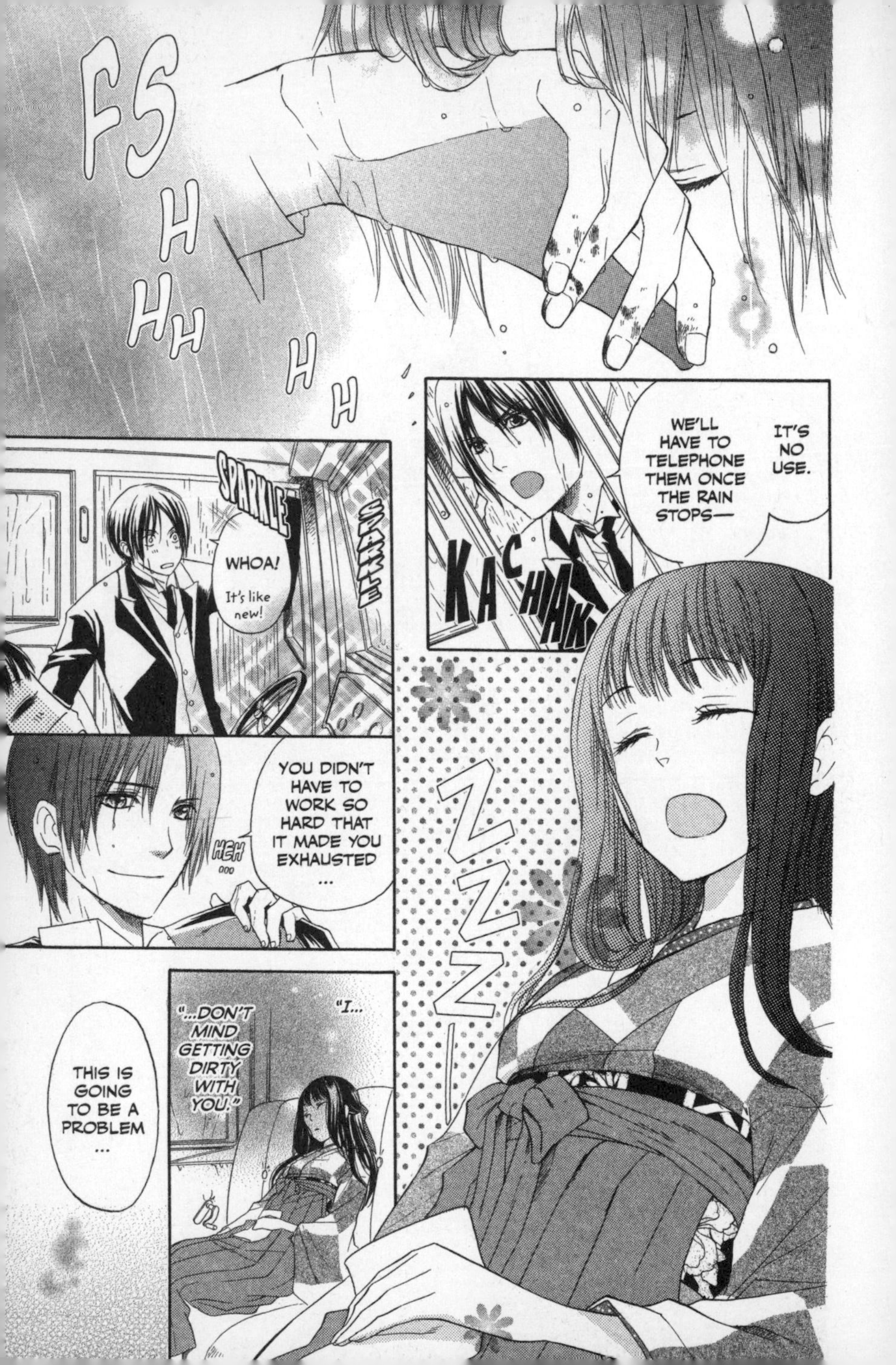
FSHHHHHH
IT'S NO USE.
WE'LL HAVE TO TELEPHONE THEM ONCE THE RAIN STOPS—
KACHAK
SPARKLE
SPARKLE
WHOA!
It's like new!
ZZZ
YOU DIDN'T HAVE TO WORK SO HARD THAT IT MADE YOU EXHAUSTED...
HEH...
"I...
"...DON'T MIND GETTING DIRTY WITH YOU."
THIS IS GOING TO BE A PROBLEM...

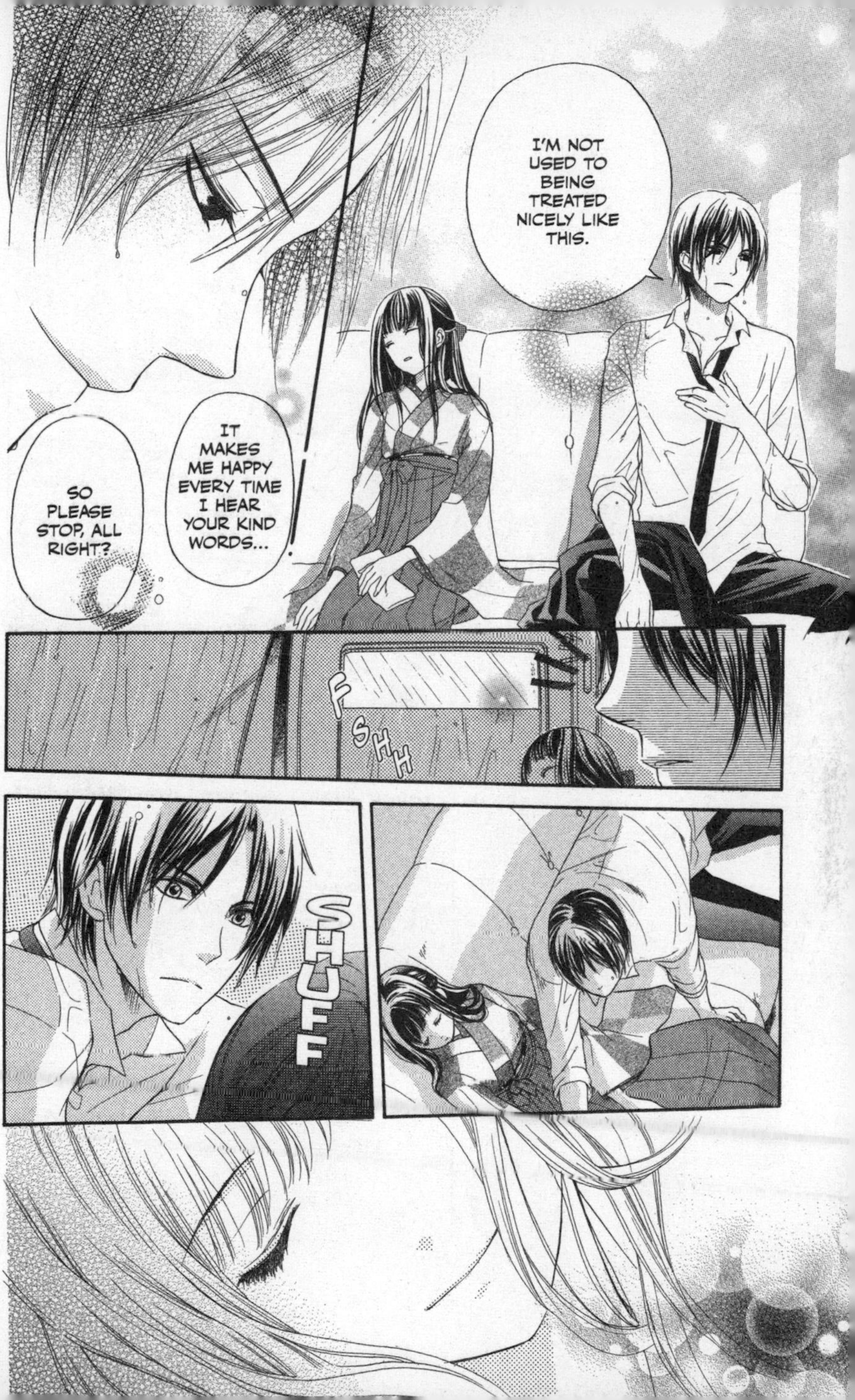
I'M NOT USED TO BEING TREATED NICELY LIKE THIS.
IT MAKES ME HAPPY EVERY TIME I HEAR YOUR KIND WORDS...
SO PLEASE STOP, ALL RIGHT?
FSHH
SHUFF

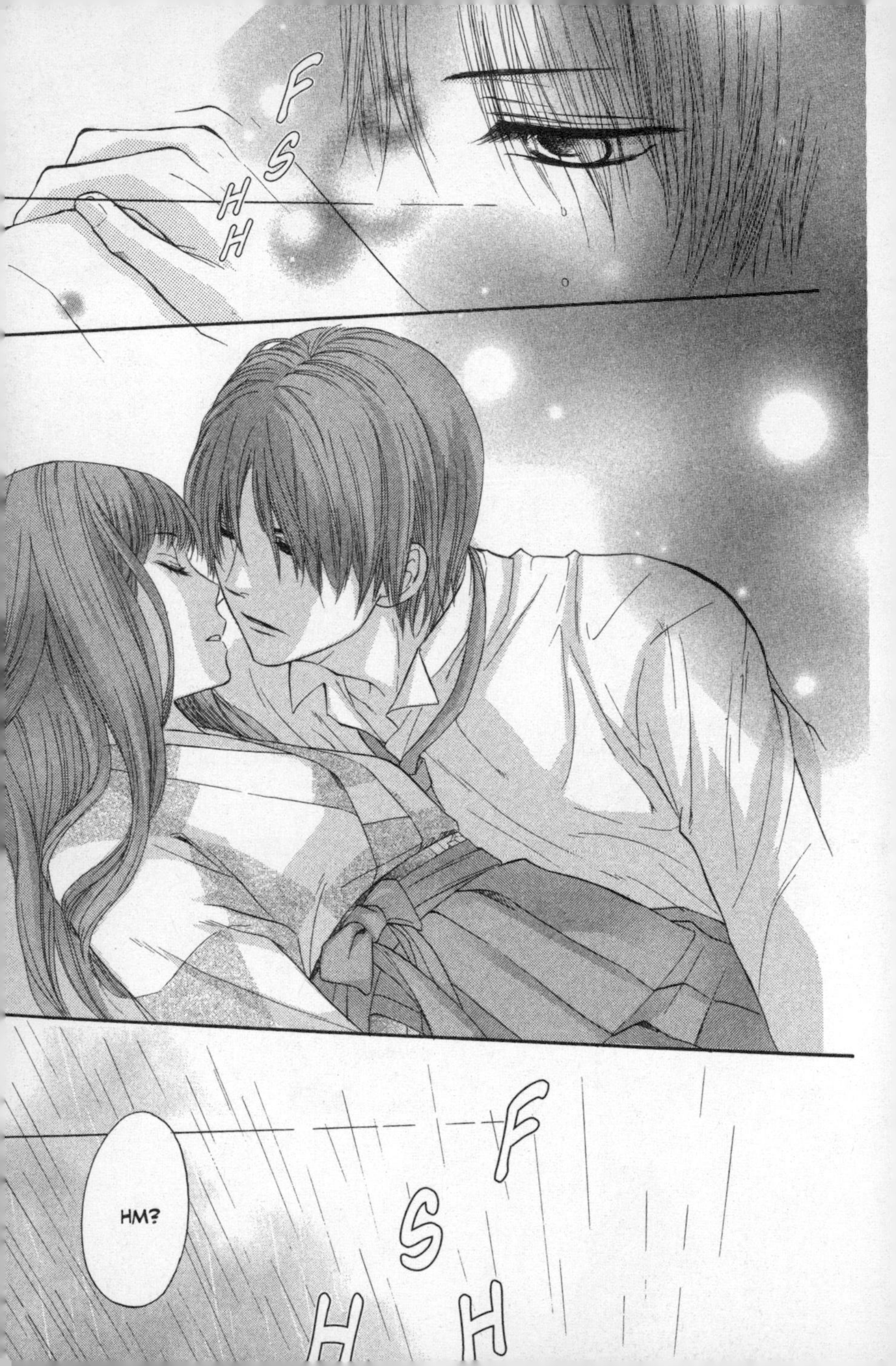
FSHH
FSHH
HM?

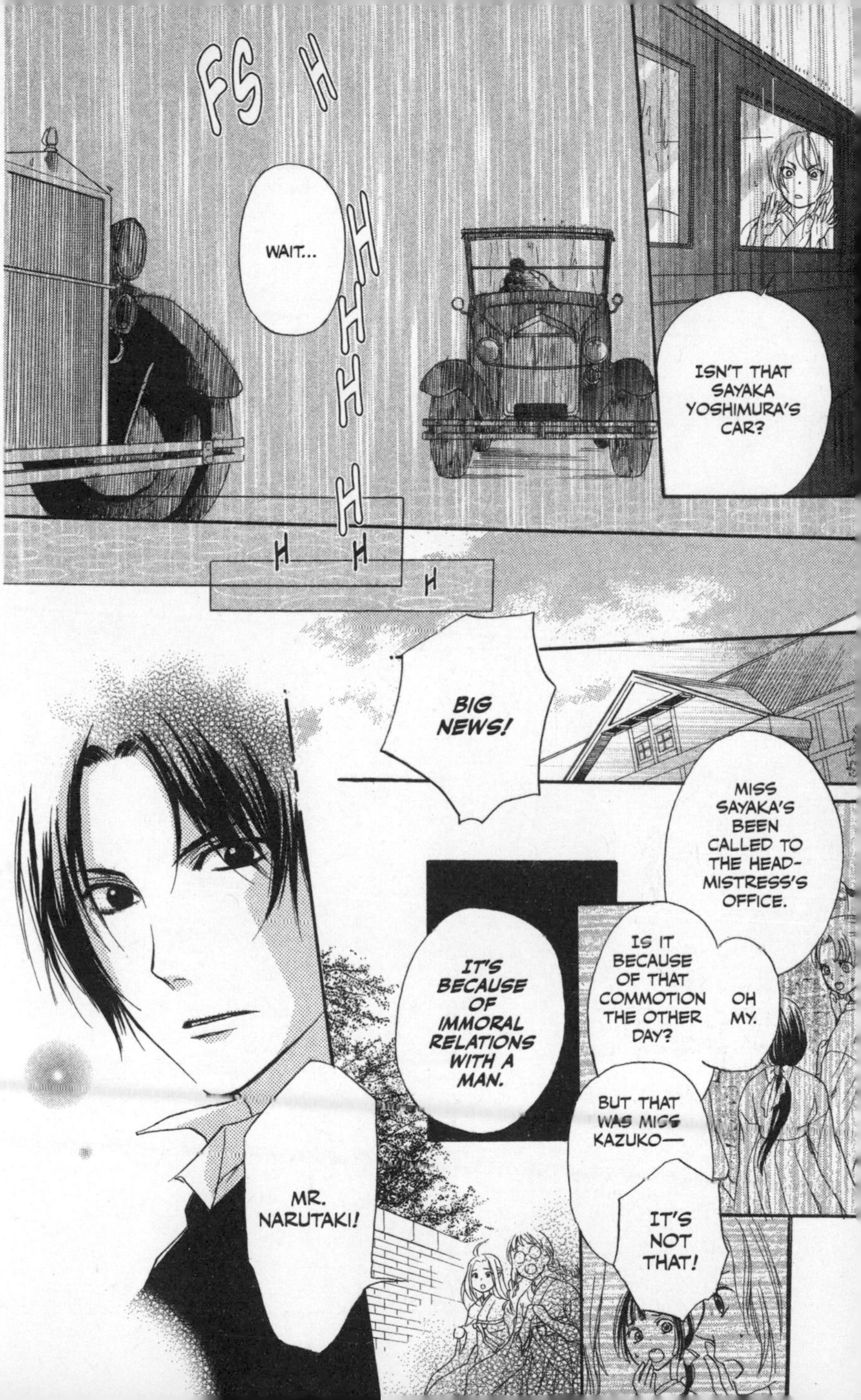
ISN'T THAT SAYAKA YOSHIMURA'S CAR?
WAIT...
FSHHHHHHHHHHHH
BIG NEWS!
MISS SAYAKA'S BEEN CALLED TO THE HEAD-MISTRESS'S OFFICE.
OH MY.
IS IT BECAUSE OF THAT COMMOTION THE OTHER DAY?
IT'S BECAUSE OF IMMORAL RELATIONS WITH A MAN.
BUT THAT WAS MISS KAZUKO—
IT'S NOT THAT!
MR. NARUTAKI!

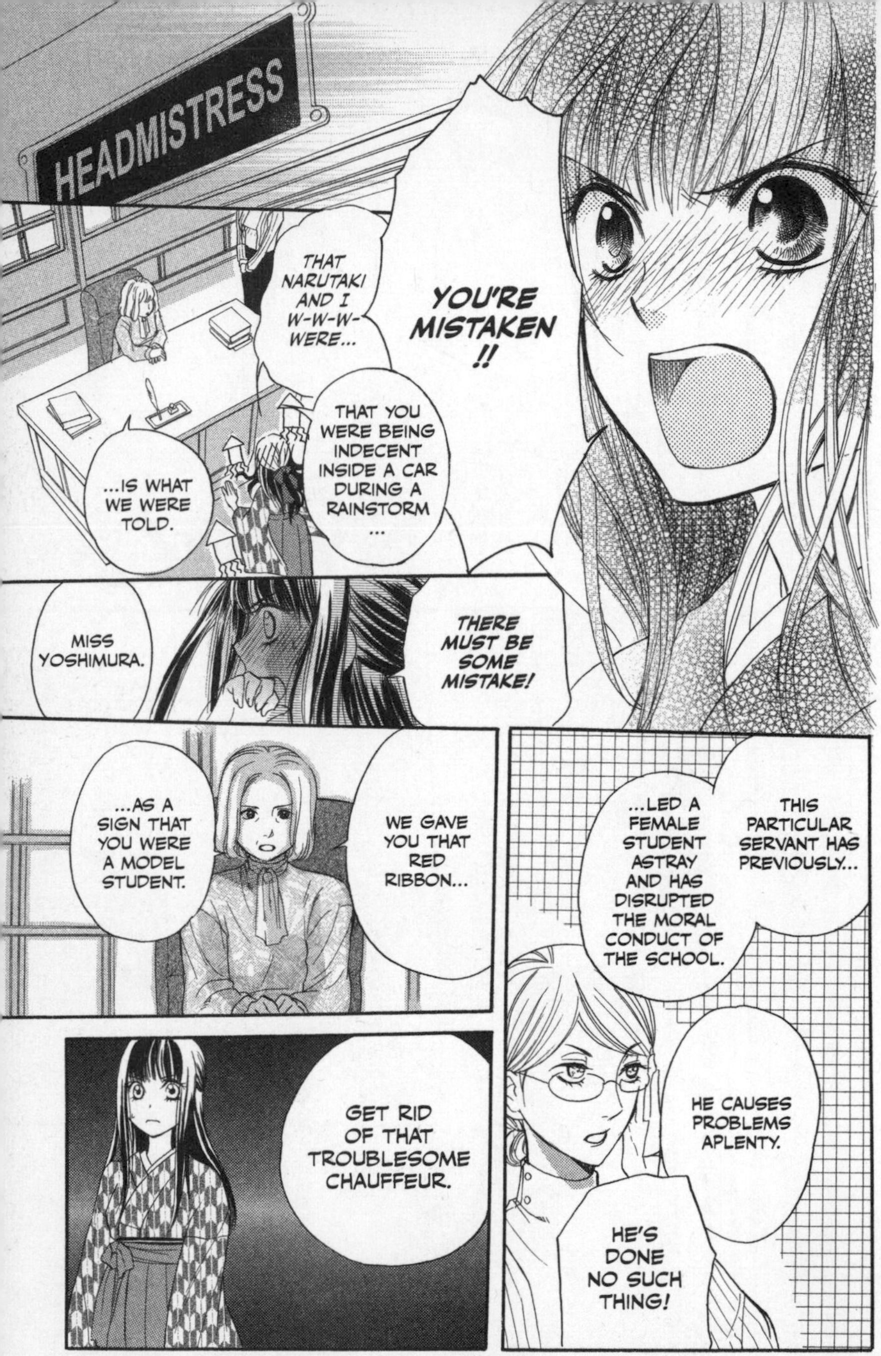
HEADMISTRESS
THAT YOU WERE BEING INDECENT INSIDE A CAR DURING A RAINSTORM ...
...IS WHAT WE WERE TOLD.
THAT NARUTAKI AND I W-W-W-WERE...
YOU'RE MISTAKEN !!
THERE MUST BE SOME MISTAKE!
MISS YOSHIMURA.
THIS PARTICULAR SERVANT HAS PREVIOUSLY...
...LED A FEMALE STUDENT ASTRAY AND HAS DISRUPTED THE MORAL CONDUCT OF THE SCHOOL.
HE CAUSES PROBLEMS APLENTY.
HE'S DONE NO SUCH THING!
WE GAVE YOU THAT RED RIBBON...
...AS A SIGN THAT YOU WERE A MODEL STUDENT.
GET RID OF THAT TROUBLESOME CHAUFFEUR.

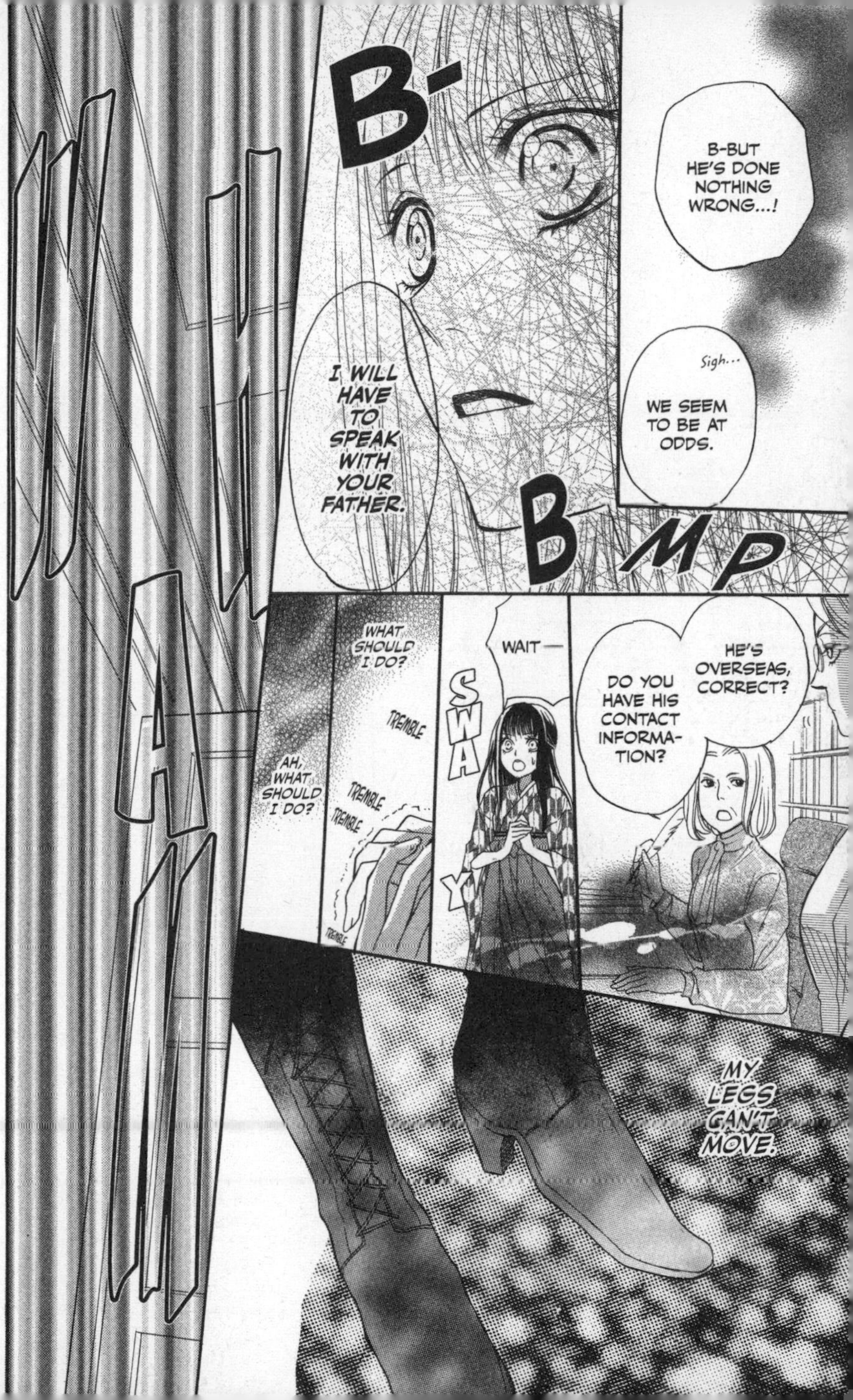
B-BUT HE'S DONE NOTHING WRONG...!
Sigh...
WE SEEM TO BE AT ODDS.
B-
I WILL HAVE TO SPEAK WITH YOUR FATHER.
B MP
HE'S OVERSEAS, CORRECT?
DO YOU HAVE HIS CONTACT INFORMATION?
WAIT—
SWAY
WHAT SHOULD I DO?
TREMBLE
AH, WHAT SHOULD I DO?
TREMBLE
TREMBLE
TREMBLE
MY LEGS CAN'T MOVE.

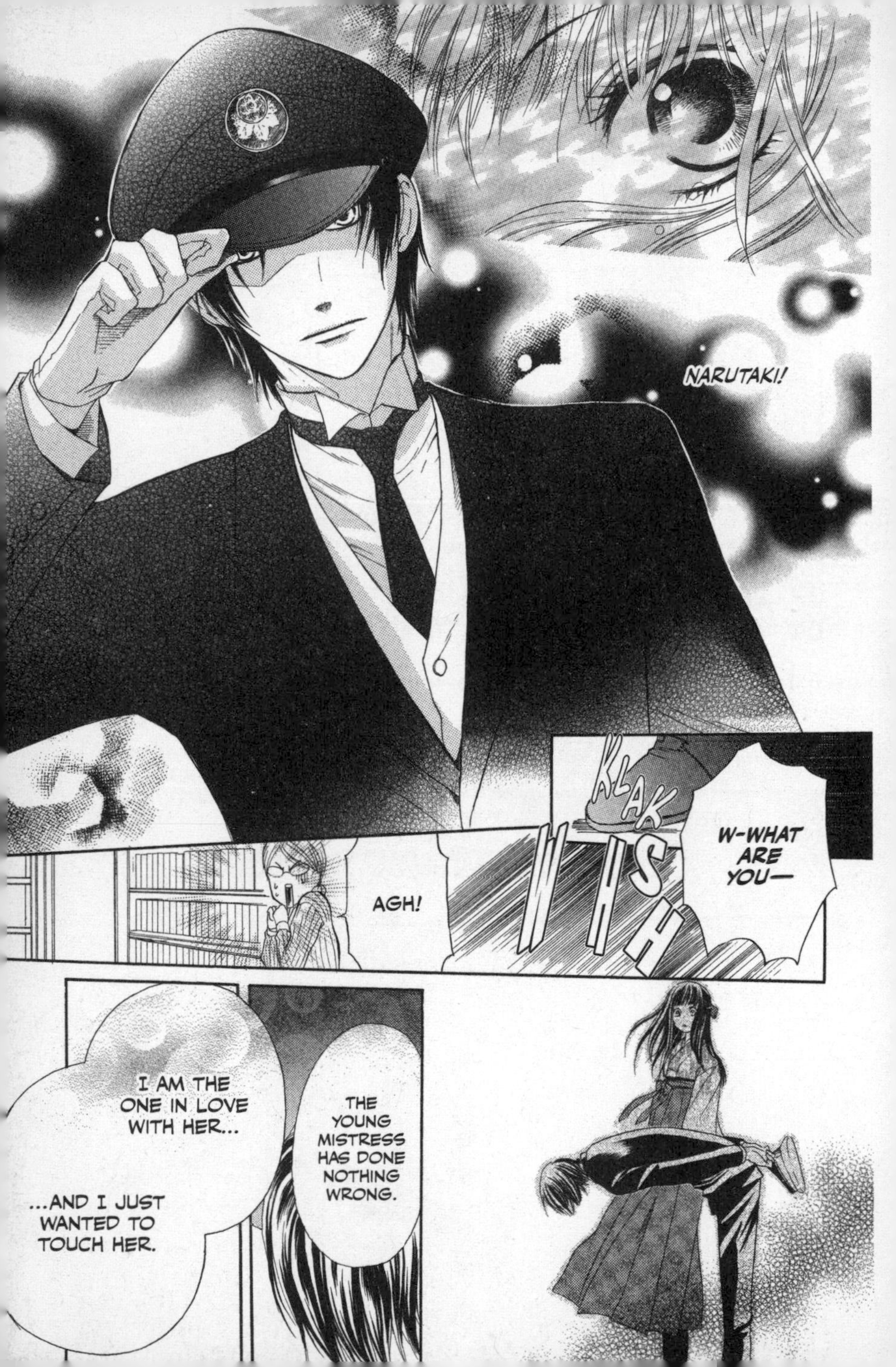
NARUTAKI!
KLAK
W-WHAT ARE YOU—
WHISH
AGH!
THE YOUNG MISTRESS HAS DONE NOTHING WRONG.
I AM THE ONE IN LOVE WITH HER...
...AND I JUST WANTED TO TOUCH HER.

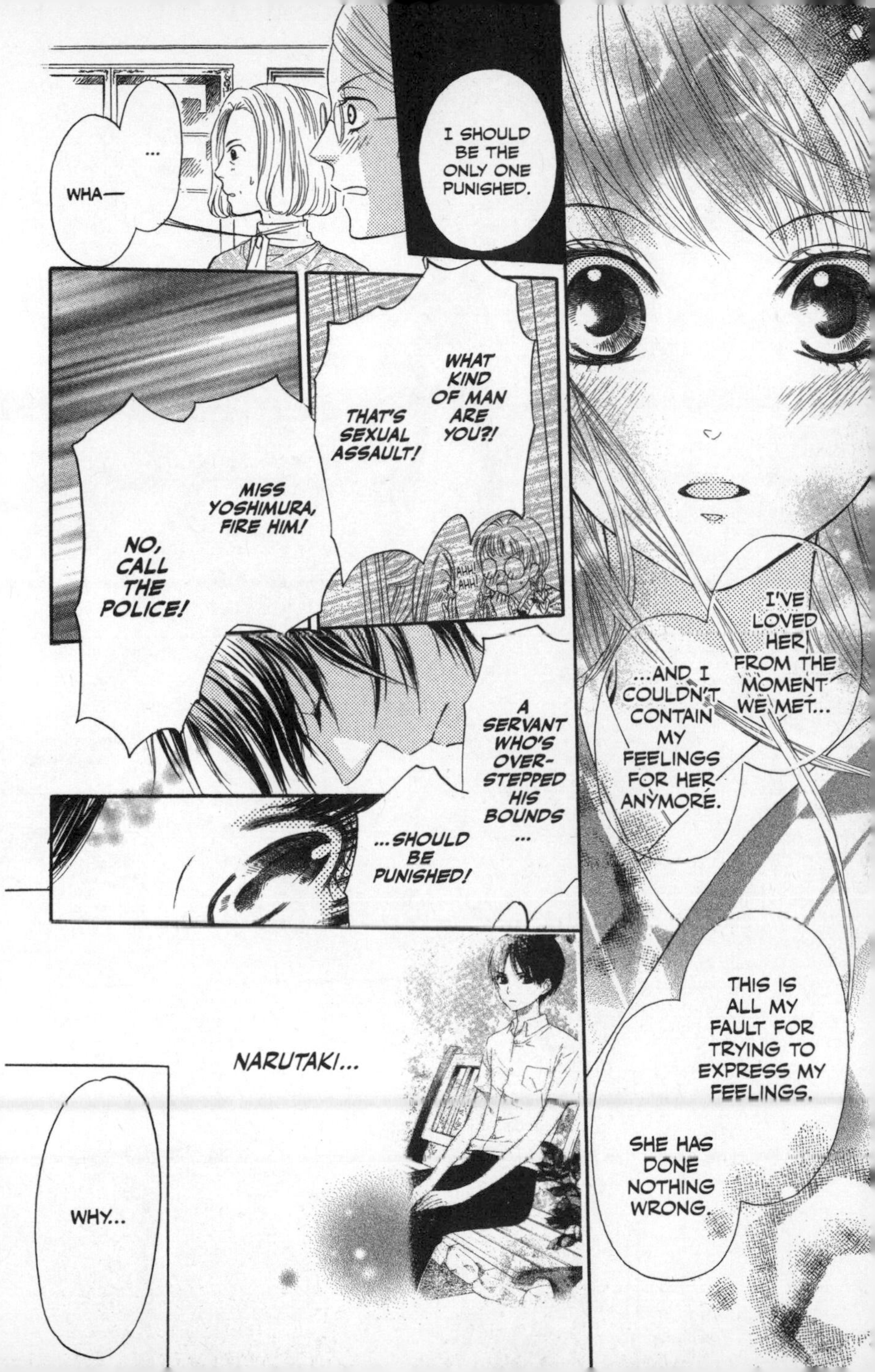

I'VE LOVED HER FROM THE MOMENT WE MET...
...AND I COULDN'T CONTAIN MY FEELINGS FOR HER ANYMORE.
THIS IS ALL MY FAULT FOR TRYING TO EXPRESS MY FEELINGS.
SHE HAS DONE NOTHING WRONG.
I SHOULD BE THE ONLY ONE PUNISHED.
...
WHA—
WHAT KIND OF MAN ARE YOU?!
THAT'S SEXUAL ASSAULT!
MISS YOSHIMURA, FIRE HIM!
NO, CALL THE POLICE!
AHH! AHH!
A SERVANT WHO'S OVER-STEPPED HIS BOUNDS ...
...SHOULD BE PUNISHED!
NARUTAKI...
WHY...

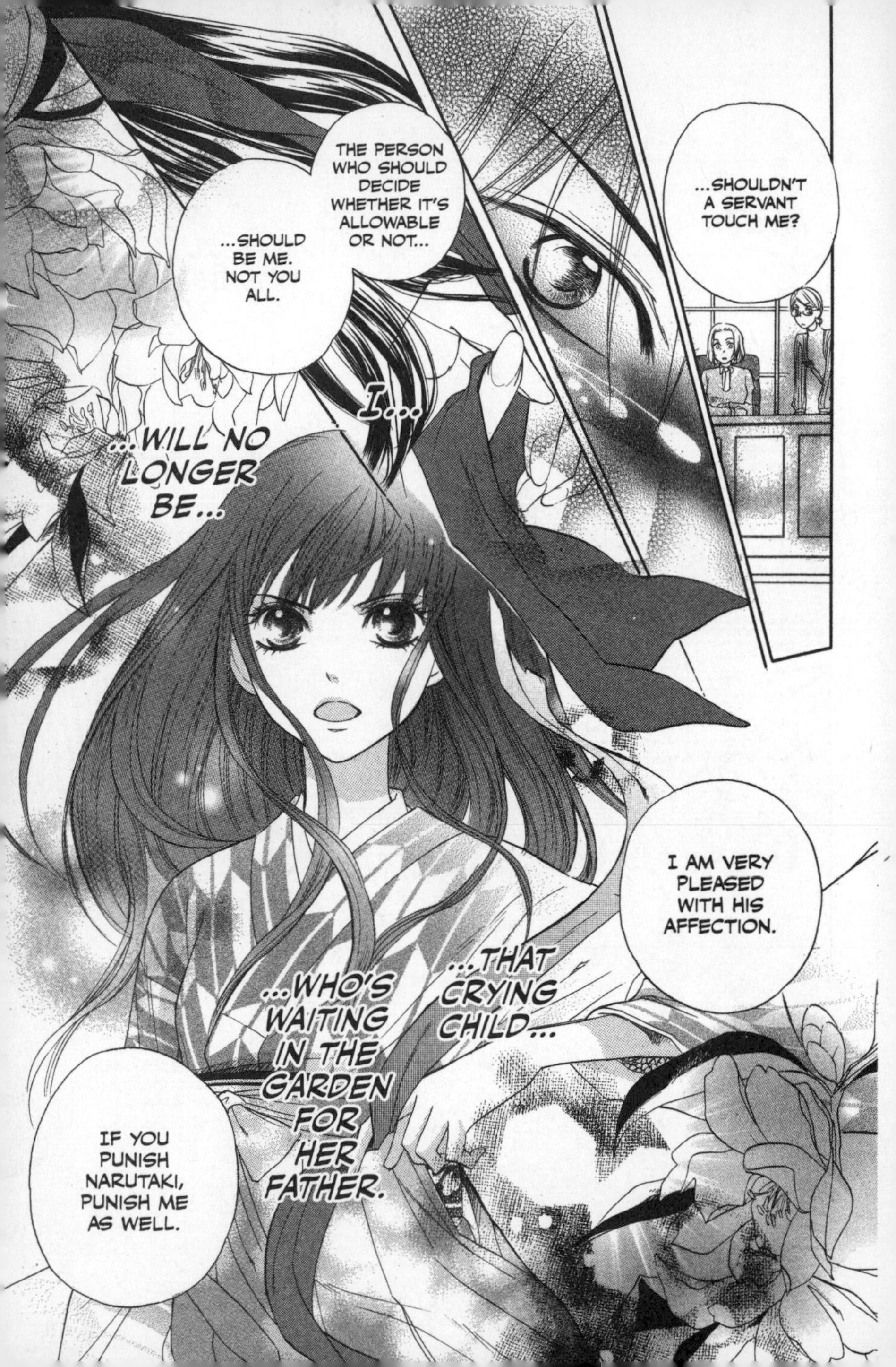
...SHOULDN'T A SERVANT TOUCH ME?
THE PERSON WHO SHOULD DECIDE WHETHER IT'S ALLOWABLE OR NOT...
...SHOULD BE ME. NOT YOU ALL.
I...
...WILL NO LONGER BE...
I AM VERY PLEASED WITH HIS AFFECTION.
...THAT CRYING CHILD...
...WHO'S WAITING IN THE GARDEN FOR HER FATHER.
IF YOU PUNISH NARUTAKI, PUNISH ME AS WELL.

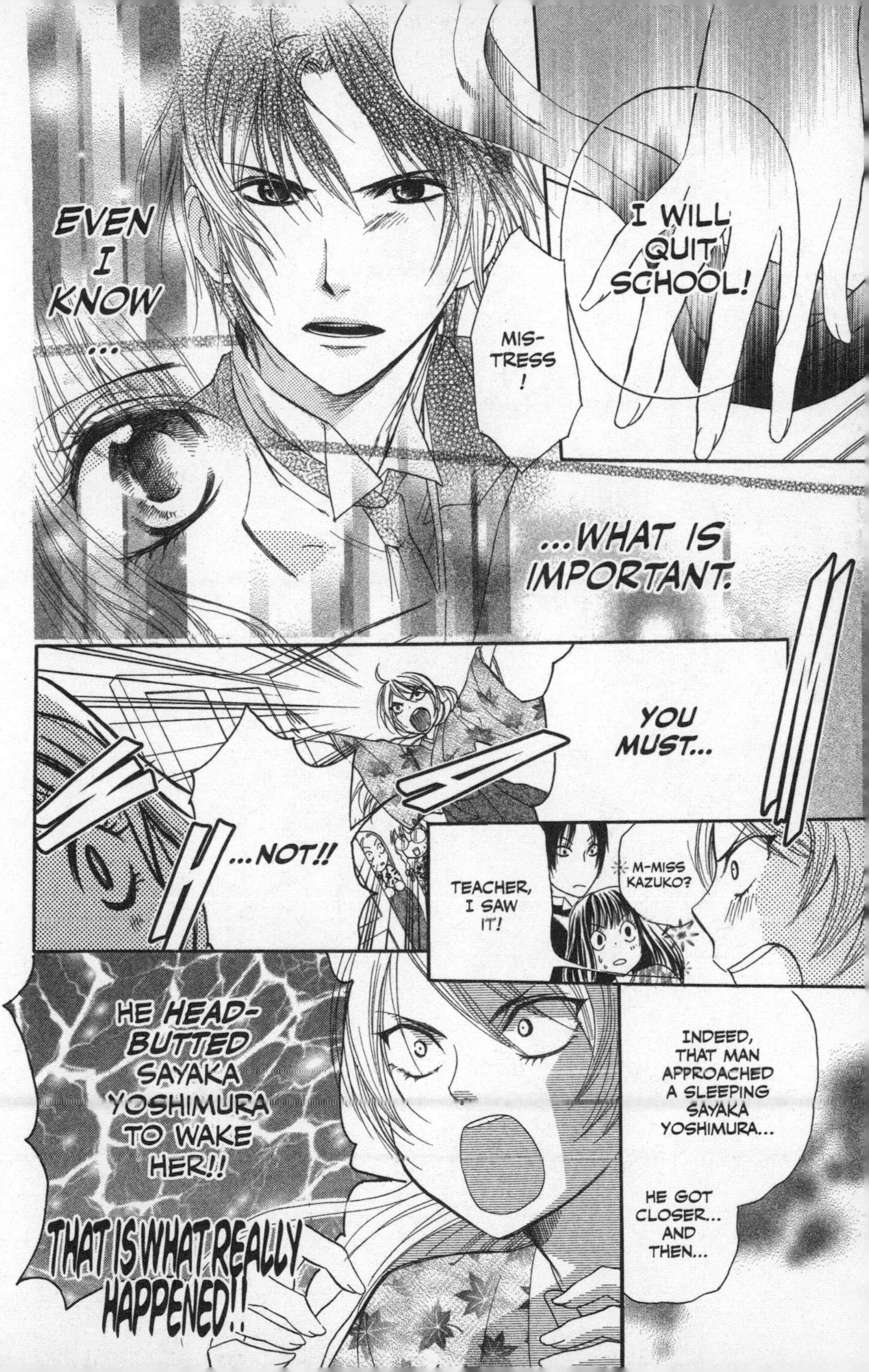
I WILL QUIT SCHOOL!
MIS-TRESS!
EVEN I KNOW...
...WHAT IS IMPORTANT.
YOU MUST...
...NOT!!
M-MISS KAZUKO?
TEACHER, I SAW IT!
INDEED, THAT MAN APPROACHED A SLEEPING SAYAKA YOSHIMURA...
HE GOT CLOSER... AND THEN...
HE HEAD-BUTTED SAYAKA YOSHIMURA TO WAKE HER!!
THAT IS WHAT REALLY HAPPENED!!

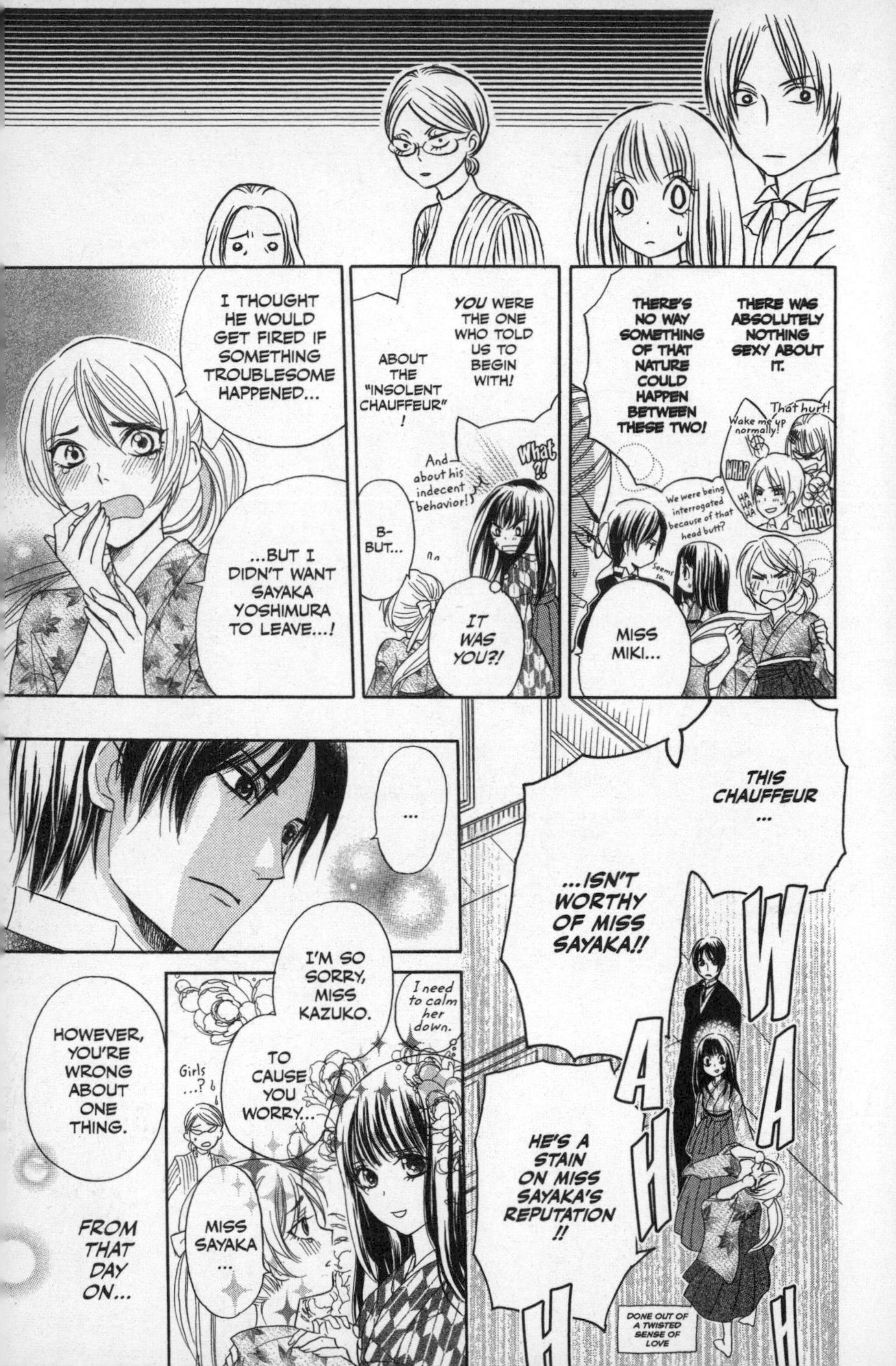
THERE WAS ABSOLUTELY NOTHING SEXY ABOUT IT.
THERE'S NO WAY SOMETHING OF THAT NATURE COULD HAPPEN BETWEEN THESE TWO!
That hurt!
Wake me up normally!
WHAP
HA HA HA
WHAP
We were being interrogated because of that head butt?
Seems so.
MISS MIKI...
YOU WERE THE ONE WHO TOLD US TO BEGIN WITH!
ABOUT THE "INSOLENT CHAUFFEUR"!
What ?!
And about his indecent behavior!
B-BUT...
IT WAS YOU?!
I THOUGHT HE WOULD GET FIRED IF SOMETHING TROUBLESOME HAPPENED...
...BUT I DIDN'T WANT SAYAKA YOSHIMURA TO LEAVE...!
THIS CHAUFFEUR ...
...ISN'T WORTHY OF MISS SAYAKA!!
WAAHHH
HE'S A STAIN ON MISS SAYAKA'S REPUTATION !!
DONE OUT OF A TWISTED SENSE OF LOVE
...
I'M SO SORRY, MISS KAZUKO.
I need to calm her down.
TO CAUSE YOU WORRY...
HOWEVER, YOU'RE WRONG ABOUT ONE THING.
Girls ...?
MISS SAYAKA ...
FROM THAT DAY ON...

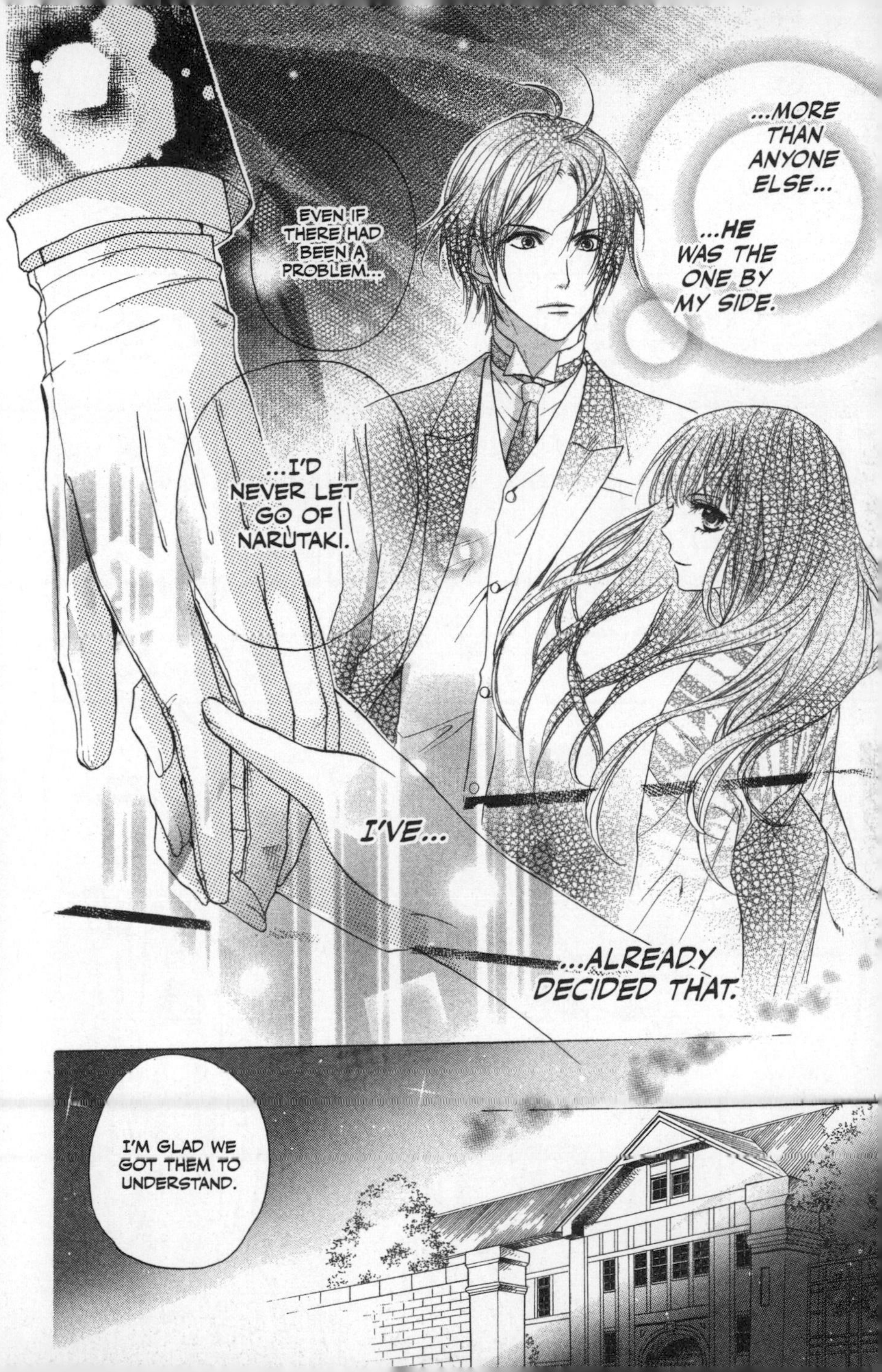
...MORE THAN ANYONE ELSE...
...HE WAS THE ONE BY MY SIDE.
EVEN IF THERE HAD BEEN A PROBLEM...
...I'D NEVER LET GO OF NARUTAKI.
I'VE...
...ALREADY DECIDED THAT.
I'M GLAD WE GOT THEM TO UNDERSTAND.

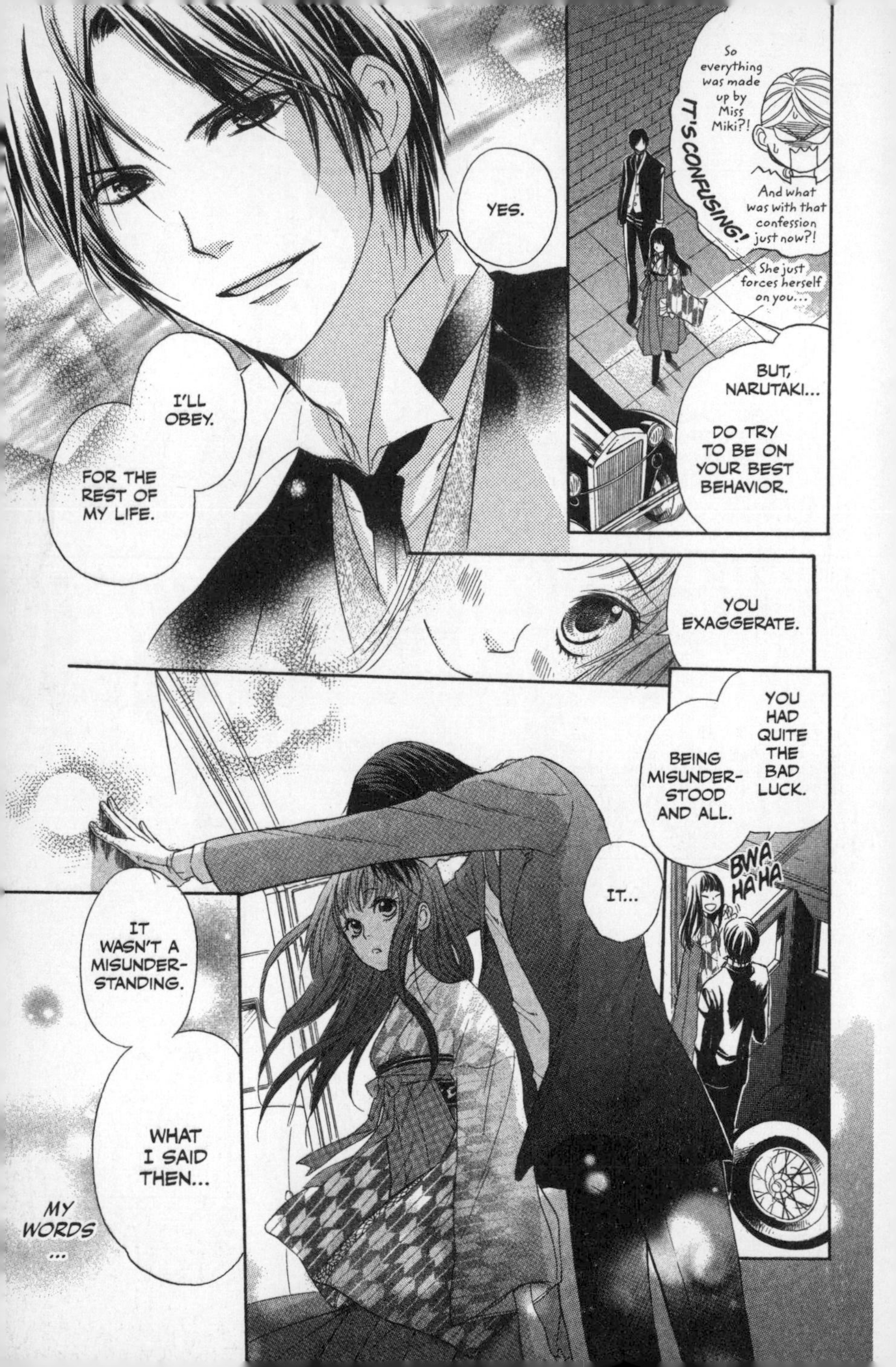
So everything was made up by Miss Miki?!
IT'S CONFUSING!
And what was with that confession just now?!
She just forces herself on you...
BUT, NARUTAKI...
DO TRY TO BE ON YOUR BEST BEHAVIOR.
YES.
I'LL OBEY.
FOR THE REST OF MY LIFE.
YOU EXAGGERATE.
YOU HAD QUITE THE BAD LUCK.
BEING MISUNDER-STOOD AND ALL.
BWA HA HA
IT...
IT WASN'T A MISUNDER-STANDING.
WHAT I SAID THEN...
MY WORDS...

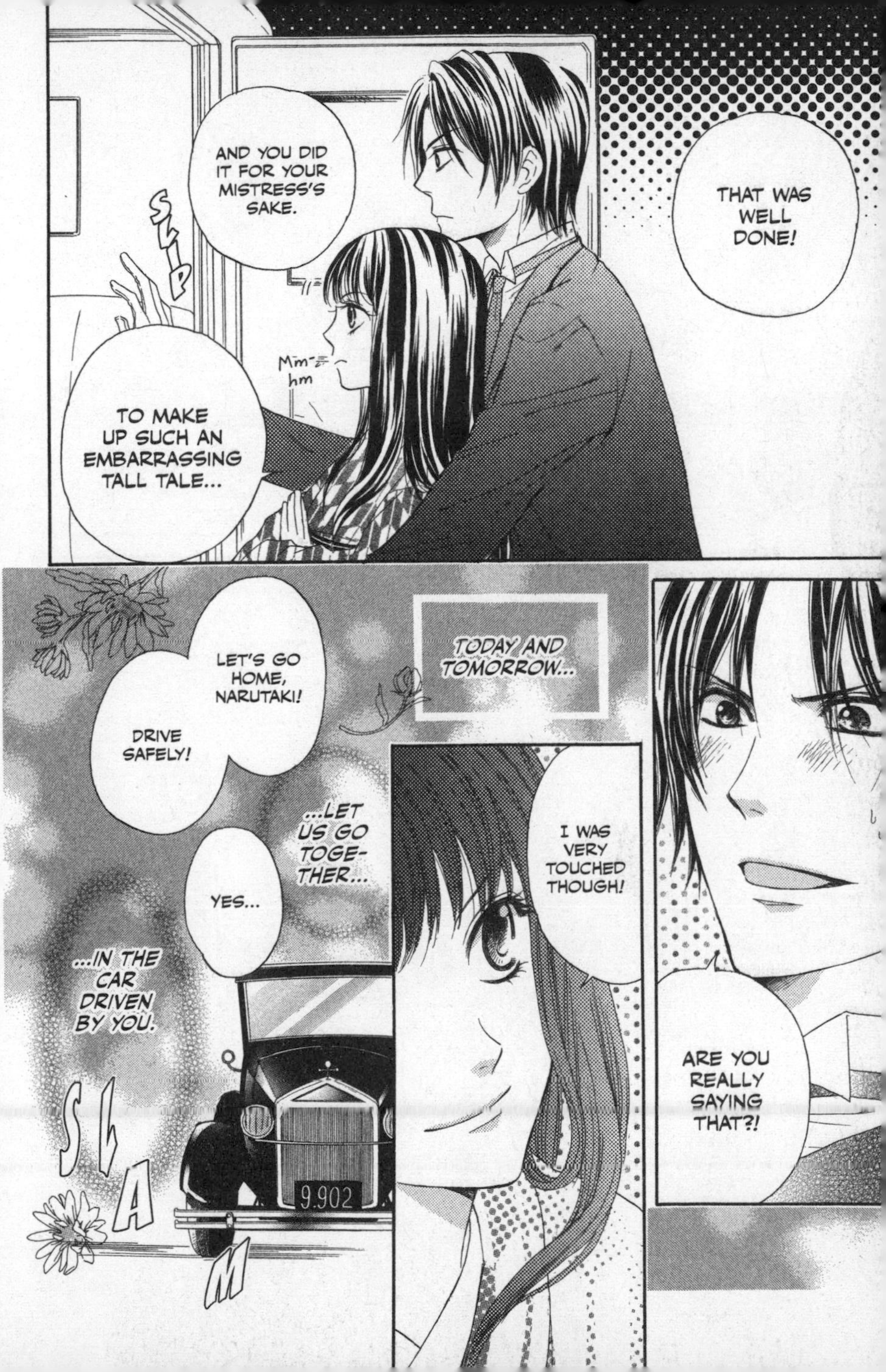
THAT WAS WELL DONE!
AND YOU DID IT FOR YOUR MISTRESS'S SAKE.
SLIP
Mm-hm
TO MAKE UP SUCH AN EMBARRASSING TALL TALE...
ARE YOU REALLY SAYING THAT?!
I WAS VERY TOUCHED THOUGH!
TODAY AND TOMORROW...
LET'S GO HOME, NARUTAKI!
DRIVE SAFELY!
...LET US GO TOGETHER...
YES...
...IN THE CAR DRIVEN BY YOU.
9.902
SLAM

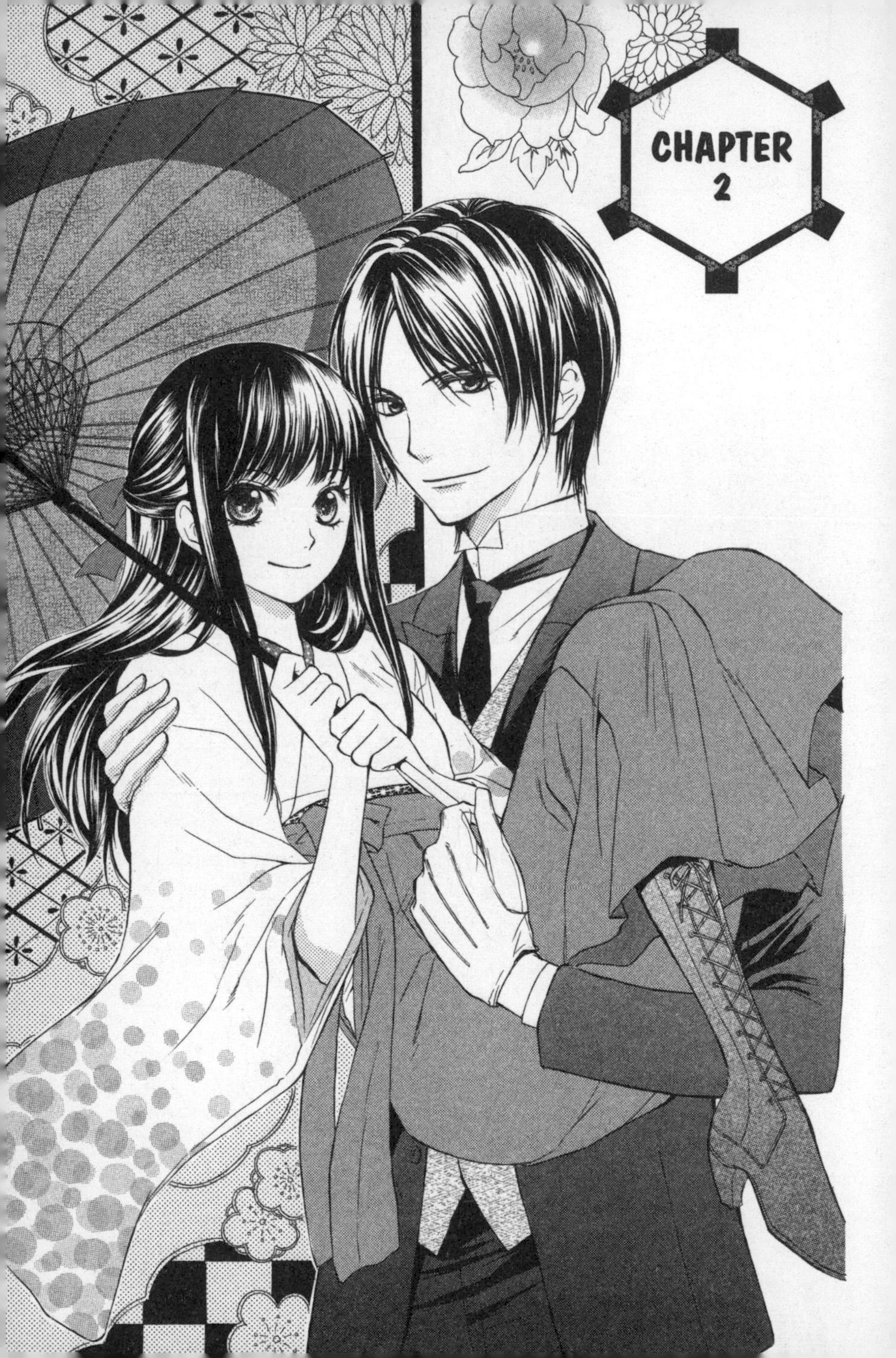
CHAPTER 2

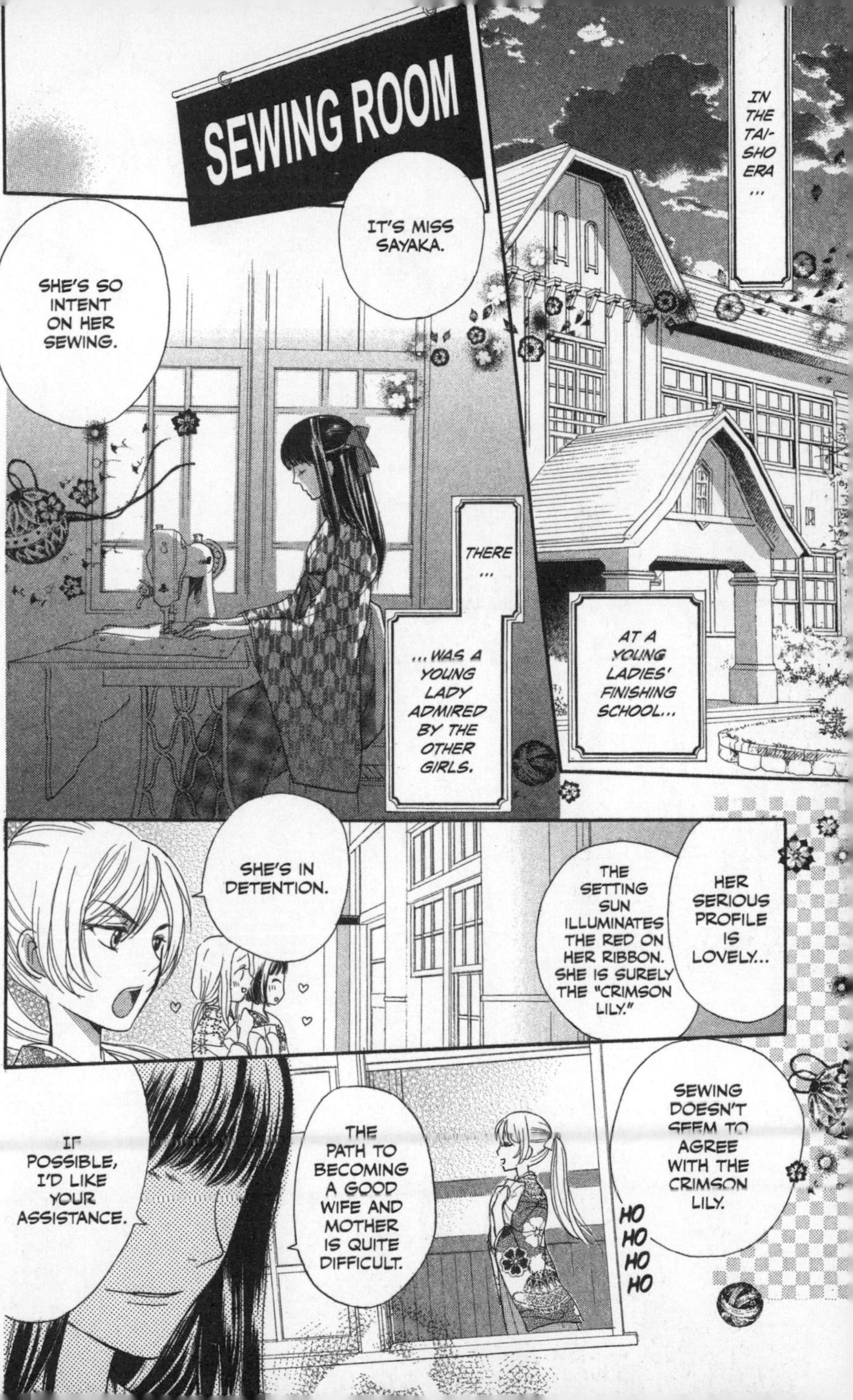
IN THE TAI-SHO ERA...
AT A YOUNG LADIES' FINISHING SCHOOL...
SEWING ROOM
THERE...
...WAS A YOUNG LADY ADMIRED BY THE OTHER GIRLS.
IT'S MISS SAYAKA.
SHE'S SO INTENT ON HER SEWING.
HER SERIOUS PROFILE IS LOVELY...
THE SETTING SUN ILLUMINATES THE RED ON HER RIBBON. SHE IS SURELY THE "CRIMSON LILY."
SHE'S IN DETENTION.
SEWING DOESN'T SEEM TO AGREE WITH THE CRIMSON LILY.
HO HO HO HO
THE PATH TO BECOMING A GOOD WIFE AND MOTHER IS QUITE DIFFICULT.
IF POSSIBLE, I'D LIKE YOUR ASSISTANCE.

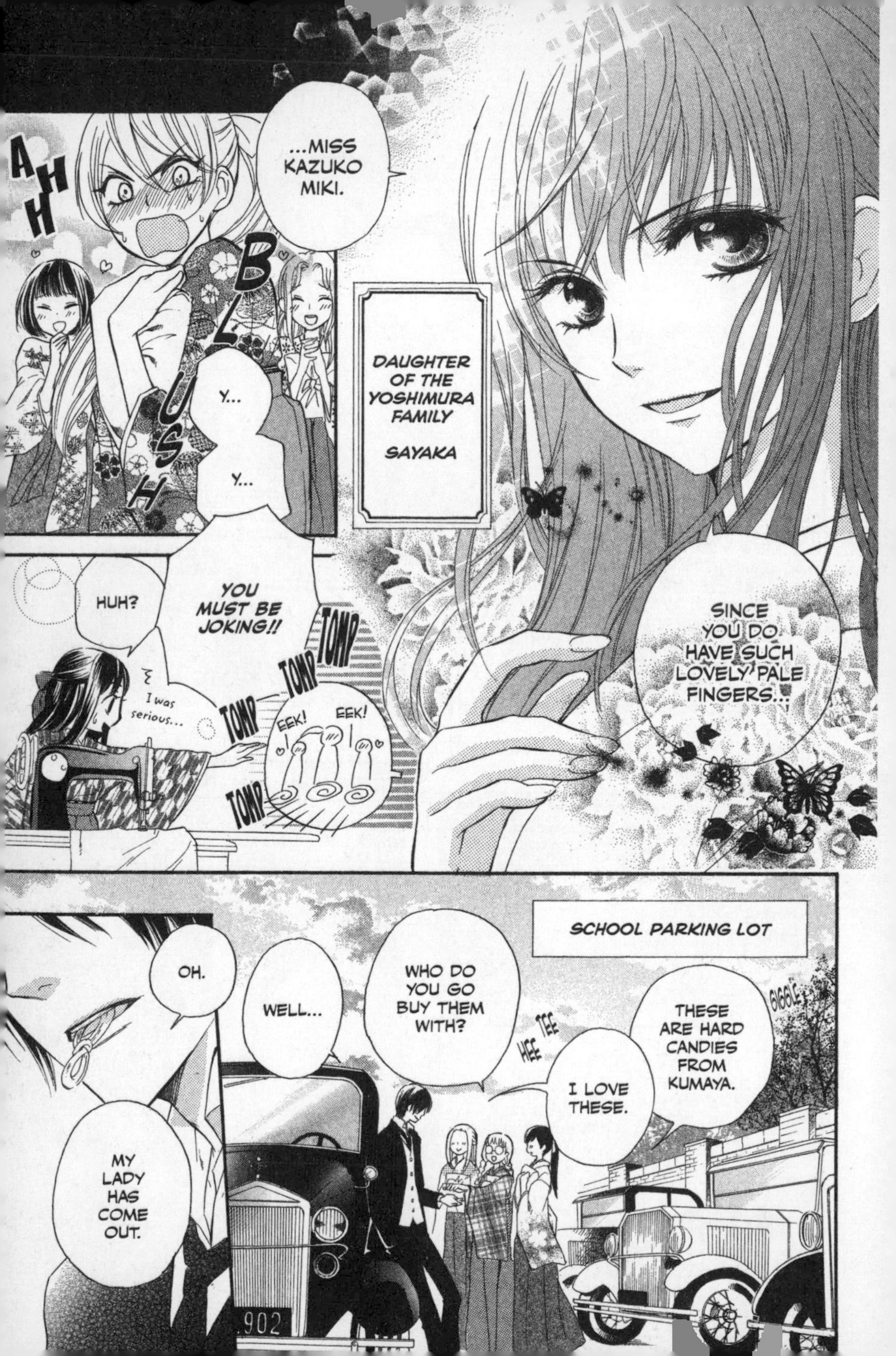
DAUGHTER OF THE YOSHIMURA FAMILY
SAYAKA
SINCE YOU DO HAVE SUCH LOVELY PALE FINGERS...
...MISS KAZUKO MIKI.
AHH
BLUSH
Y...
Y...
YOU MUST BE JOKING!!
HUH?
I was serious...
TOMP
TOMP
TOMP
TOMP
EEK!
EEK!
SCHOOL PARKING LOT
THESE ARE HARD CANDIES FROM KUMAYA.
GIGGLE
I LOVE THESE.
HEE TEE
WHO DO YOU GO BUY THEM WITH?
WELL...
OH.
MY LADY HAS COME OUT.
902

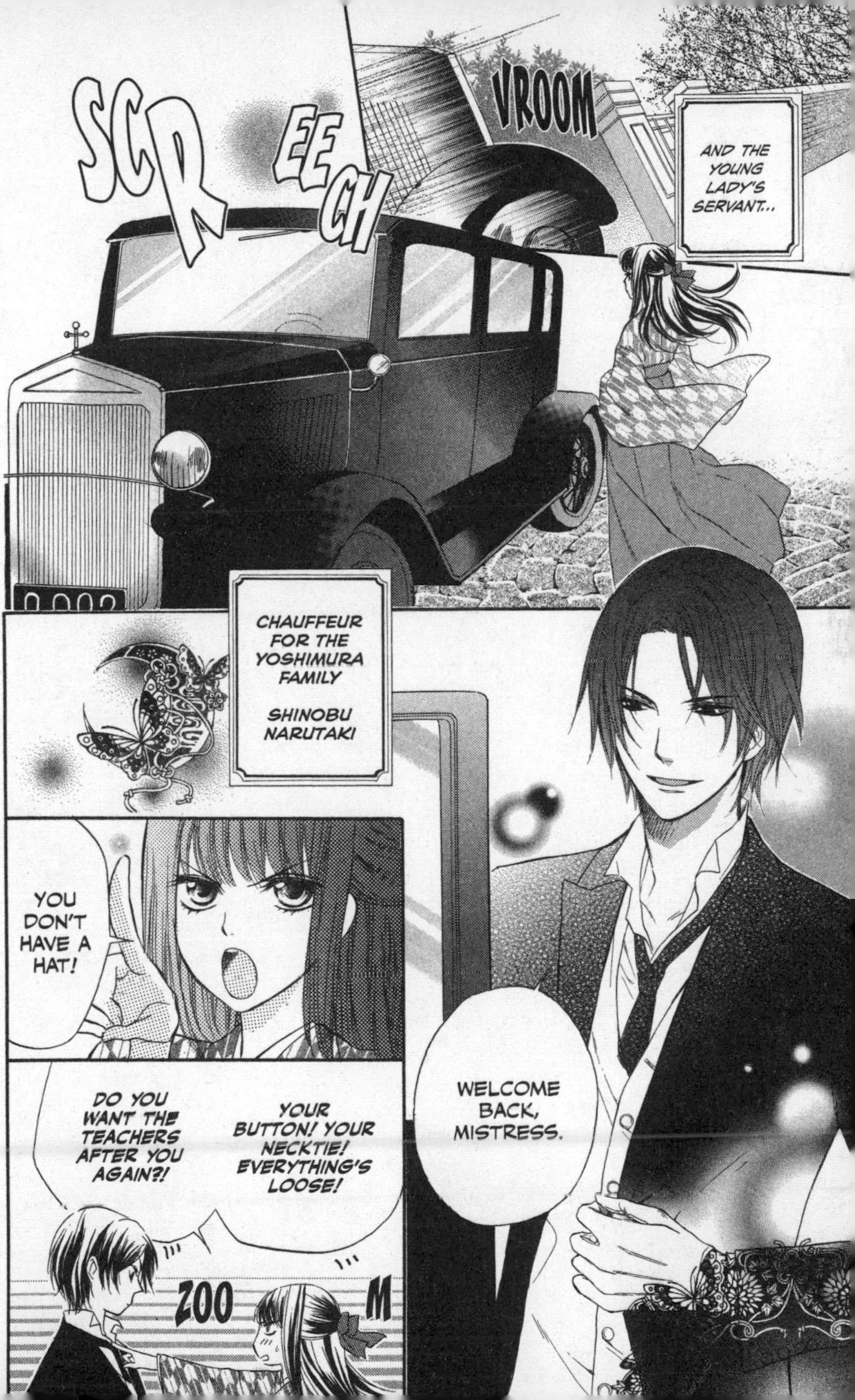
AND THE YOUNG LADY'S SERVANT...
VROOM
SCREECH
WELCOME BACK, MISTRESS.
CHAUFFEUR FOR THE YOSHIMURA FAMILY
SHINOBU NARUTAKI
YOU DON'T HAVE A HAT!
YOUR BUTTON! YOUR NECKTIE! EVERYTHING'S LOOSE!
DO YOU WANT THE TEACHERS AFTER YOU AGAIN?!
ZOOM

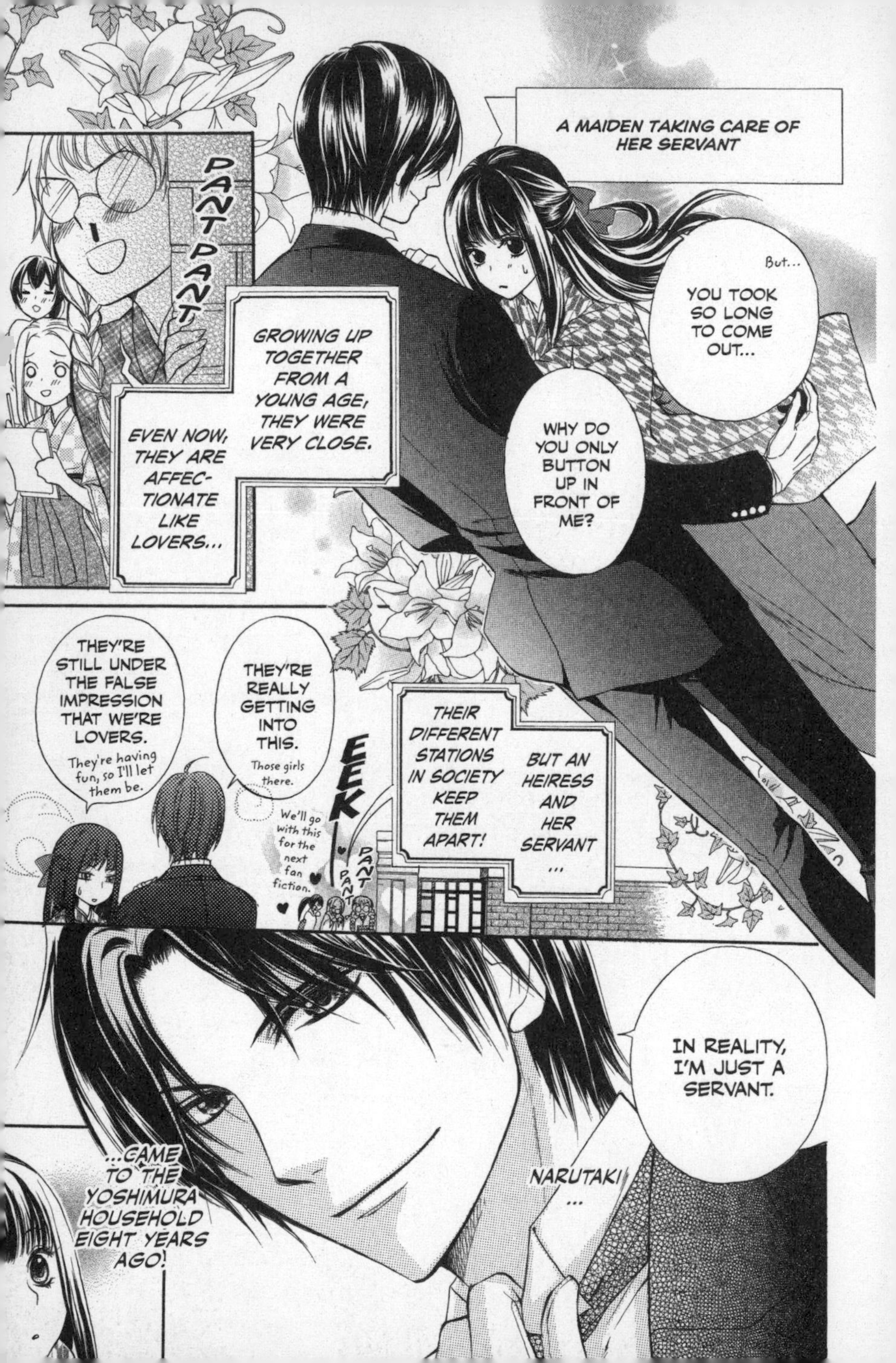
A MAIDEN TAKING CARE OF HER SERVANT
But...
YOU TOOK SO LONG TO COME OUT...
WHY DO YOU ONLY BUTTON UP IN FRONT OF ME?
GROWING UP TOGETHER FROM A YOUNG AGE, THEY WERE VERY CLOSE.
EVEN NOW, THEY ARE AFFEC-TIONATE LIKE LOVERS...
PANT PANT PANT
THEIR DIFFERENT STATIONS IN SOCIETY KEEP THEM APART!
BUT AN HEIRESS AND HER SERVANT ...
EEK
PANT PANT
We'll go with this for the next fan fiction.
THEY'RE REALLY GETTING INTO THIS.
Those girls there.
THEY'RE STILL UNDER THE FALSE IMPRESSION THAT WE'RE LOVERS.
They're having fun, so I'll let them be.
IN REALITY, I'M JUST A SERVANT.
NARUTAKI ...
...CAME TO THE YOSHIMURA HOUSEHOLD EIGHT YEARS AGO!

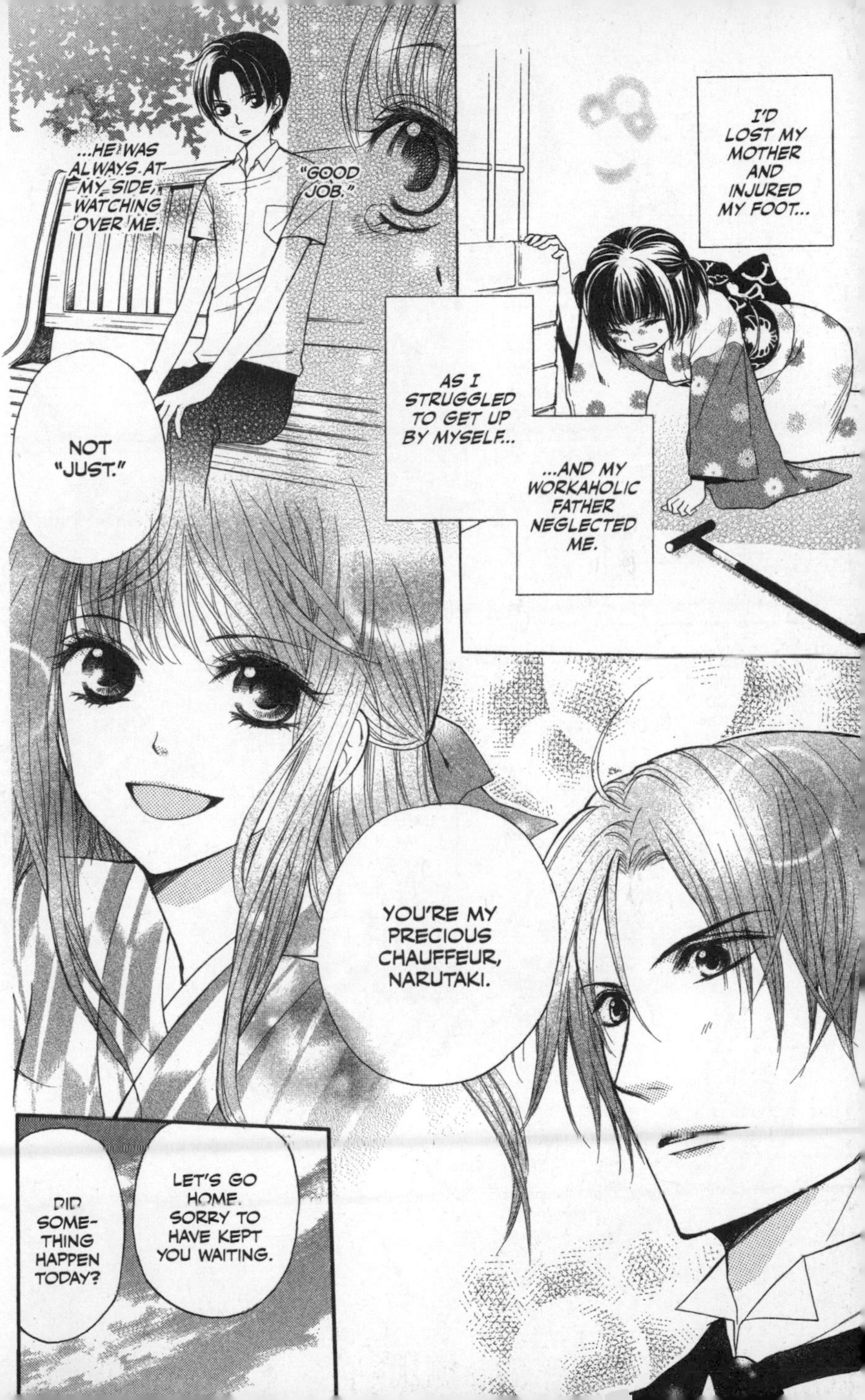
I'D LOST MY MOTHER AND INJURED MY FOOT...
AS I STRUGGLED TO GET UP BY MYSELF...
...AND MY WORKAHOLIC FATHER NEGLECTED ME.
...HE WAS ALWAYS AT MY SIDE, WATCHING OVER ME.
"GOOD JOB."
NOT "JUST."
YOU'RE MY PRECIOUS CHAUFFEUR, NARUTAKI.
LET'S GO HOME. SORRY TO HAVE KEPT YOU WAITING.
DID SOMETHING HAPPEN TODAY?

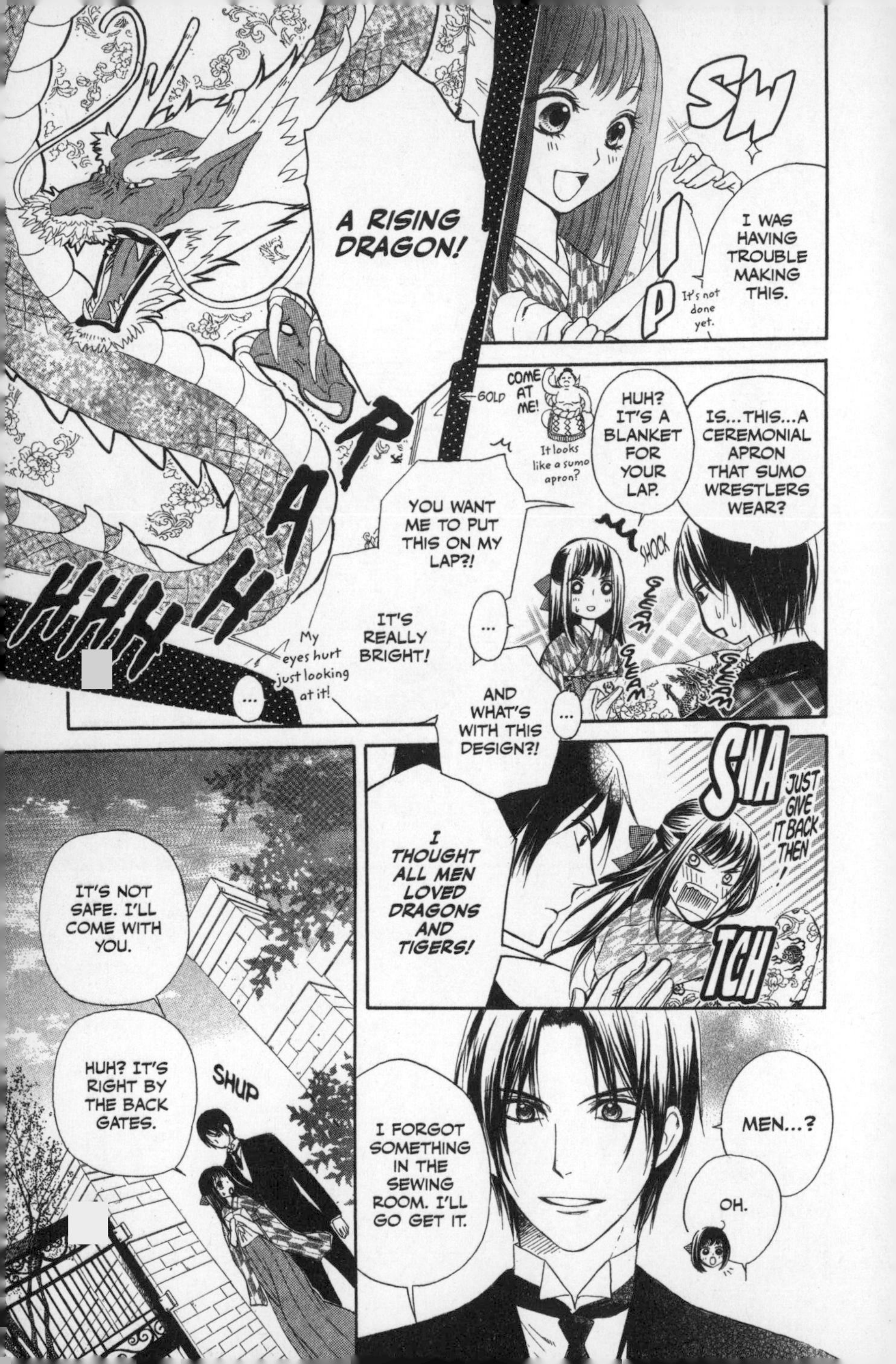
SWIP
I WAS HAVING TROUBLE MAKING THIS.
It's not done yet.
A RISING DRAGON!
PAHHHH
IS...THIS...A CEREMONIAL APRON THAT SUMO WRESTLERS WEAR?
HUH? IT'S A BLANKET FOR YOUR LAP.
COME AT ME!
It looks like a sumo apron?
GOLD
YOU WANT ME TO PUT THIS ON MY LAP?!
SHOCK
GLEAM GLEAM GLEAM GLEAM
...
IT'S REALLY BRIGHT!
My eyes hurt just looking at it!
...
AND WHAT'S WITH THIS DESIGN?!
...
SNATCH
JUST GIVE IT BACK THEN!
I THOUGHT ALL MEN LOVED DRAGONS AND TIGERS!
MEN...?
OH.
I FORGOT SOMETHING IN THE SEWING ROOM. I'LL GO GET IT.
IT'S NOT SAFE. I'LL COME WITH YOU.
HUH? IT'S RIGHT BY THE BACK GATES.
SHUP

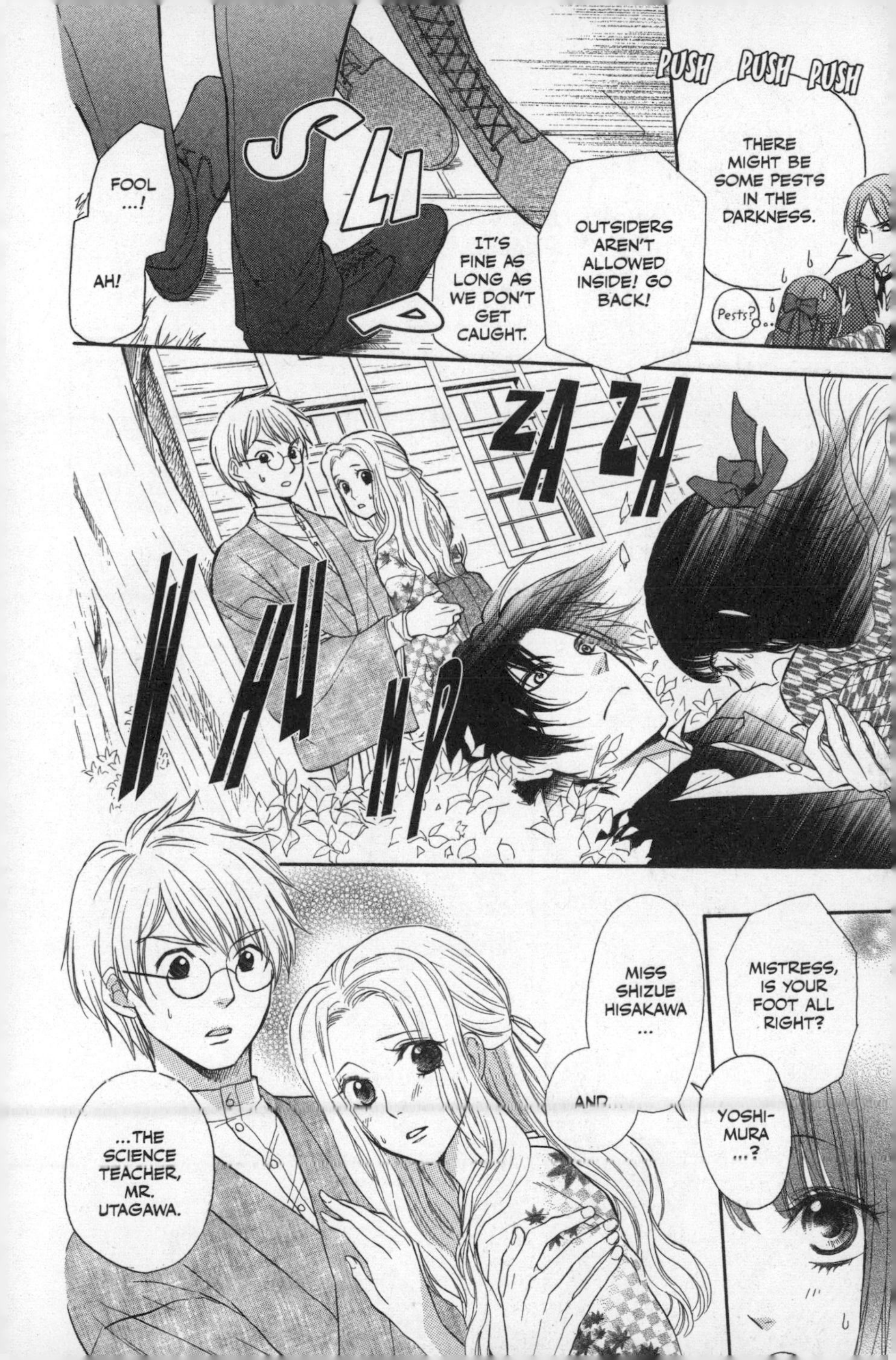
PUSH PUSH PUSH
THERE MIGHT BE SOME PESTS IN THE DARKNESS.
Pests?...
OUTSIDERS AREN'T ALLOWED INSIDE! GO BACK!
IT'S FINE AS LONG AS WE DON'T GET CAUGHT.
SLIP
FOOL ...!
AH!
ZA ZA
WHUMP
MISTRESS, IS YOUR FOOT ALL RIGHT?
YOSHI-MURA ...?
MISS SHIZUE HISAKAWA ...
AND...
...THE SCIENCE TEACHER, MR. UTAGAWA.

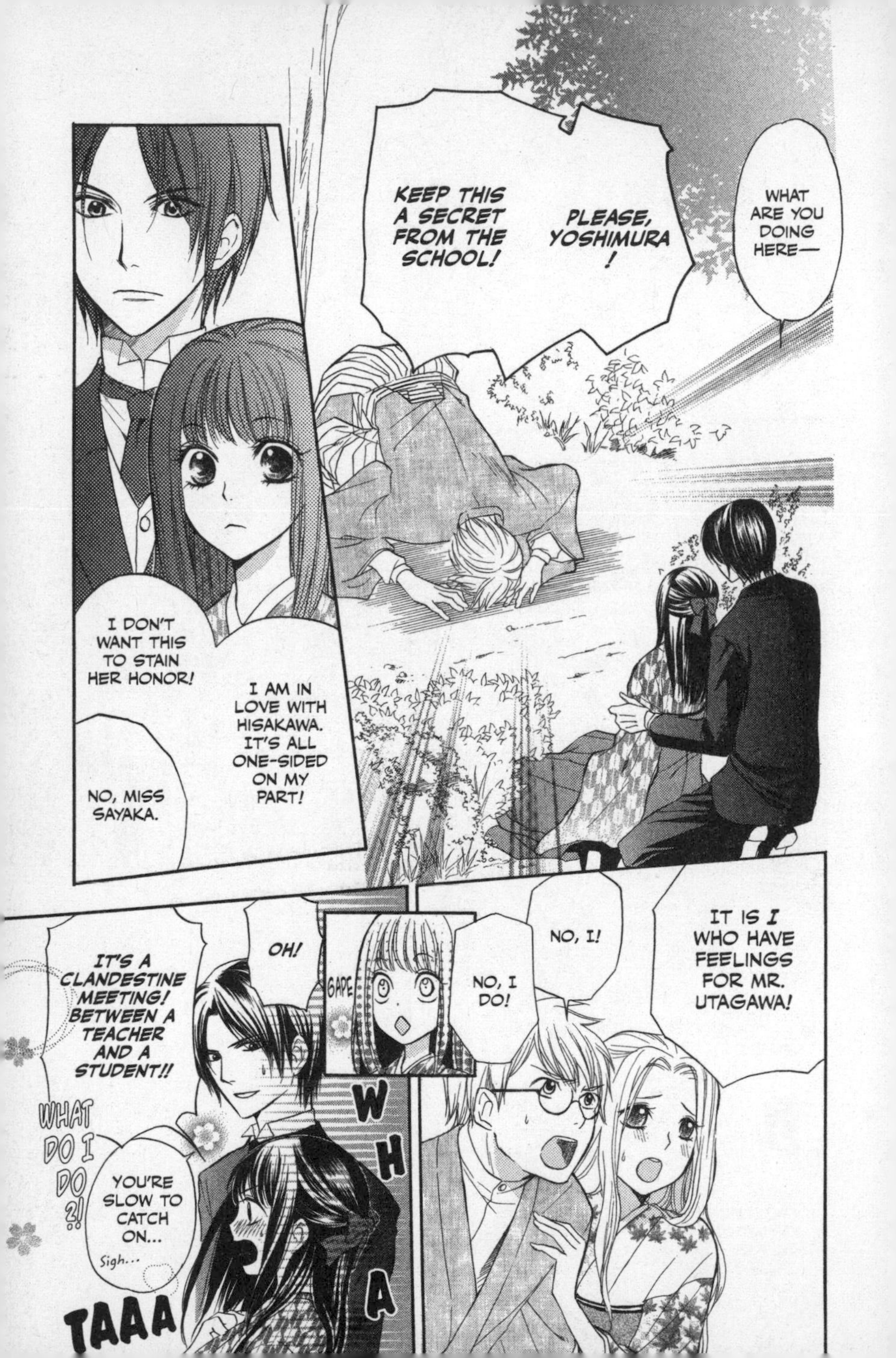
WHAT ARE YOU DOING HERE—
PLEASE, YOSHIMURA!
KEEP THIS A SECRET FROM THE SCHOOL!
I AM IN LOVE WITH HISAKAWA. IT'S ALL ONE-SIDED ON MY PART!
I DON'T WANT THIS TO STAIN HER HONOR!
NO, MISS SAYAKA.
IT IS I WHO HAVE FEELINGS FOR MR. UTAGAWA!
NO, I!
NO, I DO!
GAPE
WHA
OH!
IT'S A CLANDESTINE MEETING! BETWEEN A TEACHER AND A STUDENT!!
WHAT DO I DO?!
YOU'RE SLOW TO CATCH ON...
Sigh...
TAAA

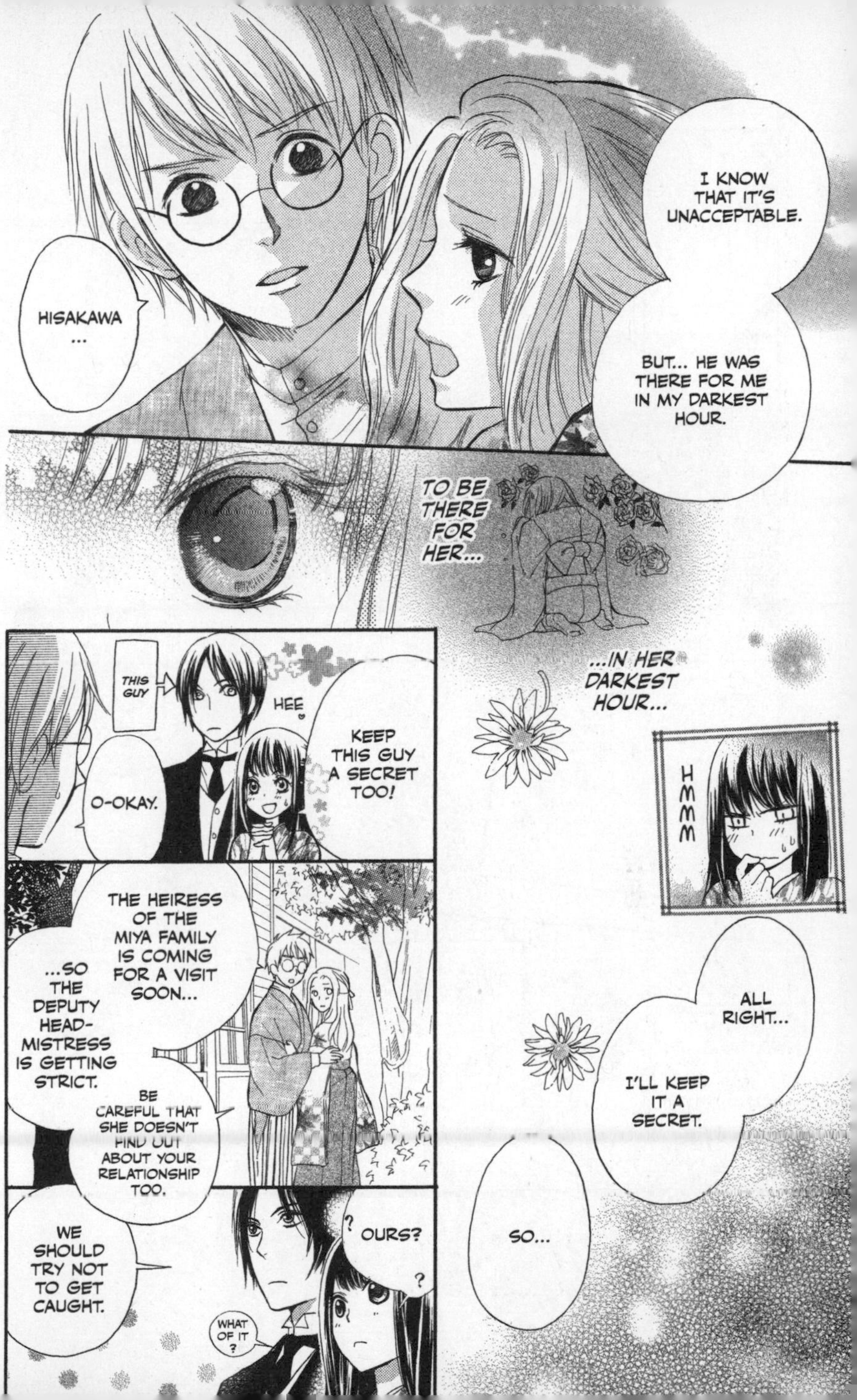

I KNOW THAT IT'S UNACCEPTABLE.
BUT... HE WAS THERE FOR ME IN MY DARKEST HOUR.
HISAKAWA ...
TO BE THERE FOR HER...
...IN HER DARKEST HOUR...
HMMM
ALL RIGHT...
I'LL KEEP IT A SECRET.
SO...
KEEP THIS GUY A SECRET TOO!
HEE
THIS GUY
O-OKAY.
THE HEIRESS OF THE MIYA FAMILY IS COMING FOR A VISIT SOON...
...SO THE DEPUTY HEAD-MISTRESS IS GETTING STRICT.
BE CAREFUL THAT SHE DOESN'T FIND OUT ABOUT YOUR RELATIONSHIP TOO.
OURS?
WE SHOULD TRY NOT TO GET CAUGHT.
WHAT OF IT?

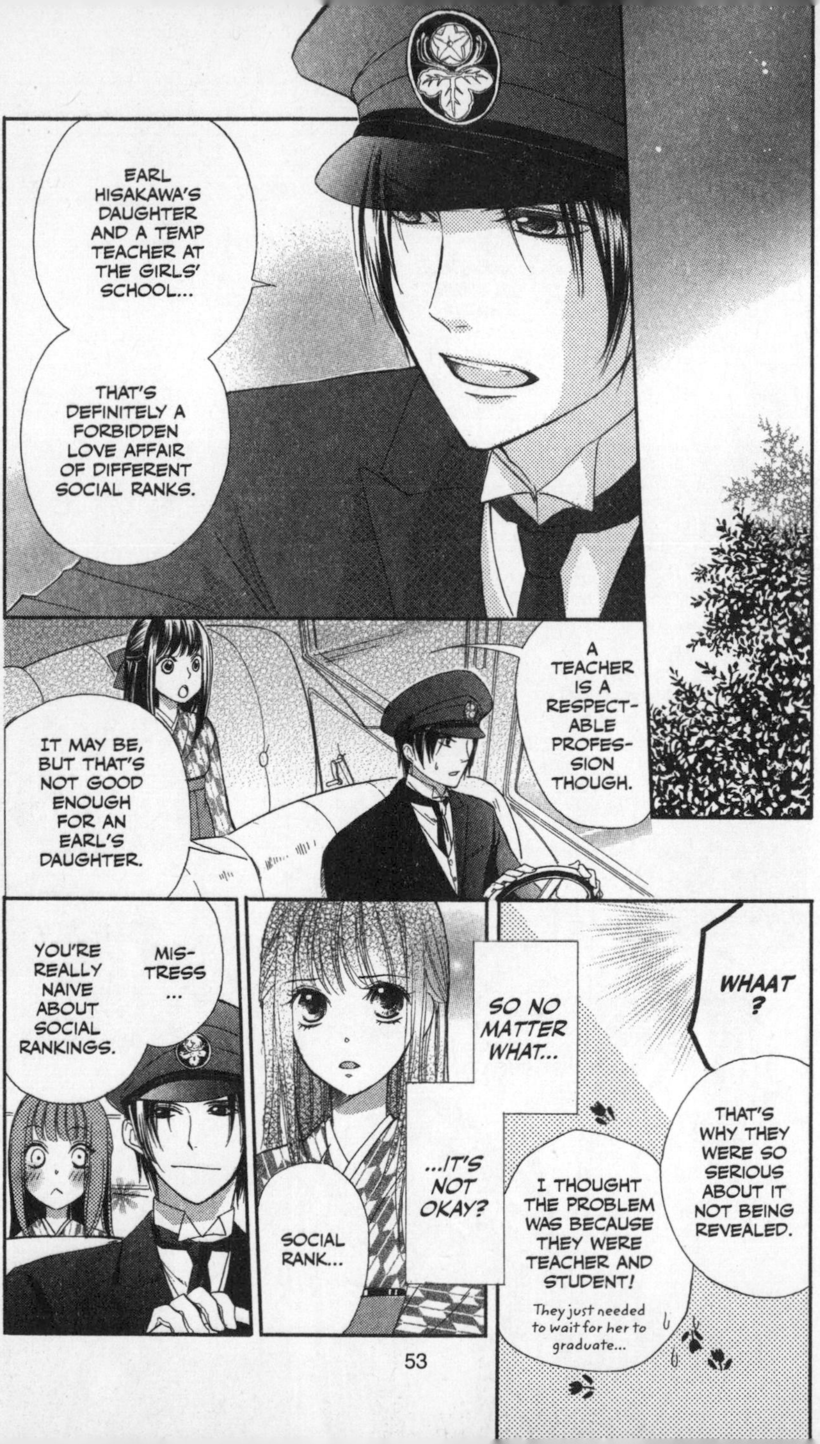
EARL HISAKAWA'S DAUGHTER AND A TEMP TEACHER AT THE GIRLS' SCHOOL...
THAT'S DEFINITELY A FORBIDDEN LOVE AFFAIR OF DIFFERENT SOCIAL RANKS.
A TEACHER IS A RESPECT-ABLE PROFES-SION THOUGH.
IT MAY BE, BUT THAT'S NOT GOOD ENOUGH FOR AN EARL'S DAUGHTER.
WHAAT?
THAT'S WHY THEY WERE SO SERIOUS ABOUT IT NOT BEING REVEALED.
I THOUGHT THE PROBLEM WAS BECAUSE THEY WERE TEACHER AND STUDENT!
They just needed to wait for her to graduate...
SO NO MATTER WHAT...
...IT'S NOT OKAY?
SOCIAL RANK...
MIS-TRESS...
YOU'RE REALLY NAIVE ABOUT SOCIAL RANKINGS.

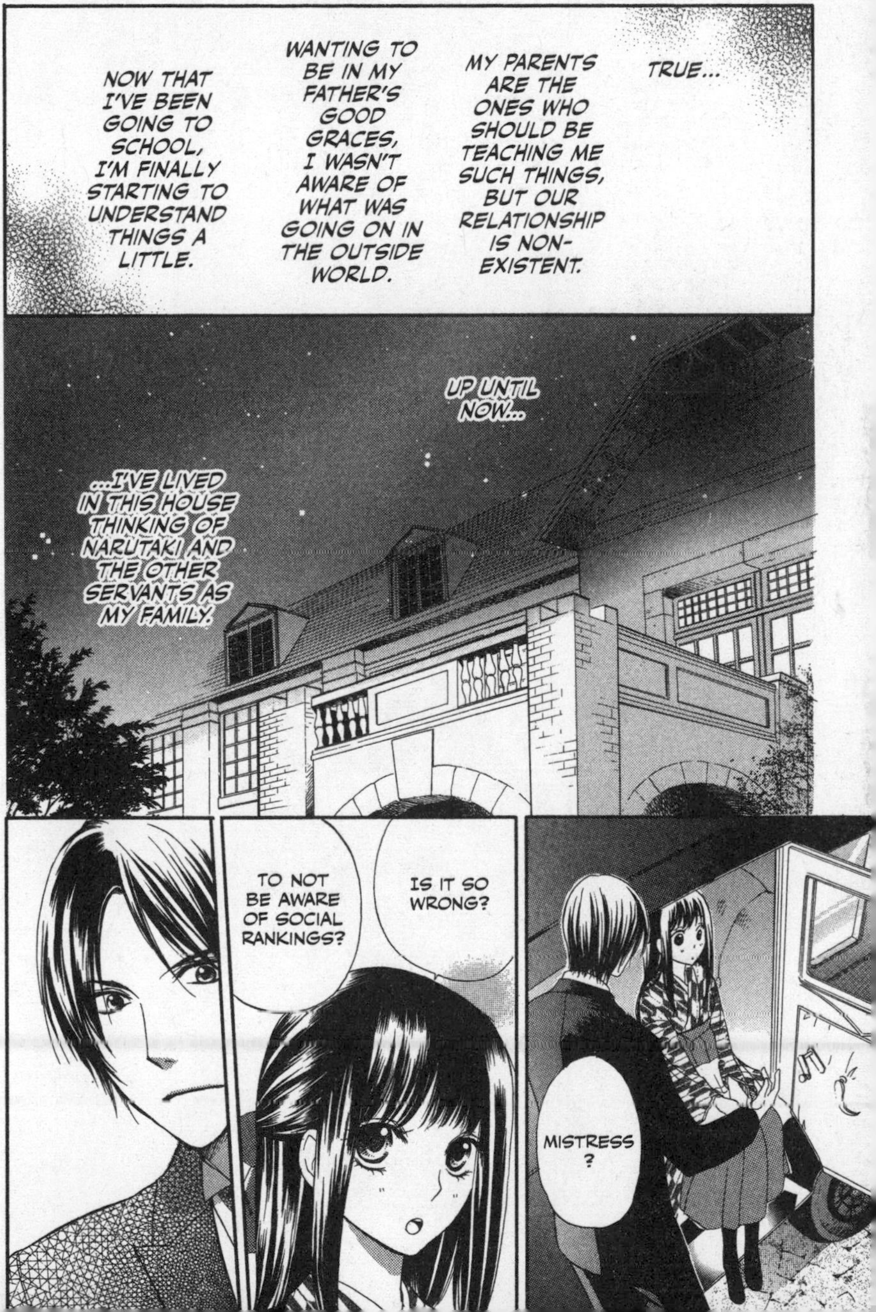
TRUE...
MY PARENTS ARE THE ONES WHO SHOULD BE TEACHING ME SUCH THINGS, BUT OUR RELATIONSHIP IS NON-EXISTENT.
WANTING TO BE IN MY FATHER'S GOOD GRACES, I WASN'T AWARE OF WHAT WAS GOING ON IN THE OUTSIDE WORLD.
NOW THAT I'VE BEEN GOING TO SCHOOL, I'M FINALLY STARTING TO UNDERSTAND THINGS A LITTLE.
UP UNTIL NOW...
...I'VE LIVED IN THIS HOUSE THINKING OF NARUTAKI AND THE OTHER SERVANTS AS MY FAMILY.
MISTRESS ?
IS IT SO WRONG?
TO NOT BE AWARE OF SOCIAL RANKINGS?

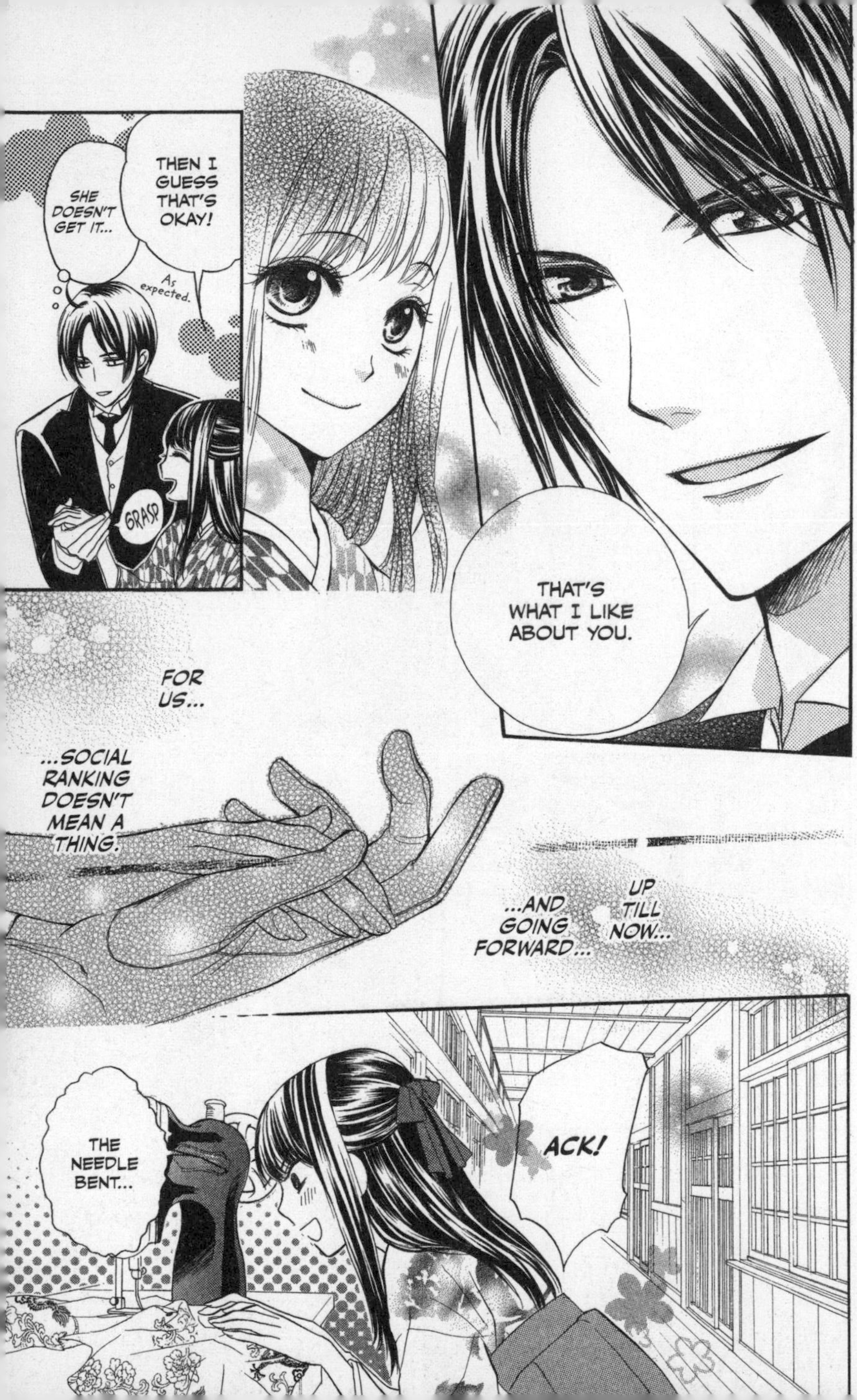
THAT'S WHAT I LIKE ABOUT YOU.
THEN I GUESS THAT'S OKAY!
SHE DOESN'T GET IT...
As expected.
GRASP
UP TILL NOW...
...AND GOING FORWARD...
FOR US...
...SOCIAL RANKING DOESN'T MEAN A THING.
ACK!
THE NEEDLE BENT...

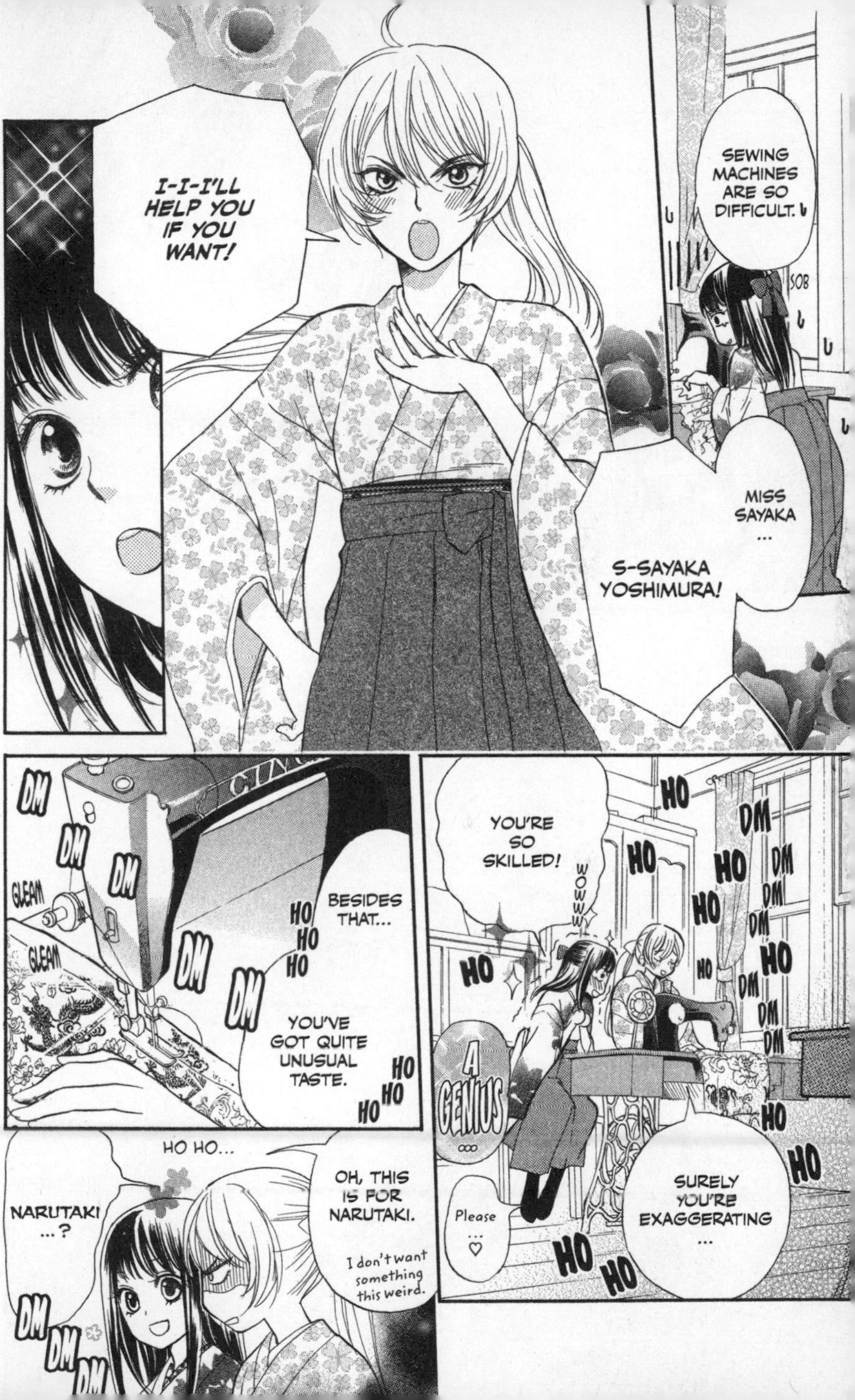
SEWING MACHINES ARE SO DIFFICULT.
SOB
MISS SAYAKA ...
S-SAYAKA YOSHIMURA!
I-I-I'LL HELP YOU IF YOU WANT!
HO HO HO HO HO HO HO HO HO HO HO HO HO
DM DM DM DM DM DM DM DM DM
YOU'RE SO SKILLED!
WOWWW
A GENIUS ...
Please ... ♡
SURELY YOU'RE EXAGGERATING ...
DM DM DM DM DM
GLEAM
GLEAM
BESIDES THAT...
HO HO HO
YOU'VE GOT QUITE UNUSUAL TASTE.
HO HO HO
HO HO...
OH, THIS IS FOR NARUTAKI.
I don't want something this weird.
NARUTAKI ...?
DM DM DM

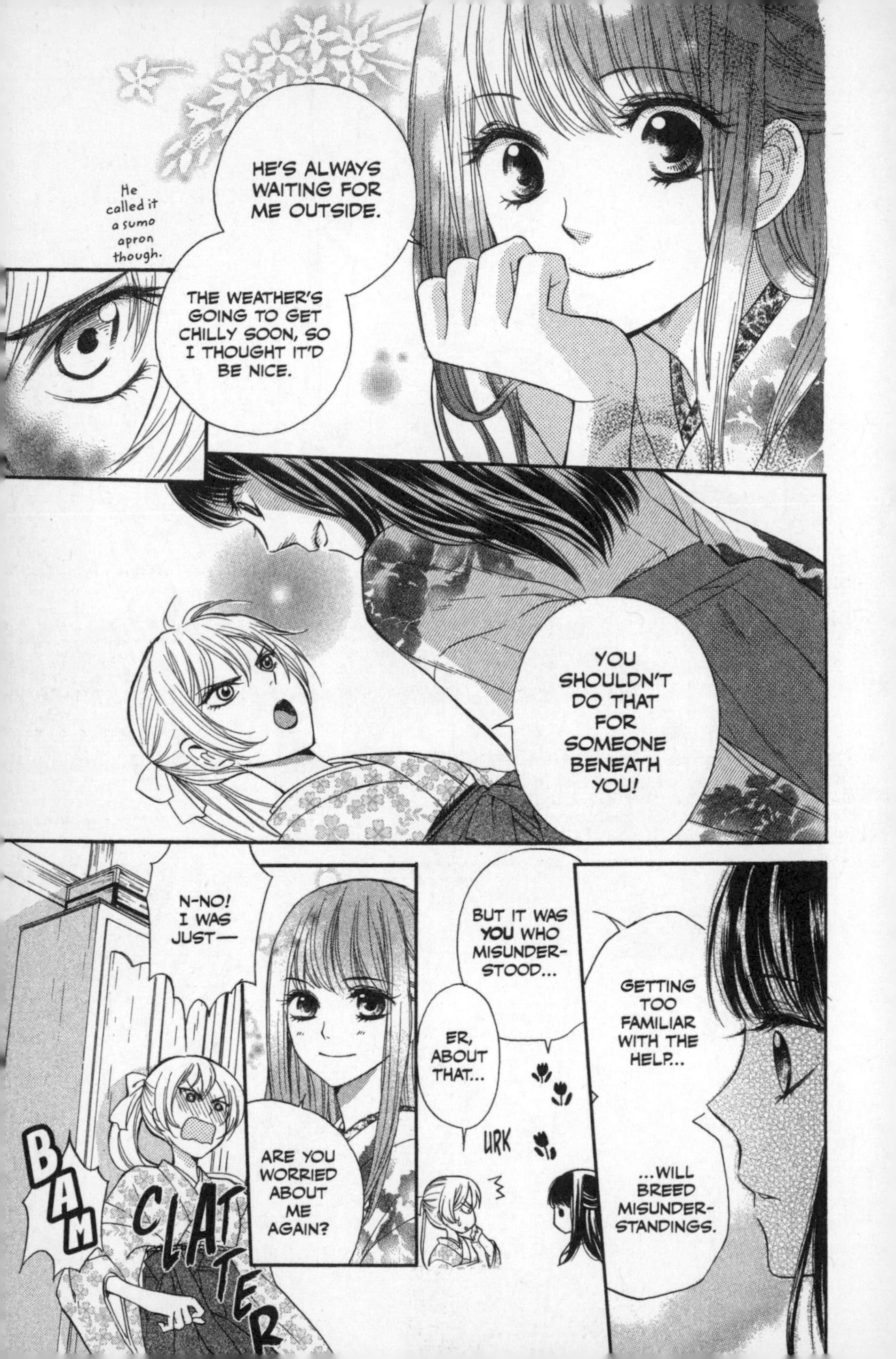

HE'S ALWAYS WAITING FOR ME OUTSIDE.
THE WEATHER'S GOING TO GET CHILLY SOON, SO I THOUGHT IT'D BE NICE.
He called it a sumo apron though.
YOU SHOULDN'T DO THAT FOR SOMEONE BENEATH YOU!
GETTING TOO FAMILIAR WITH THE HELP...
...WILL BREED MISUNDERSTANDINGS.
BUT IT WAS YOU WHO MISUNDERSTOOD...
ER, ABOUT THAT...
URK
N-NO! I WAS JUST—
ARE YOU WORRIED ABOUT ME AGAIN?
BAM
CLATTER

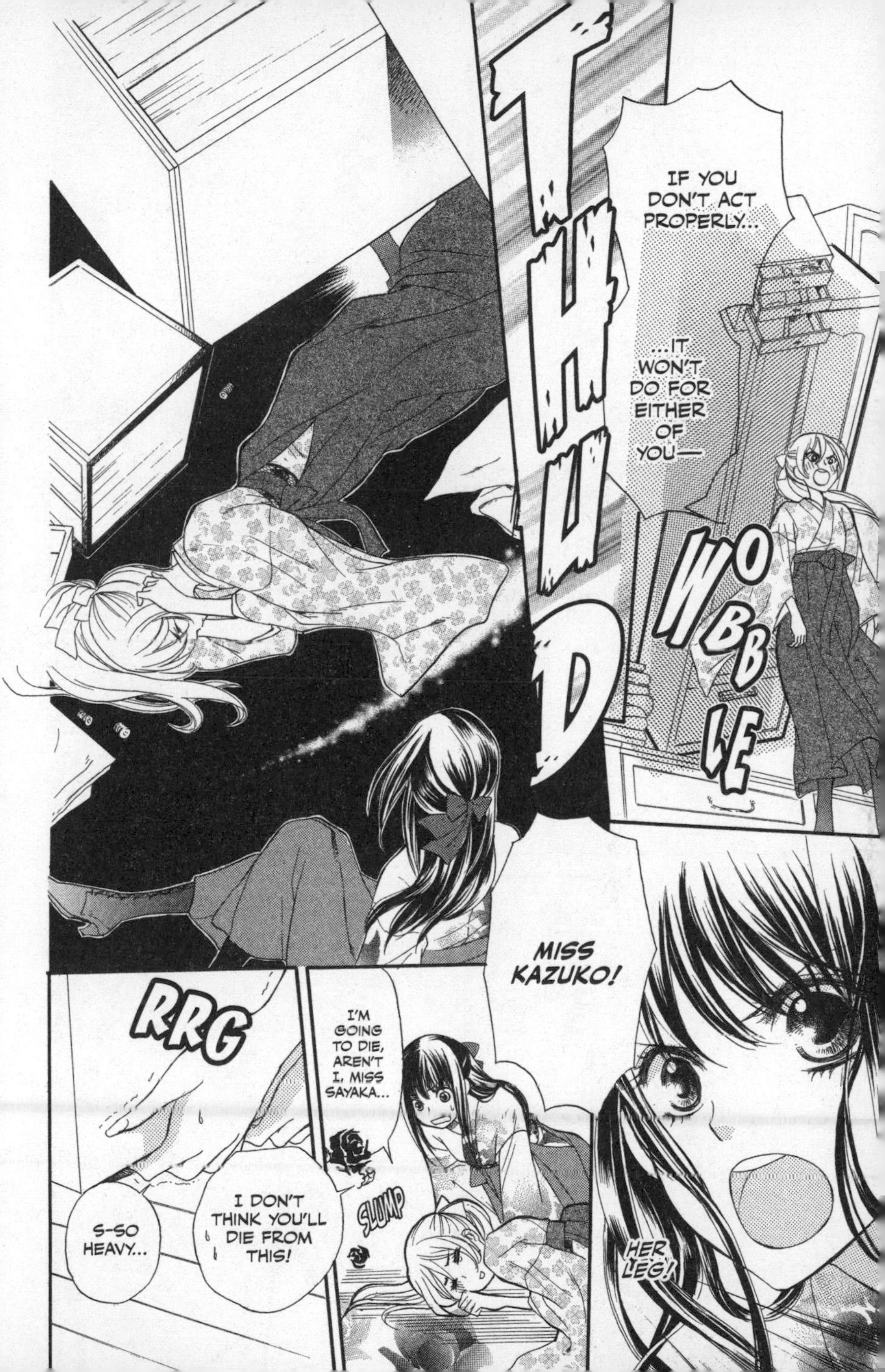
IF YOU DON'T ACT PROPERLY...
...IT WON'T DO FOR EITHER OF YOU—
WOBBLE
THUD
MISS KAZUKO!
HER LEG!
I'M GOING TO DIE, AREN'T I, MISS SAYAKA...
SLUMP
I DON'T THINK YOU'LL DIE FROM THIS!
RRG
S-SO HEAVY...

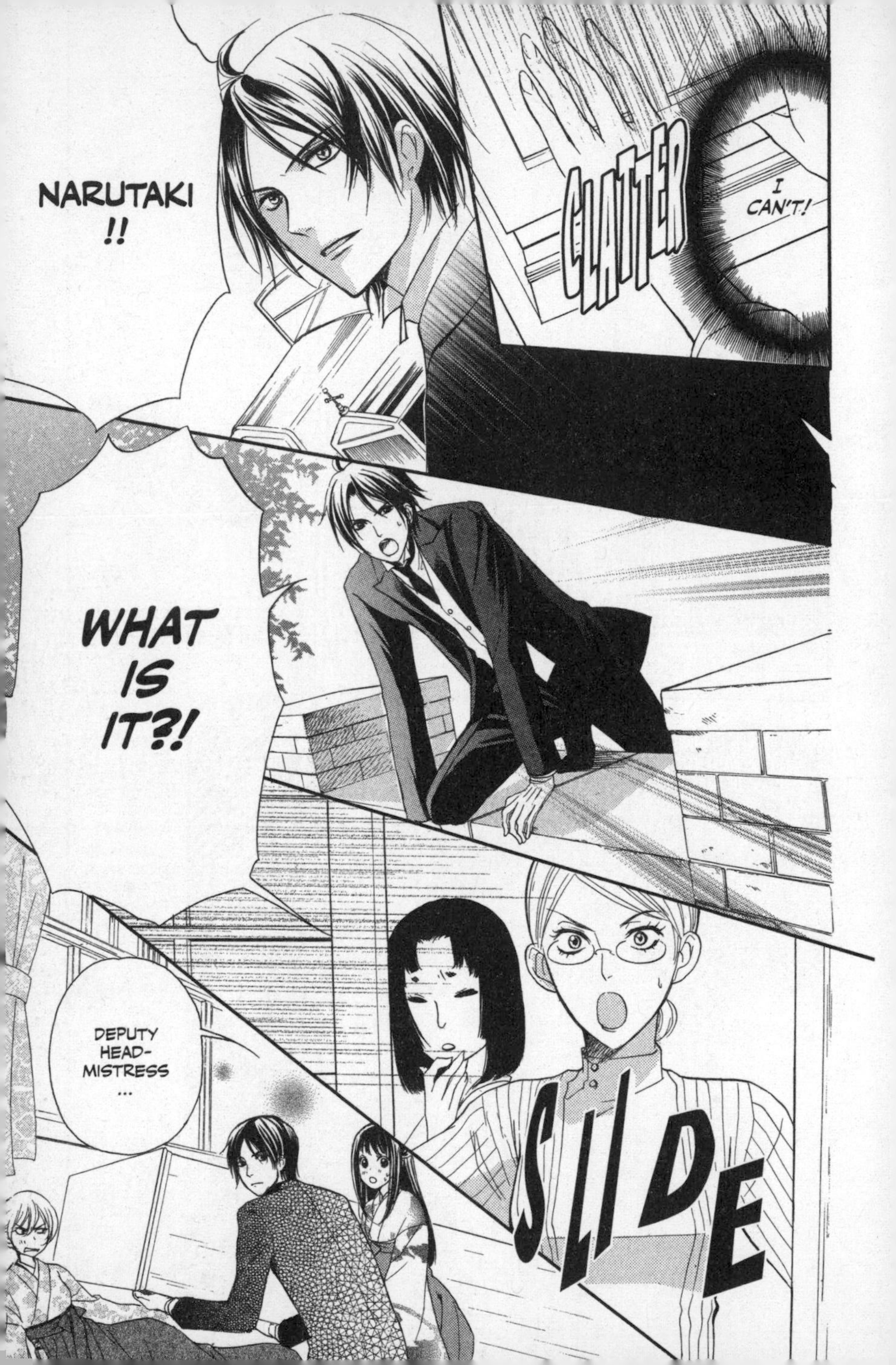
CLATTER
I CAN'T!
NARUTAKI !!
WHAT IS IT?!
SLIDE
DEPUTY HEAD-MISTRESS ...

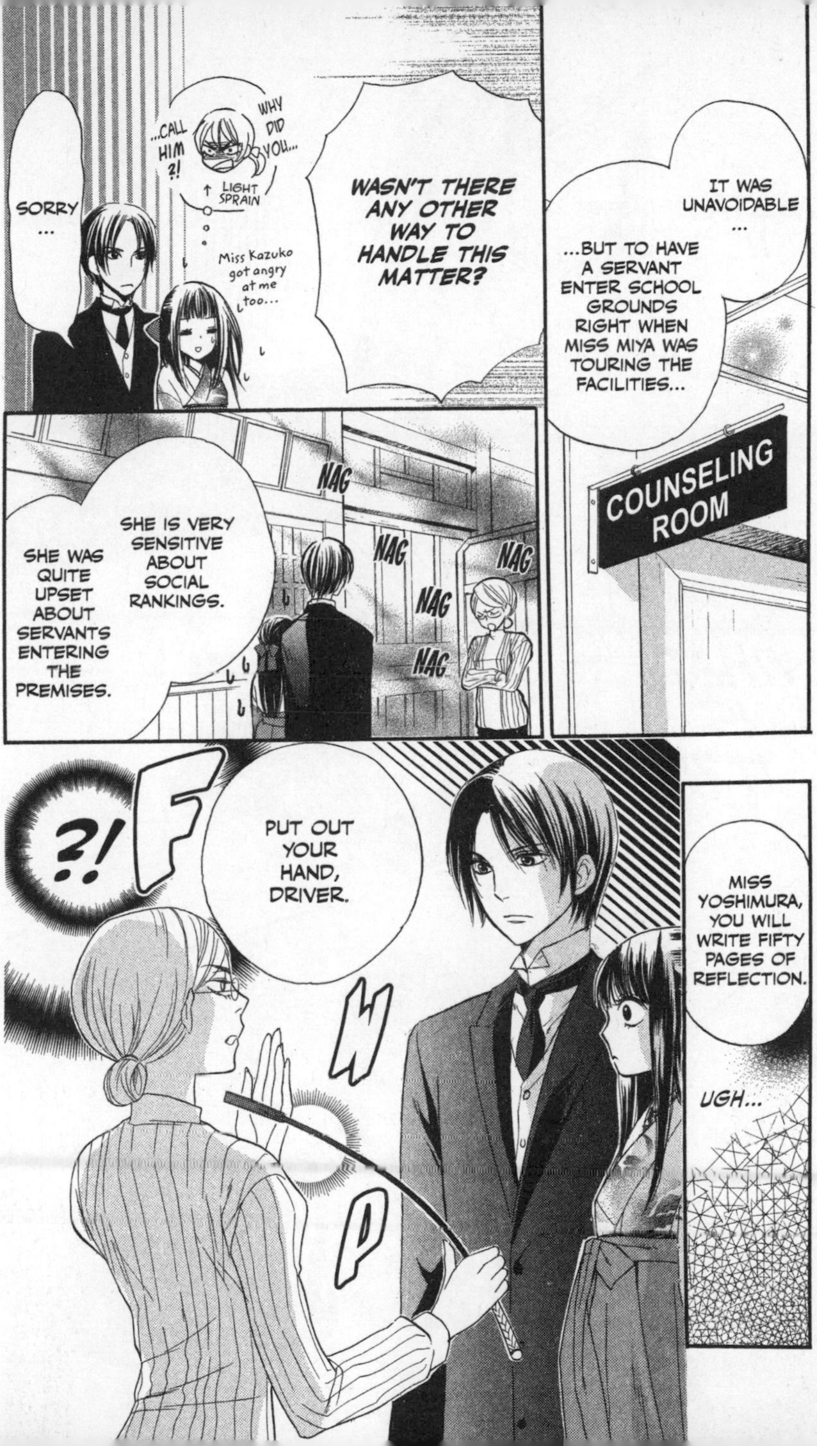

IT WAS UNAVOIDABLE ...
...BUT TO HAVE A SERVANT ENTER SCHOOL GROUNDS RIGHT WHEN MISS MIYA WAS TOURING THE FACILITIES...
WASN'T THERE ANY OTHER WAY TO HANDLE THIS MATTER?
WHY DID YOU...
...CALL HIM ?!
↑ LIGHT SPRAIN
Miss Kazuko got angry at me too...
SORRY ...
COUNSELING ROOM
NAG
NAG
NAG
NAG
NAG
SHE IS VERY SENSITIVE ABOUT SOCIAL RANKINGS.
SHE WAS QUITE UPSET ABOUT SERVANTS ENTERING THE PREMISES.
MISS YOSHIMURA, YOU WILL WRITE FIFTY PAGES OF REFLECTION.
UGH...
PUT OUT YOUR HAND, DRIVER.
F
W
P
?!

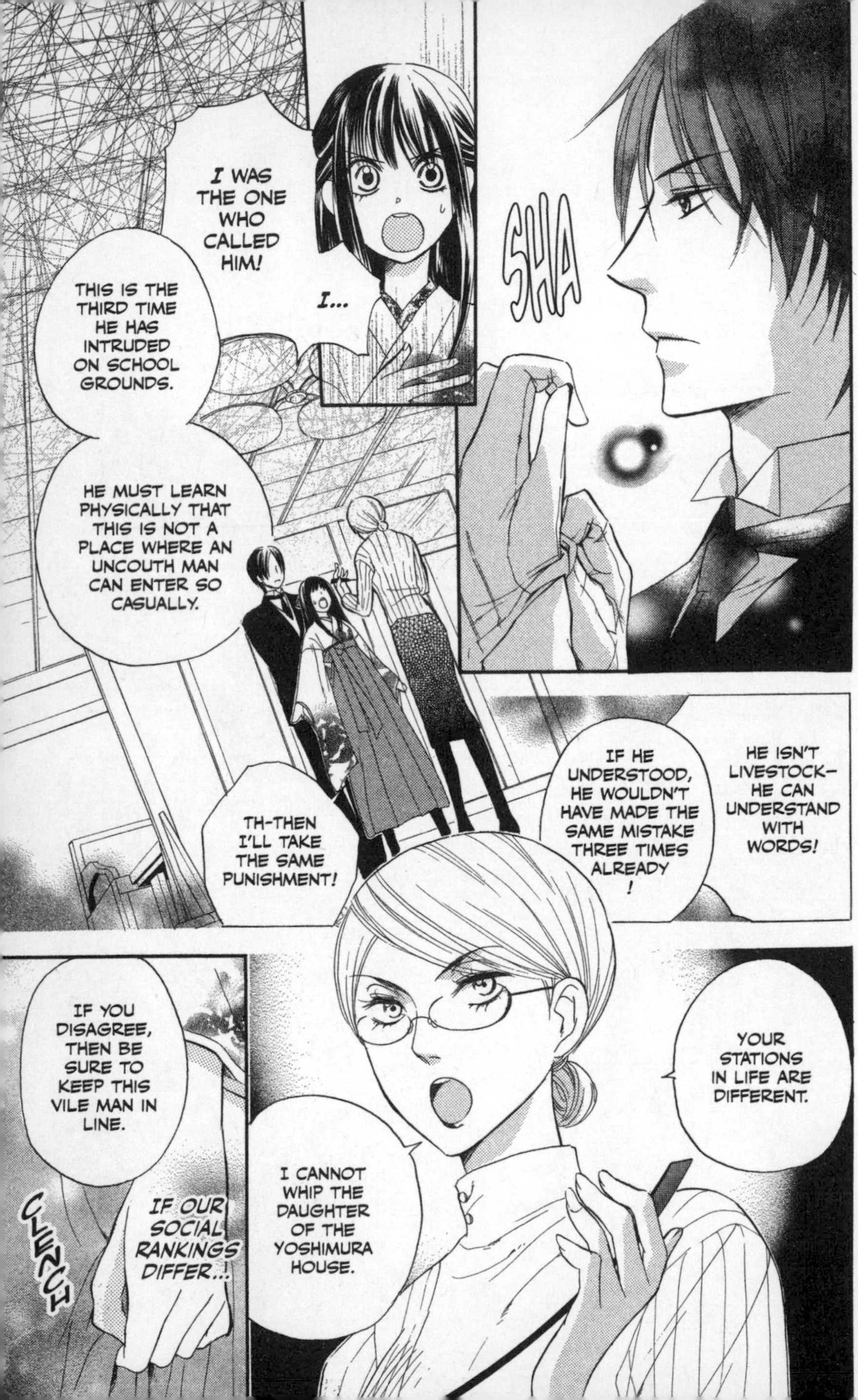
SHA
I WAS THE ONE WHO CALLED HIM!
I...
THIS IS THE THIRD TIME HE HAS INTRUDED ON SCHOOL GROUNDS.
HE MUST LEARN PHYSICALLY THAT THIS IS NOT A PLACE WHERE AN UNCOUTH MAN CAN ENTER SO CASUALLY.
HE ISN'T LIVESTOCK—HE CAN UNDERSTAND WITH WORDS!
IF HE UNDERSTOOD, HE WOULDN'T HAVE MADE THE SAME MISTAKE THREE TIMES ALREADY!
TH-THEN I'LL TAKE THE SAME PUNISHMENT!
YOUR STATIONS IN LIFE ARE DIFFERENT.
I CANNOT WHIP THE DAUGHTER OF THE YOSHIMURA HOUSE.
IF YOU DISAGREE, THEN BE SURE TO KEEP THIS VILE MAN IN LINE.
IF OUR SOCIAL RANKINGS DIFFER...!
CLENCH

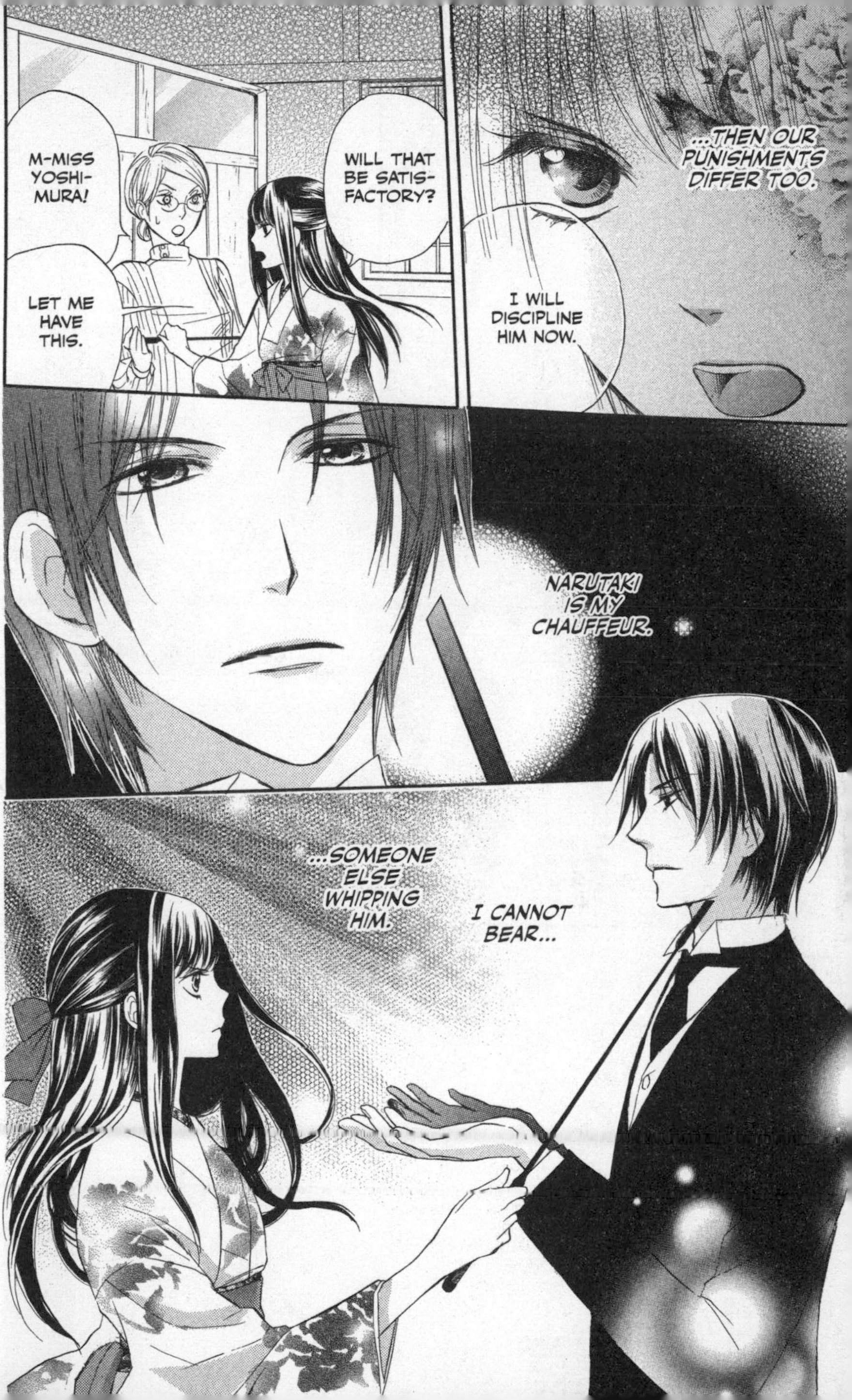
...THEN OUR PUNISHMENTS DIFFER TOO.
I WILL DISCIPLINE HIM NOW.
WILL THAT BE SATIS-FACTORY?
M-MISS YOSHI-MURA!
LET ME HAVE THIS.
NARUTAKI IS MY CHAUFFEUR.
I CANNOT BEAR...
...SOMEONE ELSE WHIPPING HIM.

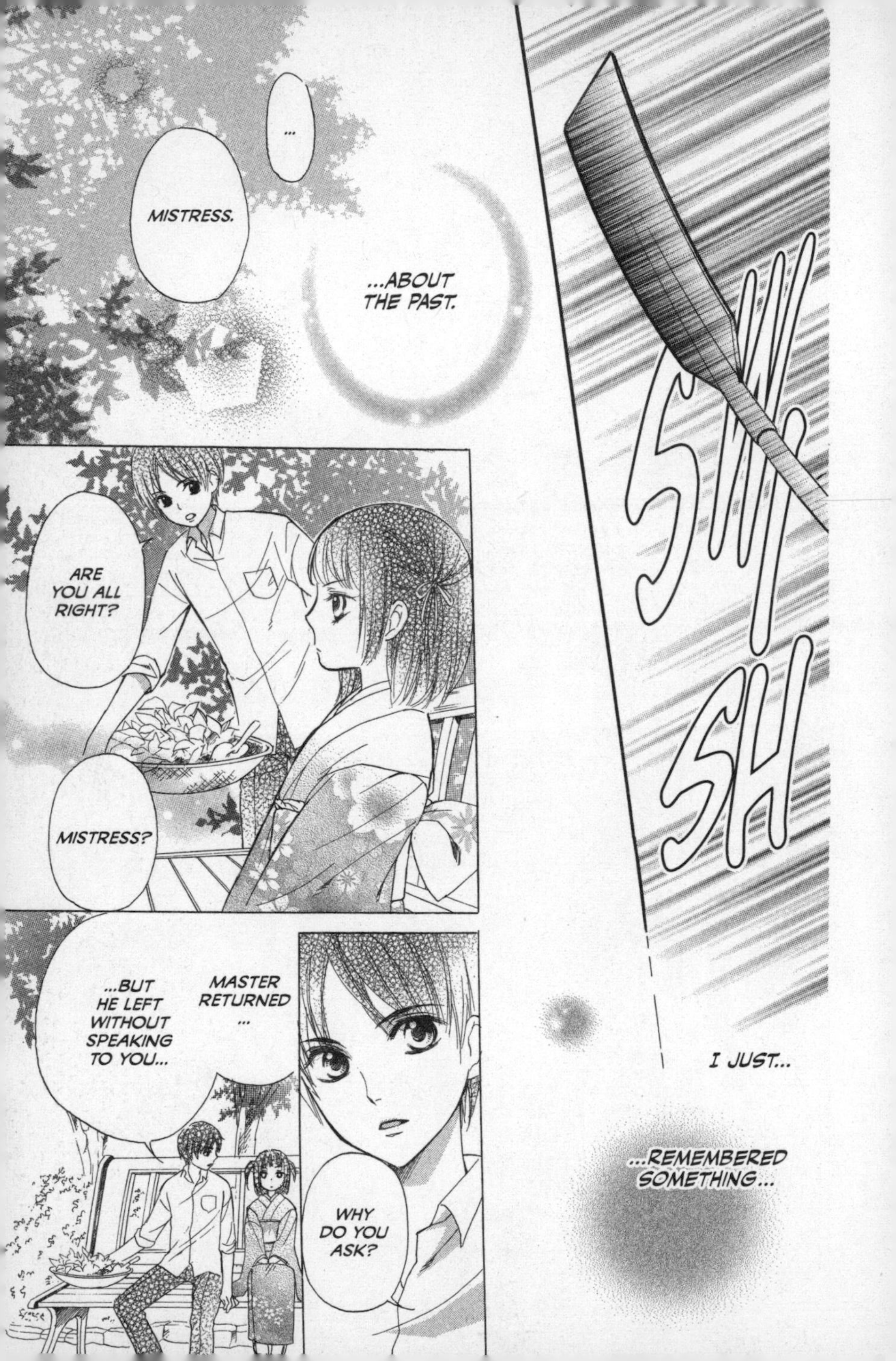
SWISH
I JUST...
...REMEMBERED SOMETHING...
...ABOUT THE PAST.
...
MISTRESS.
ARE YOU ALL RIGHT?
MISTRESS?
MASTER RETURNED... ...BUT HE LEFT WITHOUT SPEAKING TO YOU...
WHY DO YOU ASK?

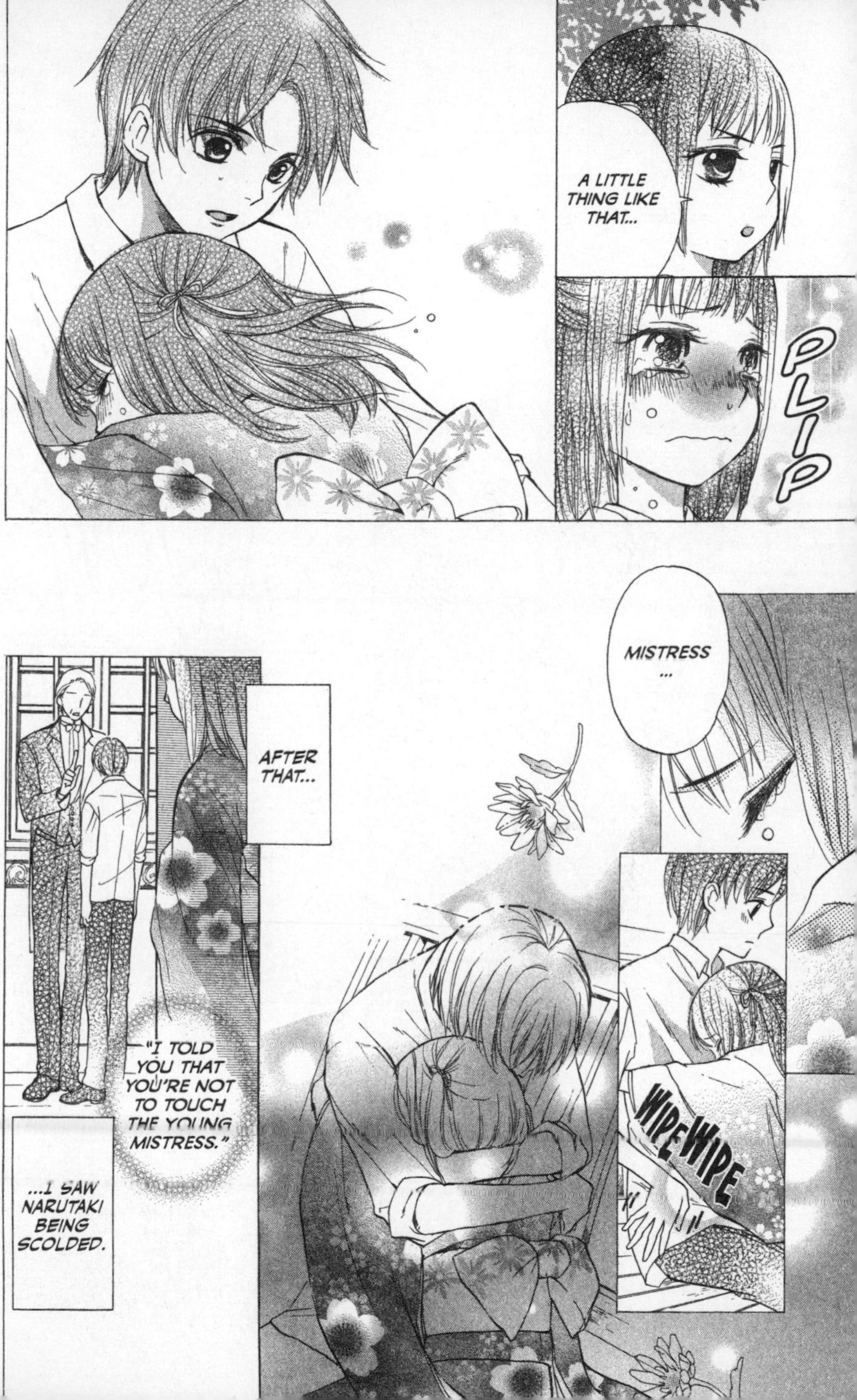
A LITTLE THING LIKE THAT...
PLIP
MISTRESS ...
WIPE WIPE
AFTER THAT...
"I TOLD YOU THAT YOU'RE NOT TO TOUCH THE YOUNG MISTRESS."
...I SAW NARUTAKI BEING SCOLDED.

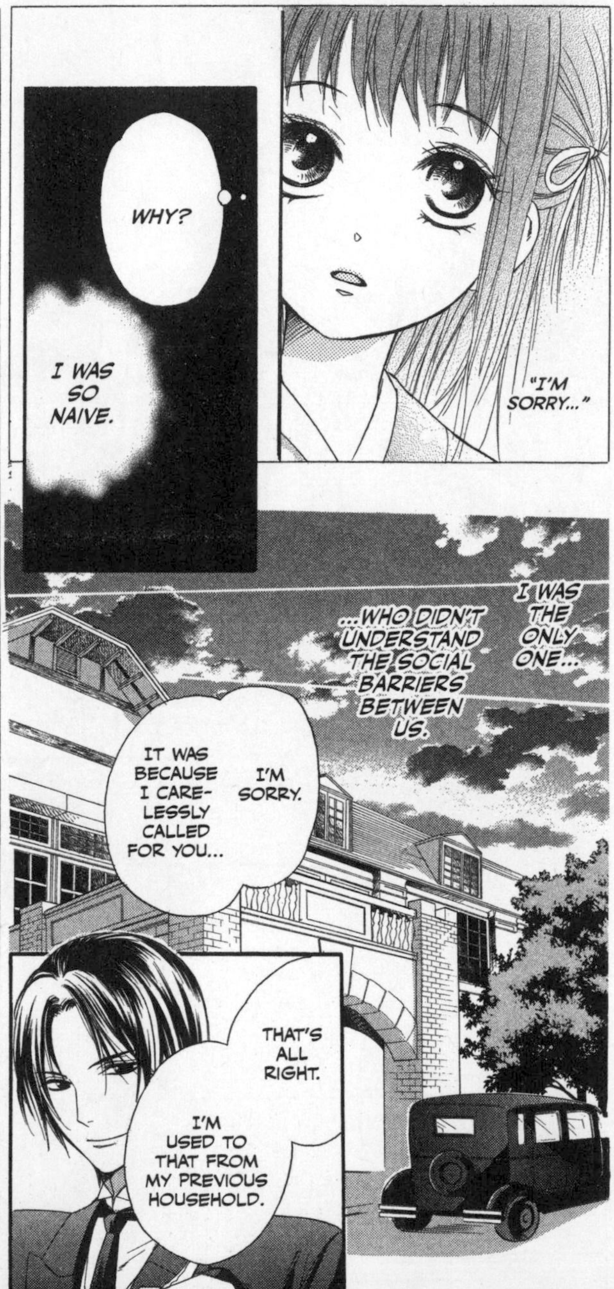
"I'M SORRY..."
WHY?
I WAS SO NAIVE.
I WAS THE ONLY ONE...
...WHO DIDN'T UNDERSTAND THE SOCIAL BARRIERS BETWEEN US.
I'M SORRY.
IT WAS BECAUSE I CARELESSLY CALLED FOR YOU...
THAT'S ALL RIGHT.
I'M USED TO THAT FROM MY PREVIOUS HOUSEHOLD.

CHAPTER 2

This is my first manga series. I was so happy when I was told, "Why don't you submit a continuation of this one-shot?"

But, well, it might end with the second chapter too. I drew what I wanted without thinking too much about it. I was just so happy to be doing the continuation and I had a lot of fun working on it. It's my favorite chapter ever.

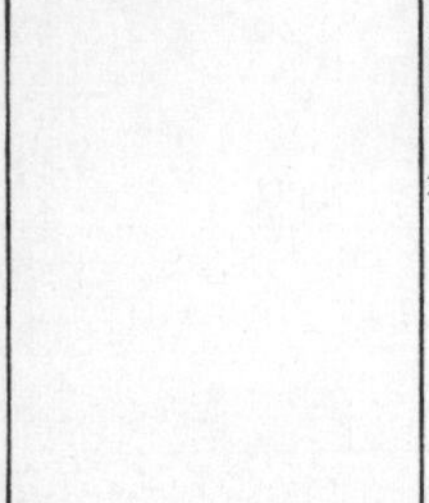
This guy's such a masochist.
MY ASSISTANT Y-DA
↓

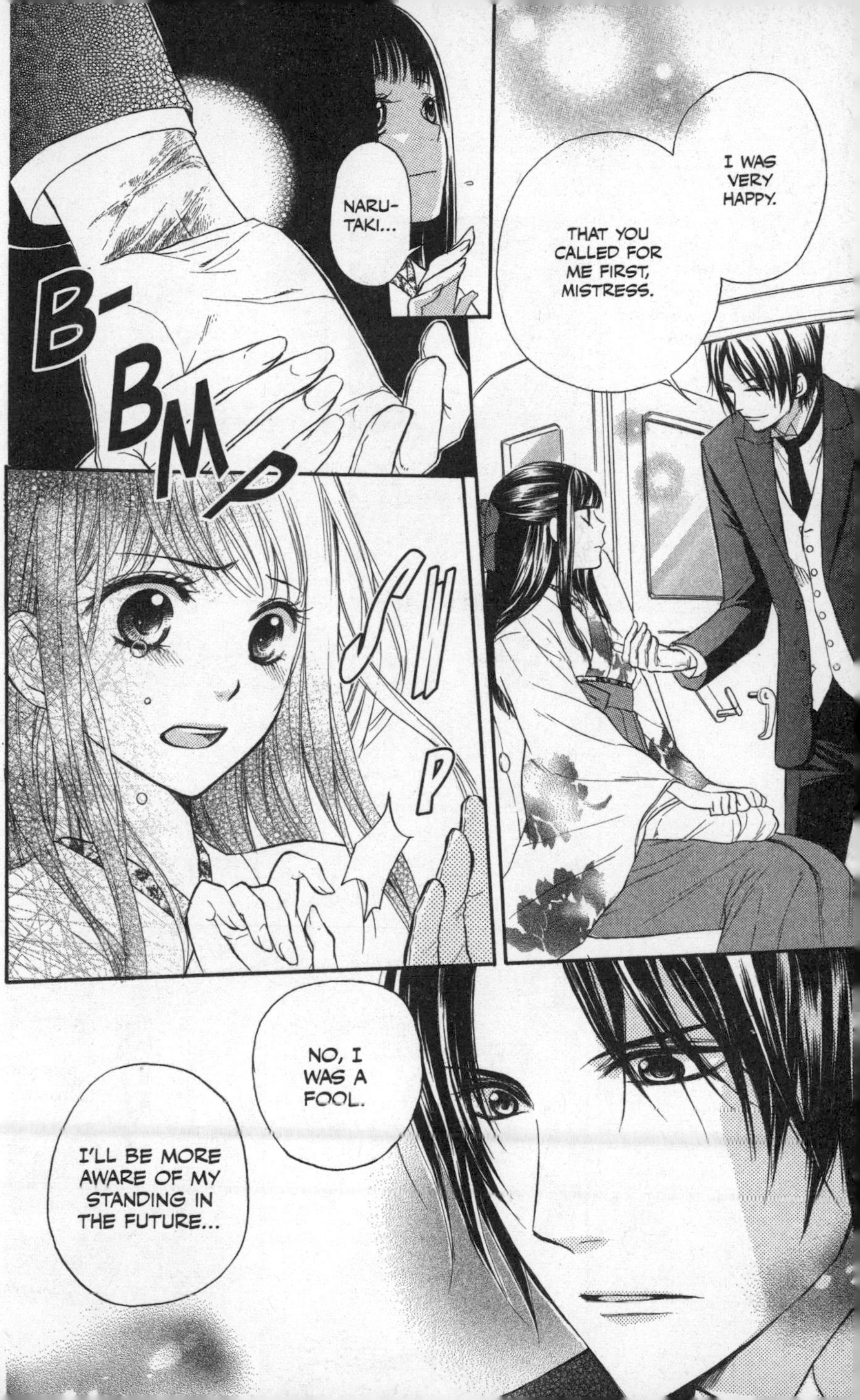
I WAS VERY HAPPY.
THAT YOU CALLED FOR ME FIRST, MISTRESS.
NARU-TAKI...
B-BMP
SHP
NO, I WAS A FOOL.
I'LL BE MORE AWARE OF MY STANDING IN THE FUTURE...

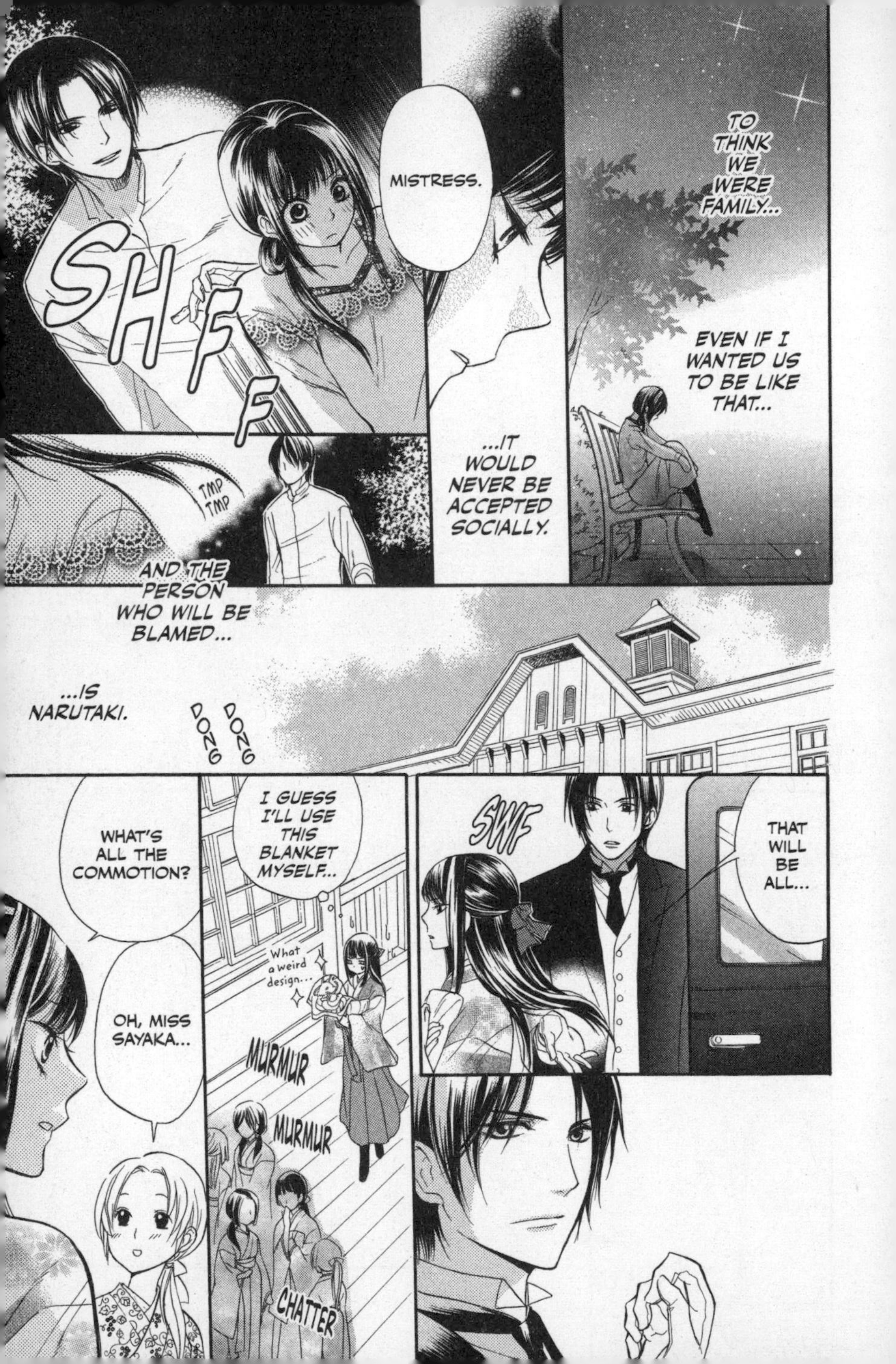
TO THINK WE WERE FAMILY...
EVEN IF I WANTED US TO BE LIKE THAT...
...IT WOULD NEVER BE ACCEPTED SOCIALLY.
MISTRESS.
SHFF
TMP TMP
AND THE PERSON WHO WILL BE BLAMED...
...IS NARUTAKI.
DONG DONG
SWF
THAT WILL BE ALL...
I GUESS I'LL USE THIS BLANKET MYSELF...
What a weird design...
MURMUR
MURMUR
CHATTER
WHAT'S ALL THE COMMOTION?
OH, MISS SAYAKA...

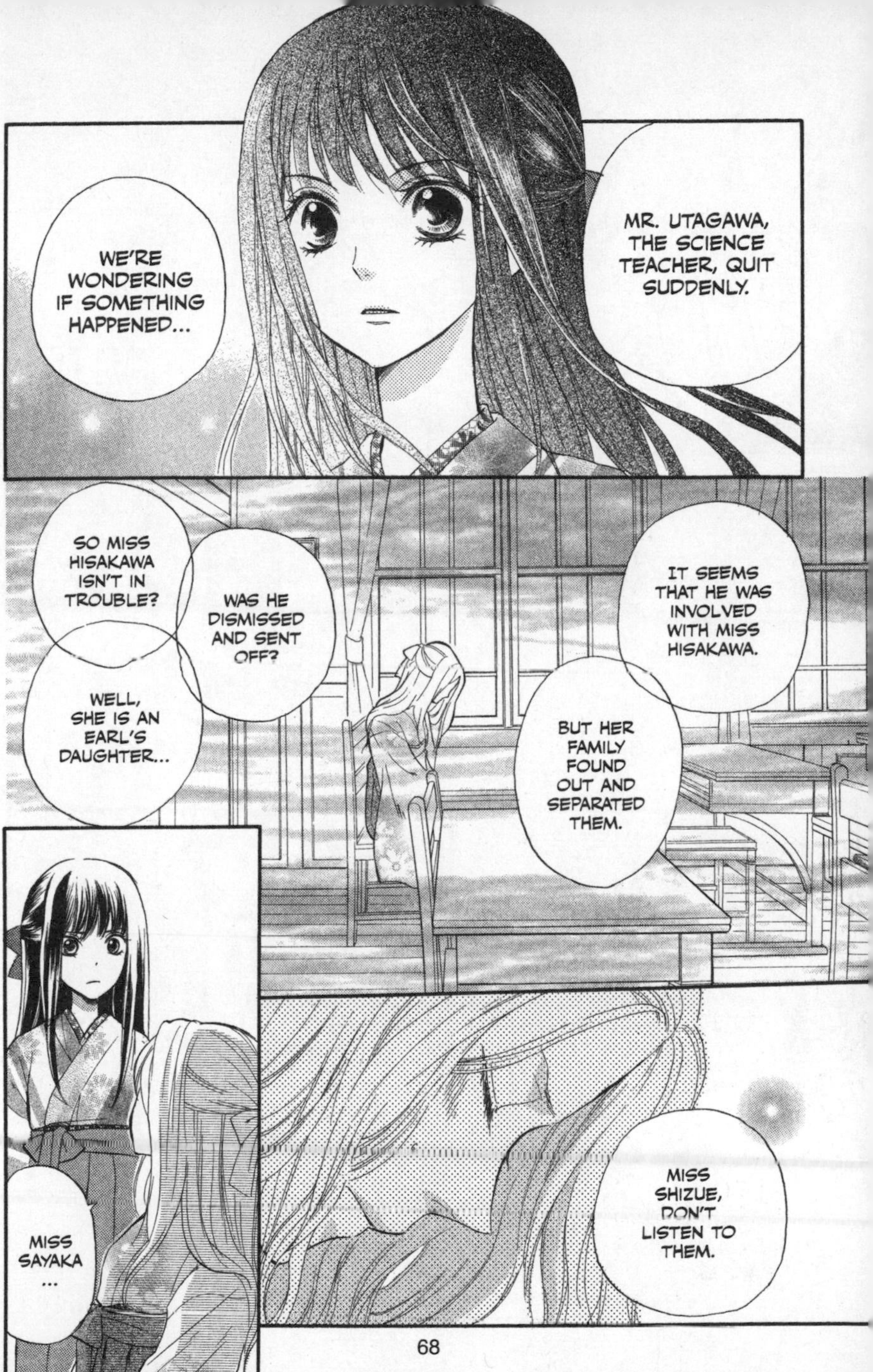
MR. UTAGAWA, THE SCIENCE TEACHER, QUIT SUDDENLY.
WE'RE WONDERING IF SOMETHING HAPPENED...
IT SEEMS THAT HE WAS INVOLVED WITH MISS HISAKAWA.
BUT HER FAMILY FOUND OUT AND SEPARATED THEM.
WAS HE DISMISSED AND SENT OFF?
SO MISS HISAKAWA ISN'T IN TROUBLE?
WELL, SHE IS AN EARL'S DAUGHTER...
MISS SHIZUE, DON'T LISTEN TO THEM.
MISS SAYAKA ...

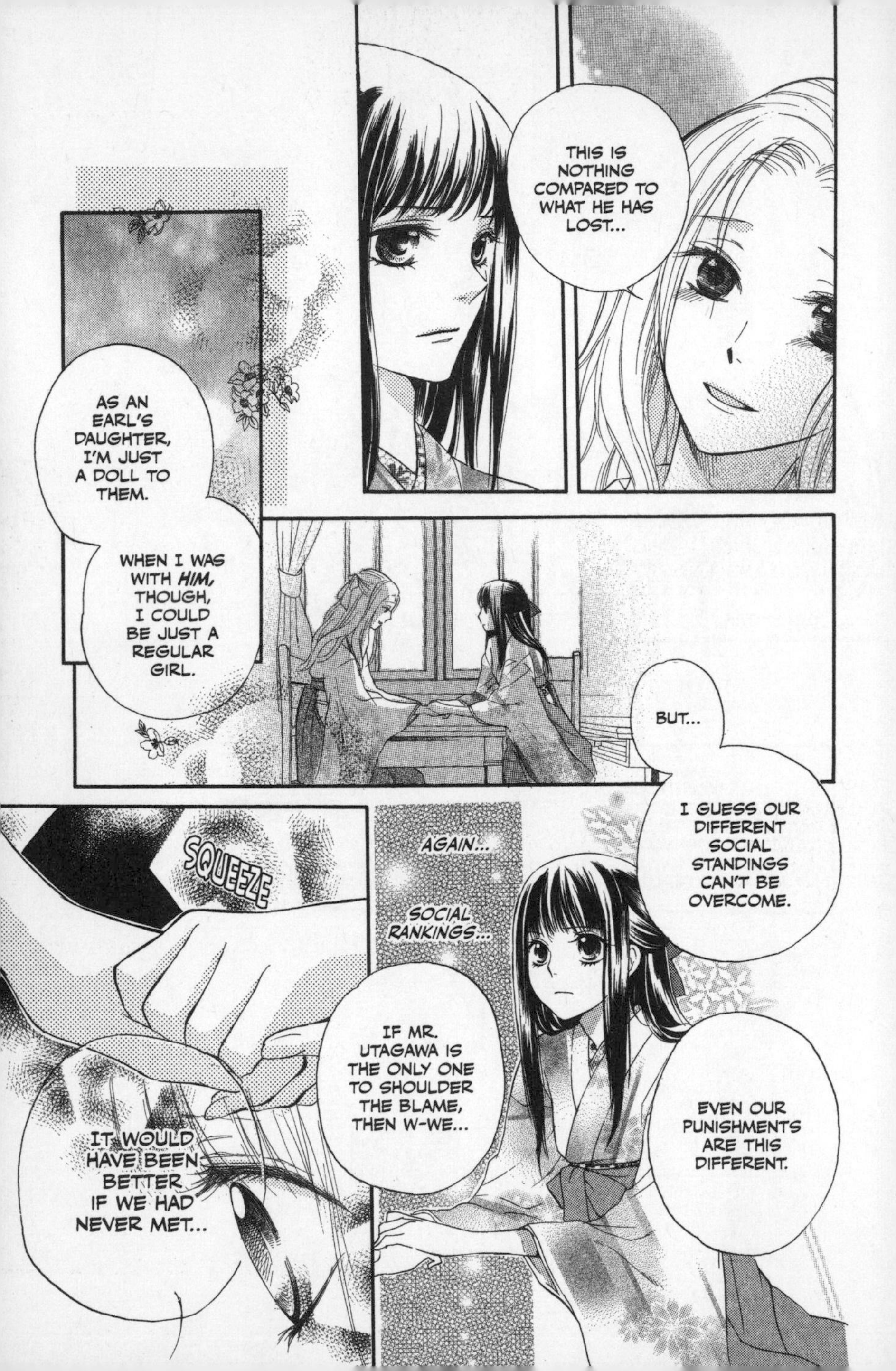
THIS IS NOTHING COMPARED TO WHAT HE HAS LOST...
AS AN EARL'S DAUGHTER, I'M JUST A DOLL TO THEM.
WHEN I WAS WITH *HIM,* THOUGH, I COULD BE JUST A REGULAR GIRL.
BUT...
I GUESS OUR DIFFERENT SOCIAL STANDINGS CAN'T BE OVERCOME.
AGAIN...
SOCIAL RANKINGS...
EVEN OUR PUNISHMENTS ARE THIS DIFFERENT.
IF MR. UTAGAWA IS THE ONLY ONE TO SHOULDER THE BLAME, THEN W-WE...
SQUEEZE
IT WOULD HAVE BEEN BETTER IF WE HAD NEVER MET...

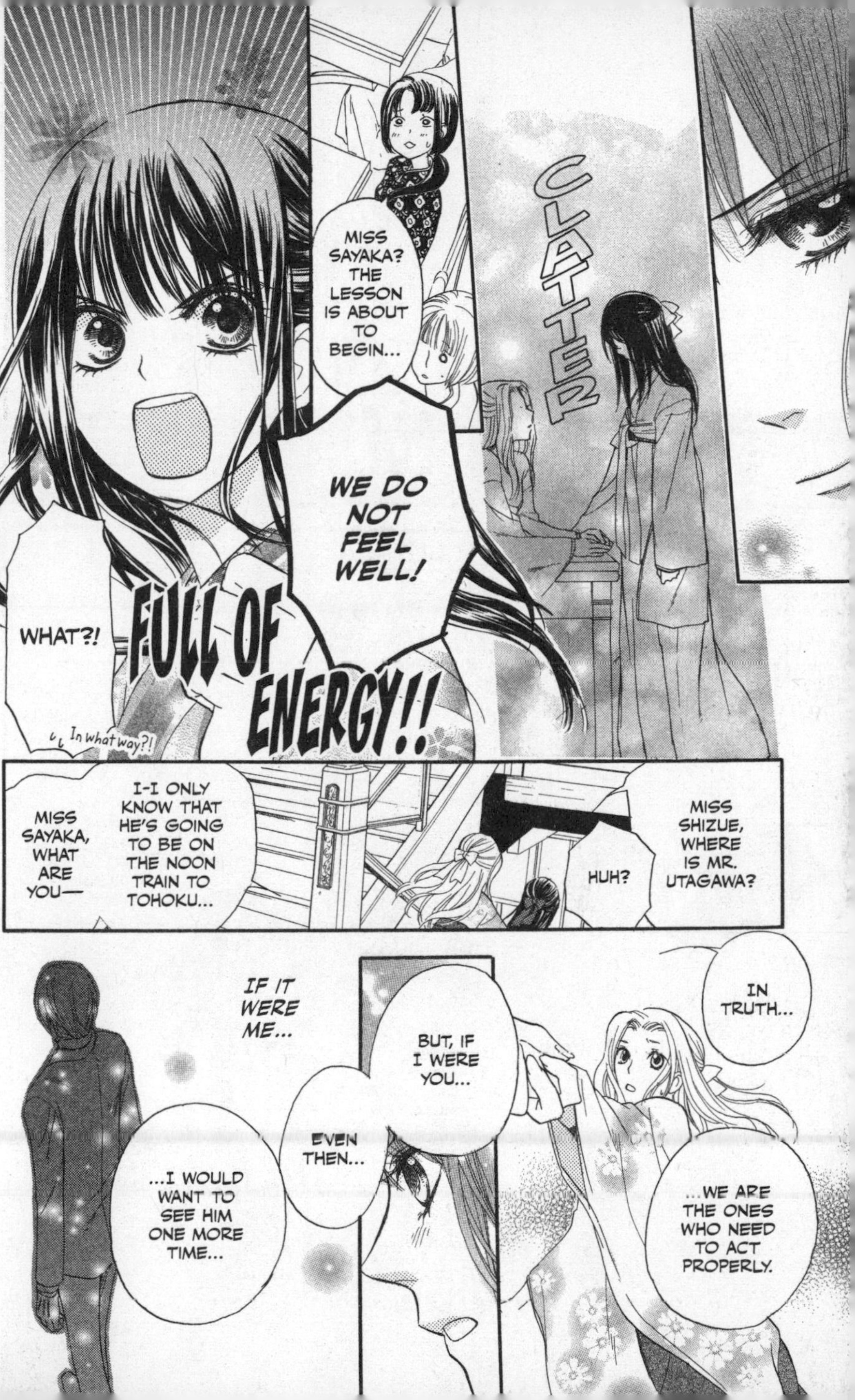
CLATTER
MISS SAYAKA? THE LESSON IS ABOUT TO BEGIN...
WE DO NOT FEEL WELL!
FULL OF ENERGY!!
WHAT?!
In what way?!
MISS SHIZUE, WHERE IS MR. UTAGAWA?
HUH?
I-I ONLY KNOW THAT HE'S GOING TO BE ON THE NOON TRAIN TO TOHOKU...
MISS SAYAKA, WHAT ARE YOU—
IN TRUTH...
...WE ARE THE ONES WHO NEED TO ACT PROPERLY.
EVEN THEN...
BUT, IF I WERE YOU...
...I WOULD WANT TO SEE HIM ONE MORE TIME...
IF IT WERE ME...

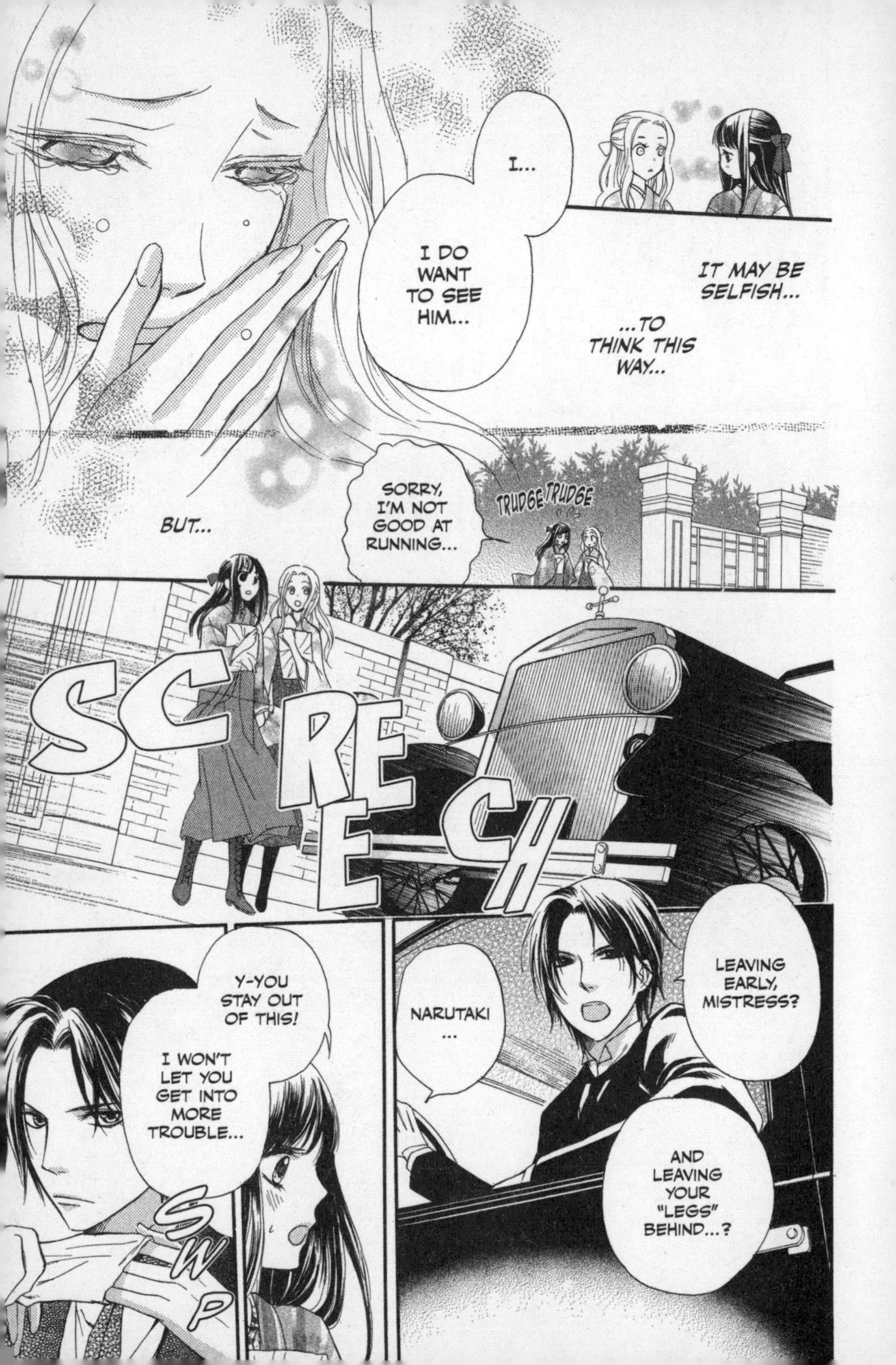
I...
IT MAY BE SELFISH...
...TO THINK THIS WAY...
I DO WANT TO SEE HIM...
BUT...
TRUDGE TRUDGE
SORRY, I'M NOT GOOD AT RUNNING...
SCREECH
LEAVING EARLY, MISTRESS?
NARUTAKI...
AND LEAVING YOUR "LEGS" BEHIND...?
Y-YOU STAY OUT OF THIS!
I WON'T LET YOU GET INTO MORE TROUBLE...
SWP

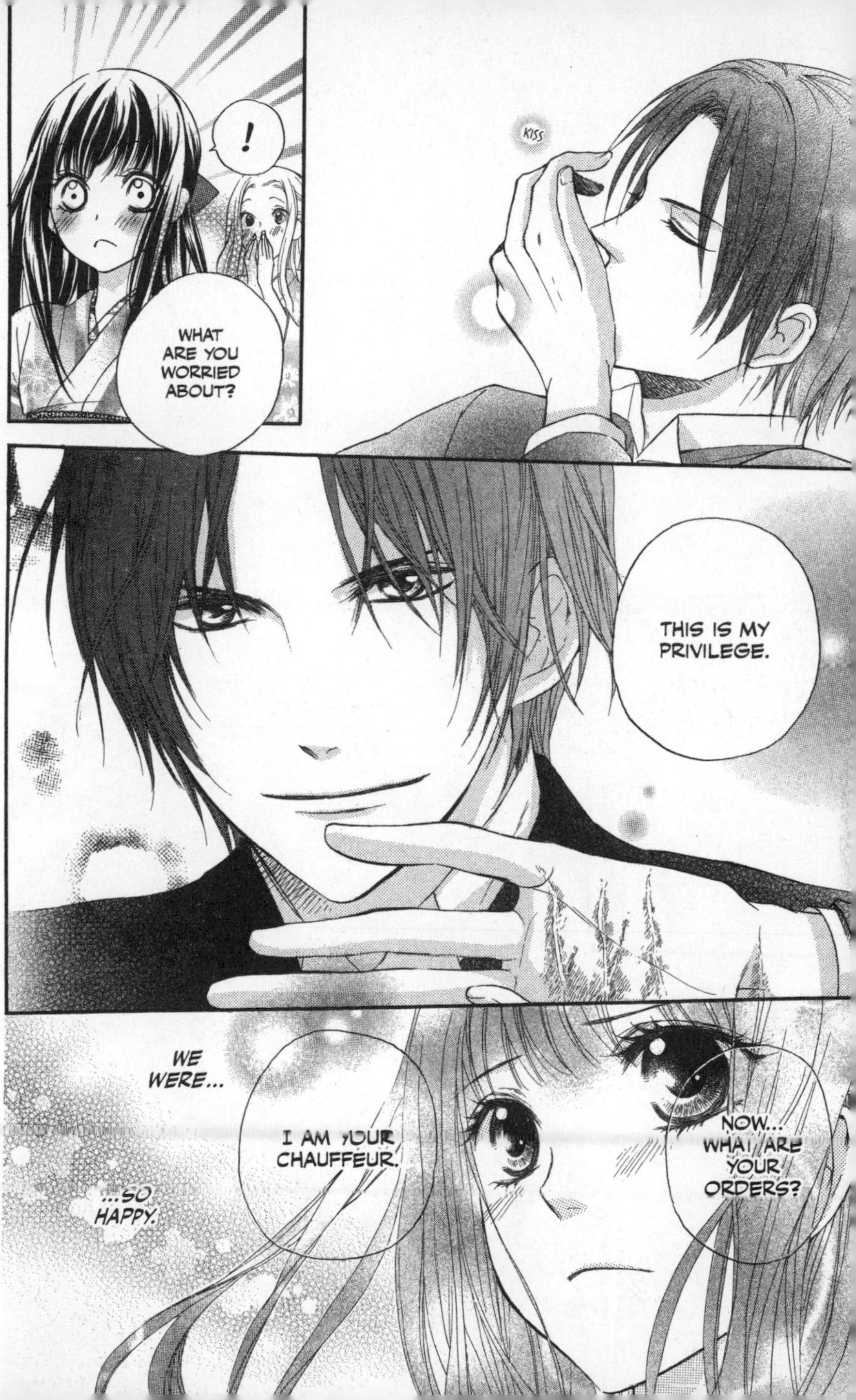
KISS
!
WHAT ARE YOU WORRIED ABOUT?
THIS IS MY PRIVILEGE.
NOW... WHAT ARE YOUR ORDERS?
I AM YOUR CHAUFFEUR.
WE WERE...
...SO HAPPY.

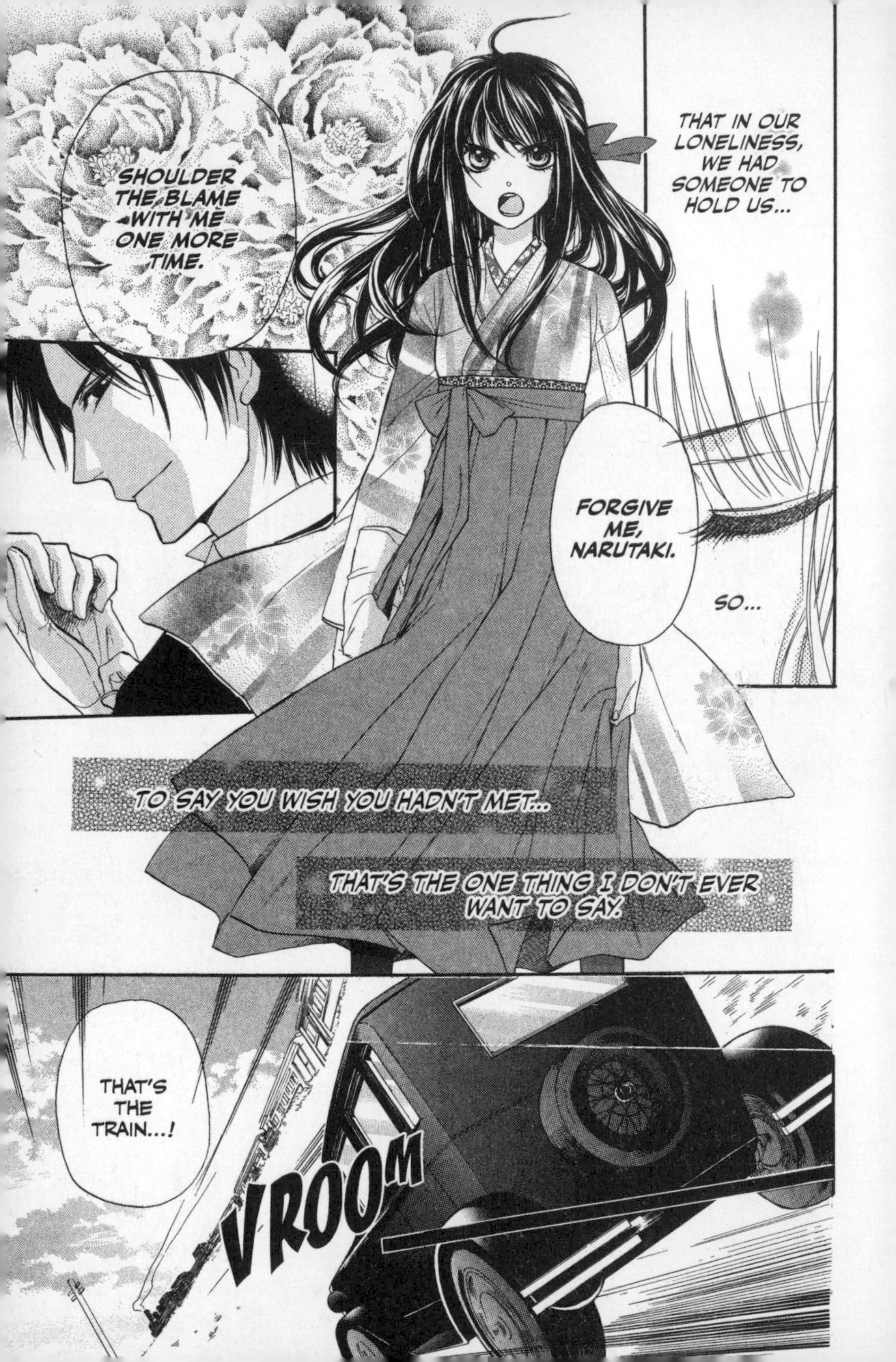
THAT IN OUR LONELINESS, WE HAD SOMEONE TO HOLD US...
SO...
FORGIVE ME, NARUTAKI.
SHOULDER THE BLAME WITH ME ONE MORE TIME.
TO SAY YOU WISH YOU HADN'T MET...
THAT'S THE ONE THING I DON'T EVER WANT TO SAY.
VROOM
THAT'S THE TRAIN...!

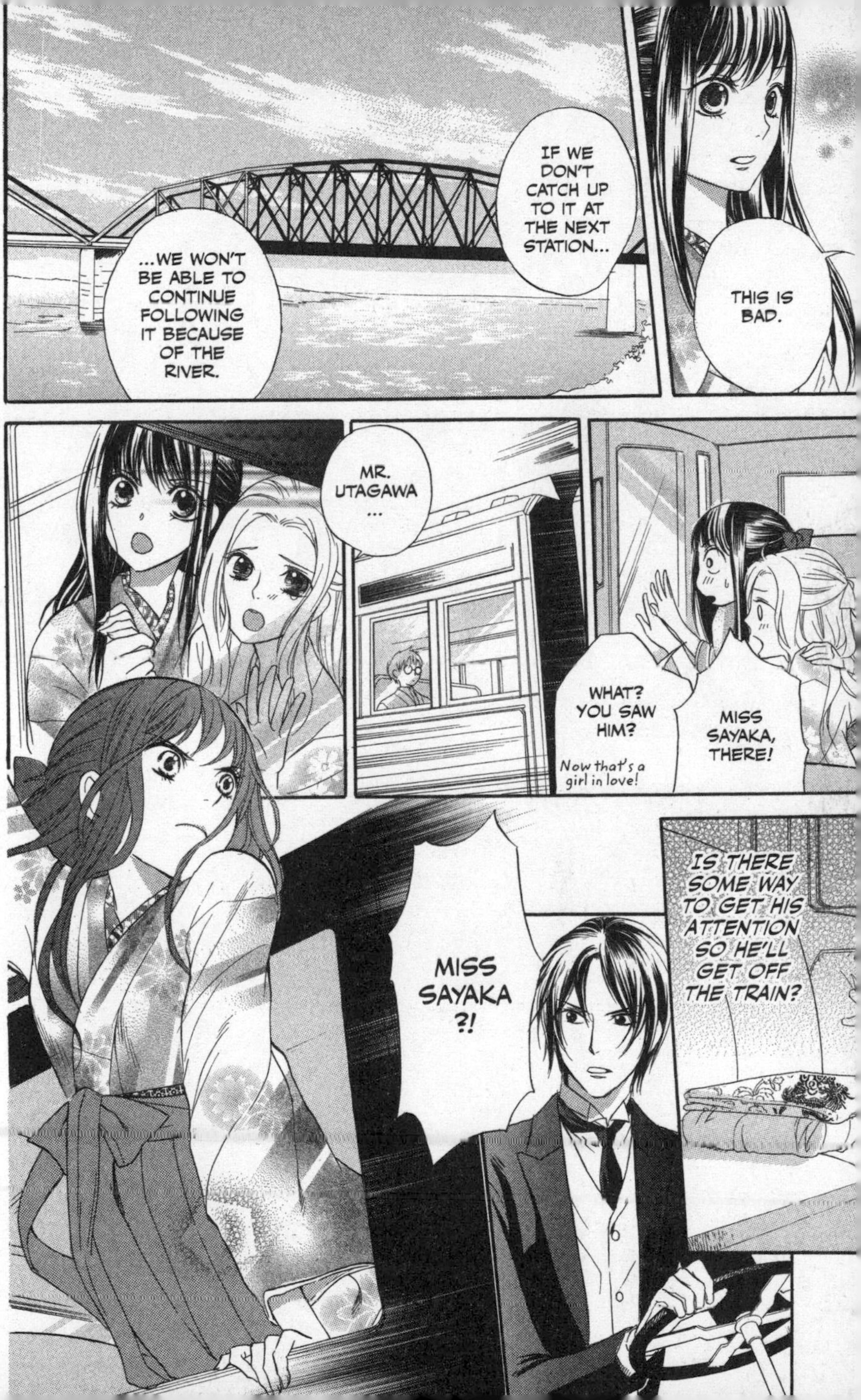
THIS IS BAD.
IF WE DON'T CATCH UP TO IT AT THE NEXT STATION...
...WE WON'T BE ABLE TO CONTINUE FOLLOWING IT BECAUSE OF THE RIVER.
MISS SAYAKA, THERE!
WHAT? YOU SAW HIM?
Now that's a girl in love!
MR. UTAGAWA ...
IS THERE SOME WAY TO GET HIS ATTENTION SO HE'LL GET OFF THE TRAIN?
MISS SAYAKA ?!

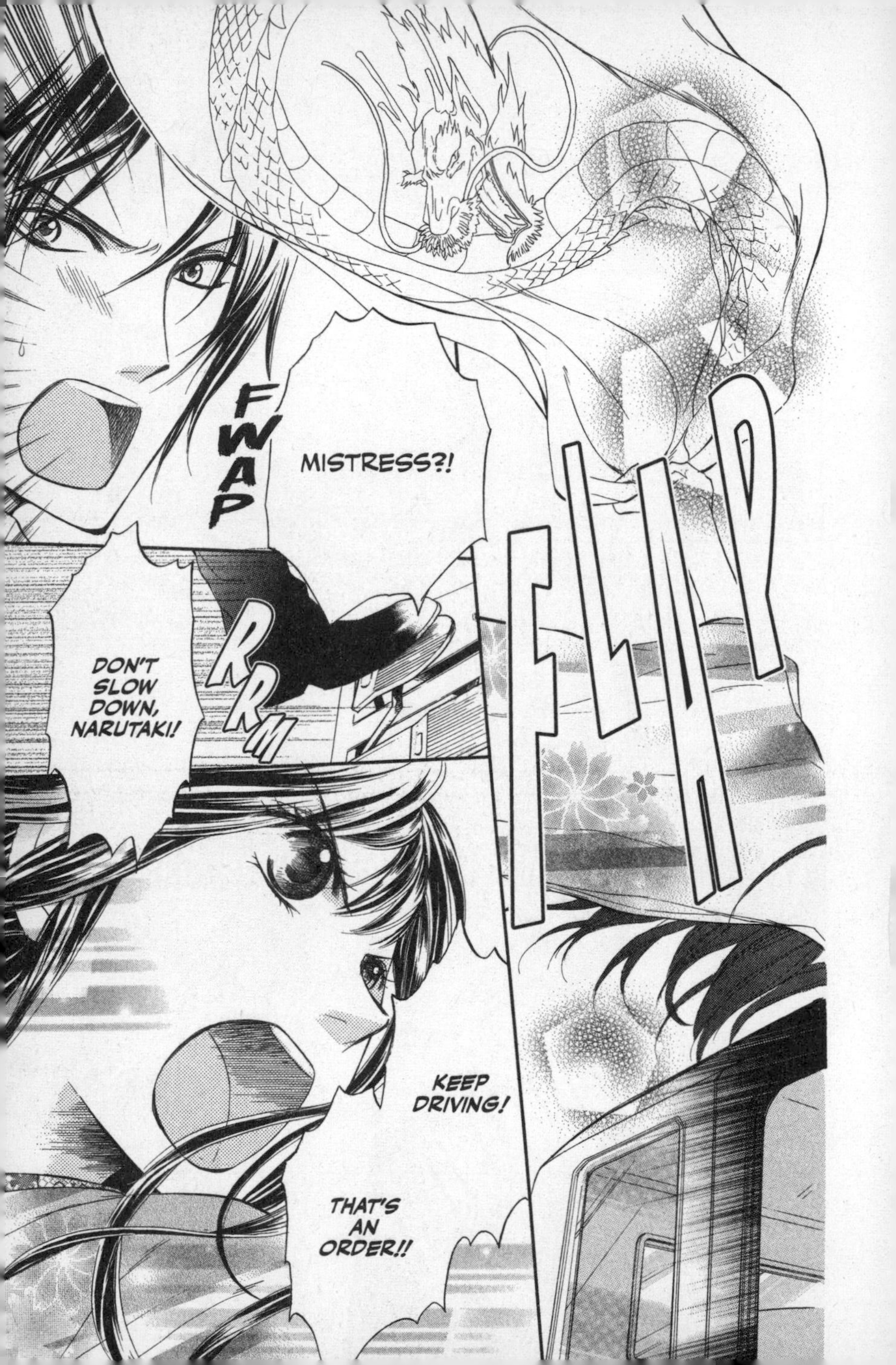
MISTRESS?!
FWAP
FLAP
RRM
DON'T SLOW DOWN, NARUTAKI!
KEEP DRIVING!
THAT'S AN ORDER!!

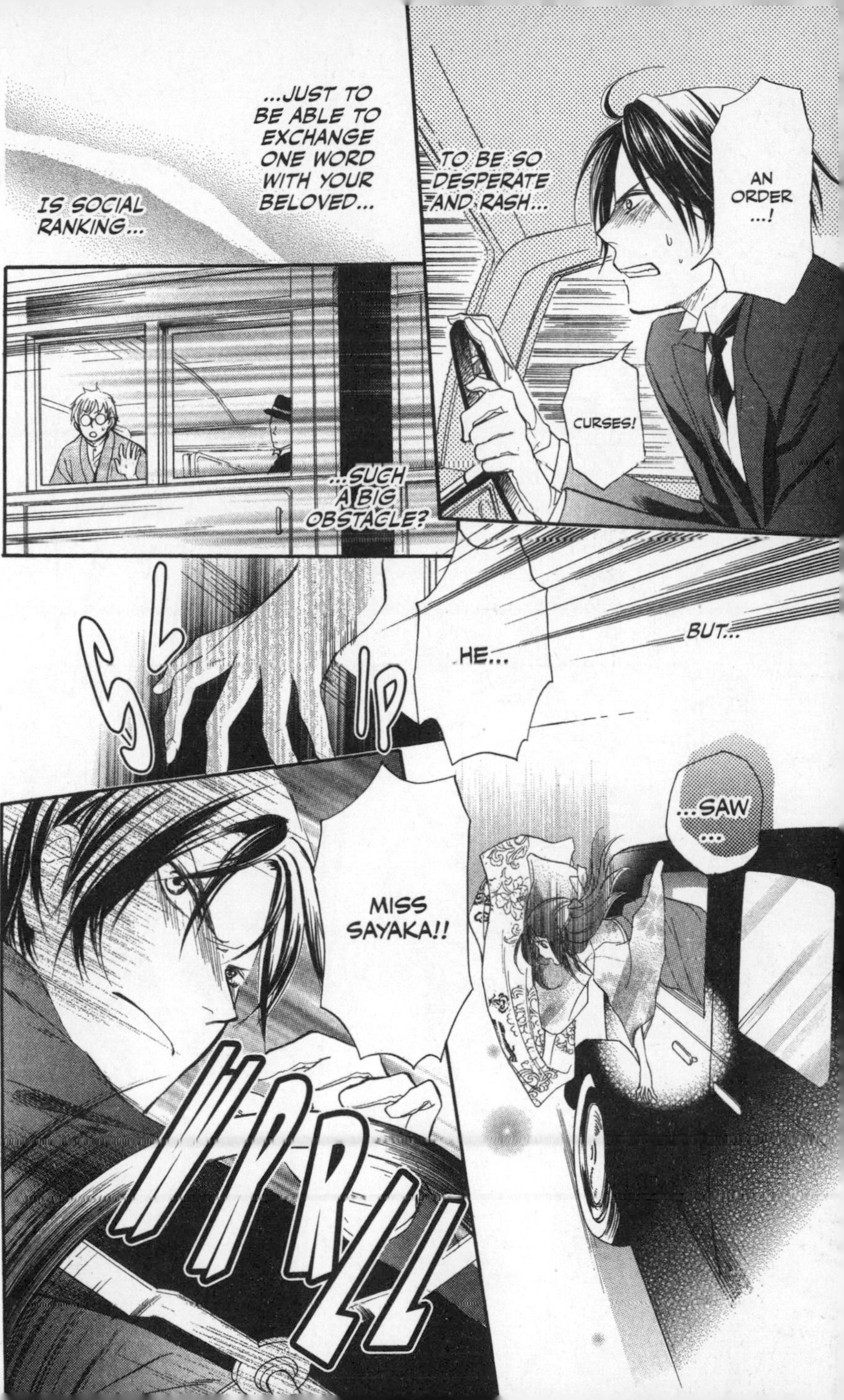
AN ORDER ...!
CURSES!
TO BE SO DESPERATE AND RASH...
...JUST TO BE ABLE TO EXCHANGE ONE WORD WITH YOUR BELOVED...
IS SOCIAL RANKING...
...SUCH A BIG OBSTACLE?
BUT...
HE...
SLIP
...SAW ...
MISS SAYAKA!!

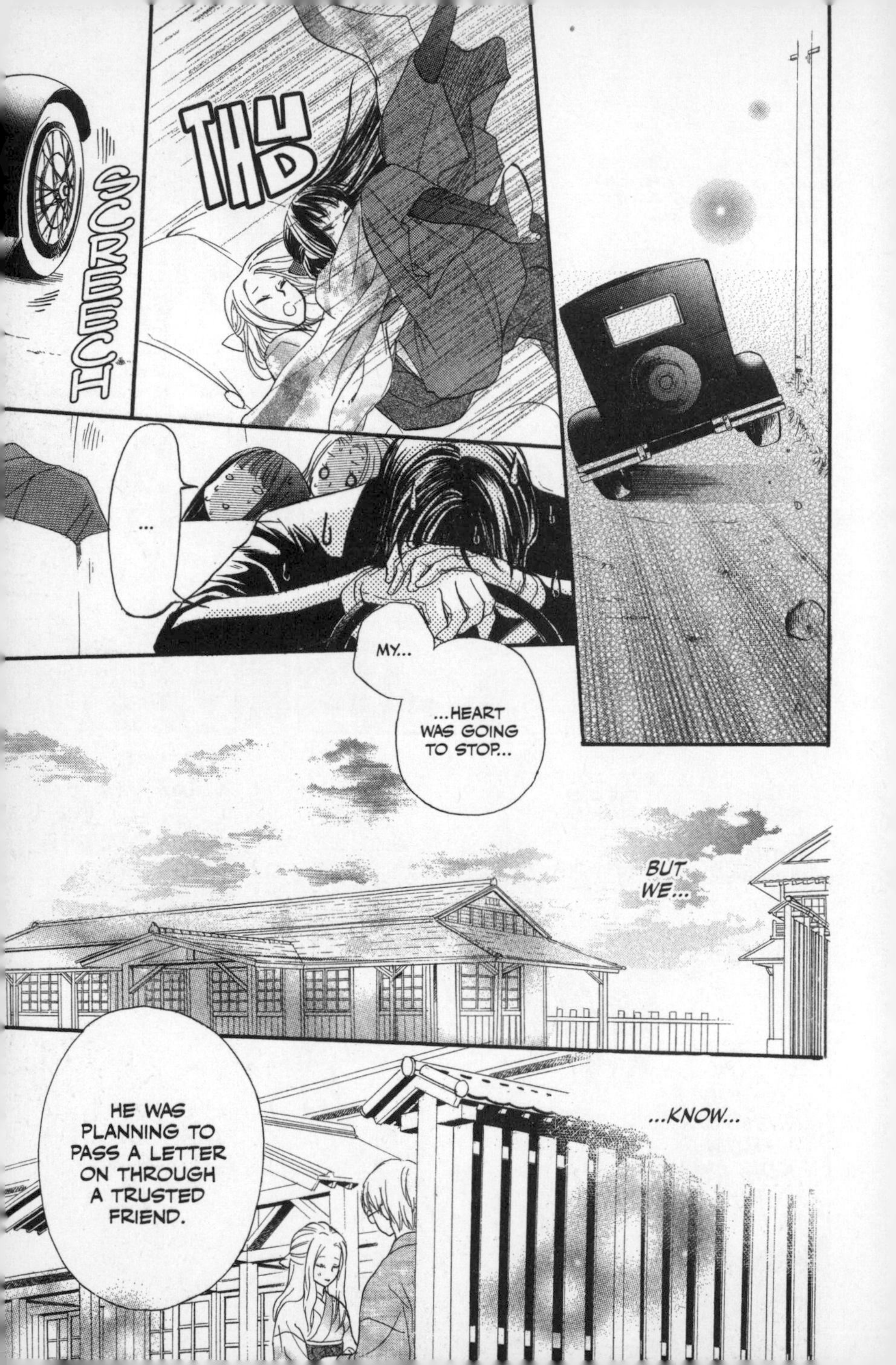
THUD
SCREECH
...
MY...
...HEART WAS GOING TO STOP...
BUT WE...
...KNOW...
HE WAS PLANNING TO PASS A LETTER ON THROUGH A TRUSTED FRIEND.

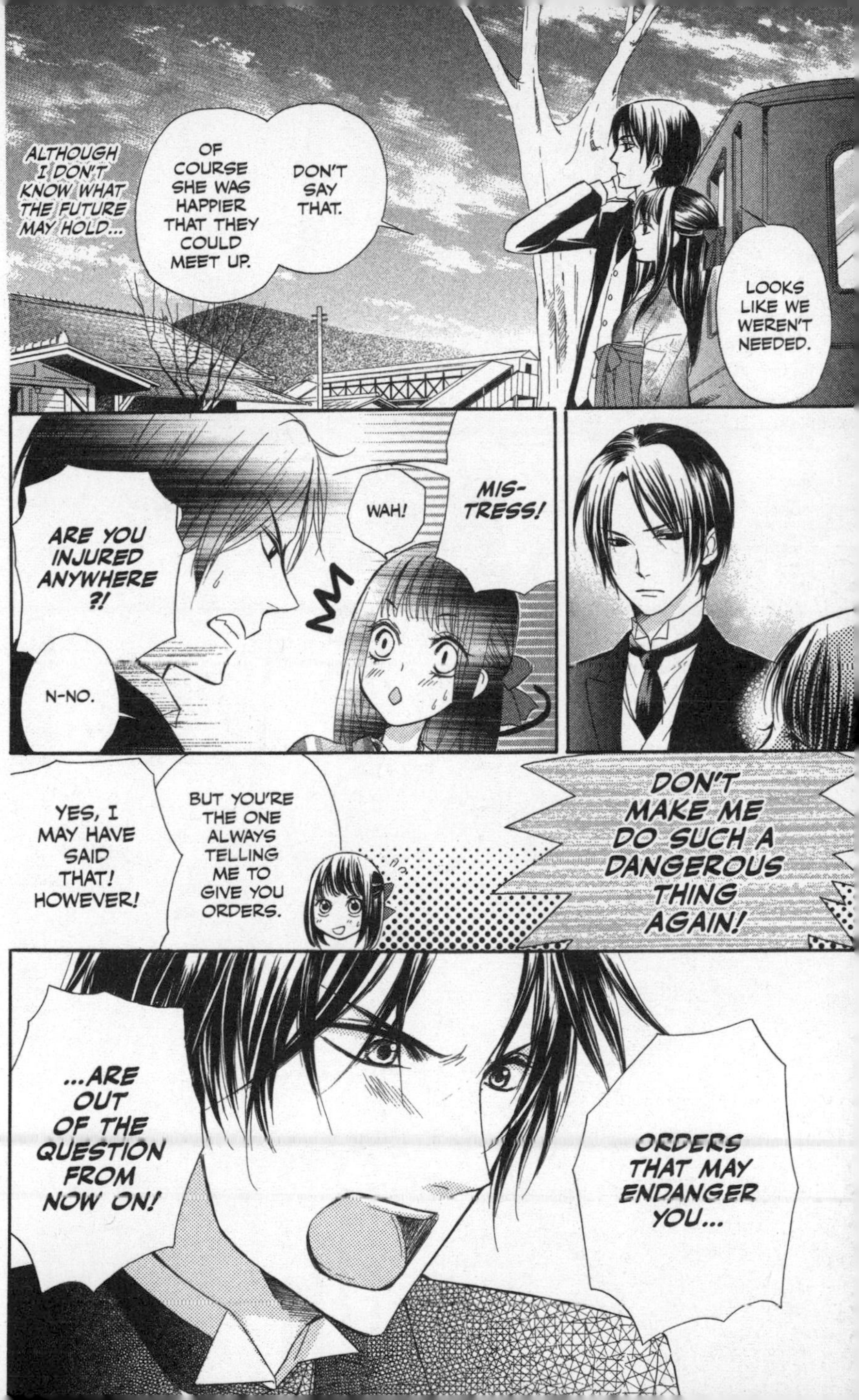
LOOKS LIKE WE WEREN'T NEEDED.
DON'T SAY THAT.
OF COURSE SHE WAS HAPPIER THAT THEY COULD MEET UP.
ALTHOUGH I DON'T KNOW WHAT THE FUTURE MAY HOLD...
MIS-TRESS!
WAH!
ARE YOU INJURED ANYWHERE ?!
N-NO.
DON'T MAKE ME DO SUCH A DANGEROUS THING AGAIN!
BUT YOU'RE THE ONE ALWAYS TELLING ME TO GIVE YOU ORDERS.
YES, I MAY HAVE SAID THAT! HOWEVER!
ORDERS THAT MAY ENDANGER YOU...
...ARE OUT OF THE QUESTION FROM NOW ON!

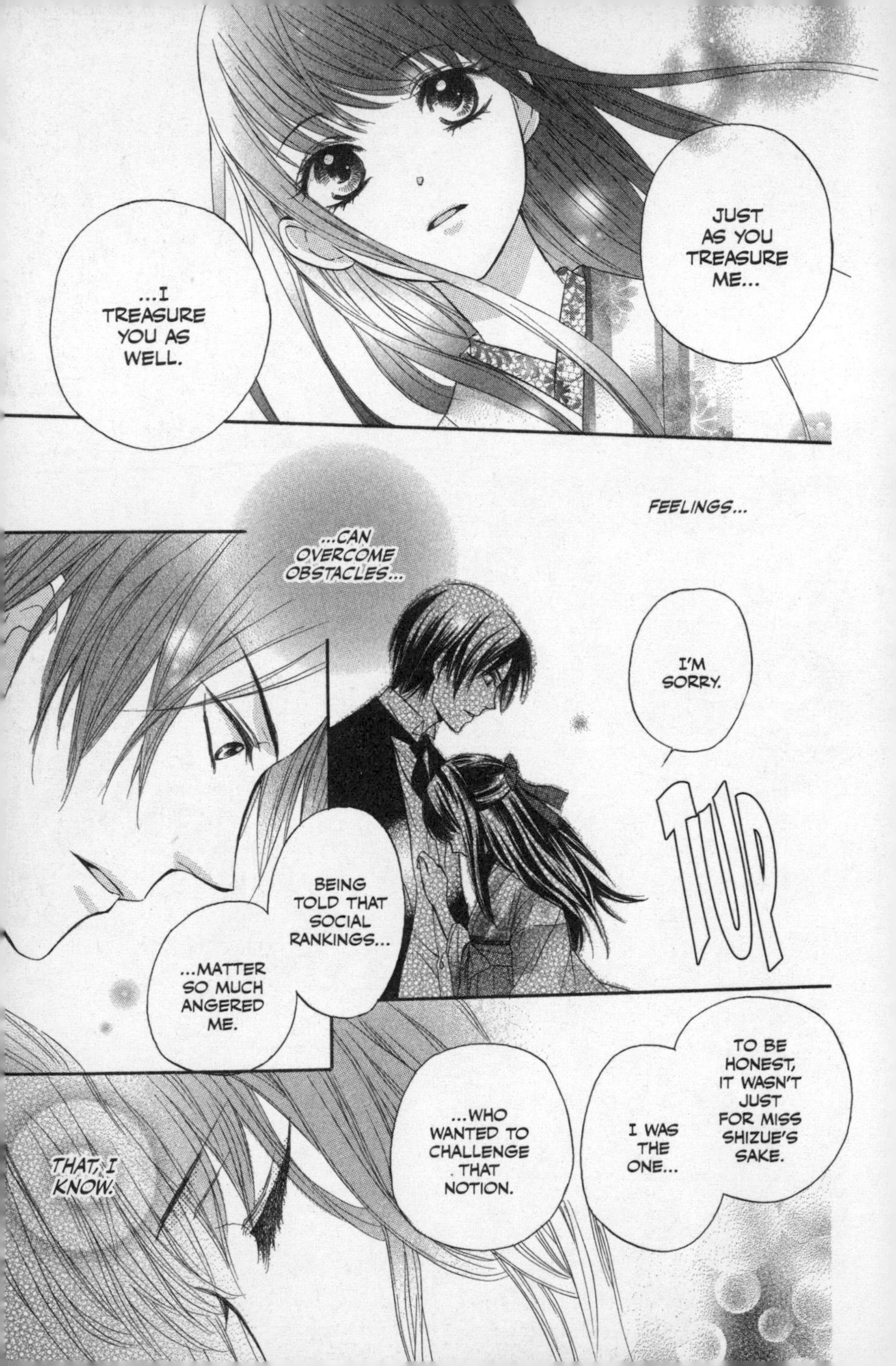
JUST AS YOU TREASURE ME...
...I TREASURE YOU AS WELL.
FEELINGS...
...CAN OVERCOME OBSTACLES...
I'M SORRY.
TUP
BEING TOLD THAT SOCIAL RANKINGS...
...MATTER SO MUCH ANGERED ME.
TO BE HONEST, IT WASN'T JUST FOR MISS SHIZUE'S SAKE.
I WAS THE ONE...
...WHO WANTED TO CHALLENGE THAT NOTION.
THAT, I KNOW.

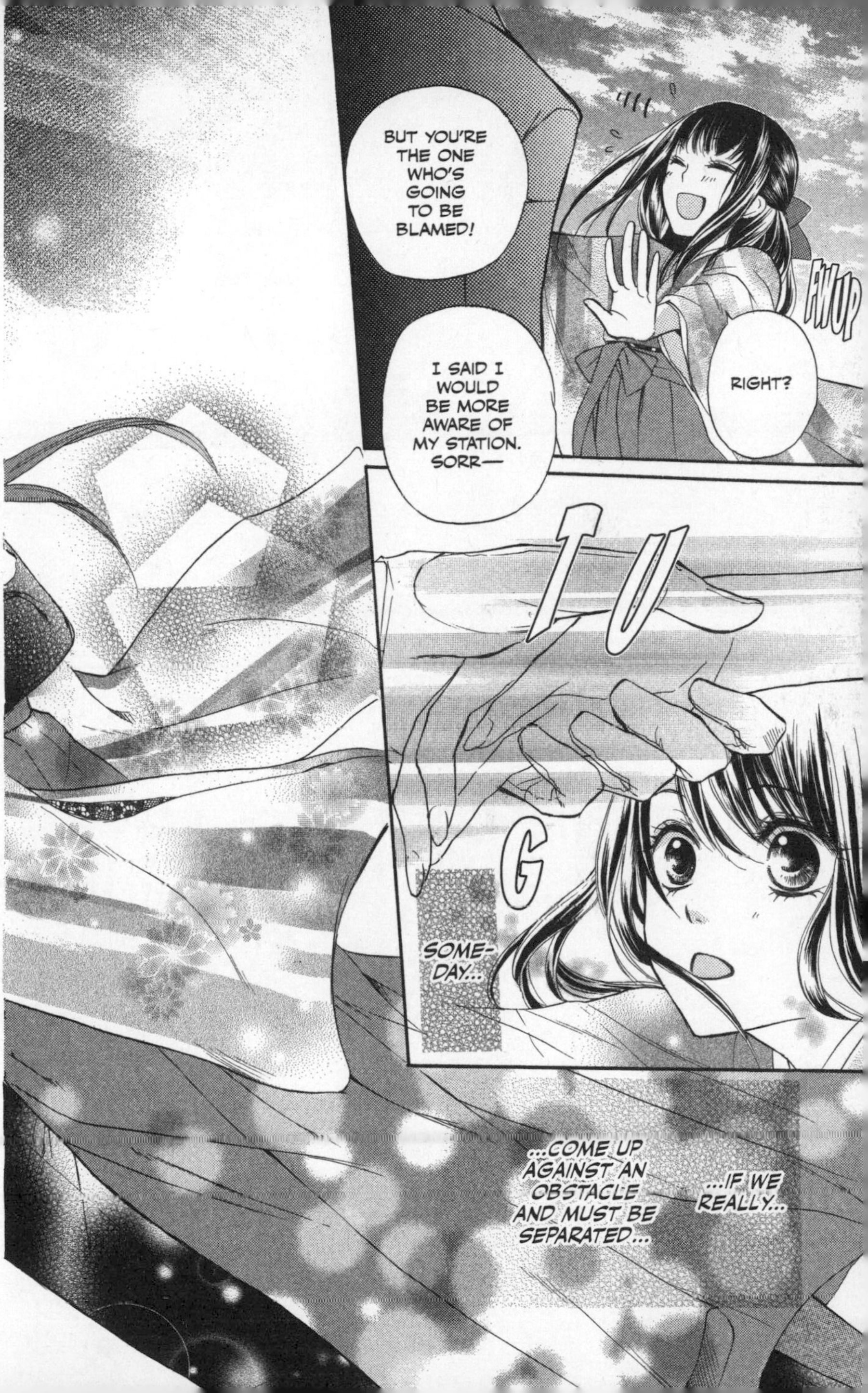
FWUP
BUT YOU'RE THE ONE WHO'S GOING TO BE BLAMED!
RIGHT?
I SAID I WOULD BE MORE AWARE OF MY STATION. SORR—
TUG
SOME-DAY...
...IF WE REALLY...
...COME UP AGAINST AN OBSTACLE AND MUST BE SEPARATED...

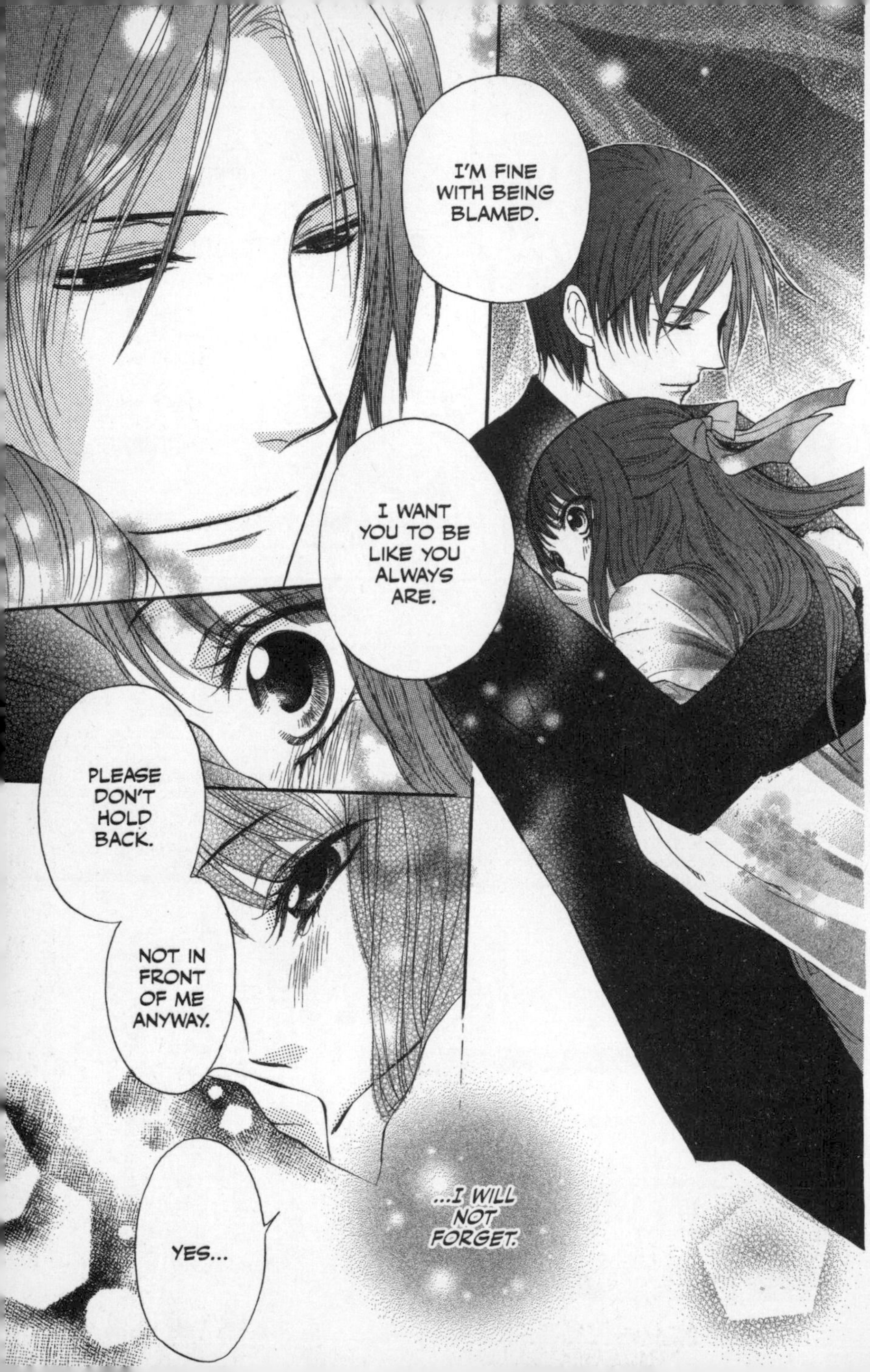
I'M FINE WITH BEING BLAMED.
I WANT YOU TO BE LIKE YOU ALWAYS ARE.
PLEASE DON'T HOLD BACK.
NOT IN FRONT OF ME ANYWAY.
...I WILL NOT FORGET.
YES...

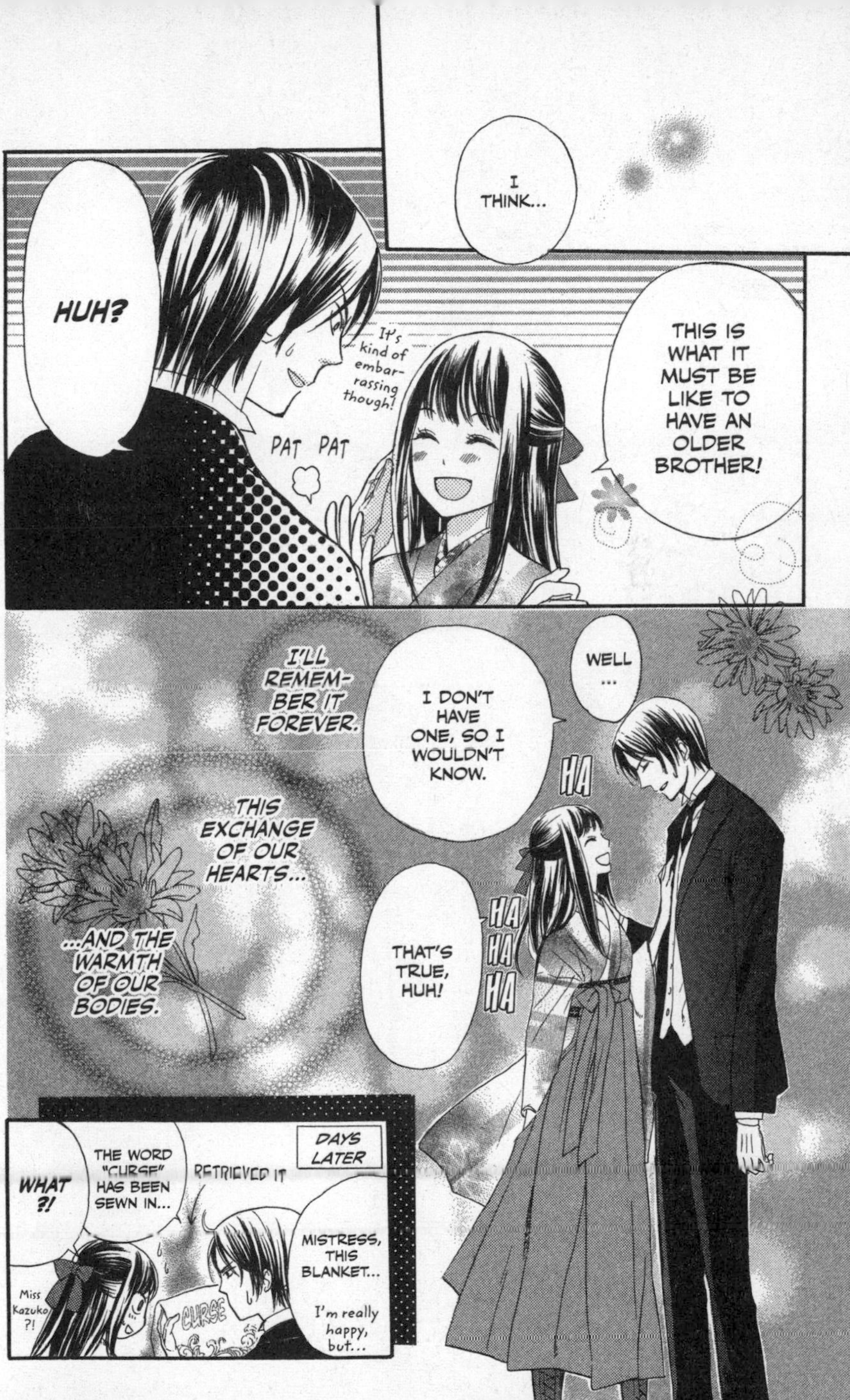
I THINK...
THIS IS WHAT IT MUST BE LIKE TO HAVE AN OLDER BROTHER!
It's kind of embarrassing though!
PAT PAT
HUH?
WELL ...
I DON'T HAVE ONE, SO I WOULDN'T KNOW.
HA HA HA HA
THAT'S TRUE, HUH!
I'LL REMEMBER IT FOREVER.
THIS EXCHANGE OF OUR HEARTS...
...AND THE WARMTH OF OUR BODIES.
DAYS LATER
MISTRESS, THIS BLANKET...
I'm really happy, but...
CURSE
THE WORD "CURSE" HAS BEEN SEWN IN...
WHAT ?!
Miss Kazuko ?!

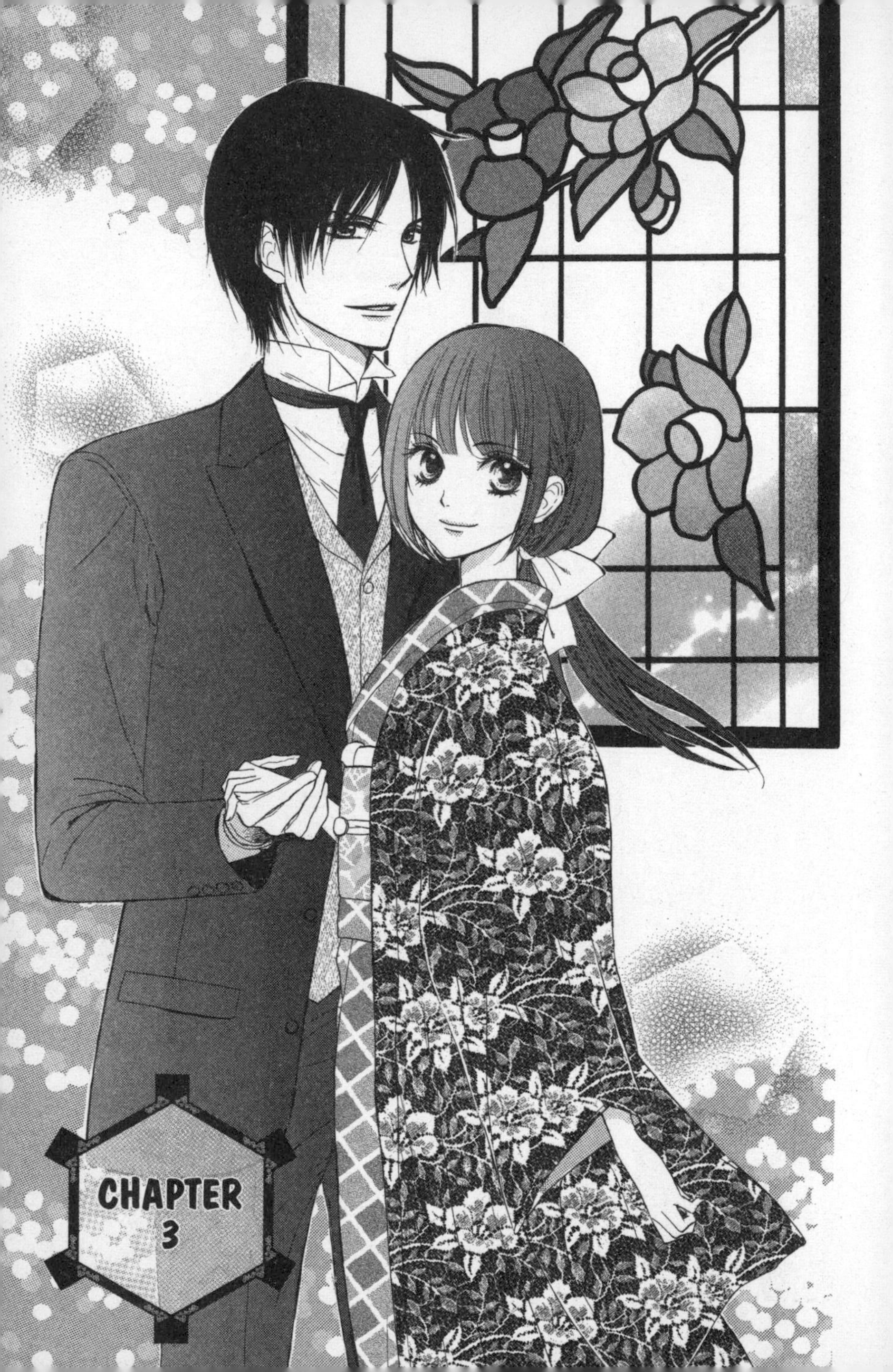
CHAPTER
3

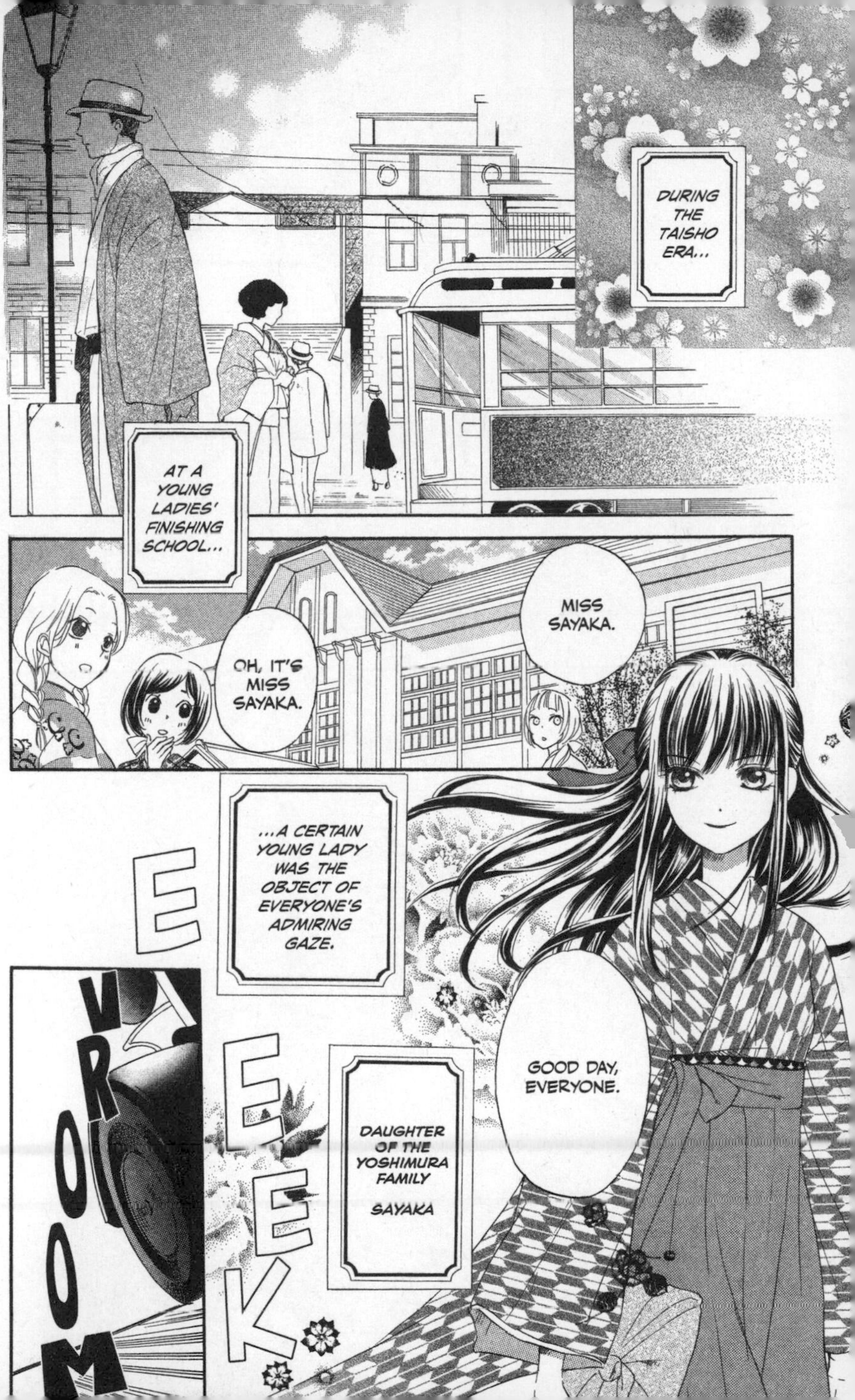
DURING THE TAISHO ERA...
AT A YOUNG LADIES' FINISHING SCHOOL...
MISS SAYAKA.
OH, IT'S MISS SAYAKA.
...A CERTAIN YOUNG LADY WAS THE OBJECT OF EVERYONE'S ADMIRING GAZE.
GOOD DAY, EVERYONE.
DAUGHTER OF THE YOSHIMURA FAMILY
SAYAKA
EEEEK
VROOOOM

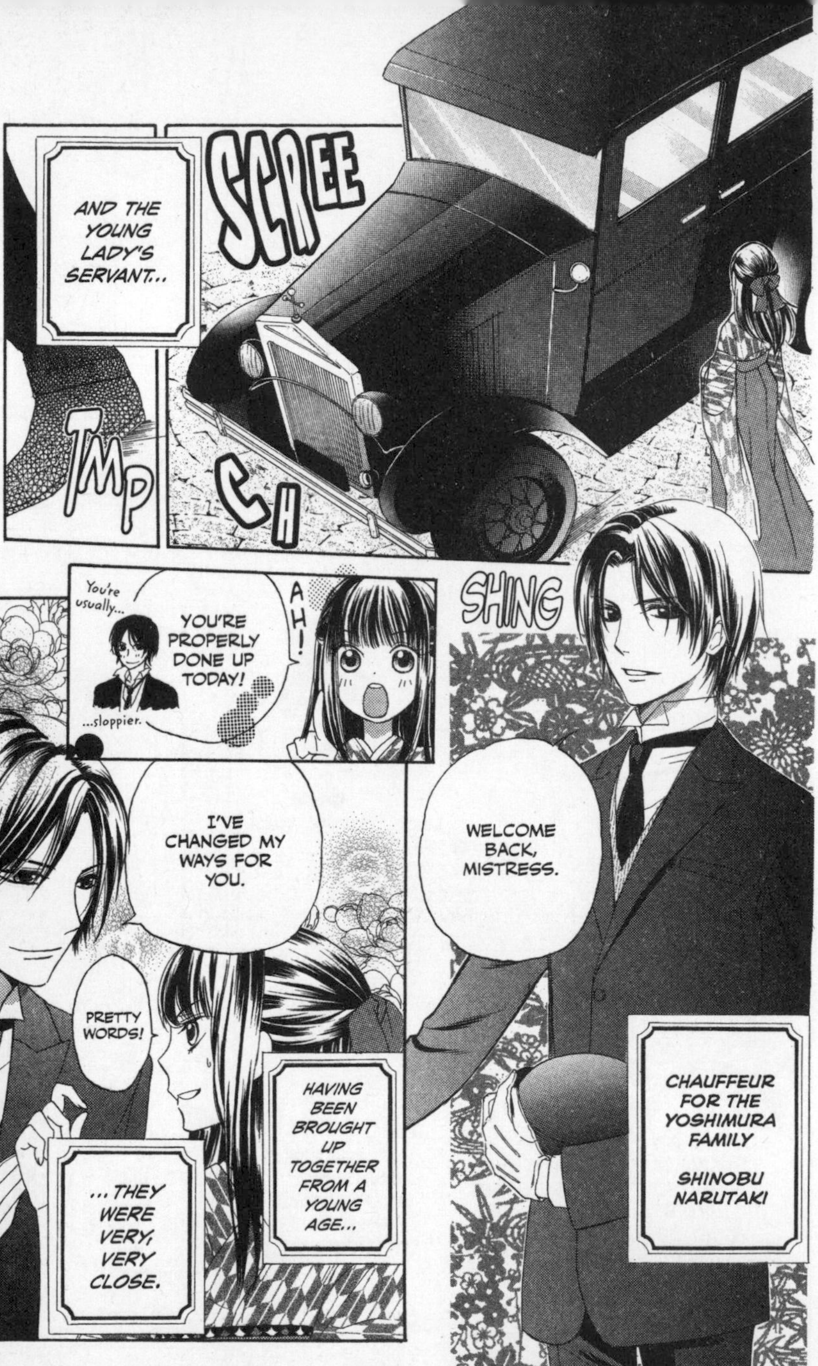
SCREE
CH
AND THE YOUNG LADY'S SERVANT...
TMP
SHING
WELCOME BACK, MISTRESS.
CHAUFFEUR FOR THE YOSHIMURA FAMILY
SHINOBU NARUTAKI
AH!
YOU'RE PROPERLY DONE UP TODAY!
You're usually...
...sloppier.
I'VE CHANGED MY WAYS FOR YOU.
HAVING BEEN BROUGHT UP TOGETHER FROM A YOUNG AGE...
PRETTY WORDS!
...THEY WERE VERY, VERY CLOSE.

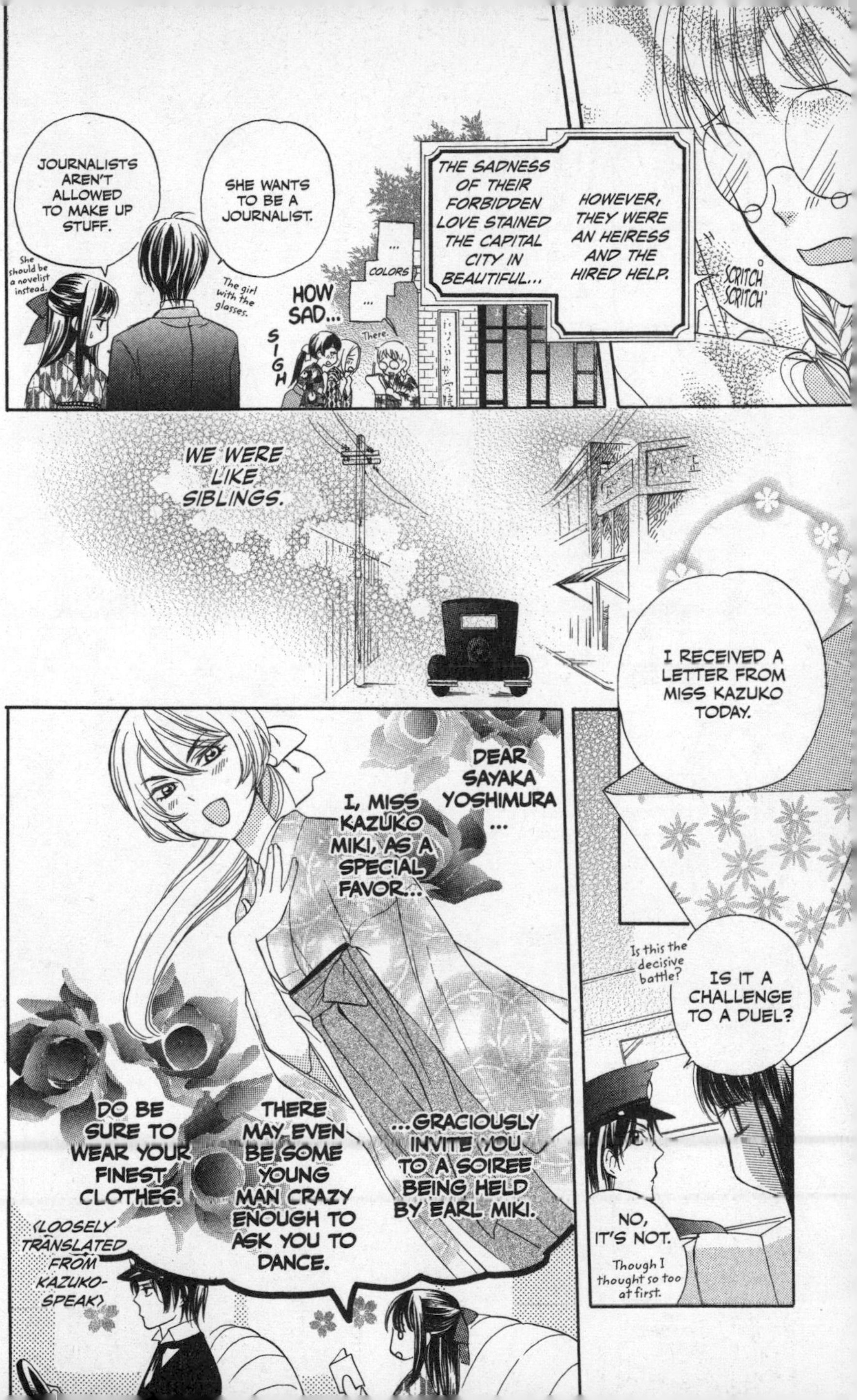

HOWEVER, THEY WERE AN HEIRESS AND THE HIRED HELP.
THE SADNESS OF THEIR FORBIDDEN LOVE STAINED THE CAPITAL CITY IN BEAUTIFUL...
SCRITCH SCRITCH
...
COLORS
...
HOW SAD...
SIGH
There.
The girl with the glasses.
SHE WANTS TO BE A JOURNALIST.
JOURNALISTS AREN'T ALLOWED TO MAKE UP STUFF.
She should be a novelist instead.
WE WERE LIKE SIBLINGS.
I RECEIVED A LETTER FROM MISS KAZUKO TODAY.
IS IT A CHALLENGE TO A DUEL?
Is this the decisive battle?
NO, IT'S NOT.
Though I thought so too at first.
DEAR SAYAKA YOSHIMURA...
I, MISS KAZUKO MIKI, AS A SPECIAL FAVOR...
...GRACIOUSLY INVITE YOU TO A SOIREE BEING HELD BY EARL MIKI.
THERE MAY EVEN BE SOME YOUNG MAN CRAZY ENOUGH TO ASK YOU TO DANCE.
DO BE SURE TO WEAR YOUR FINEST CLOTHES.
<LOOSELY TRANSLATED FROM KAZUKO-SPEAK>

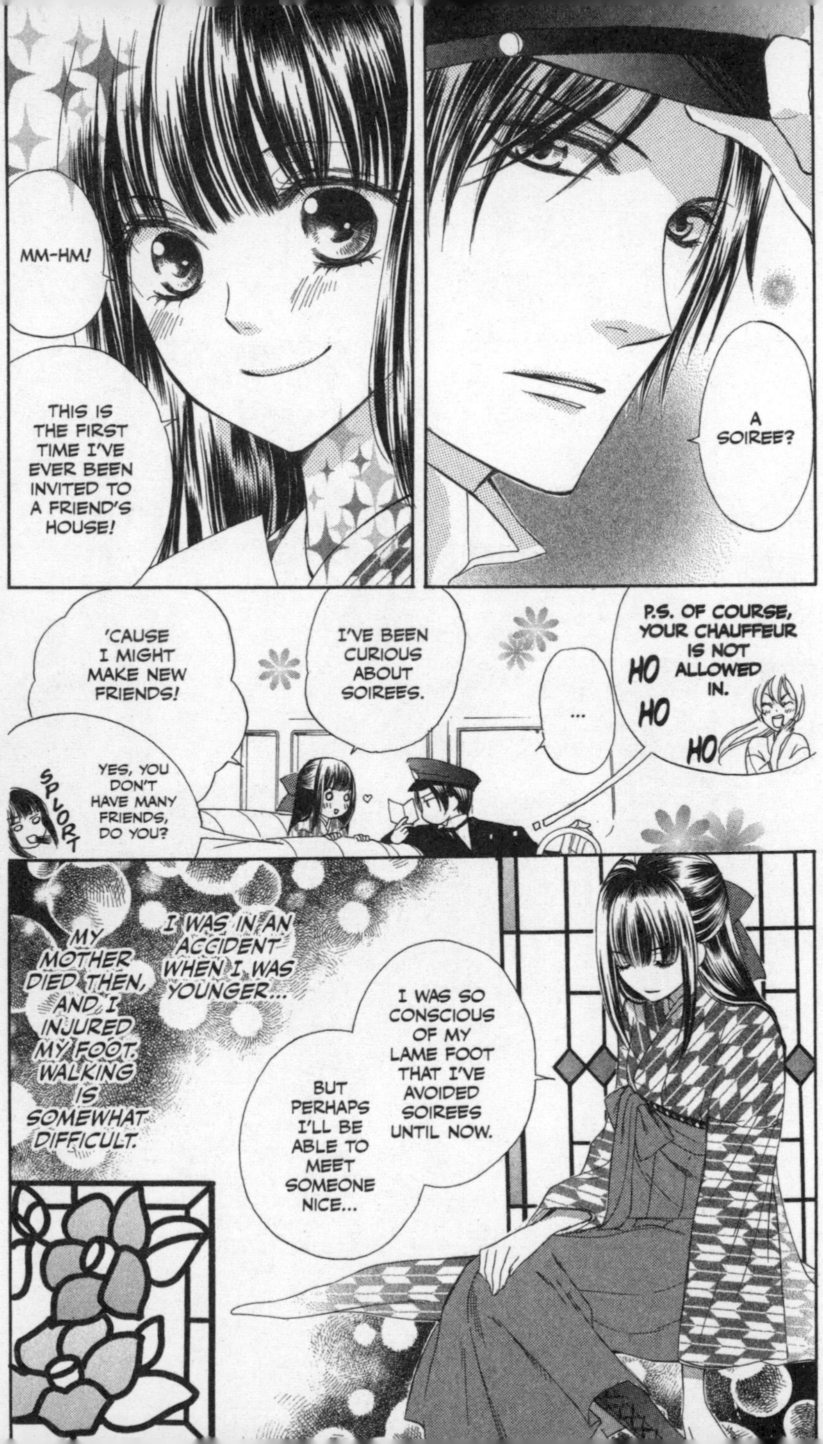
A SOIREE?
MM-HM!
THIS IS THE FIRST TIME I'VE EVER BEEN INVITED TO A FRIEND'S HOUSE!
P.S. OF COURSE, YOUR CHAUFFEUR IS NOT ALLOWED IN.
HO HO HO
...
I'VE BEEN CURIOUS ABOUT SOIREES.
'CAUSE I MIGHT MAKE NEW FRIENDS!
YES, YOU DON'T HAVE MANY FRIENDS, DO YOU?
SPVORT
I WAS IN AN ACCIDENT WHEN I WAS YOUNGER...
MY MOTHER DIED THEN, AND I INJURED MY FOOT. WALKING IS SOMEWHAT DIFFICULT.
I WAS SO CONSCIOUS OF MY LAME FOOT THAT I'VE AVOIDED SOIREES UNTIL NOW.
BUT PERHAPS I'LL BE ABLE TO MEET SOMEONE NICE...

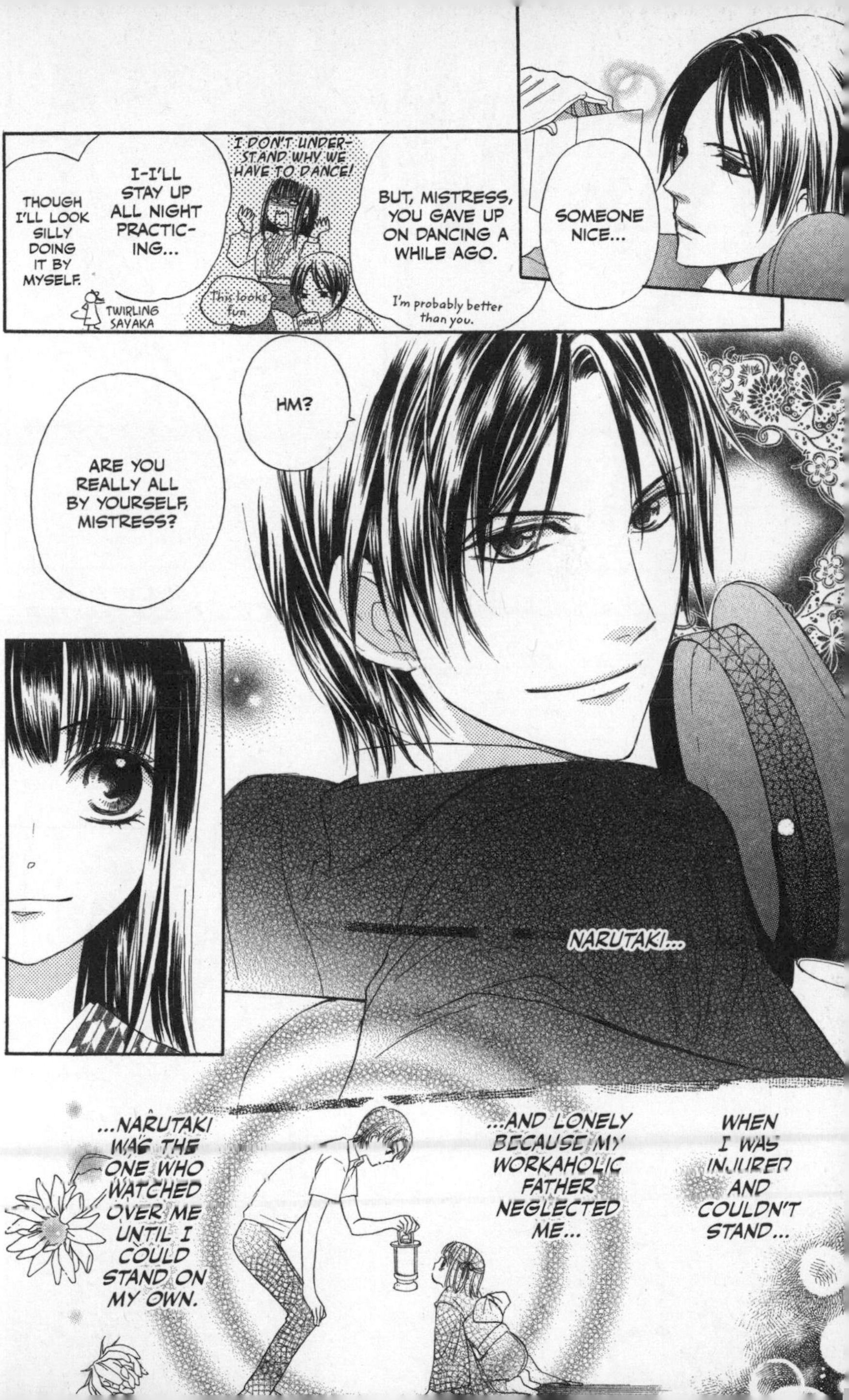
SOMEONE NICE...
BUT, MISTRESS, YOU GAVE UP ON DANCING A WHILE AGO.
I'm probably better than you.
I DON'T UNDER-STAND WHY WE HAVE TO DANCE!
This looks fun
I-I'LL STAY UP ALL NIGHT PRACTIC-ING...
THOUGH I'LL LOOK SILLY DOING IT BY MYSELF.
TWIRLING SAYAKA
HM?
ARE YOU REALLY ALL BY YOURSELF, MISTRESS?
NARUTAKI...
WHEN I WAS INJURED AND COULDN'T STAND...
...AND LONELY BECAUSE MY WORKAHOLIC FATHER NEGLECTED ME...
...NARUTAKI WAS THE ONE WHO WATCHED OVER ME UNTIL I COULD STAND ON MY OWN.

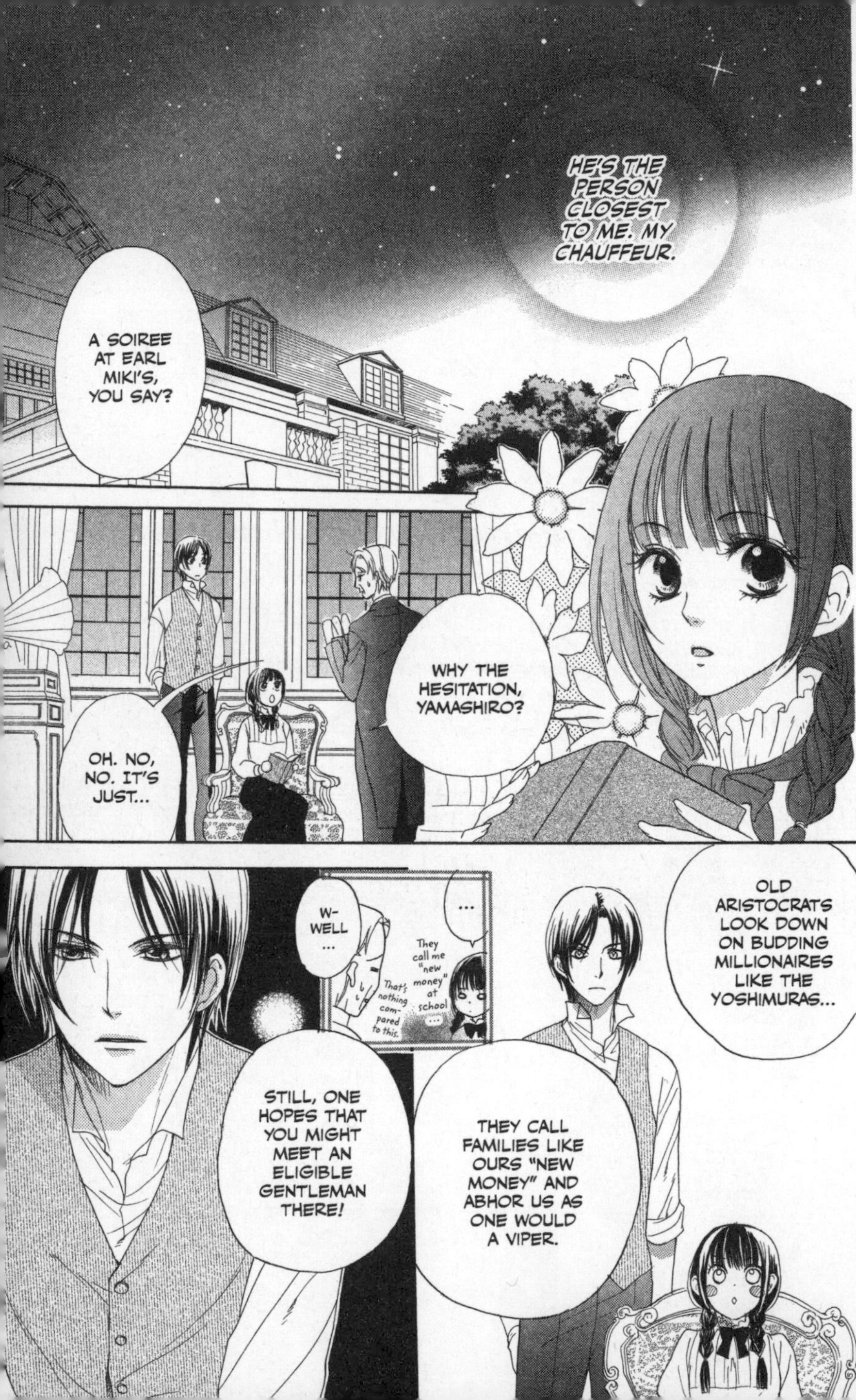

HE'S THE PERSON CLOSEST TO ME. MY CHAUFFEUR.
A SOIREE AT EARL MIKI'S, YOU SAY?
WHY THE HESITATION, YAMASHIRO?
OH. NO, NO. IT'S JUST...
OLD ARISTOCRATS LOOK DOWN ON BUDDING MILLIONAIRES LIKE THE YOSHIMURAS...
THEY CALL FAMILIES LIKE OURS "NEW MONEY" AND ABHOR US AS ONE WOULD A VIPER.
...
W-WELL...
They call me "new money" at school...
That's nothing compared to this.
STILL, ONE HOPES THAT YOU MIGHT MEET AN ELIGIBLE GENTLEMAN THERE!

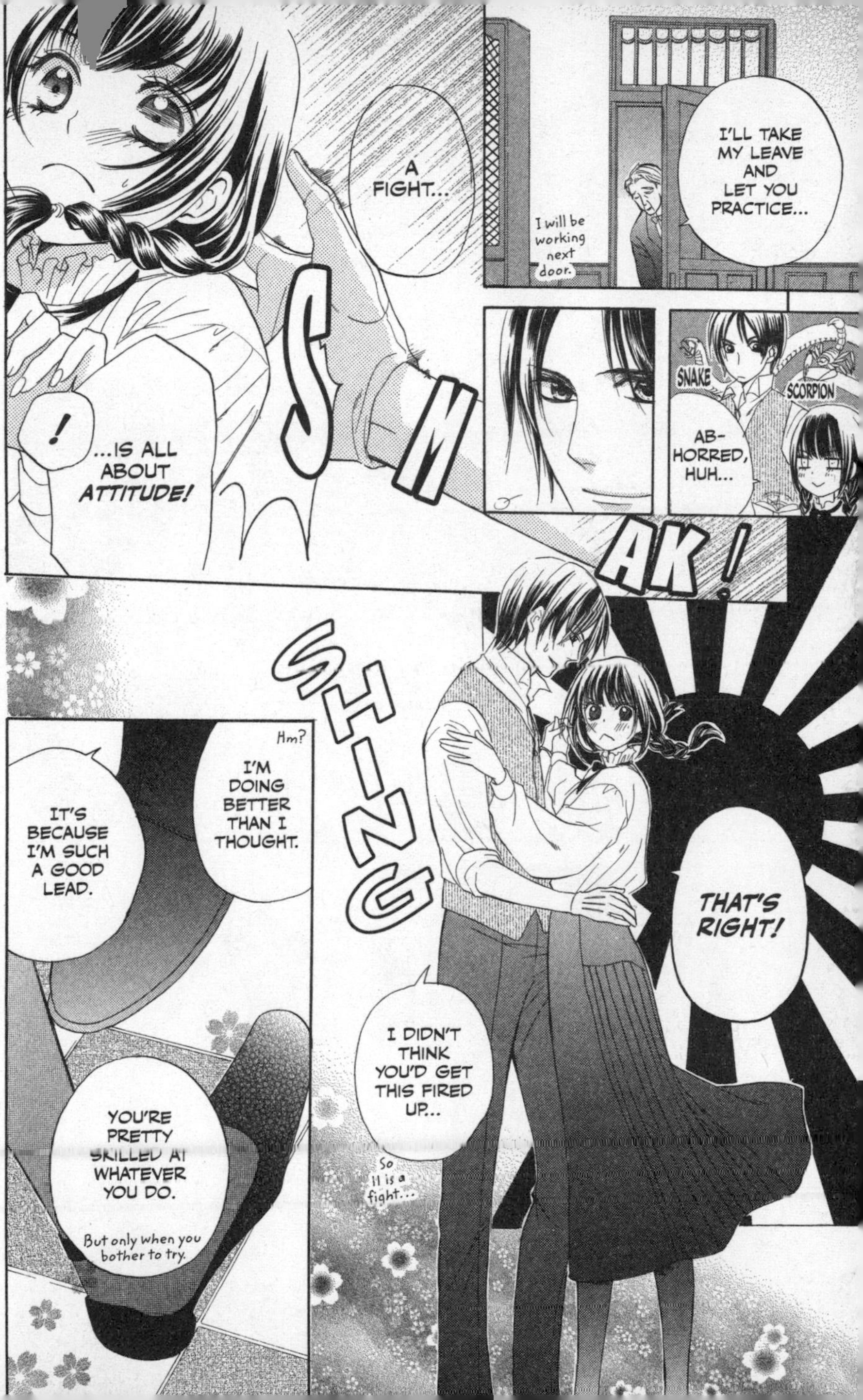
I'LL TAKE MY LEAVE AND LET YOU PRACTICE...
I will be working next door.
SNAKE
SCORPION
AB-HORRED, HUH...
A FIGHT...
!
...IS ALL ABOUT ATTITUDE!
SMAK!
THAT'S RIGHT!
SHING
I DIDN'T THINK YOU'D GET THIS FIRED UP...
So it is a fight...
Hm?
I'M DOING BETTER THAN I THOUGHT.
IT'S BECAUSE I'M SUCH A GOOD LEAD.
YOU'RE PRETTY SKILLED AT WHATEVER YOU DO.
But only when you bother to try.

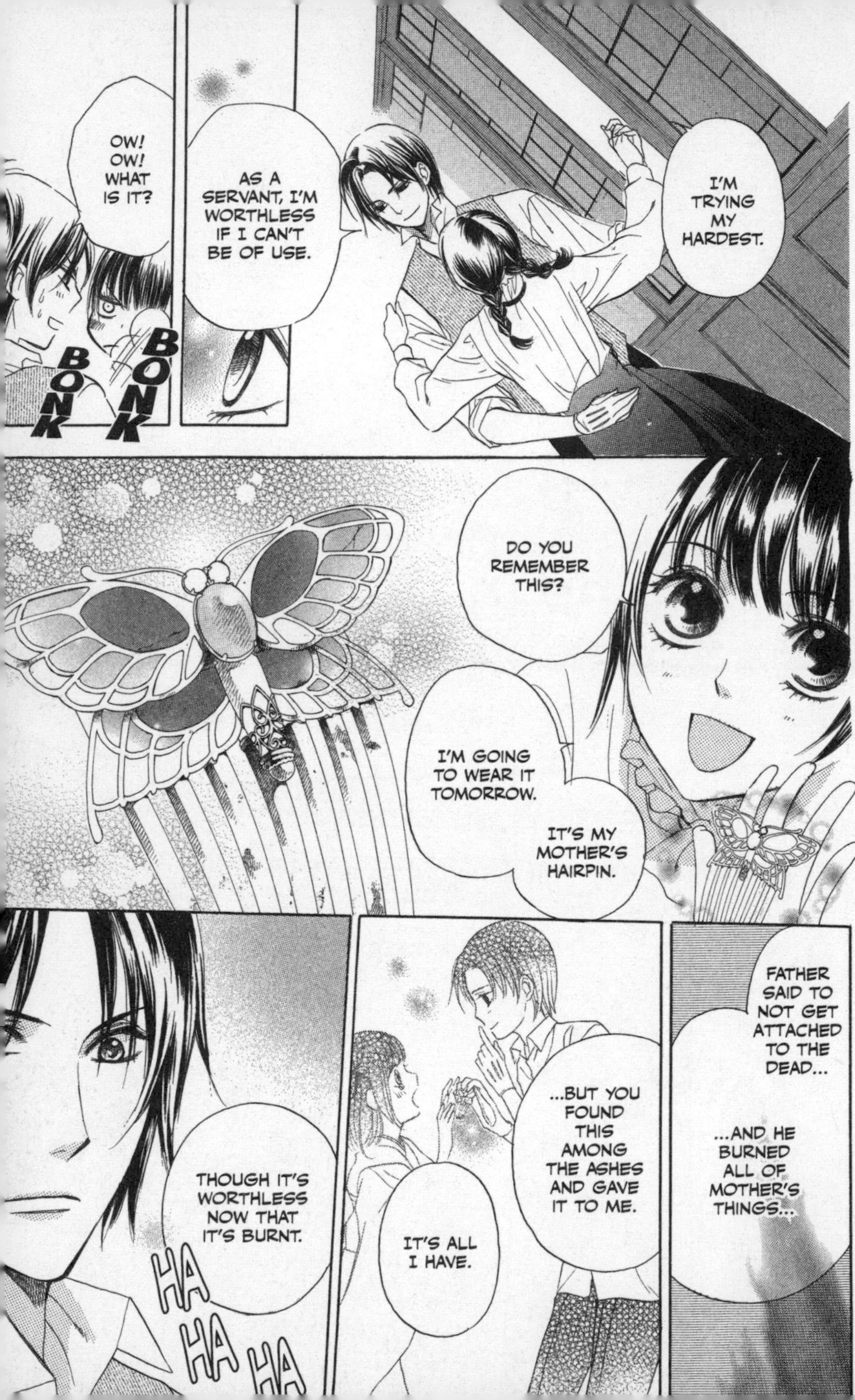
I'M TRYING MY HARDEST.
AS A SERVANT, I'M WORTHLESS IF I CAN'T BE OF USE.
OW! OW! WHAT IS IT?
BONK
BONK
DO YOU REMEMBER THIS?
IT'S MY MOTHER'S HAIRPIN.
I'M GOING TO WEAR IT TOMORROW.
FATHER SAID TO NOT GET ATTACHED TO THE DEAD...
...AND HE BURNED ALL OF MOTHER'S THINGS...
...BUT YOU FOUND THIS AMONG THE ASHES AND GAVE IT TO ME.
IT'S ALL I HAVE.
THOUGH IT'S WORTHLESS NOW THAT IT'S BURNT.
HA HA HA

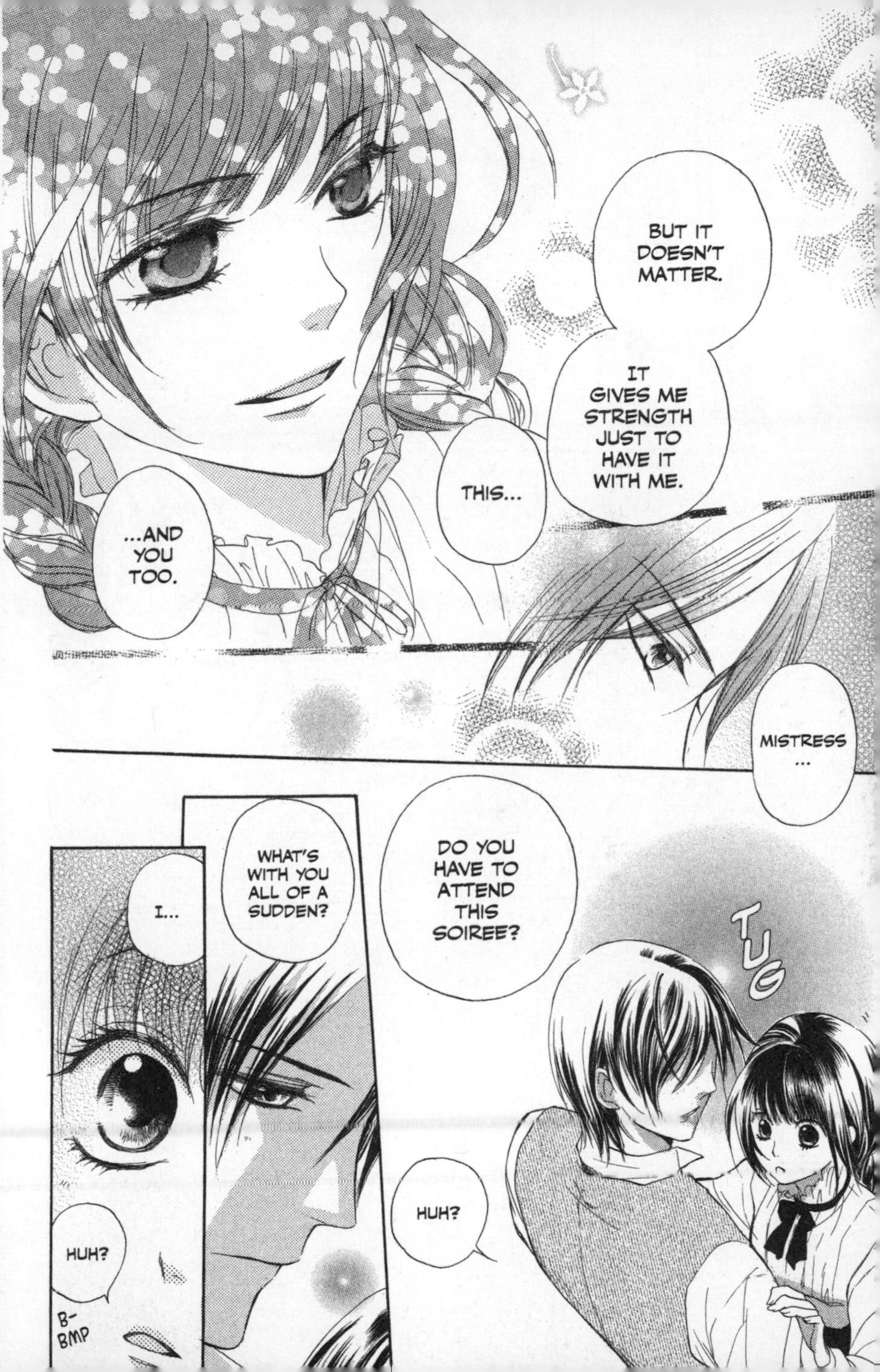
BUT IT DOESN'T MATTER.
IT GIVES ME STRENGTH JUST TO HAVE IT WITH ME.
THIS...
...AND YOU TOO.
MISTRESS...
DO YOU HAVE TO ATTEND THIS SOIREE?
TUG
HUH?
WHAT'S WITH YOU ALL OF A SUDDEN?
I...
HUH?
B-BMP

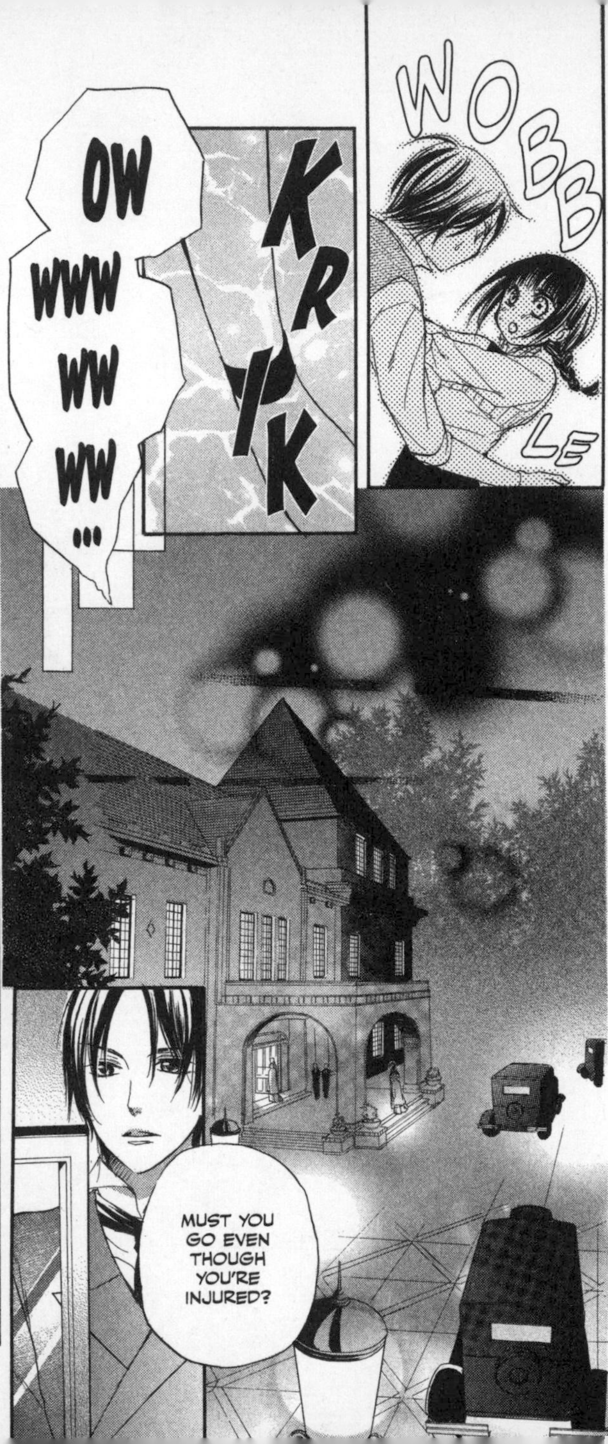
WOBBLE
OW WWW WW WW...
KRIK
MUST YOU GO EVEN THOUGH YOU'RE INJURED?

CHAPTER 3

Unlike with the second chapter, I had a really hard time with the storyboards this time. The art was difficult, and I was mentally exhausted.

I was somehow able to finish it, all thanks to my editor and friends, letters that I received from fans, and my assistant Y-da's help.

*Although I was able to finish the chapter, I didn't make it in time to mail the pages by air (the timetable had changed), so I had to send them by special delivery that cost 10,000 yen.**
This chapter was troublesome to the end.

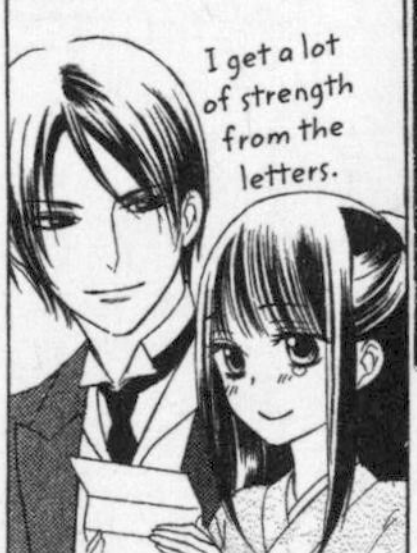
I get a lot of strength from the letters.

**About $100.00*

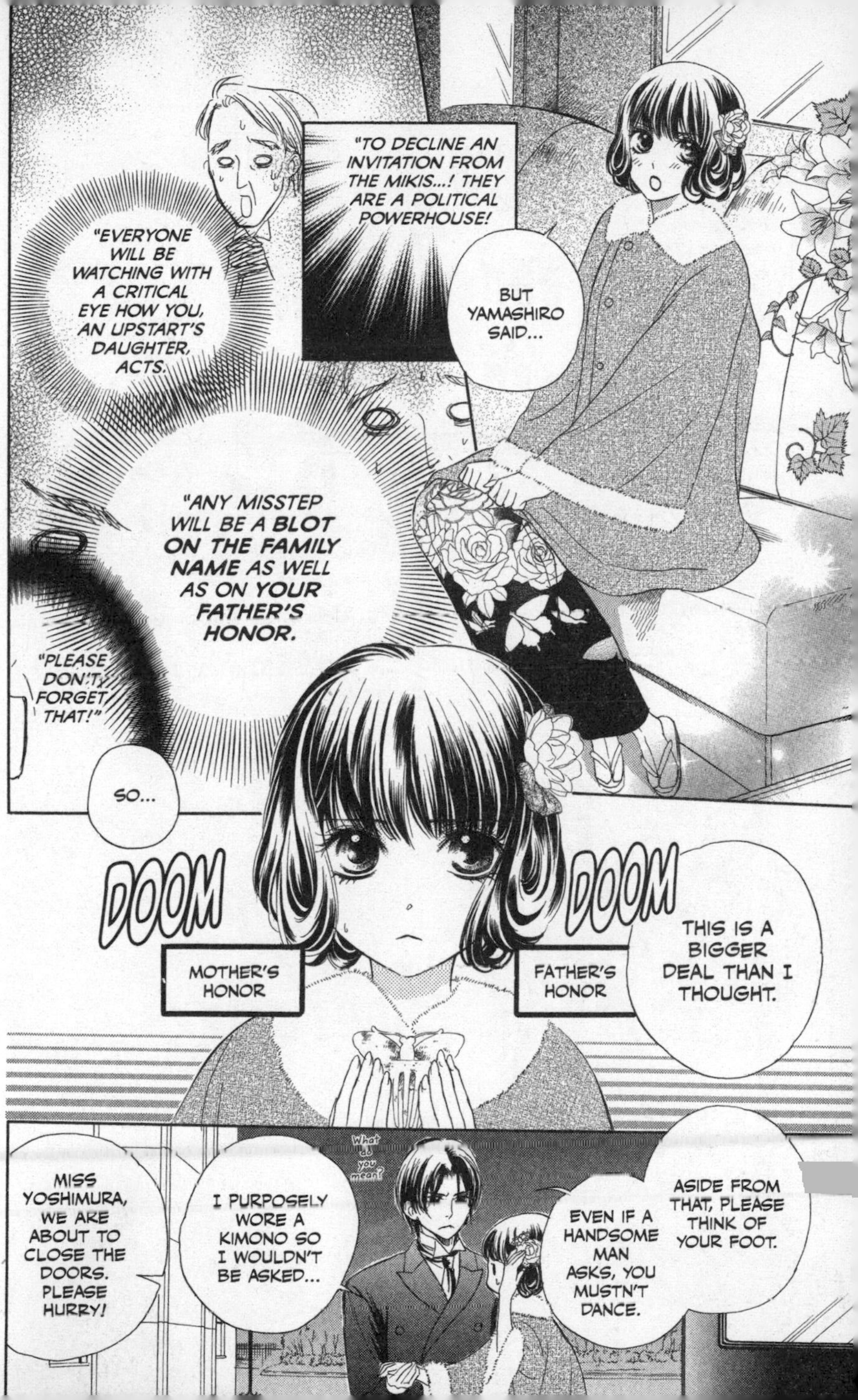
BUT YAMASHIRO SAID...
"TO DECLINE AN INVITATION FROM THE MIKIS...! THEY ARE A POLITICAL POWERHOUSE!
"EVERYONE WILL BE WATCHING WITH A CRITICAL EYE HOW YOU, AN UPSTART'S DAUGHTER, ACTS.
"ANY MISSTEP WILL BE A BLOT ON THE FAMILY NAME AS WELL AS ON YOUR FATHER'S HONOR.
"PLEASE DON'T FORGET THAT!"
SO...
THIS IS A BIGGER DEAL THAN I THOUGHT.
DOOM
FATHER'S HONOR
DOOM
MOTHER'S HONOR
ASIDE FROM THAT, PLEASE THINK OF YOUR FOOT.
EVEN IF A HANDSOME MAN ASKS, YOU MUSTN'T DANCE.
What do you mean?
I PURPOSELY WORE A KIMONO SO I WOULDN'T BE ASKED...
MISS YOSHIMURA, WE ARE ABOUT TO CLOSE THE DOORS. PLEASE HURRY!

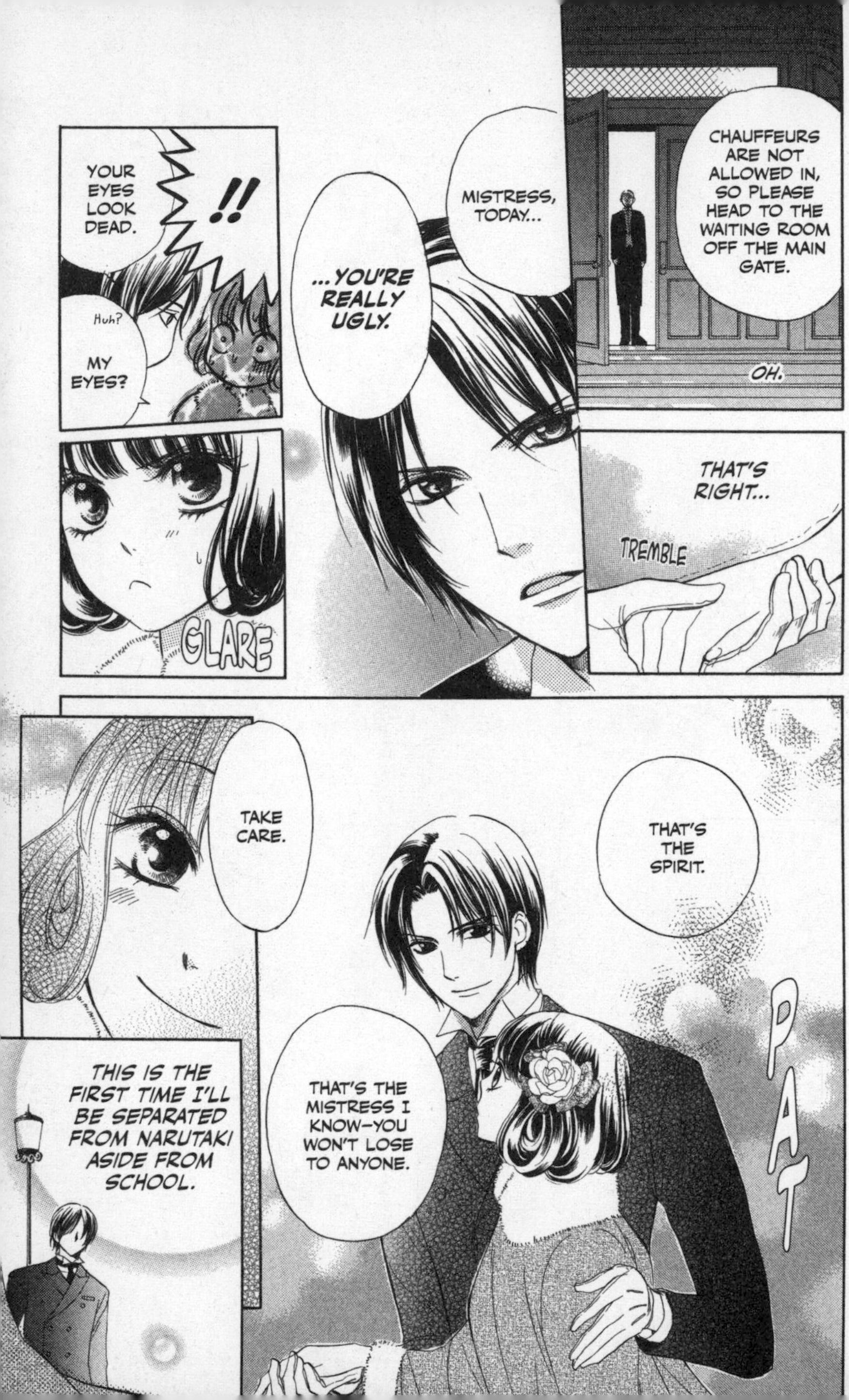
CHAUFFEURS ARE NOT ALLOWED IN, SO PLEASE HEAD TO THE WAITING ROOM OFF THE MAIN GATE.
OH.
MISTRESS, TODAY...
...YOU'RE REALLY UGLY.
!!
YOUR EYES LOOK DEAD.
Huh?
MY EYES?
THAT'S RIGHT...
TREMBLE
GLARE
THAT'S THE SPIRIT.
THAT'S THE MISTRESS I KNOW—YOU WON'T LOSE TO ANYONE.
PAT
TAKE CARE.
THIS IS THE FIRST TIME I'LL BE SEPARATED FROM NARUTAKI ASIDE FROM SCHOOL.

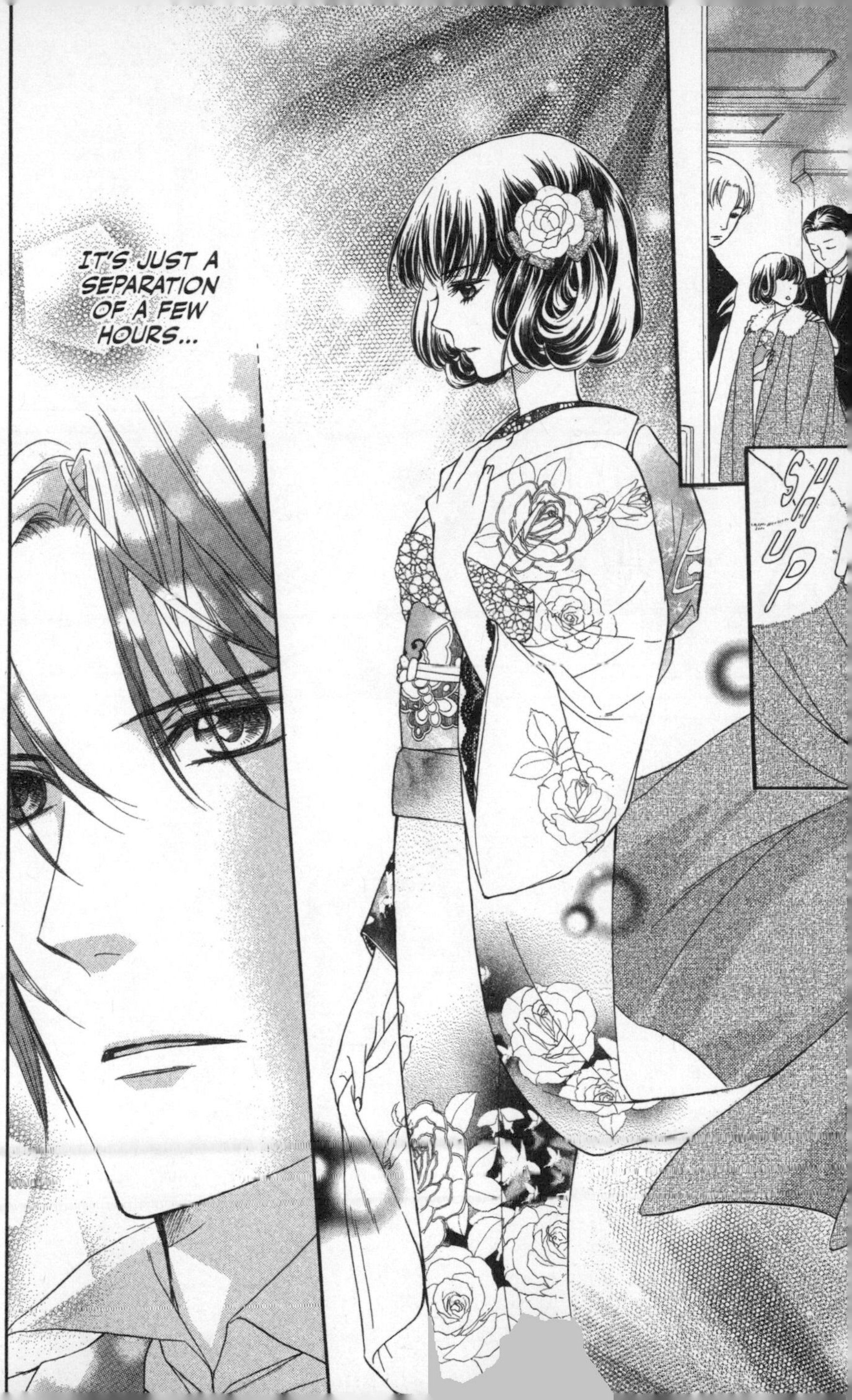
SHUP
IT'S JUST A SEPARATION OF A FEW HOURS...

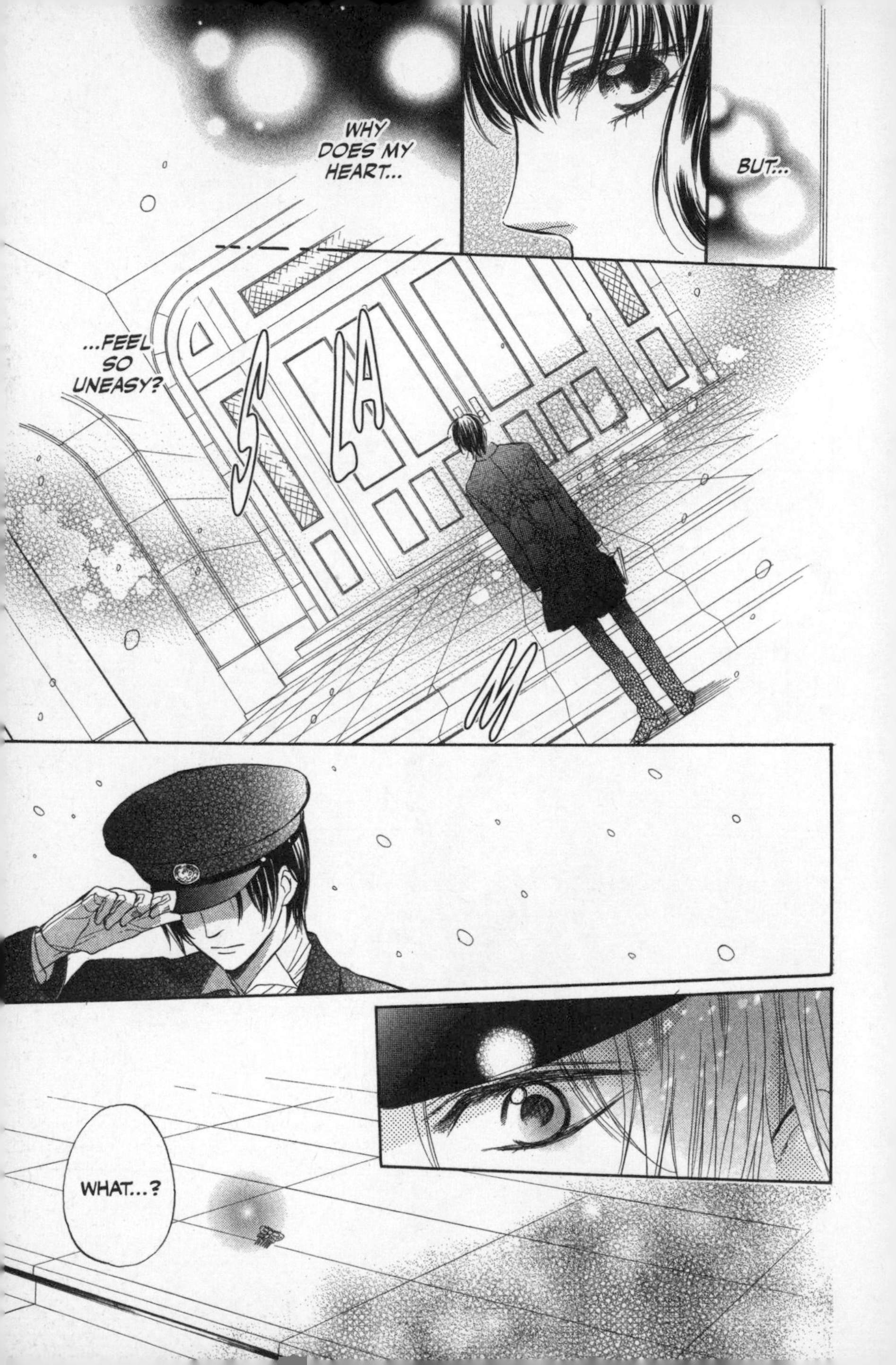
BUT...
WHY DOES MY HEART...
...FEEL SO UNEASY?
SLAM
WHAT...?

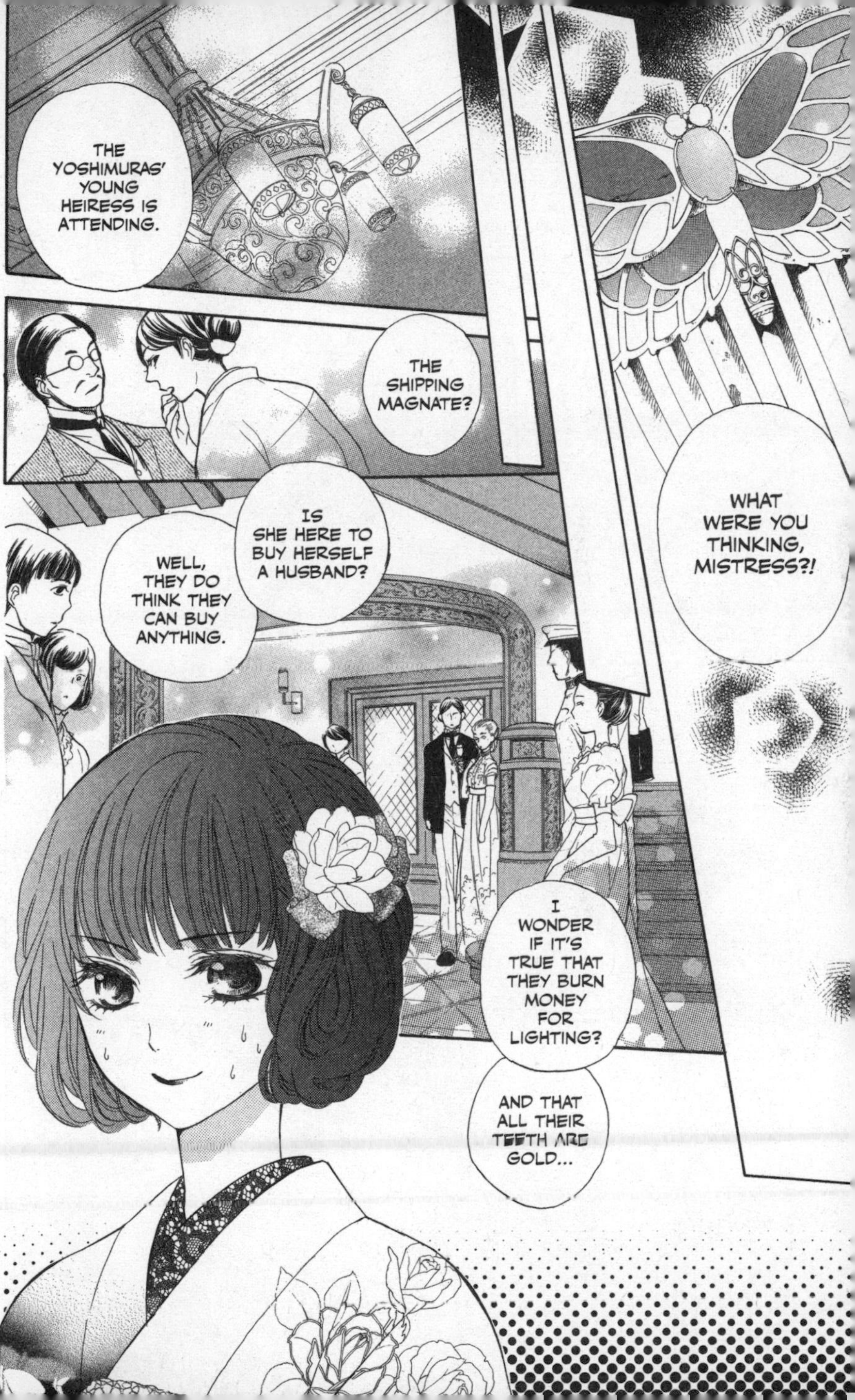
WHAT WERE YOU THINKING, MISTRESS?!
THE YOSHIMURAS' YOUNG HEIRESS IS ATTENDING.
THE SHIPPING MAGNATE?
IS SHE HERE TO BUY HERSELF A HUSBAND?
WELL, THEY DO THINK THEY CAN BUY ANYTHING.
I WONDER IF IT'S TRUE THAT THEY BURN MONEY FOR LIGHTING?
AND THAT ALL THEIR TEETH ARE GOLD...

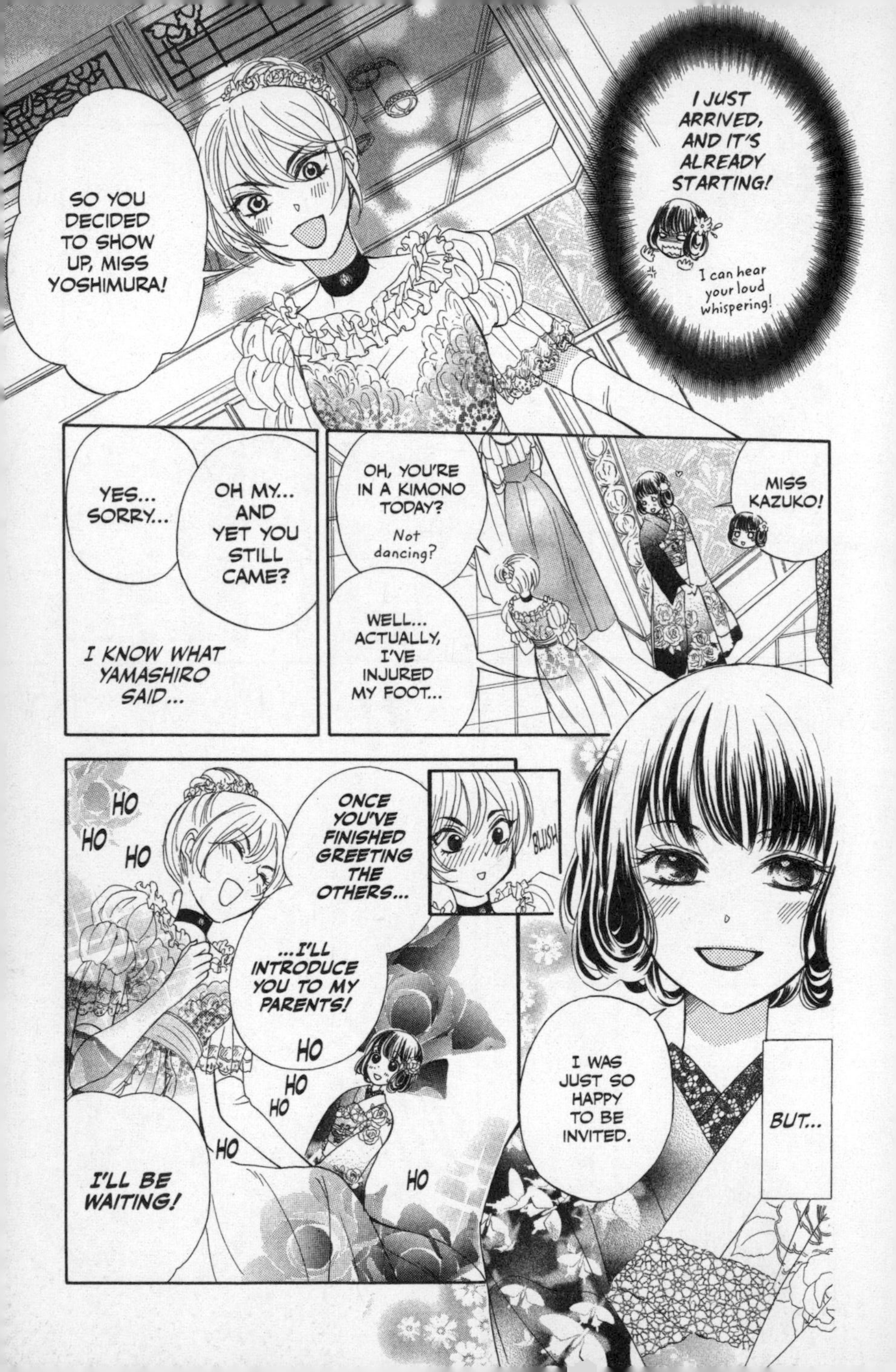
I JUST ARRIVED, AND IT'S ALREADY STARTING!
I can hear your loud whispering!
SO YOU DECIDED TO SHOW UP, MISS YOSHIMURA!
MISS KAZUKO!
OH, YOU'RE IN A KIMONO TODAY?
Not dancing?
WELL... ACTUALLY, I'VE INJURED MY FOOT...
OH MY... AND YET YOU STILL CAME?
YES... SORRY...
I KNOW WHAT YAMASHIRO SAID...
I WAS JUST SO HAPPY TO BE INVITED.
BUT...
BLUSH
ONCE YOU'VE FINISHED GREETING THE OTHERS...
HO
HO
HO
...I'LL INTRODUCE YOU TO MY PARENTS!
HO
HO
HO
HO
HO
I'LL BE WAITING!

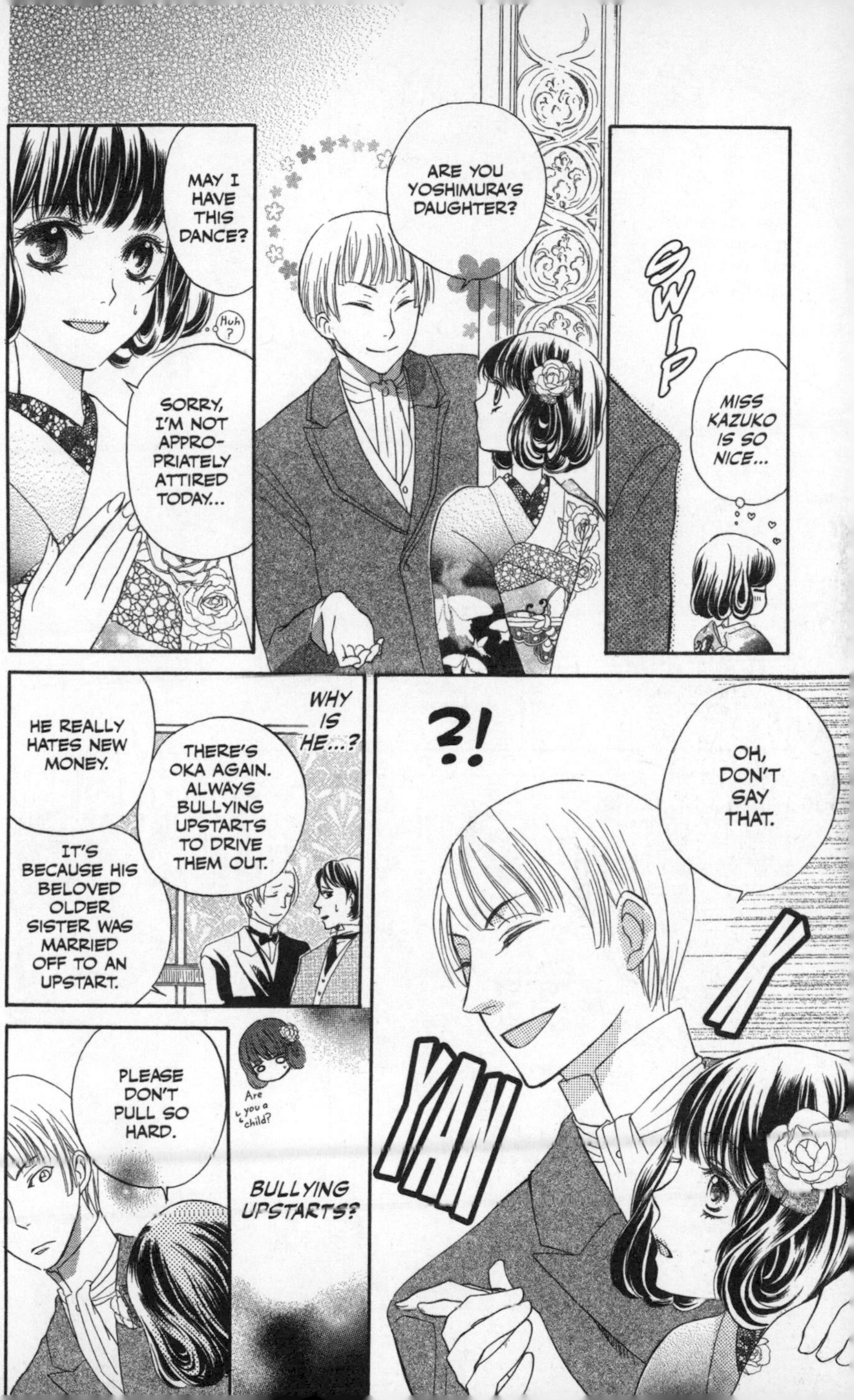
SWIP
MISS KAZUKO IS SO NICE...
ARE YOU YOSHIMURA'S DAUGHTER?
MAY I HAVE THIS DANCE?
Huh?
SORRY, I'M NOT APPROPRIATELY ATTIRED TODAY...
OH, DON'T SAY THAT.
?!
YANK
WHY IS HE...?
THERE'S OKA AGAIN. ALWAYS BULLYING UPSTARTS TO DRIVE THEM OUT.
HE REALLY HATES NEW MONEY.
IT'S BECAUSE HIS BELOVED OLDER SISTER WAS MARRIED OFF TO AN UPSTART.
PLEASE DON'T PULL SO HARD.
Are you a child?
BULLYING UPSTARTS?

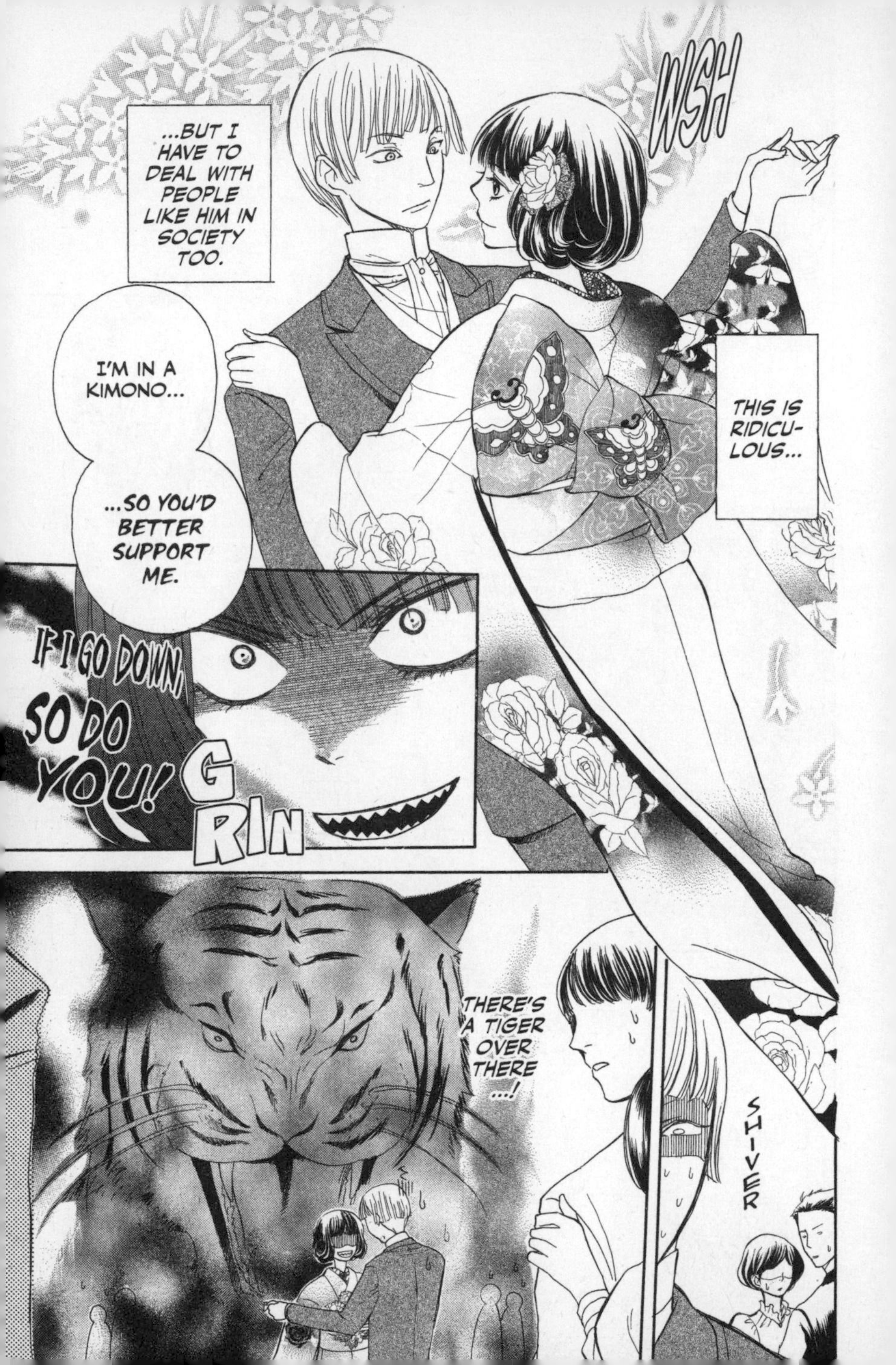
WSH
THIS IS RIDICULOUS...
...BUT I HAVE TO DEAL WITH PEOPLE LIKE HIM IN SOCIETY TOO.
I'M IN A KIMONO...
...SO YOU'D BETTER SUPPORT ME.
IF I GO DOWN, SO DO YOU!
GRIN
SHIVER
THERE'S A TIGER OVER THERE ...!

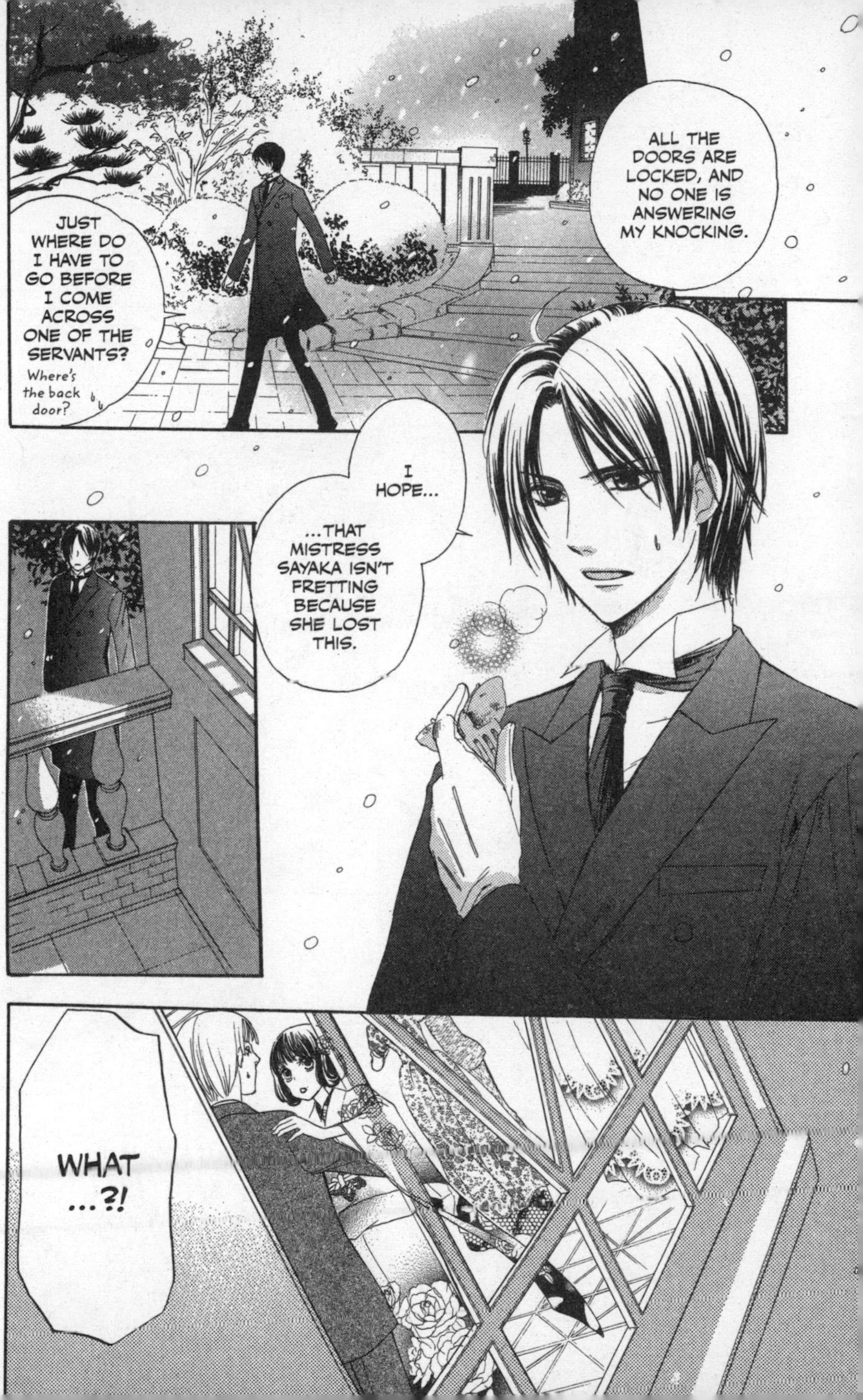
ALL THE DOORS ARE LOCKED, AND NO ONE IS ANSWERING MY KNOCKING.
JUST WHERE DO I HAVE TO GO BEFORE I COME ACROSS ONE OF THE SERVANTS?
Where's the back door?
I HOPE...
...THAT MISTRESS SAYAKA ISN'T FRETTING BECAUSE SHE LOST THIS.
WHAT ...?!

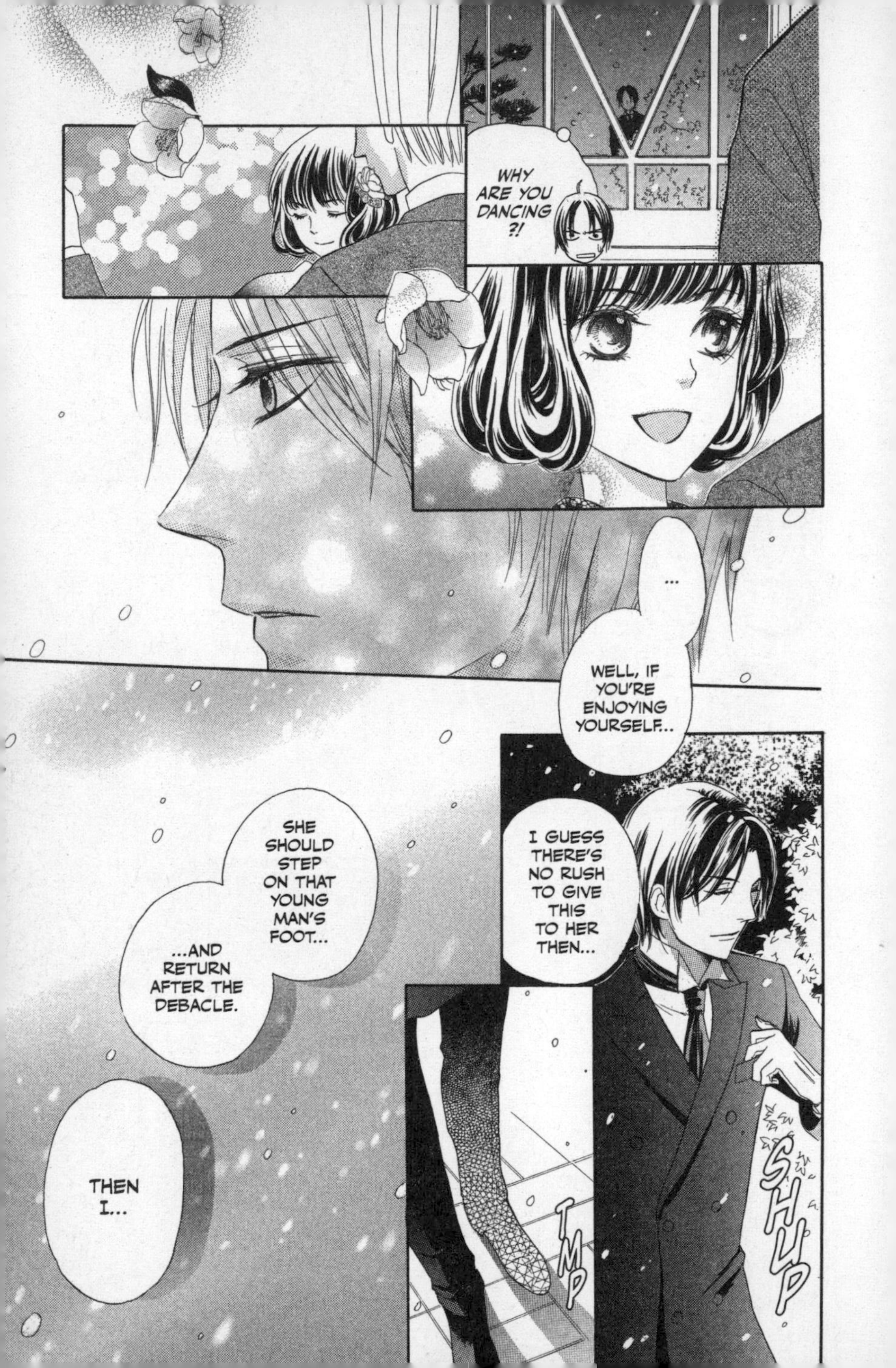
WHY ARE YOU DANCING ?!
...
WELL, IF YOU'RE ENJOYING YOURSELF...
I GUESS THERE'S NO RUSH TO GIVE THIS TO HER THEN...
SHUP
TMP
SHE SHOULD STEP ON THAT YOUNG MAN'S FOOT...
...AND RETURN AFTER THE DEBACLE.
THEN I...

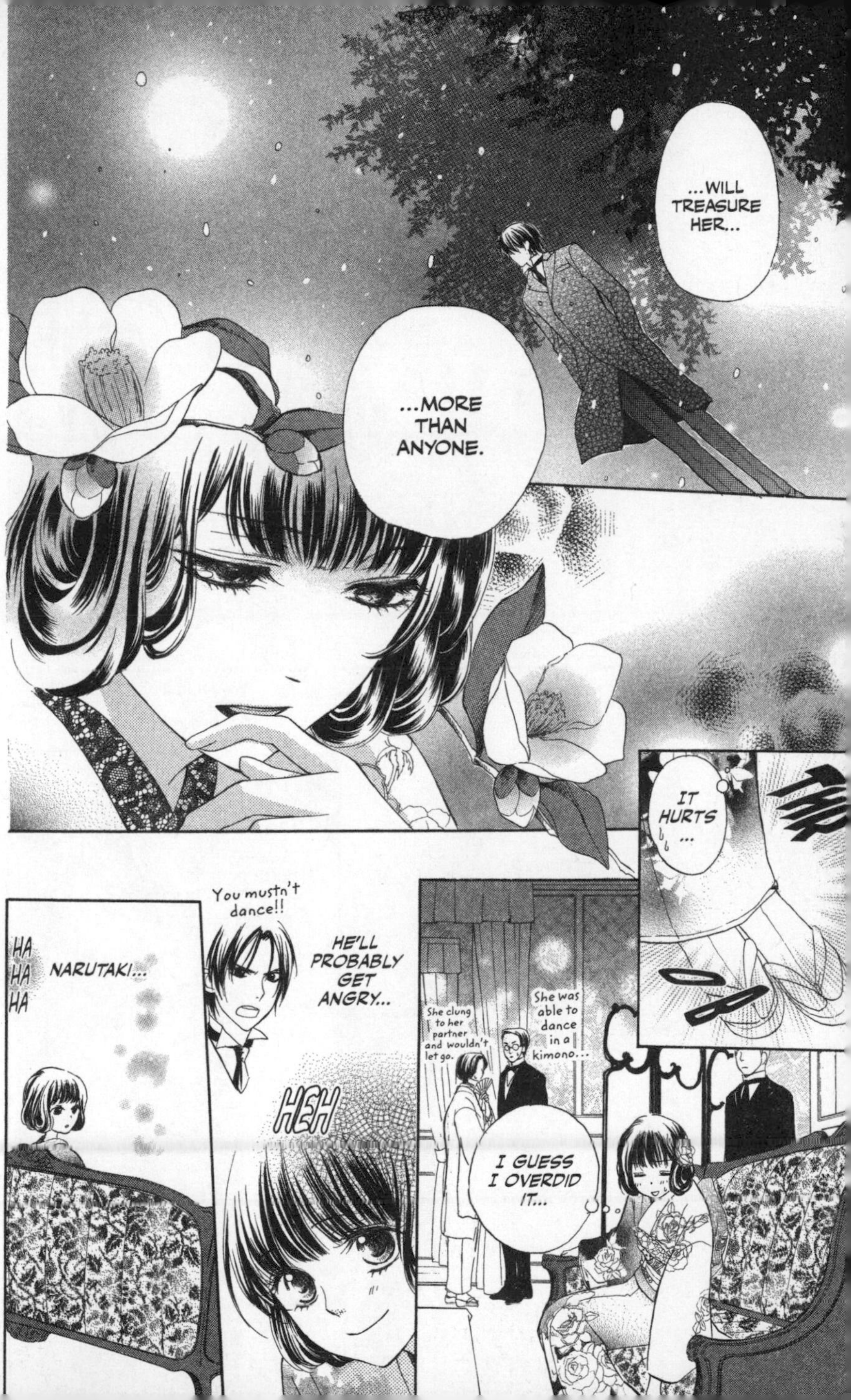
...WILL TREASURE HER...
...MORE THAN ANYONE.
IT HURTS ...
She was able to dance in a kimono...
She clung to her partner and wouldn't let go.
I GUESS I OVERDID IT...
You mustn't dance!!
HE'LL PROBABLY GET ANGRY...
NARUTAKI...
HA HA HA
HEH

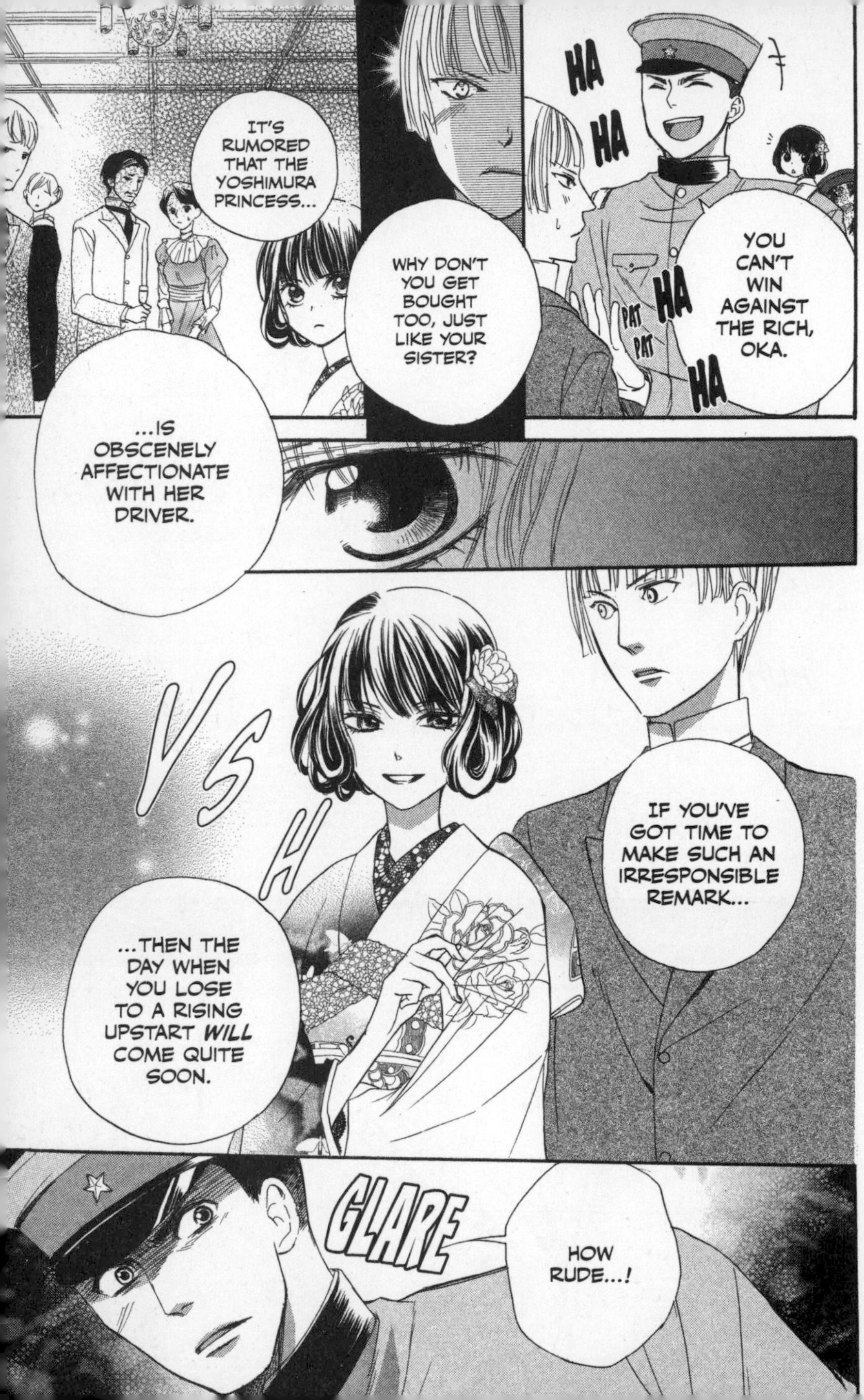
HA HA
YOU CAN'T WIN AGAINST THE RICH, OKA.
HA
PAT PAT
HA
WHY DON'T YOU GET BOUGHT TOO, JUST LIKE YOUR SISTER?
IT'S RUMORED THAT THE YOSHIMURA PRINCESS...
...IS OBSCENELY AFFECTIONATE WITH HER DRIVER.
IF YOU'VE GOT TIME TO MAKE SUCH AN IRRESPONSIBLE REMARK...
VSH
...THEN THE DAY WHEN YOU LOSE TO A RISING UPSTART *WILL* COME QUITE SOON.
GLARE
HOW RUDE...!

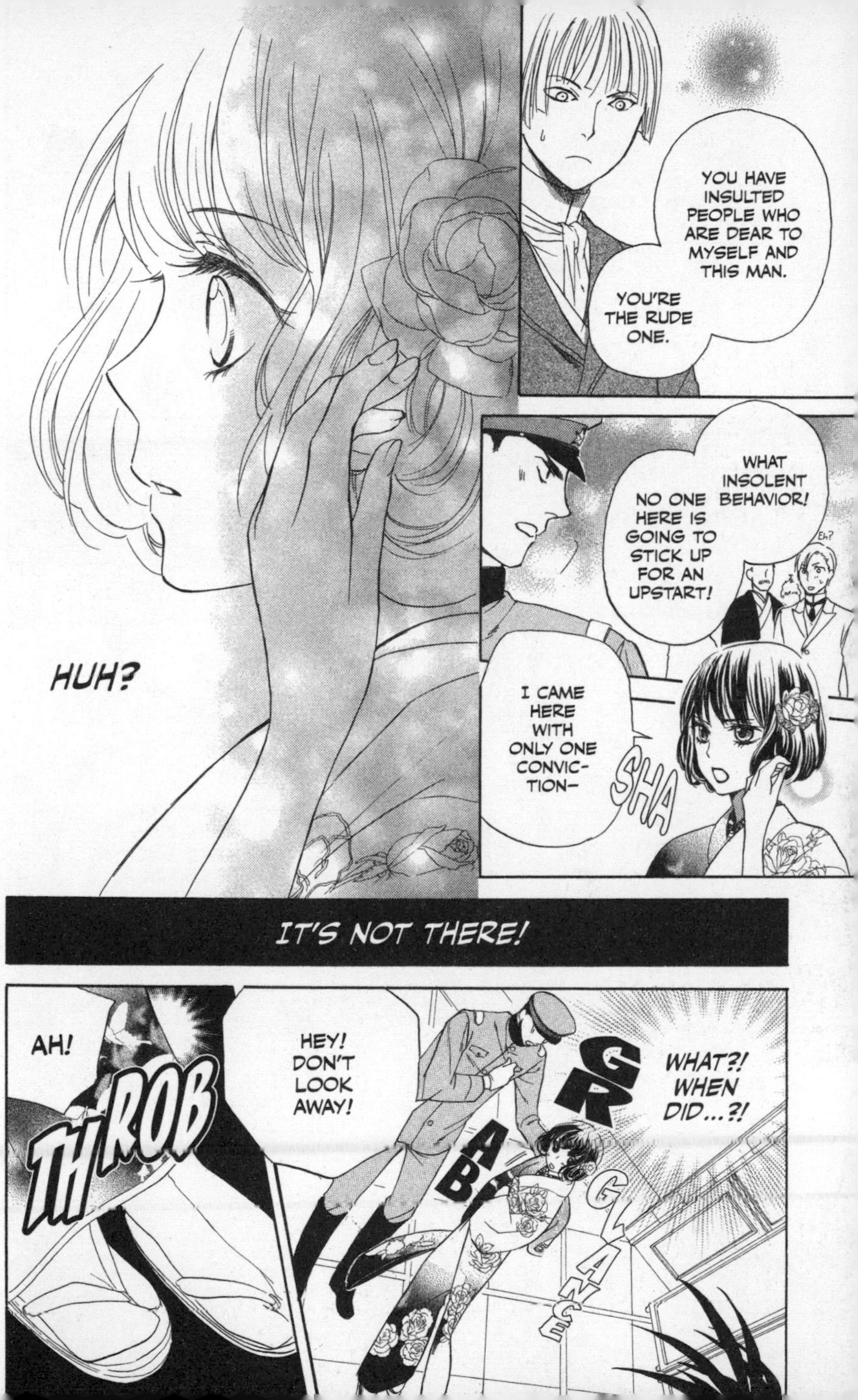
YOU HAVE INSULTED PEOPLE WHO ARE DEAR TO MYSELF AND THIS MAN.
YOU'RE THE RUDE ONE.
WHAT INSOLENT BEHAVIOR!
NO ONE HERE IS GOING TO STICK UP FOR AN UPSTART!
Eh?
I CAME HERE WITH ONLY ONE CONVIC-TION—
SHA
HUH?
IT'S NOT THERE!
WHAT?! WHEN DID...?!
GRAB
GLANCE
HEY! DON'T LOOK AWAY!
AH!
THROB

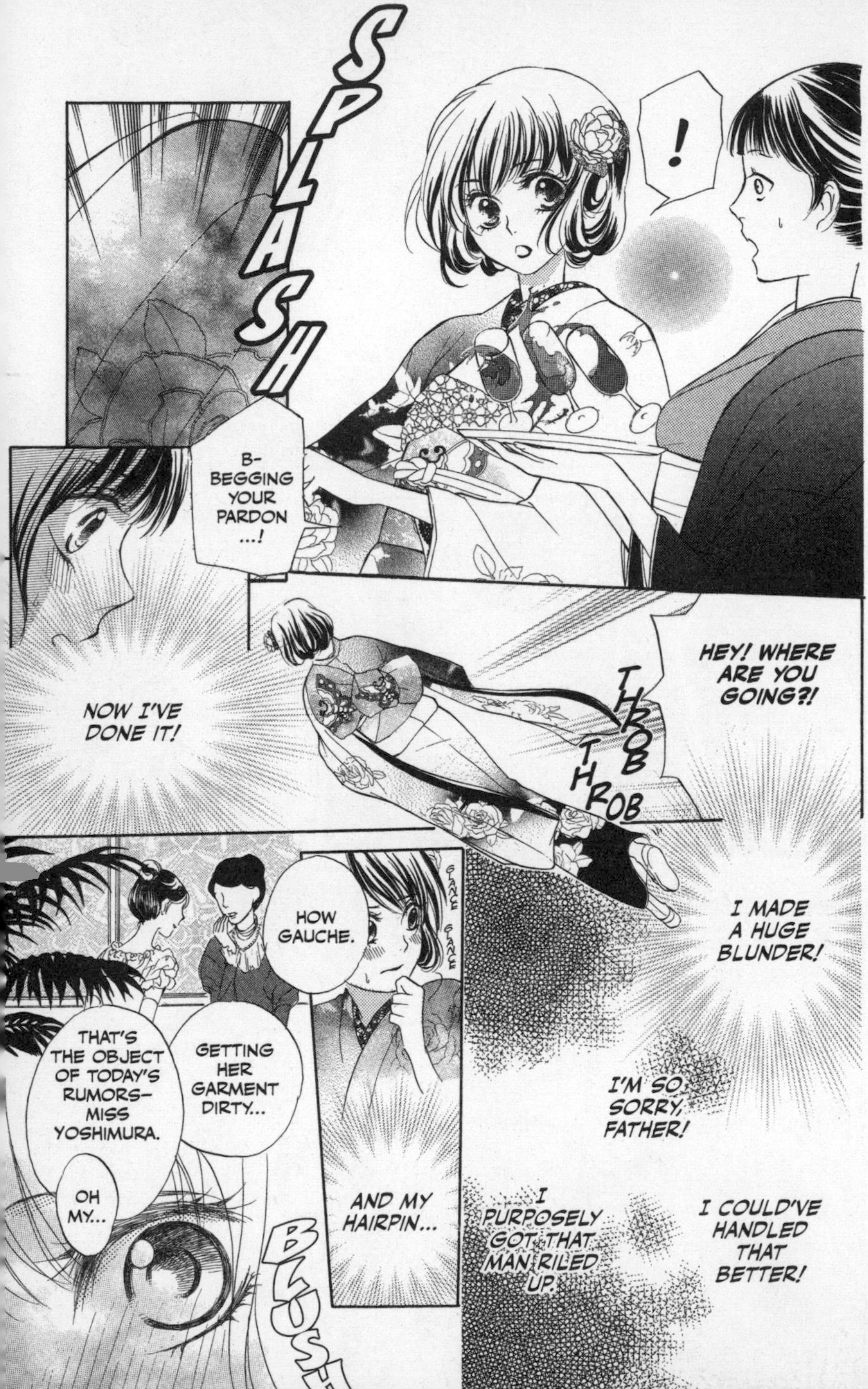
!
SPLASH
B-BEGGING YOUR PARDON...!
HEY! WHERE ARE YOU GOING?!
THROB THROB
NOW I'VE DONE IT!
I MADE A HUGE BLUNDER!
I'M SO SORRY, FATHER!
I COULD'VE HANDLED THAT BETTER!
I PURPOSELY GOT THAT MAN RILED UP.
GLANCE GLANCE
HOW GAUCHE.
AND MY HAIRPIN...
GETTING HER GARMENT DIRTY...
THAT'S THE OBJECT OF TODAY'S RUMORS- MISS YOSHIMURA.
OH MY...
BLUSH

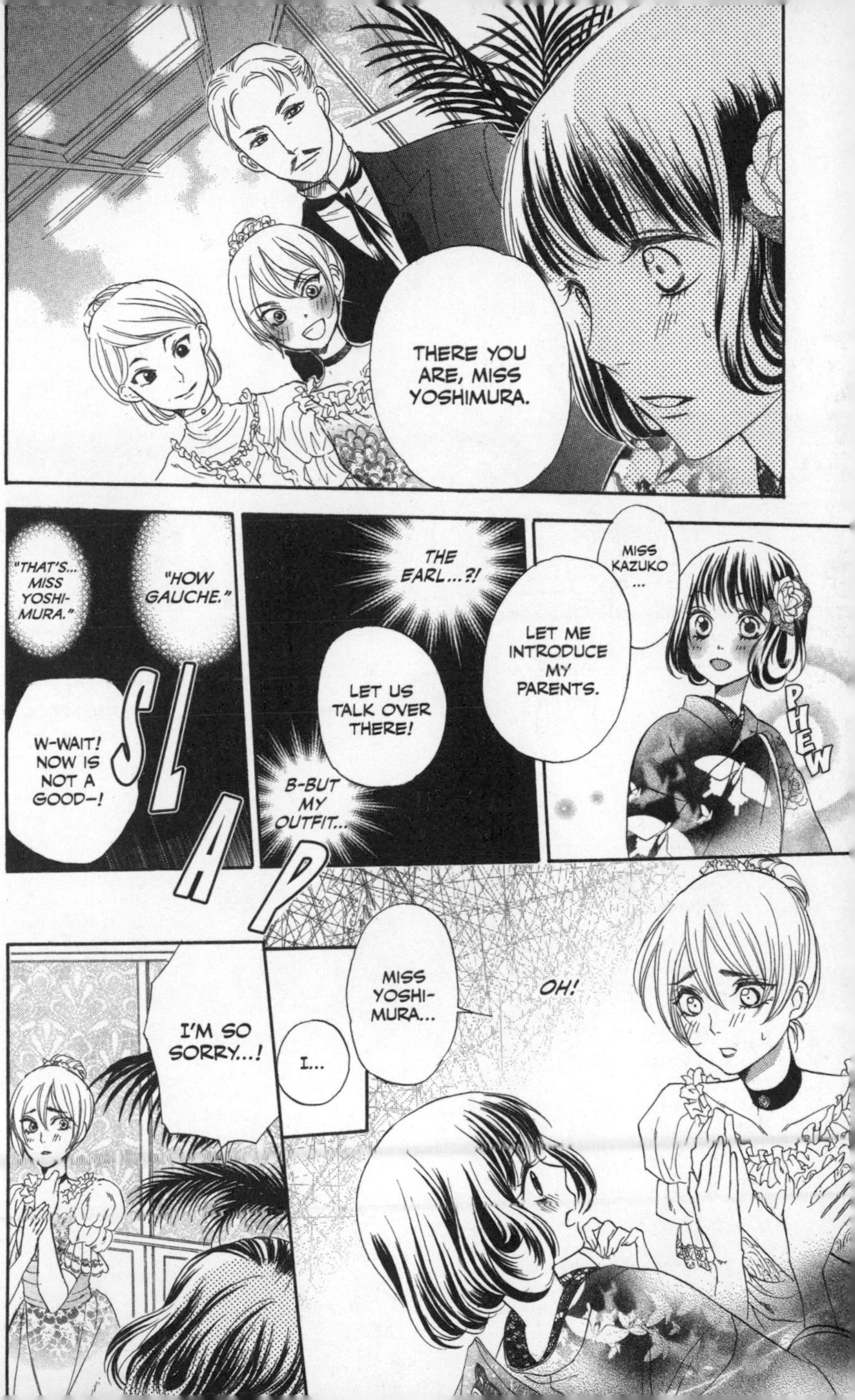
THERE YOU ARE, MISS YOSHIMURA.
MISS KAZUKO ...
LET ME INTRODUCE MY PARENTS.
PHEW
THE EARL...?!
LET US TALK OVER THERE!
B-BUT MY OUTFIT...
"THAT'S... MISS YOSHI-MURA."
"HOW GAUCHE."
W-WAIT! NOW IS NOT A GOOD-!
SLAP
OH!
MISS YOSHI-MURA...
I...
I'M SO SORRY...!

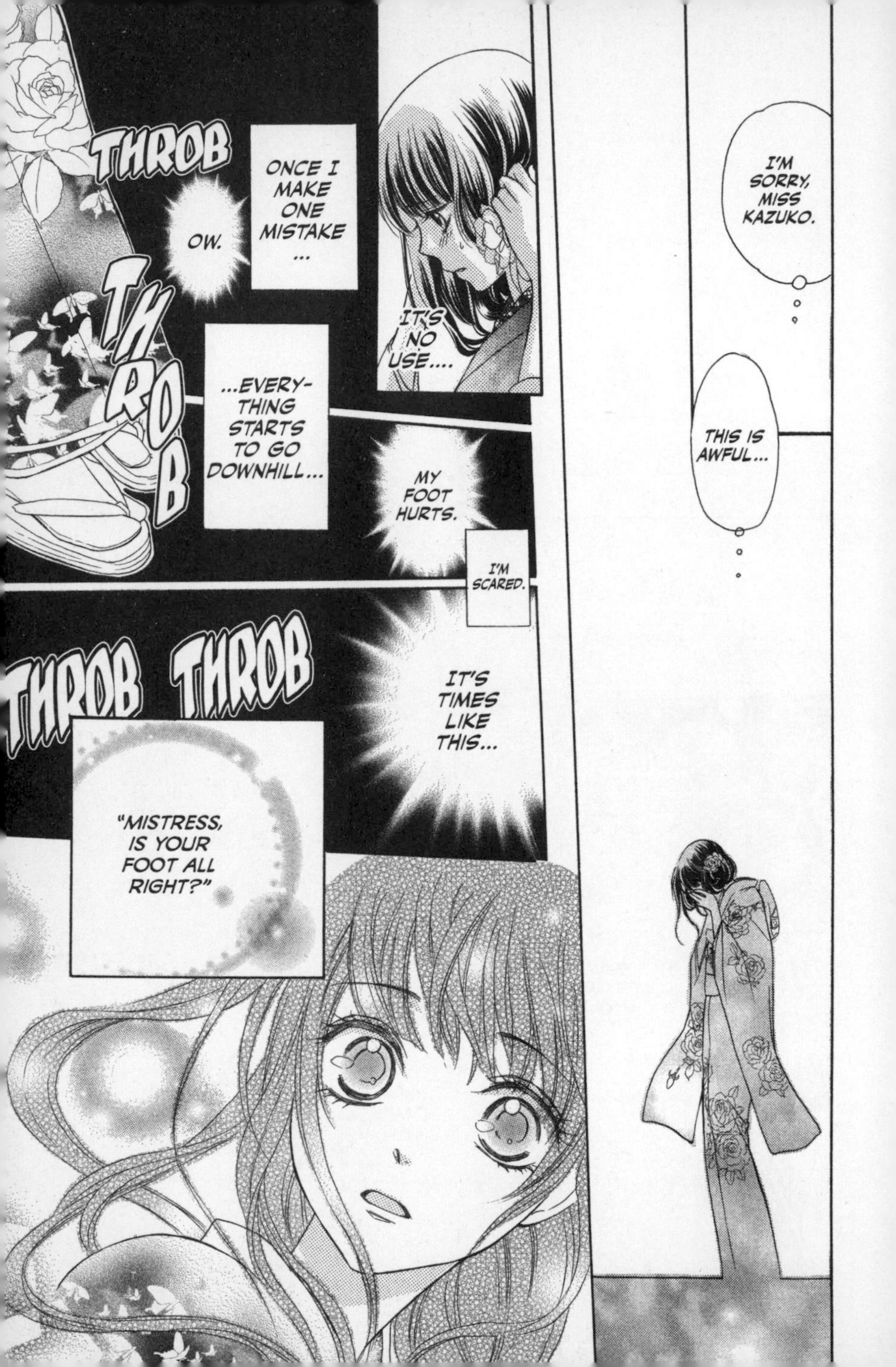
I'M SORRY, MISS KAZUKO.
THIS IS AWFUL...
IT'S NO USE....
THROB
ONCE I MAKE ONE MISTAKE...
OW.
THROB
...EVERY-THING STARTS TO GO DOWNHILL...
MY FOOT HURTS.
I'M SCARED.
IT'S TIMES LIKE THIS...
THROB THROB
"MISTRESS, IS YOUR FOOT ALL RIGHT?"

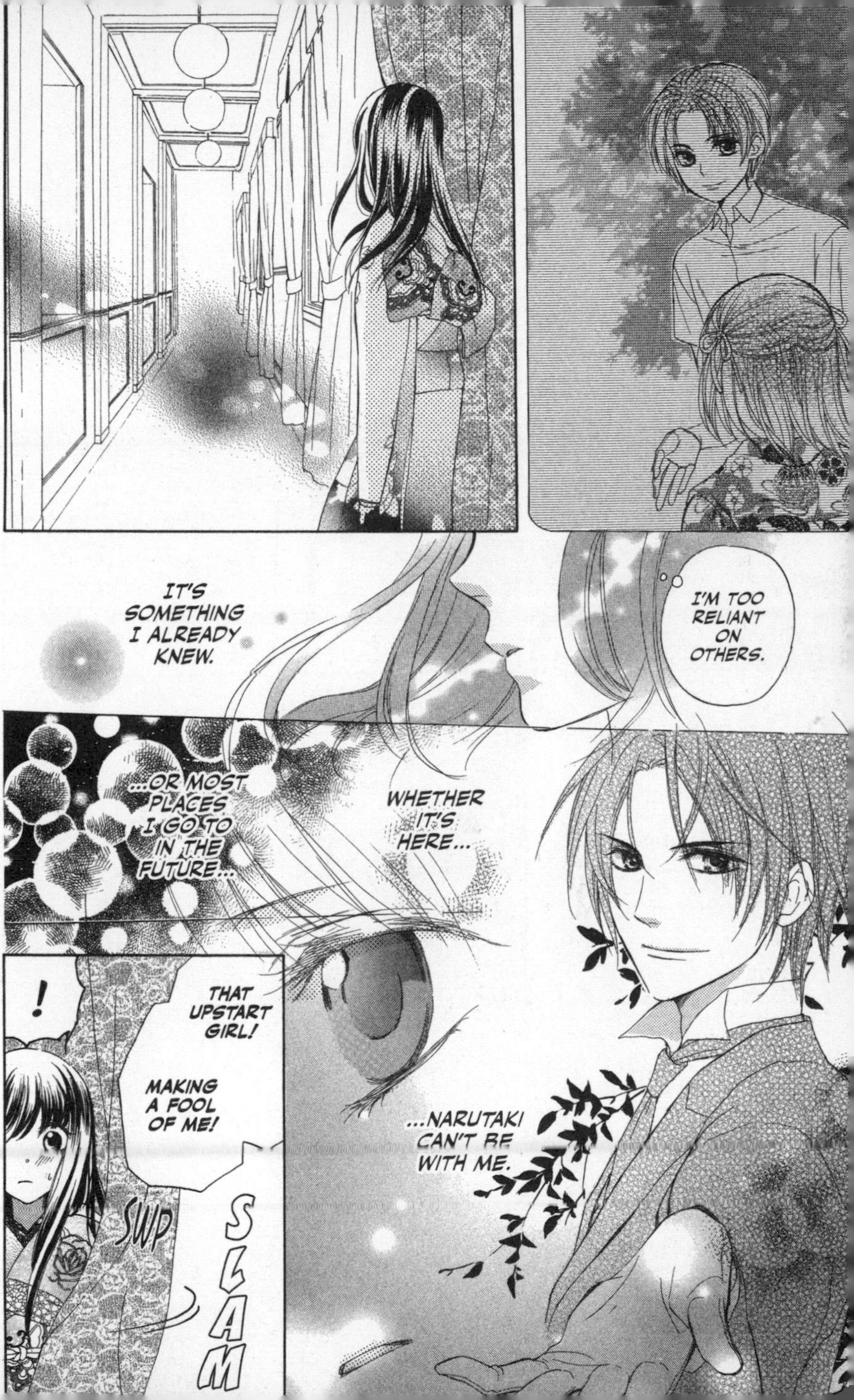
I'M TOO RELIANT ON OTHERS.
IT'S SOMETHING I ALREADY KNEW.
WHETHER IT'S HERE...
...OR MOST PLACES I GO TO IN THE FUTURE...
...NARUTAKI CAN'T BE WITH ME.
!
THAT UPSTART GIRL!
MAKING A FOOL OF ME!
SWP
SLAM

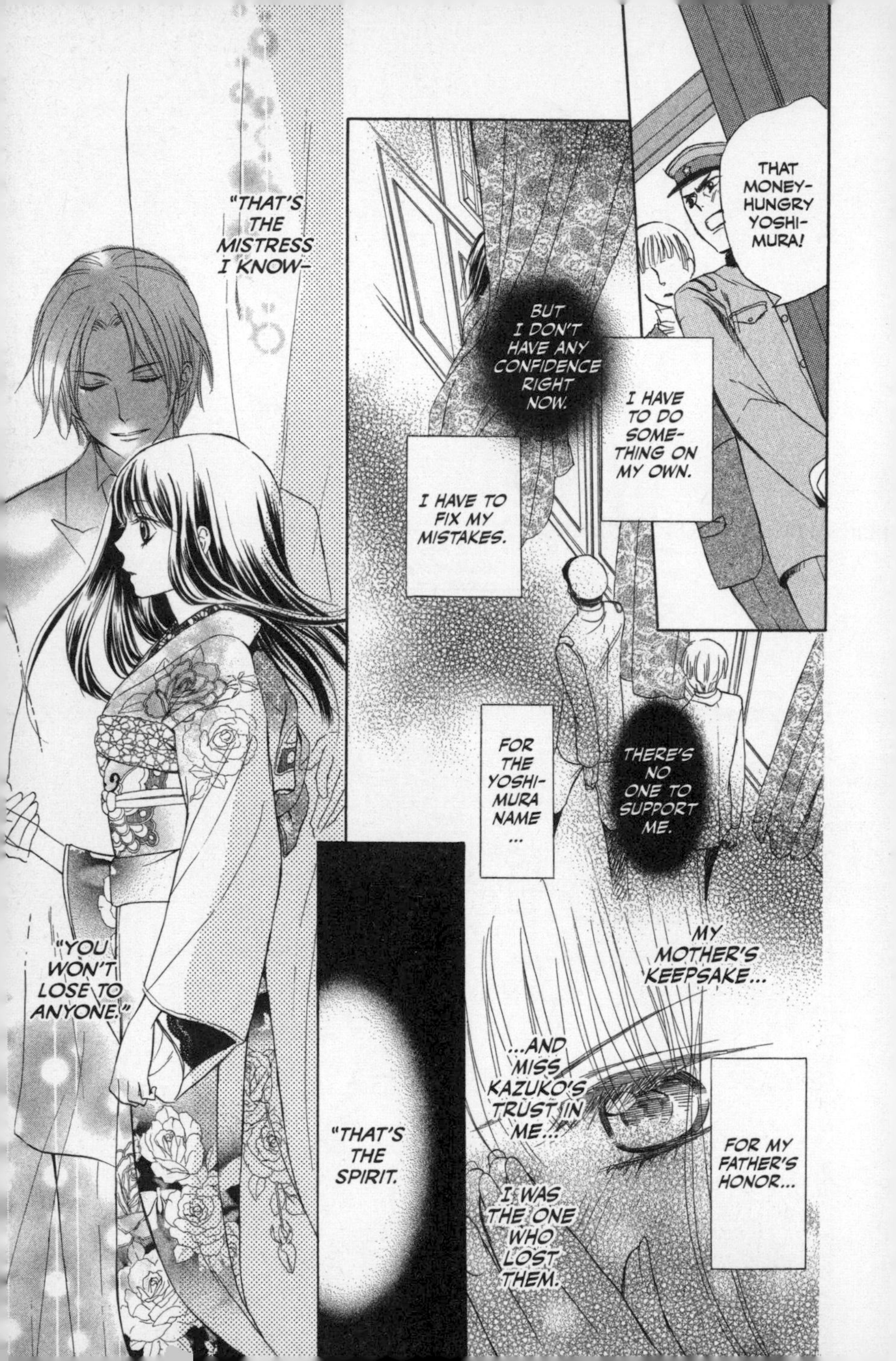
THAT MONEY-HUNGRY YOSHIMURA!
I HAVE TO DO SOMETHING ON MY OWN.
BUT I DON'T HAVE ANY CONFIDENCE RIGHT NOW.
I HAVE TO FIX MY MISTAKES.
THERE'S NO ONE TO SUPPORT ME.
FOR THE YOSHIMURA NAME...
MY MOTHER'S KEEPSAKE...
FOR MY FATHER'S HONOR...
...AND MISS KAZUKO'S TRUST IN ME...
I WAS THE ONE WHO LOST THEM.
"THAT'S THE SPIRIT.
"THAT'S THE MISTRESS I KNOW–
"YOU WON'T LOSE TO ANYONE."

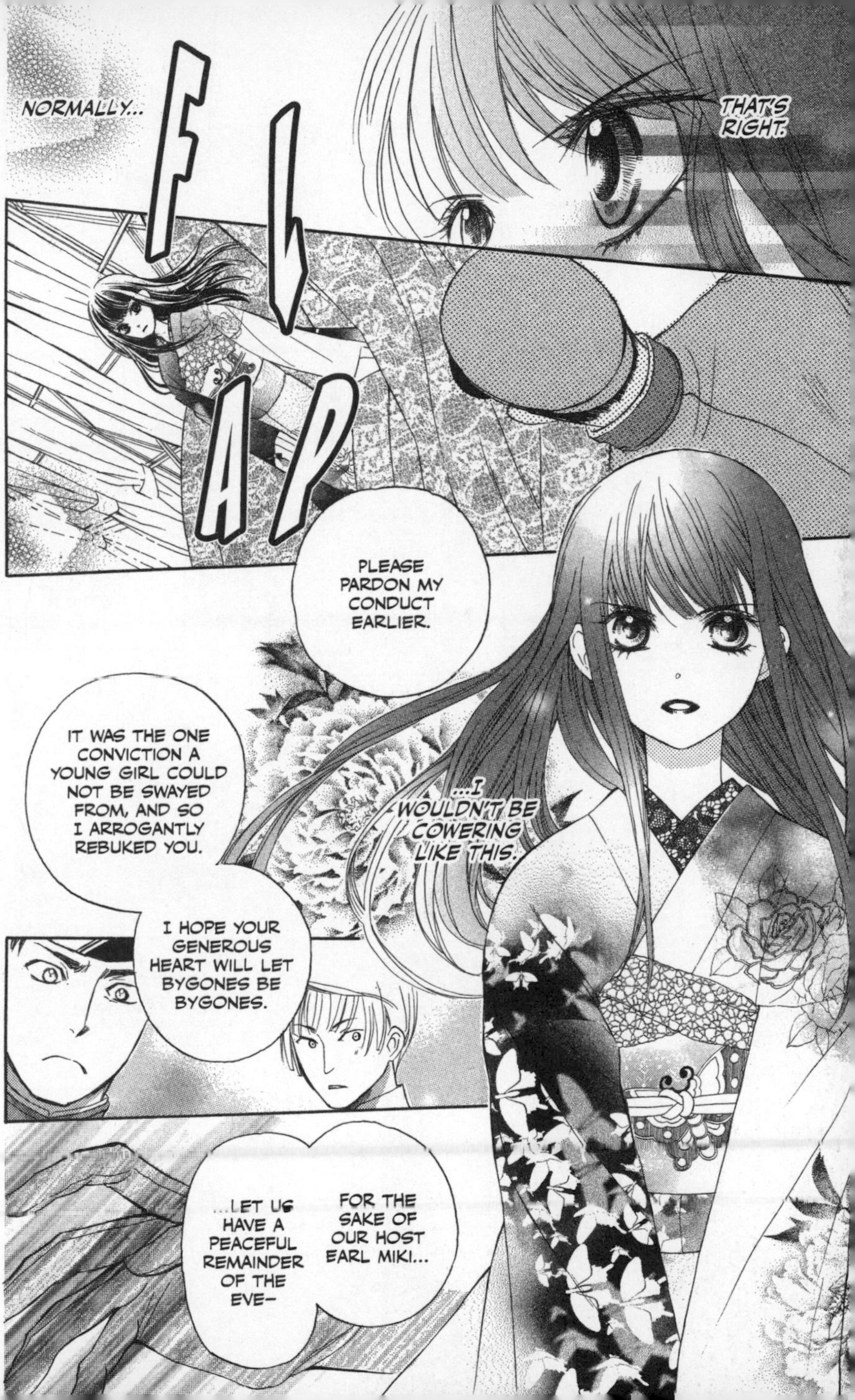
THAT'S RIGHT.
NORMALLY...
FLAP
...I WOULDN'T BE COWERING LIKE THIS.
PLEASE PARDON MY CONDUCT EARLIER.
IT WAS THE ONE CONVICTION A YOUNG GIRL COULD NOT BE SWAYED FROM, AND SO I ARROGANTLY REBUKED YOU.
I HOPE YOUR GENEROUS HEART WILL LET BYGONES BE BYGONES.
FOR THE SAKE OF OUR HOST EARL MIKI...
...LET US HAVE A PEACEFUL REMAINDER OF THE EVE-

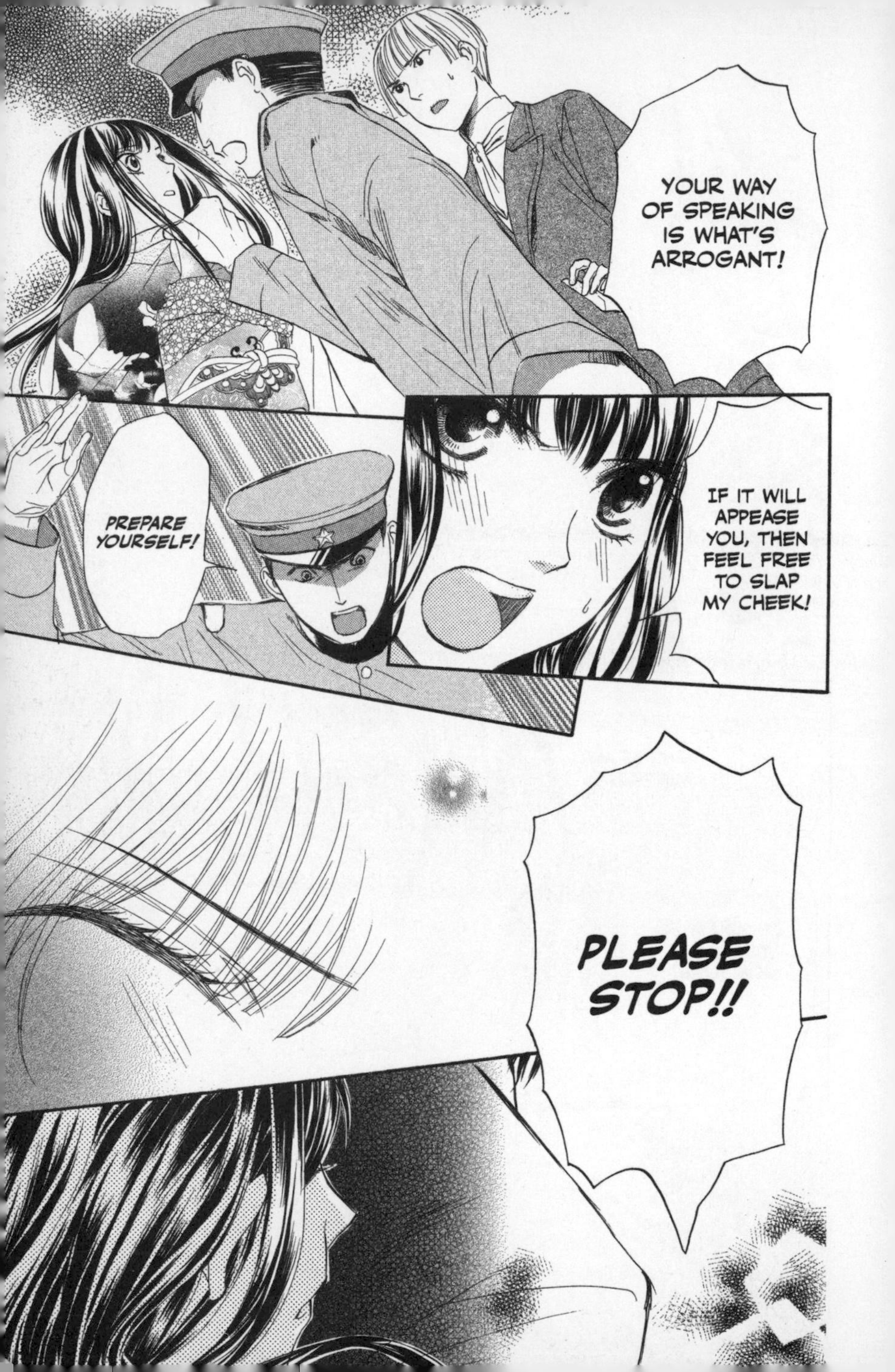
YOUR WAY OF SPEAKING IS WHAT'S ARROGANT!
IF IT WILL APPEASE YOU, THEN FEEL FREE TO SLAP MY CHEEK!
PREPARE YOURSELF!
PLEASE STOP!!

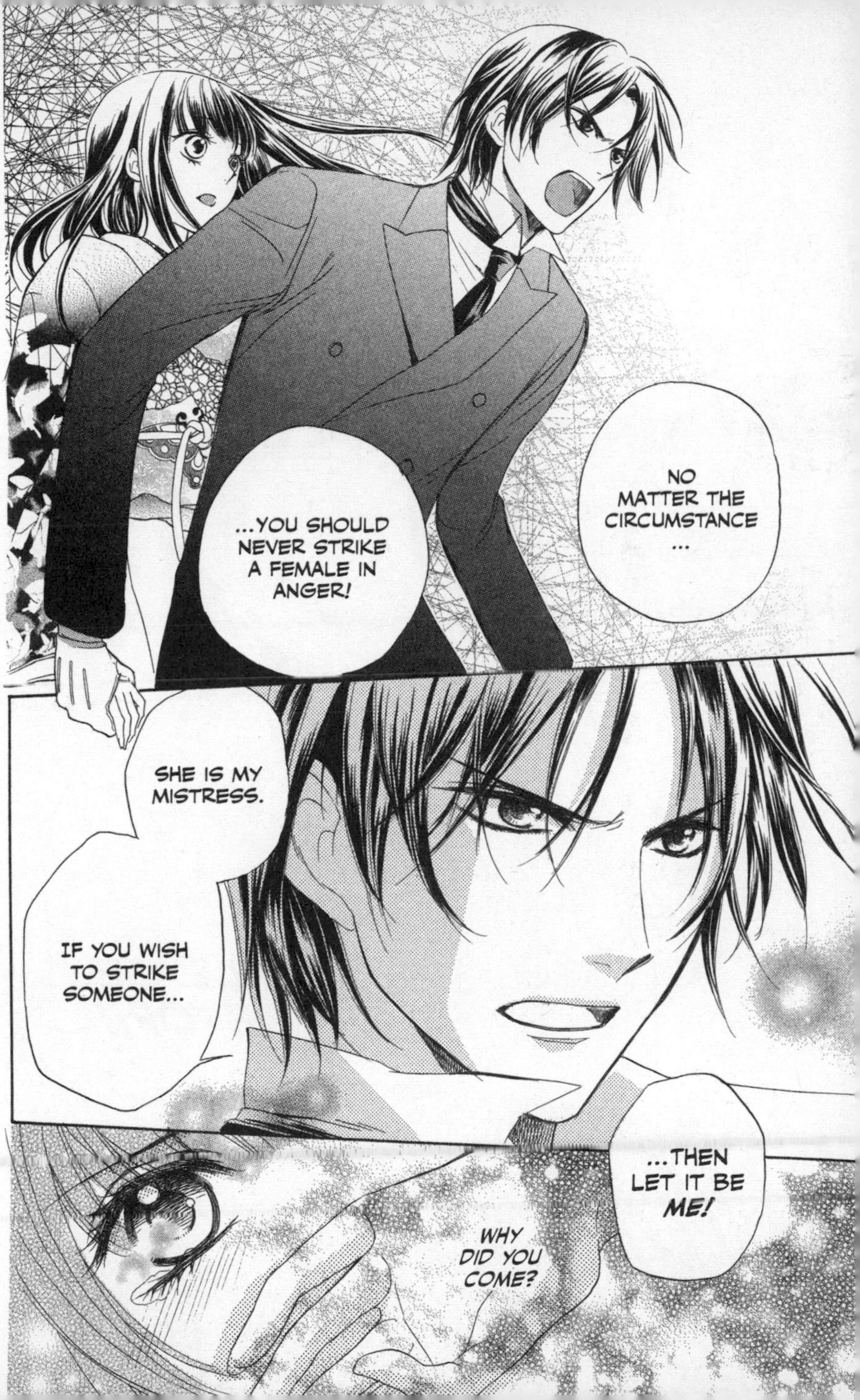
NO MATTER THE CIRCUMSTANCE...
...YOU SHOULD NEVER STRIKE A FEMALE IN ANGER!
SHE IS MY MISTRESS.
IF YOU WISH TO STRIKE SOMEONE...
...THEN LET IT BE *ME!*
WHY DID YOU COME?

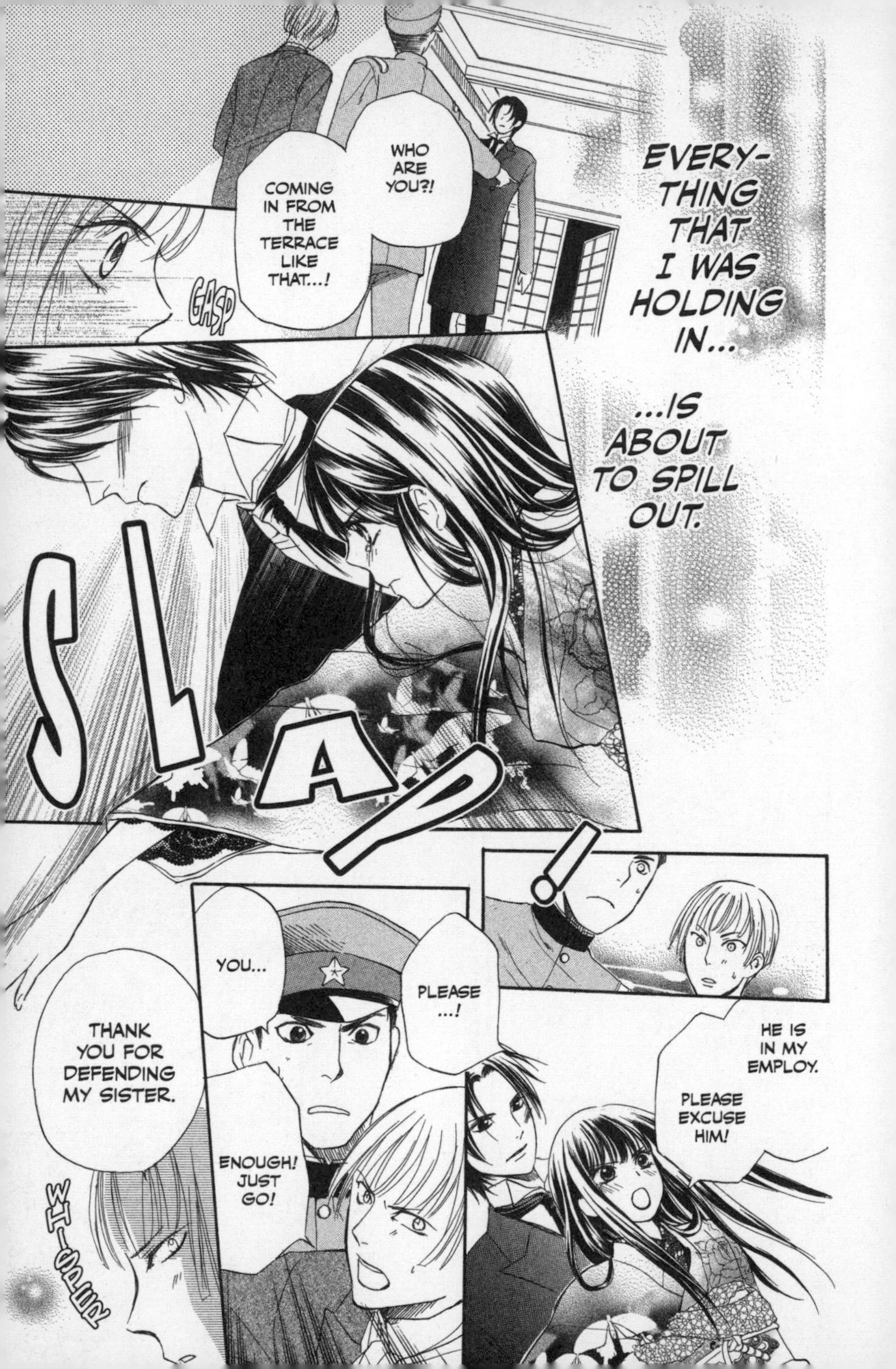
EVERY-THING THAT I WAS HOLDING IN...
WHO ARE YOU?!
COMING IN FROM THE TERRACE LIKE THAT...!
GASP
...IS ABOUT TO SPILL OUT.
SLAP!
HE IS IN MY EMPLOY.
PLEASE EXCUSE HIM!
PLEASE ...!
YOU...
ENOUGH! JUST GO!
THANK YOU FOR DEFENDING MY SISTER.

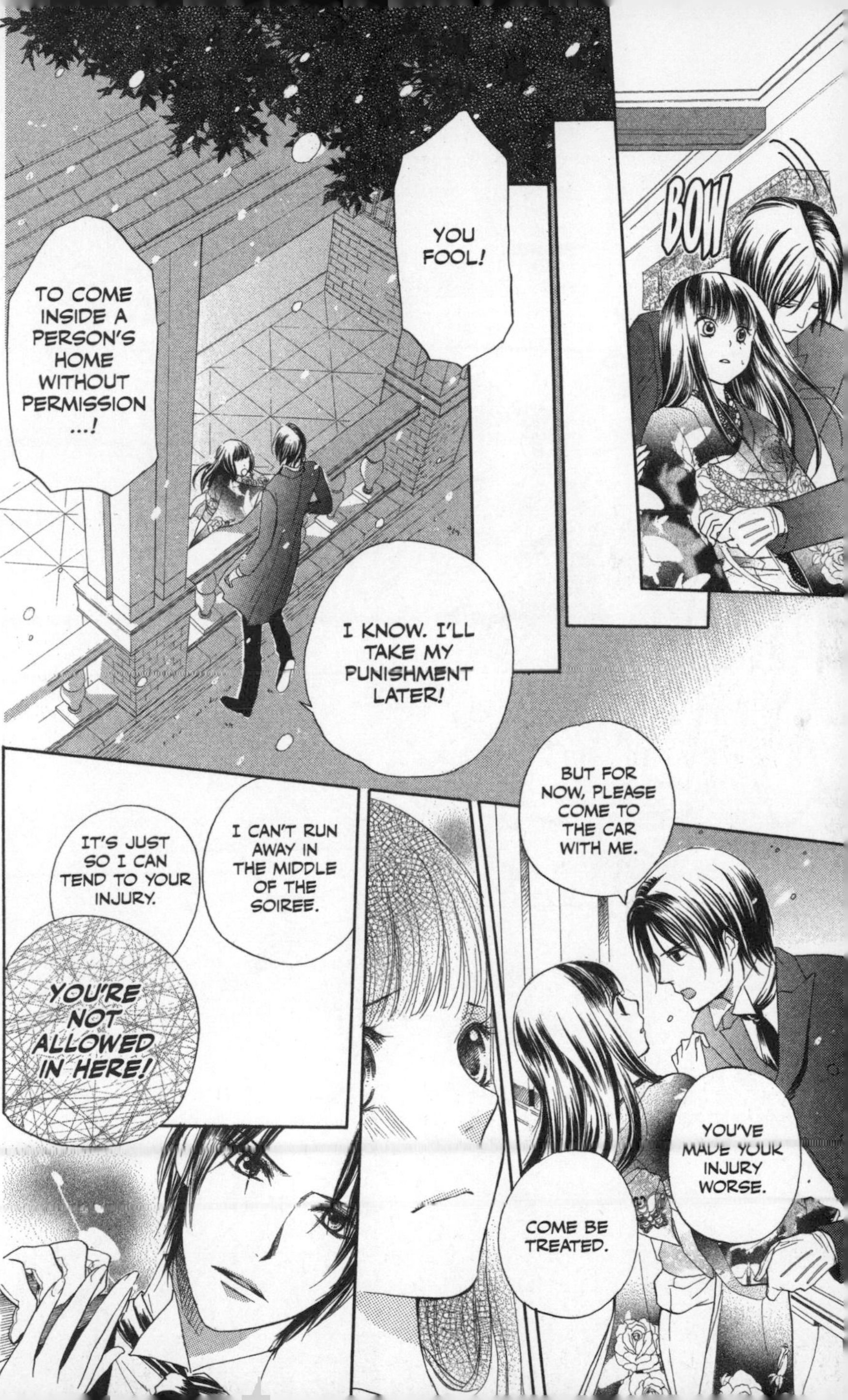
BOW
YOU FOOL!
TO COME INSIDE A PERSON'S HOME WITHOUT PERMISSION ...!
I KNOW. I'LL TAKE MY PUNISHMENT LATER!
BUT FOR NOW, PLEASE COME TO THE CAR WITH ME.
YOU'VE MADE YOUR INJURY WORSE.
COME BE TREATED.
I CAN'T RUN AWAY IN THE MIDDLE OF THE SOIREE.
IT'S JUST SO I CAN TEND TO YOUR INJURY.
YOU'RE NOT ALLOWED IN HERE!

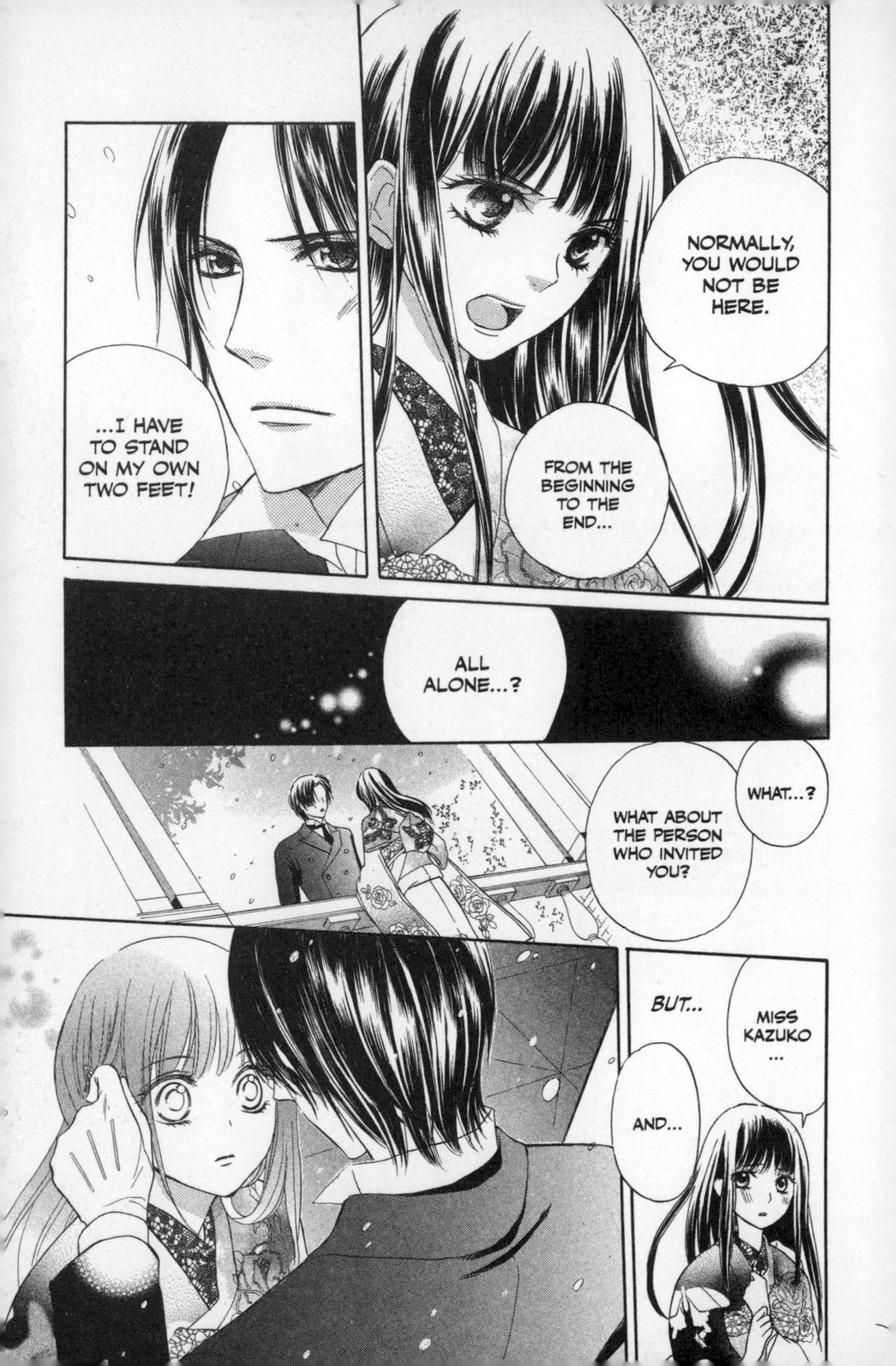
NORMALLY, YOU WOULD NOT BE HERE.
FROM THE BEGINNING TO THE END...
...I HAVE TO STAND ON MY OWN TWO FEET!
ALL ALONE...?
WHAT...?
WHAT ABOUT THE PERSON WHO INVITED YOU?
MISS KAZUKO ...
BUT...
AND...

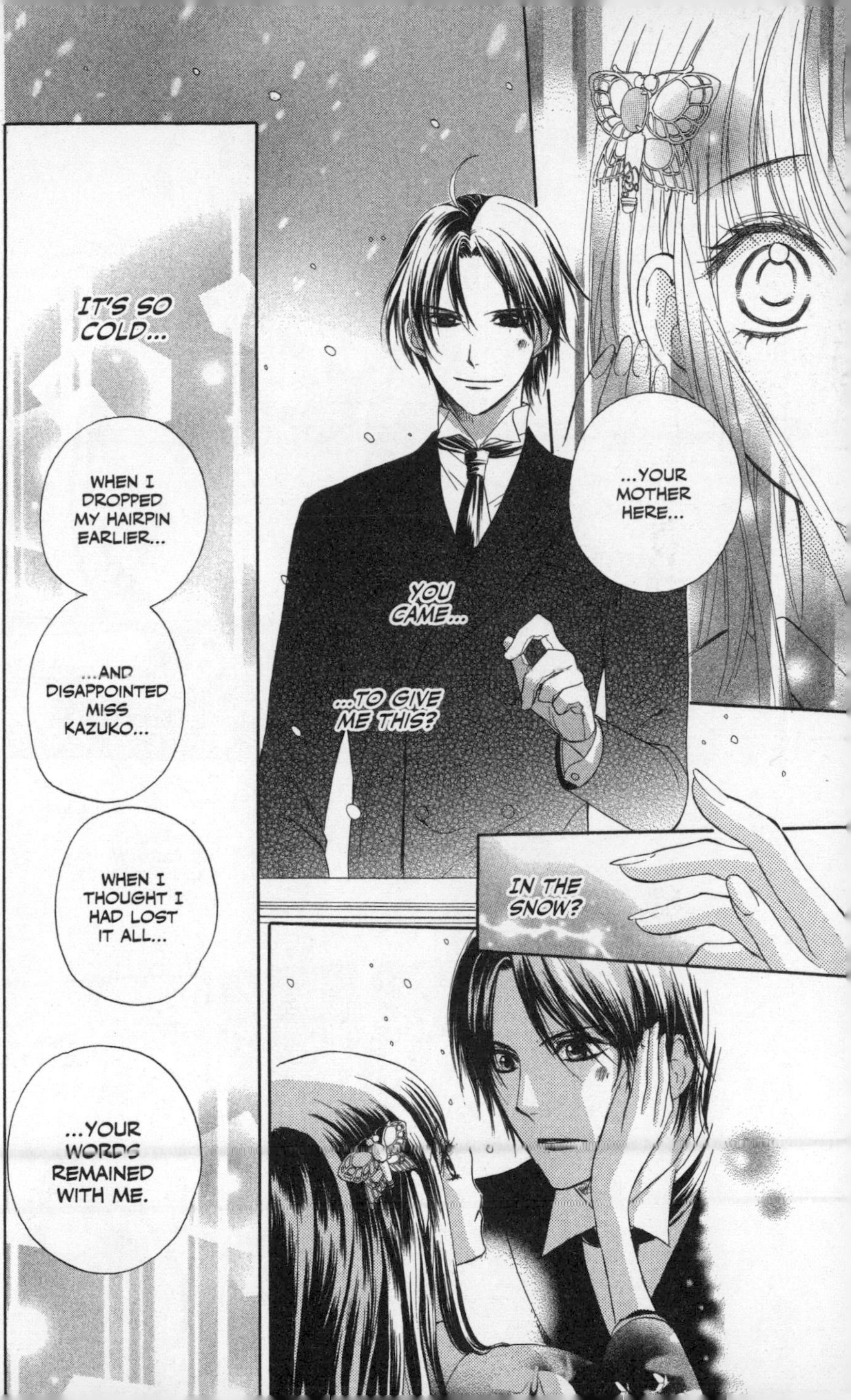
...YOUR MOTHER HERE...
YOU CAME...
...TO GIVE ME THIS?
IN THE SNOW?
IT'S SO COLD...
WHEN I DROPPED MY HAIRPIN EARLIER...
...AND DISAPPOINTED MISS KAZUKO...
WHEN I THOUGHT I HAD LOST IT ALL...
...YOUR WORDS REMAINED WITH ME.

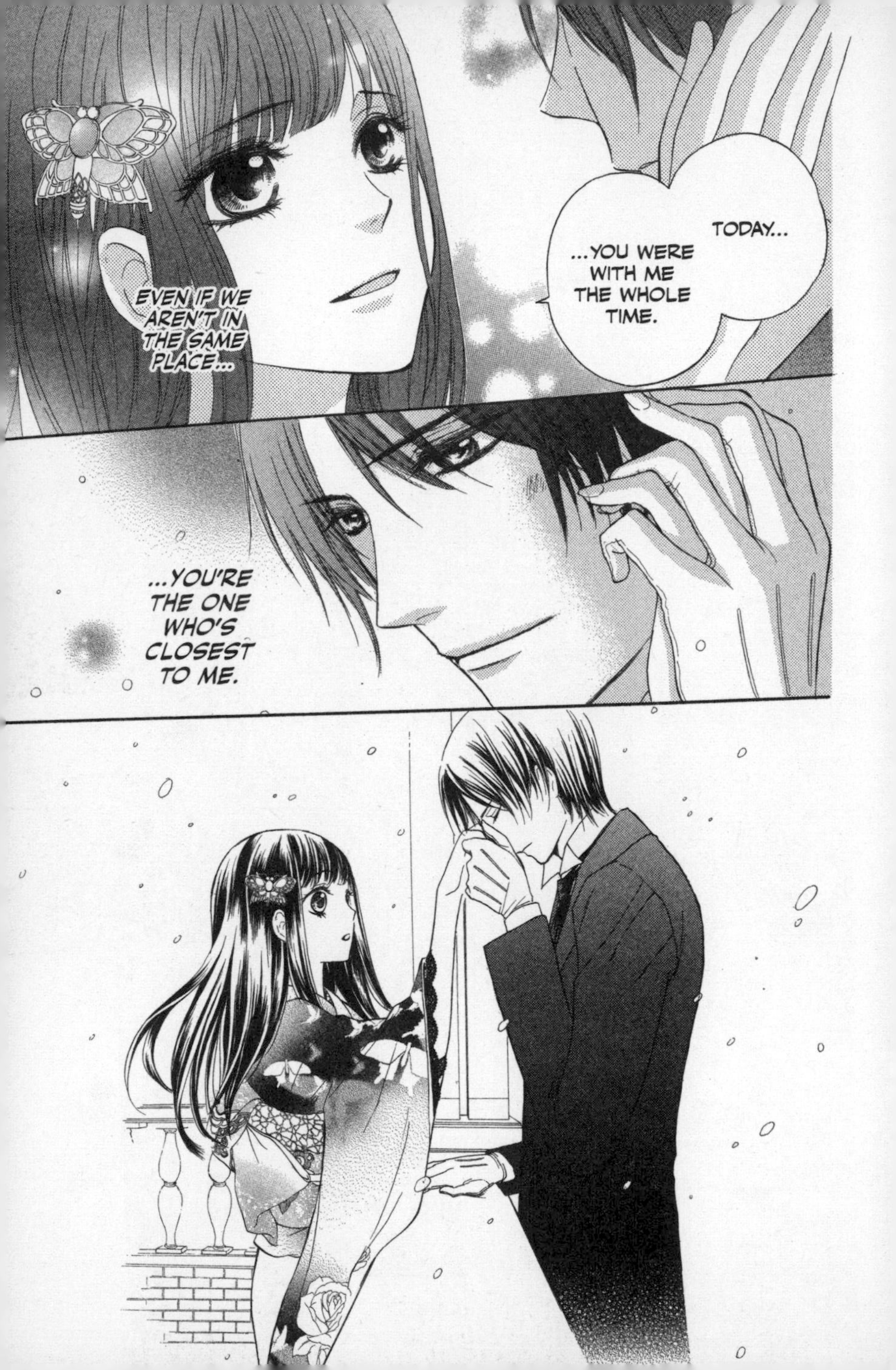
TODAY...
...YOU WERE WITH ME THE WHOLE TIME.
EVEN IF WE AREN'T IN THE SAME PLACE...
...YOU'RE THE ONE WHO'S CLOSEST TO ME.

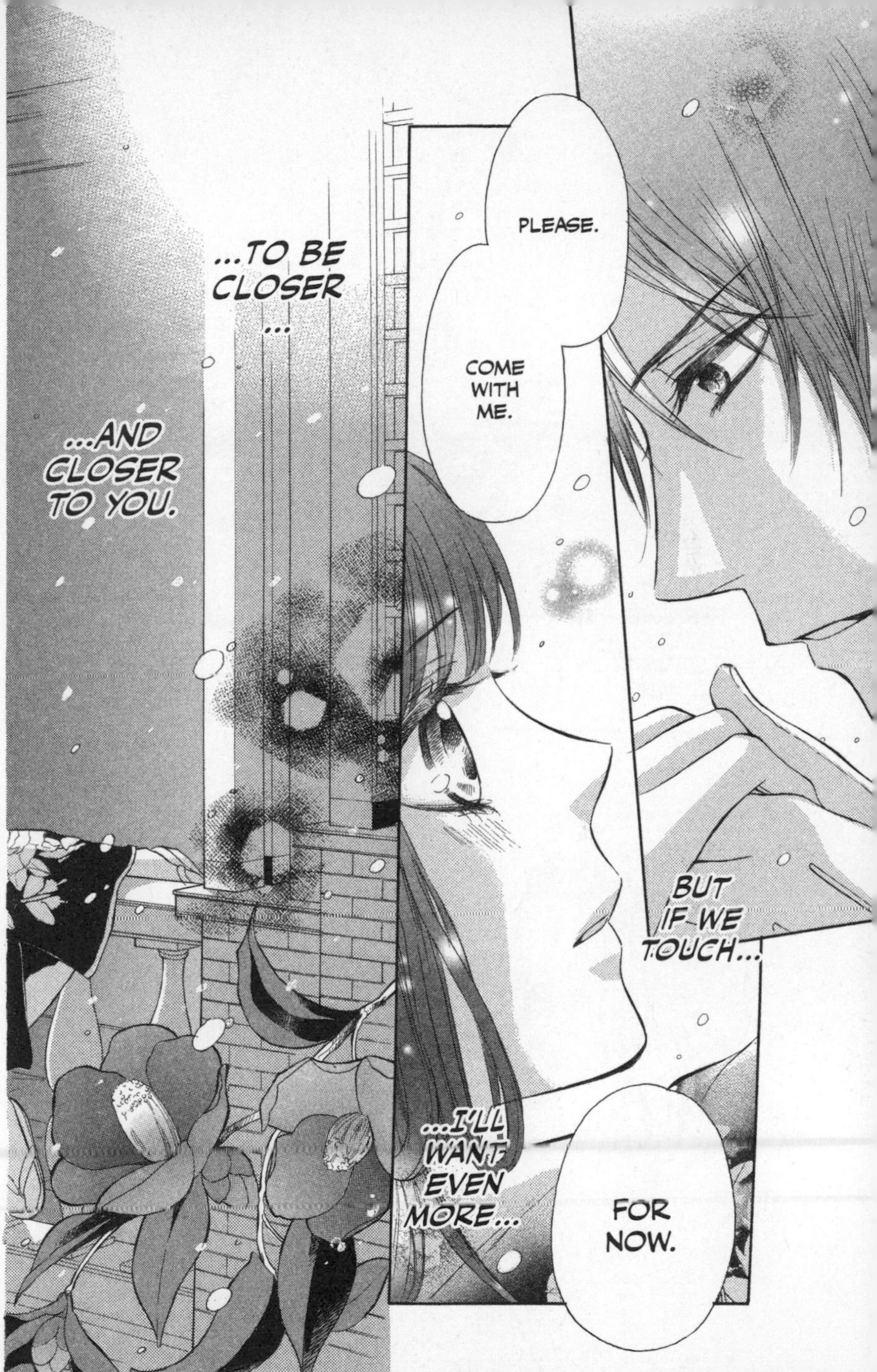
PLEASE.
COME WITH ME.
BUT IF WE TOUCH...
...I'LL WANT EVEN MORE...
FOR NOW.
...TO BE CLOSER ...
...AND CLOSER TO YOU.

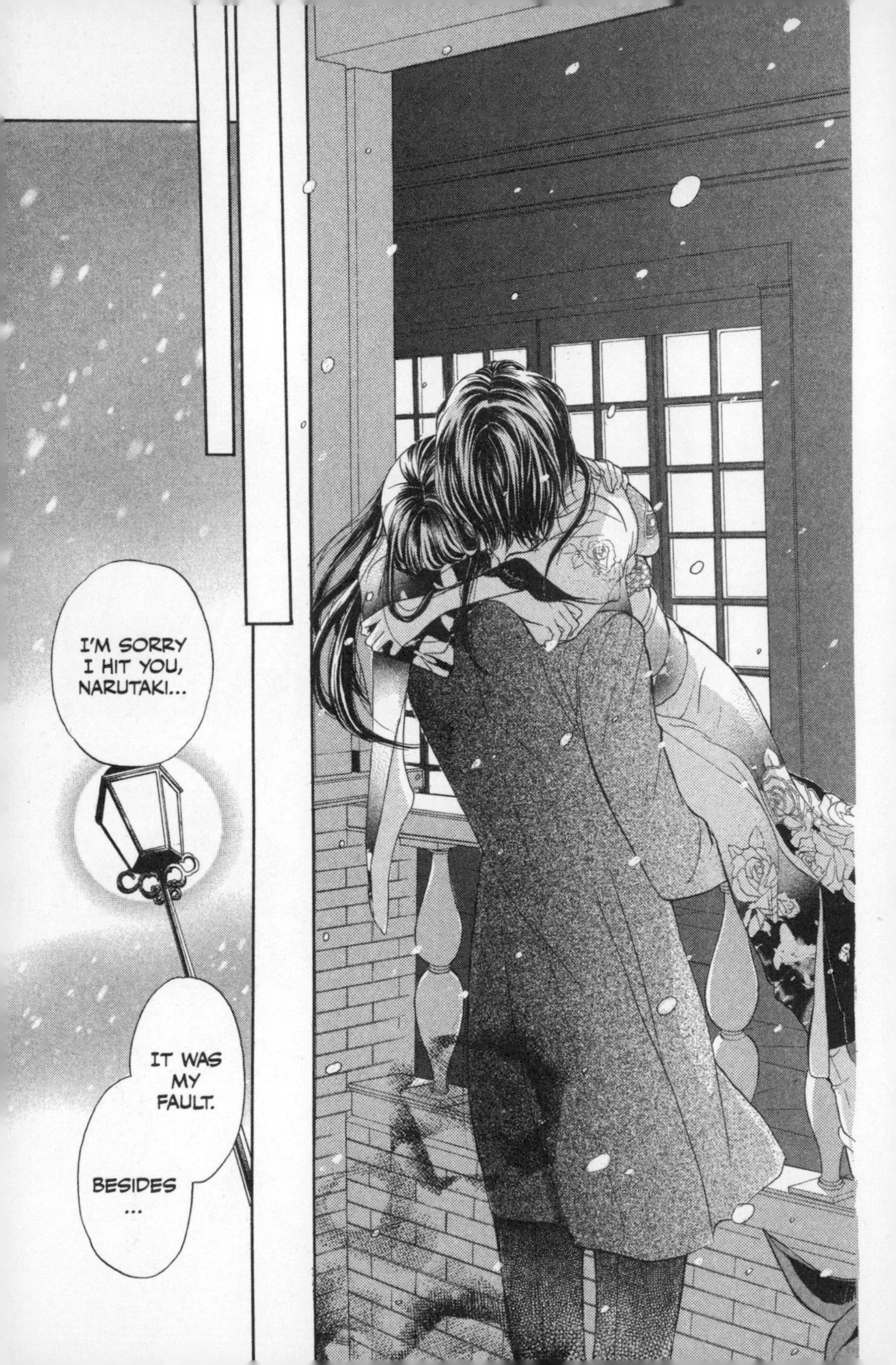
I'M SORRY I HIT YOU, NARUTAKI...
IT WAS MY FAULT.
BESIDES ...

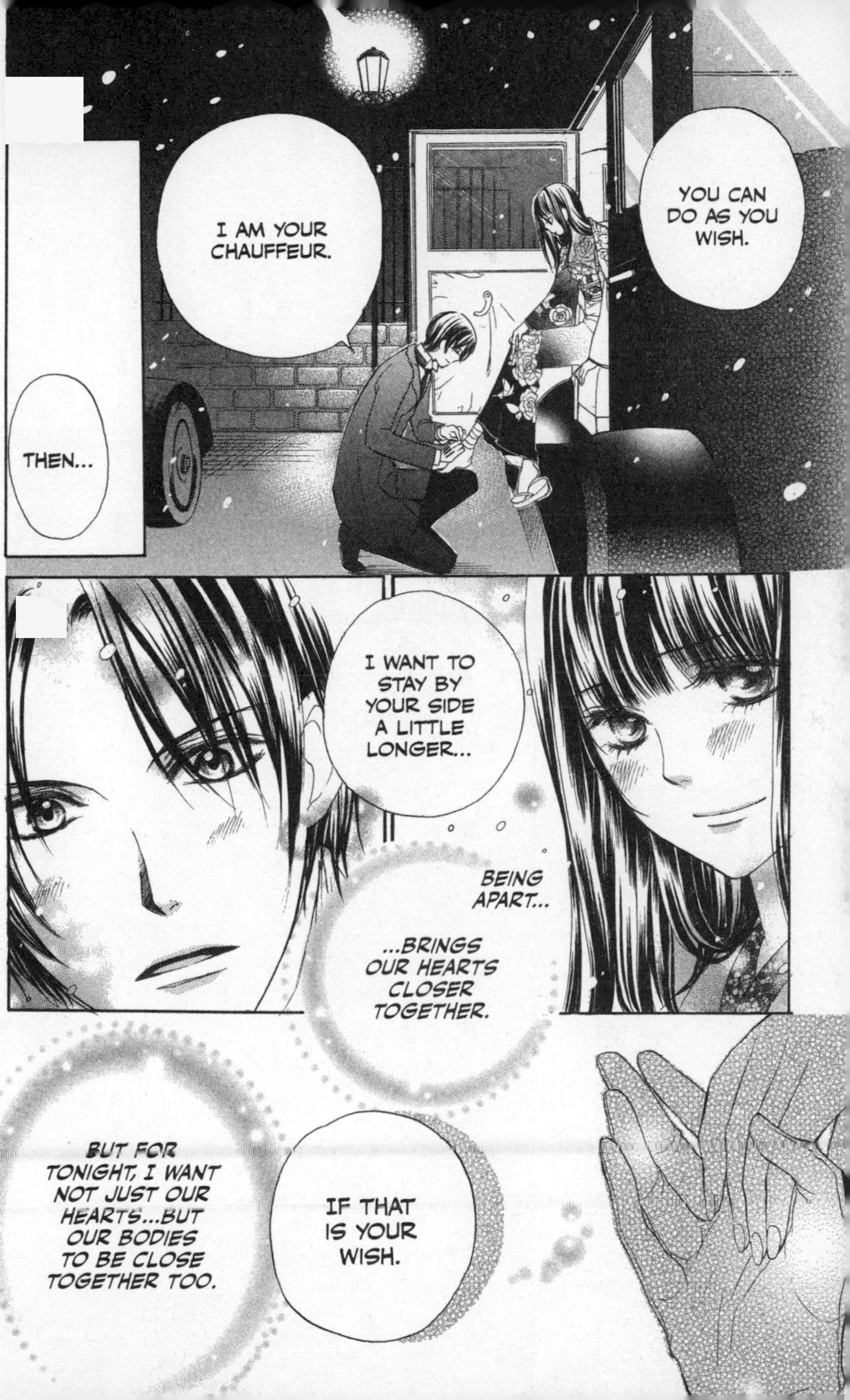
YOU CAN DO AS YOU WISH.
I AM YOUR CHAUFFEUR.
THEN...
I WANT TO STAY BY YOUR SIDE A LITTLE LONGER...
BEING APART...
...BRINGS OUR HEARTS CLOSER TOGETHER.
IF THAT IS YOUR WISH.
BUT FOR TONIGHT, I WANT NOT JUST OUR HEARTS...BUT OUR BODIES TO BE CLOSE TOGETHER TOO.

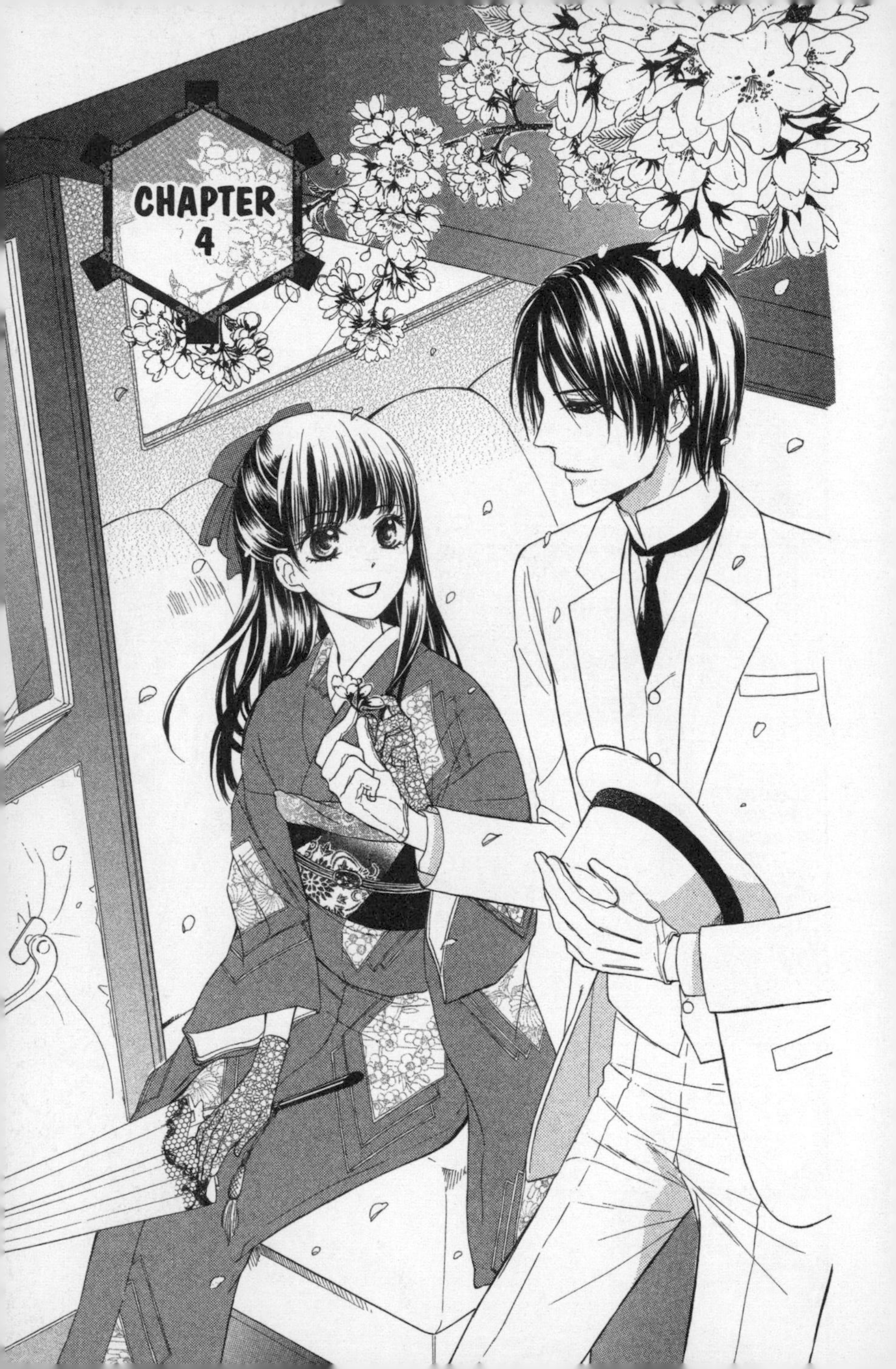
CHAPTER
4

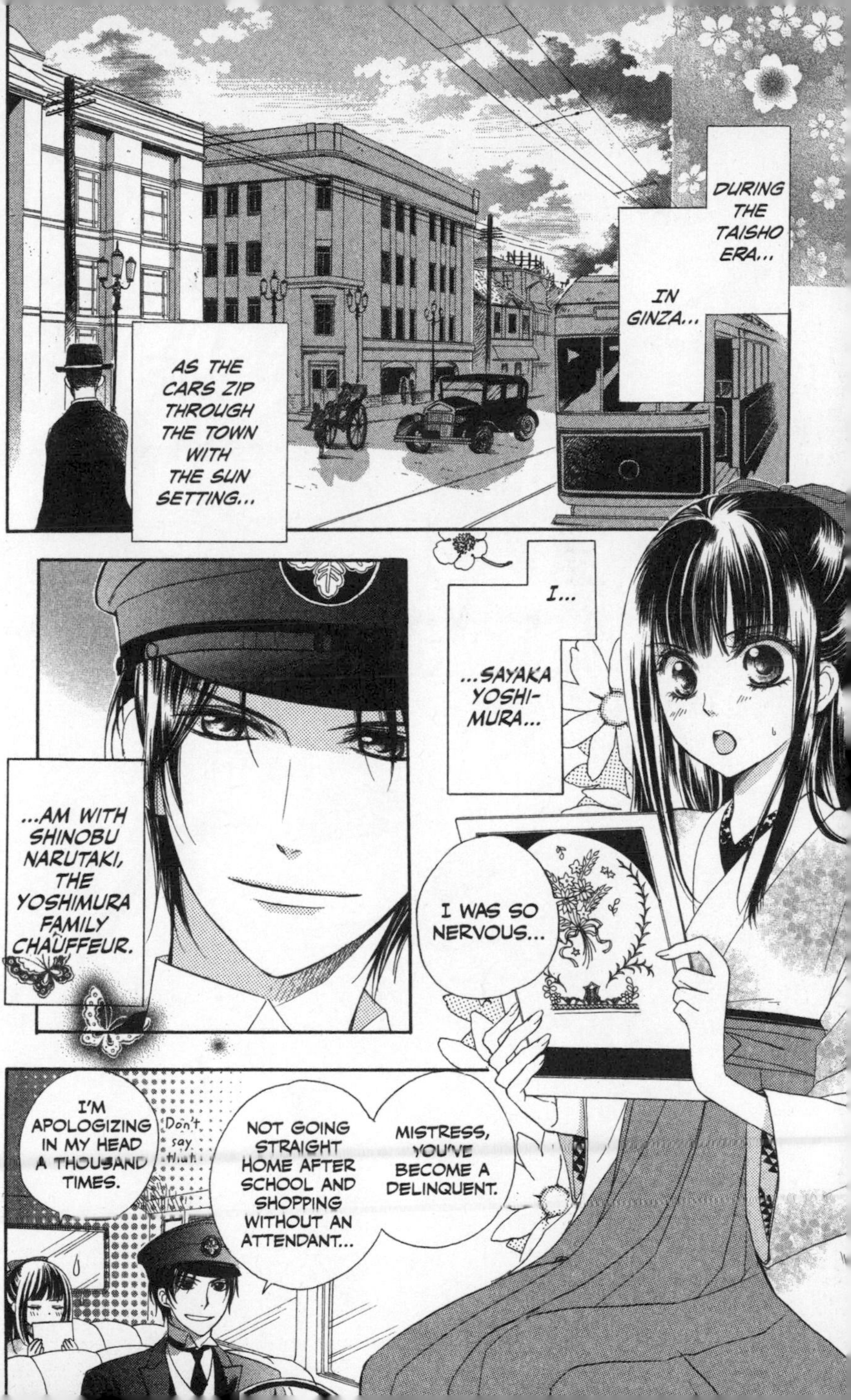

DURING THE TAISHO ERA...
IN GINZA...
AS THE CARS ZIP THROUGH THE TOWN WITH THE SUN SETTING...
I...
...SAYAKA YOSHIMURA...
...AM WITH SHINOBU NARUTAKI, THE YOSHIMURA FAMILY CHAUFFEUR.
I WAS SO NERVOUS...
MISTRESS, YOU'VE BECOME A DELINQUENT.
NOT GOING STRAIGHT HOME AFTER SCHOOL AND SHOPPING WITHOUT AN ATTENDANT...
Don't say that.
I'M APOLOGIZING IN MY HEAD A THOUSAND TIMES.

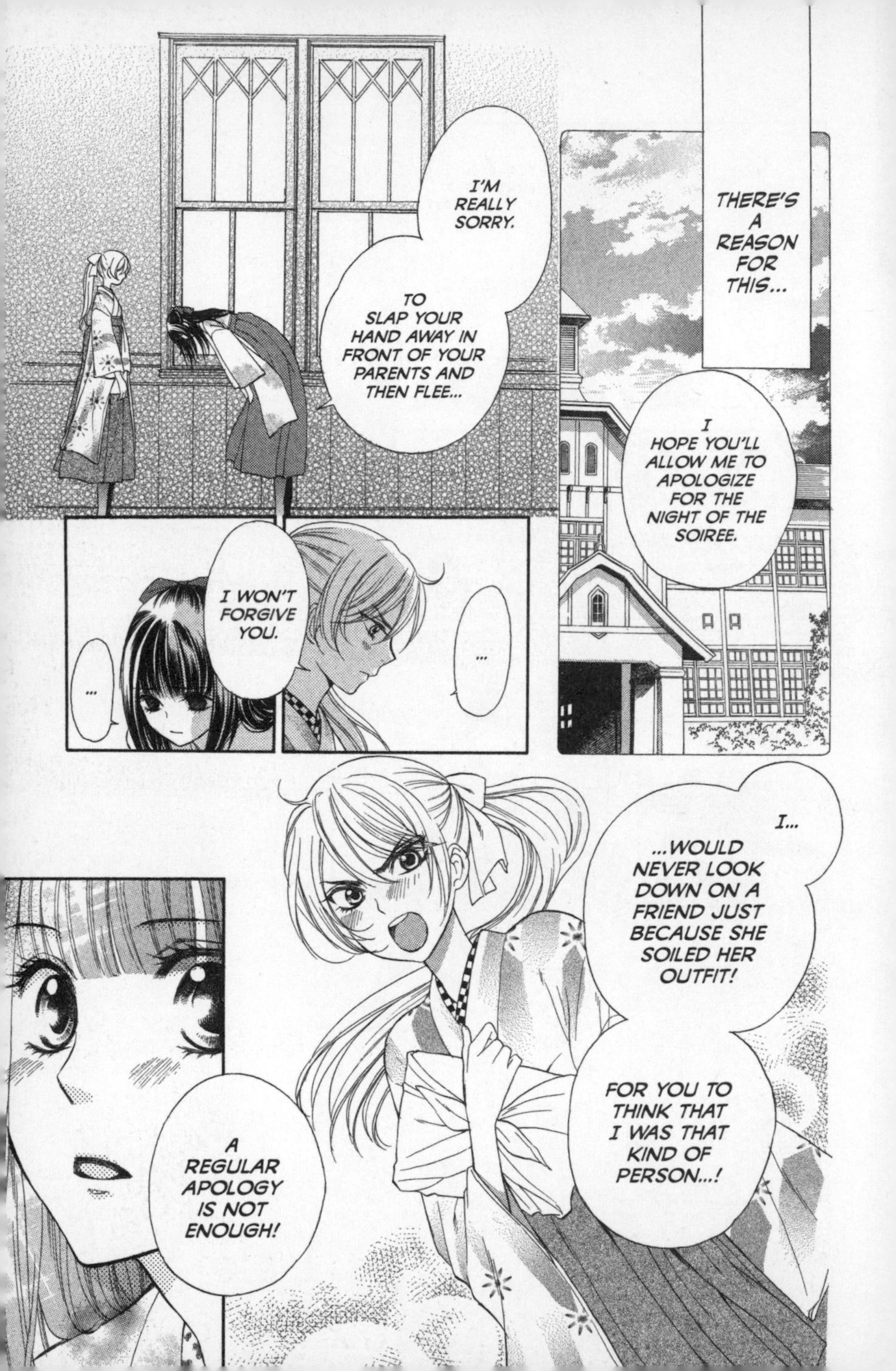

THERE'S A REASON FOR THIS...
I HOPE YOU'LL ALLOW ME TO APOLOGIZE FOR THE NIGHT OF THE SOIREE.
I'M REALLY SORRY.
TO SLAP YOUR HAND AWAY IN FRONT OF YOUR PARENTS AND THEN FLEE...
...
I WON'T FORGIVE YOU.
...
I...
...WOULD NEVER LOOK DOWN ON A FRIEND JUST BECAUSE SHE SOILED HER OUTFIT!
FOR YOU TO THINK THAT I WAS THAT KIND OF PERSON...!
A REGULAR APOLOGY IS NOT ENOUGH!

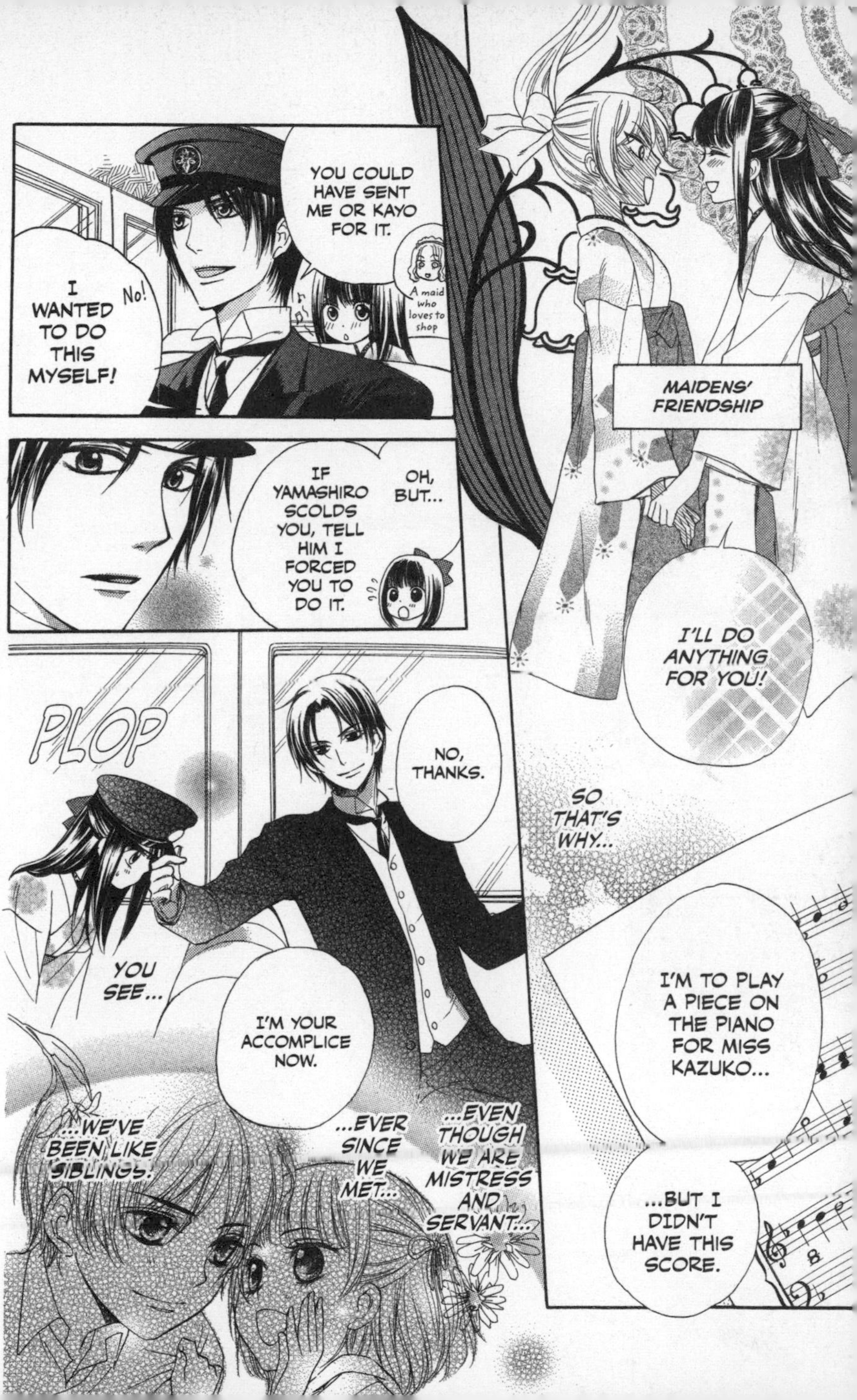

MAIDENS' FRIENDSHIP
I'LL DO ANYTHING FOR YOU!
SO THAT'S WHY...
I'M TO PLAY A PIECE ON THE PIANO FOR MISS KAZUKO...
...BUT I DIDN'T HAVE THIS SCORE.
YOU COULD HAVE SENT ME OR KAYO FOR IT.
A maid who loves to shop
No!
I WANTED TO DO THIS MYSELF!
IF YAMASHIRO SCOLDS YOU, TELL HIM I FORCED YOU TO DO IT.
OH, BUT...
PLOP
NO, THANKS.
YOU SEE...
I'M YOUR ACCOMPLICE NOW.
...EVEN THOUGH WE ARE MISTRESS AND SERVANT...
...EVER SINCE WE MET...
...WE'VE BEEN LIKE SIBLINGS.

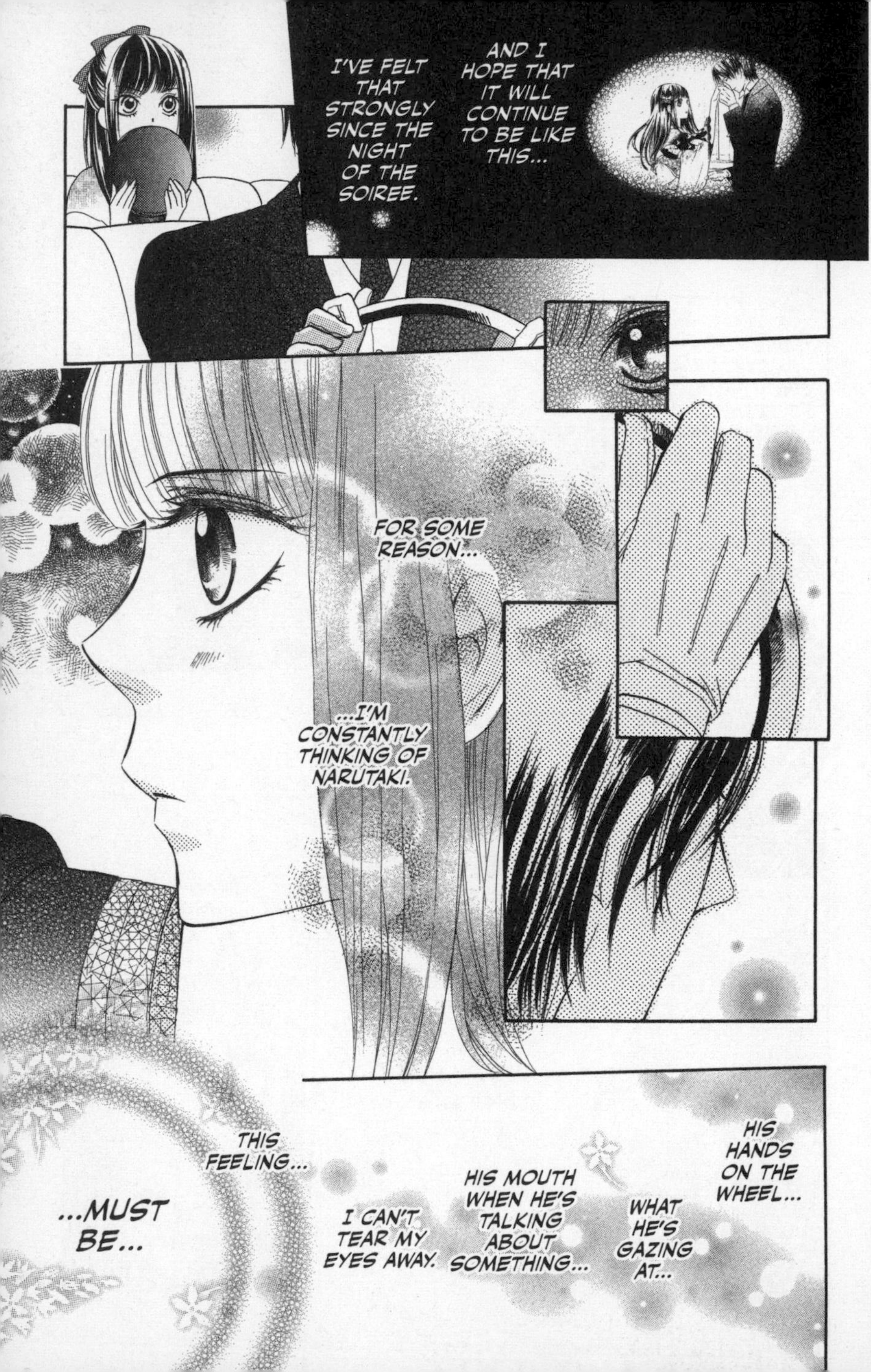
AND I HOPE THAT IT WILL CONTINUE TO BE LIKE THIS...
I'VE FELT THAT STRONGLY SINCE THE NIGHT OF THE SOIREE.
FOR SOME REASON...
...I'M CONSTANTLY THINKING OF NARUTAKI.
HIS HANDS ON THE WHEEL...
WHAT HE'S GAZING AT...
HIS MOUTH WHEN HE'S TALKING ABOUT SOMETHING...
I CAN'T TEAR MY EYES AWAY.
THIS FEELING...
...MUST BE...

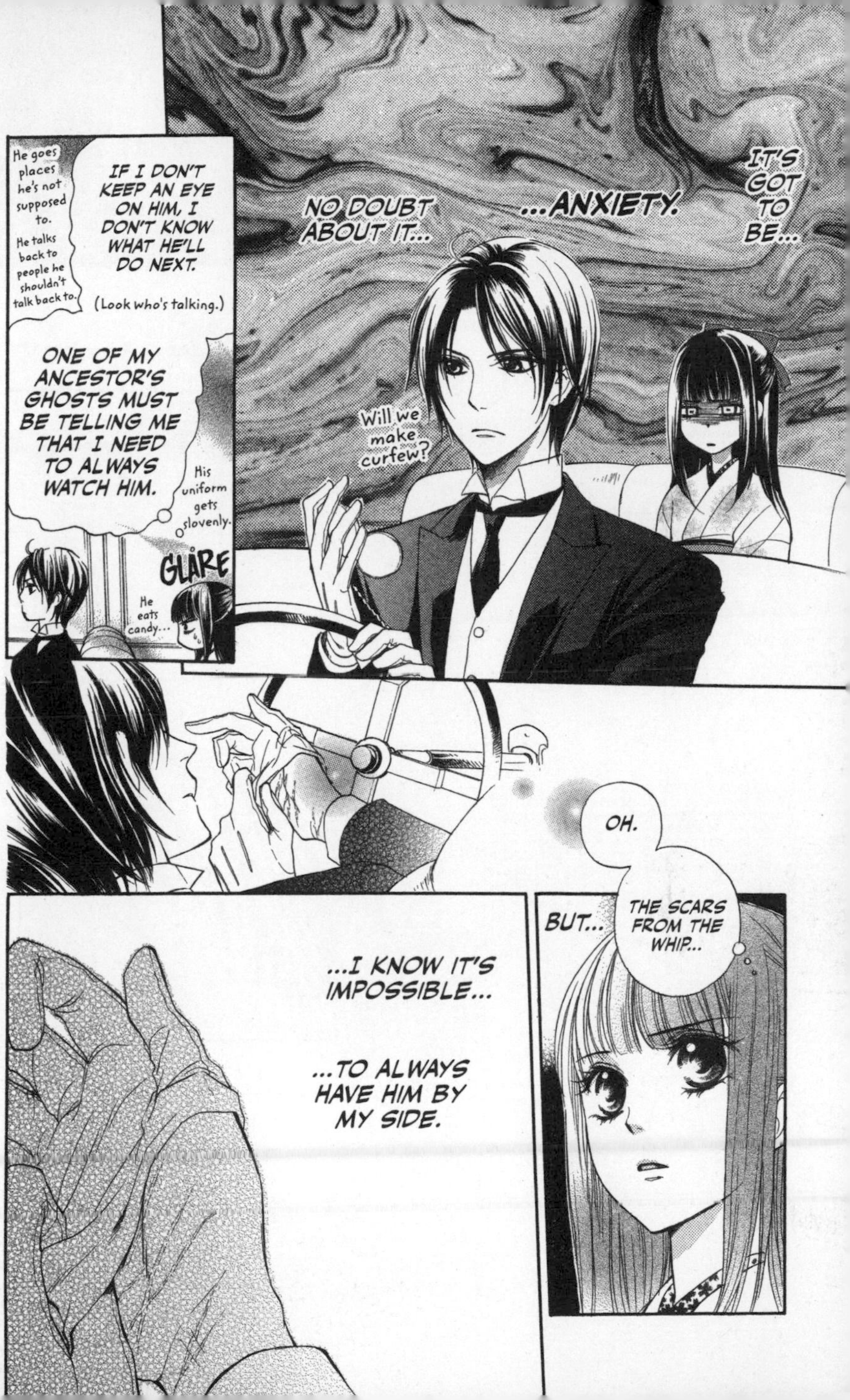

IT'S GOT TO BE...
...ANXIETY.
NO DOUBT ABOUT IT...
Will we make curfew?
IF I DON'T KEEP AN EYE ON HIM, I DON'T KNOW WHAT HE'LL DO NEXT.
He goes places he's not supposed to.
He talks back to people he shouldn't talk back to.
(Look who's talking.)
ONE OF MY ANCESTOR'S GHOSTS MUST BE TELLING ME THAT I NEED TO ALWAYS WATCH HIM.
His uniform gets slovenly.
GLARE
He eats candy...
OH.
THE SCARS FROM THE WHIP...
BUT...
...I KNOW IT'S IMPOSSIBLE...
...TO ALWAYS HAVE HIM BY MY SIDE.

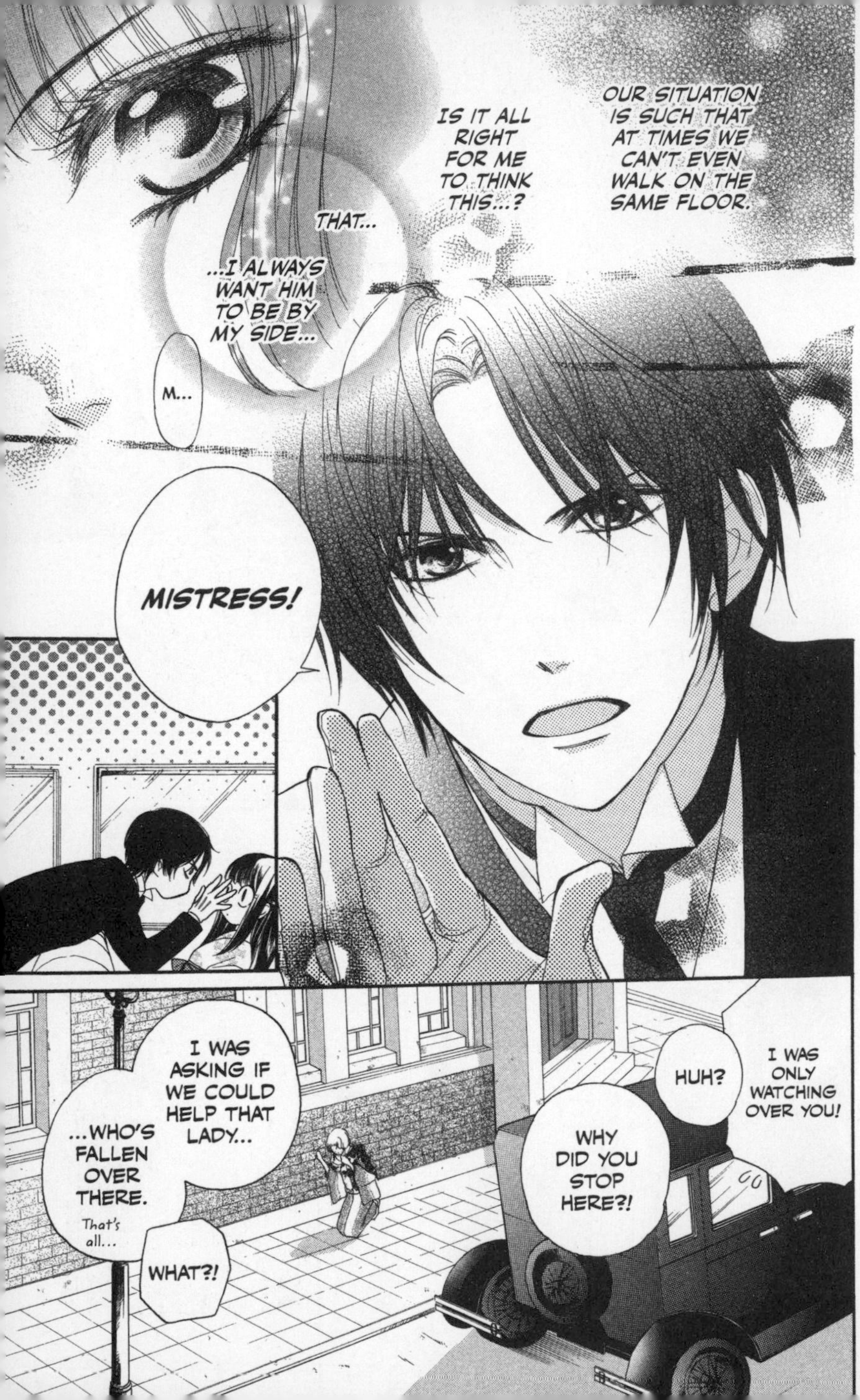
OUR SITUATION IS SUCH THAT AT TIMES WE CAN'T EVEN WALK ON THE SAME FLOOR.
IS IT ALL RIGHT FOR ME TO THINK THIS...?
THAT...
...I ALWAYS WANT HIM TO BE BY MY SIDE...
M...
MISTRESS!
I WAS ONLY WATCHING OVER YOU!
HUH?
WHY DID YOU STOP HERE?!
I WAS ASKING IF WE COULD HELP THAT LADY...
...WHO'S FALLEN OVER THERE.
That's all...
WHAT?!

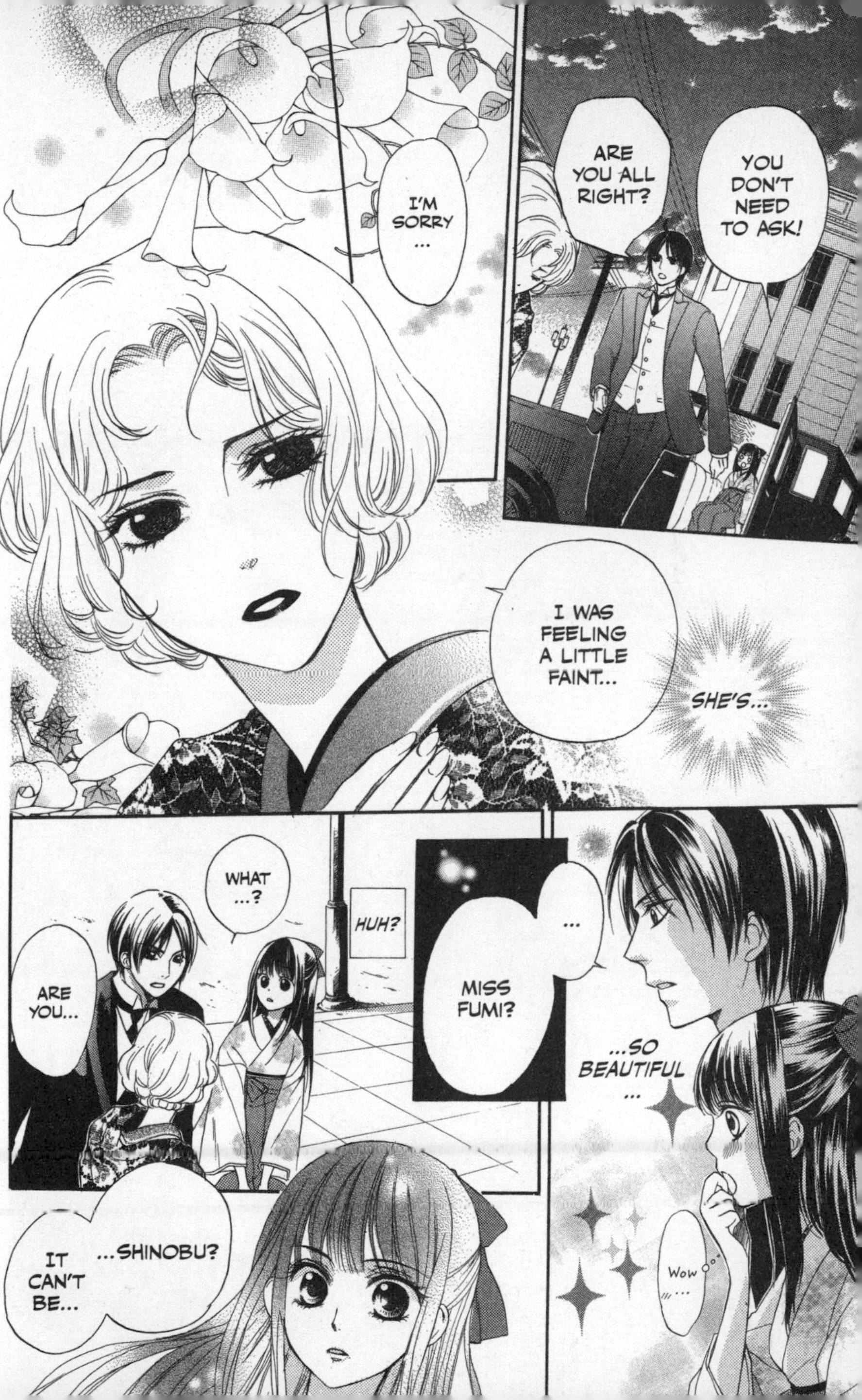
YOU DON'T NEED TO ASK!
ARE YOU ALL RIGHT?
I'M SORRY ...
I WAS FEELING A LITTLE FAINT...
SHE'S...
...SO BEAUTIFUL ...
Wow ...
...
MISS FUMI?
WHAT ...?
HUH?
ARE YOU...
...SHINOBU?
IT CAN'T BE...

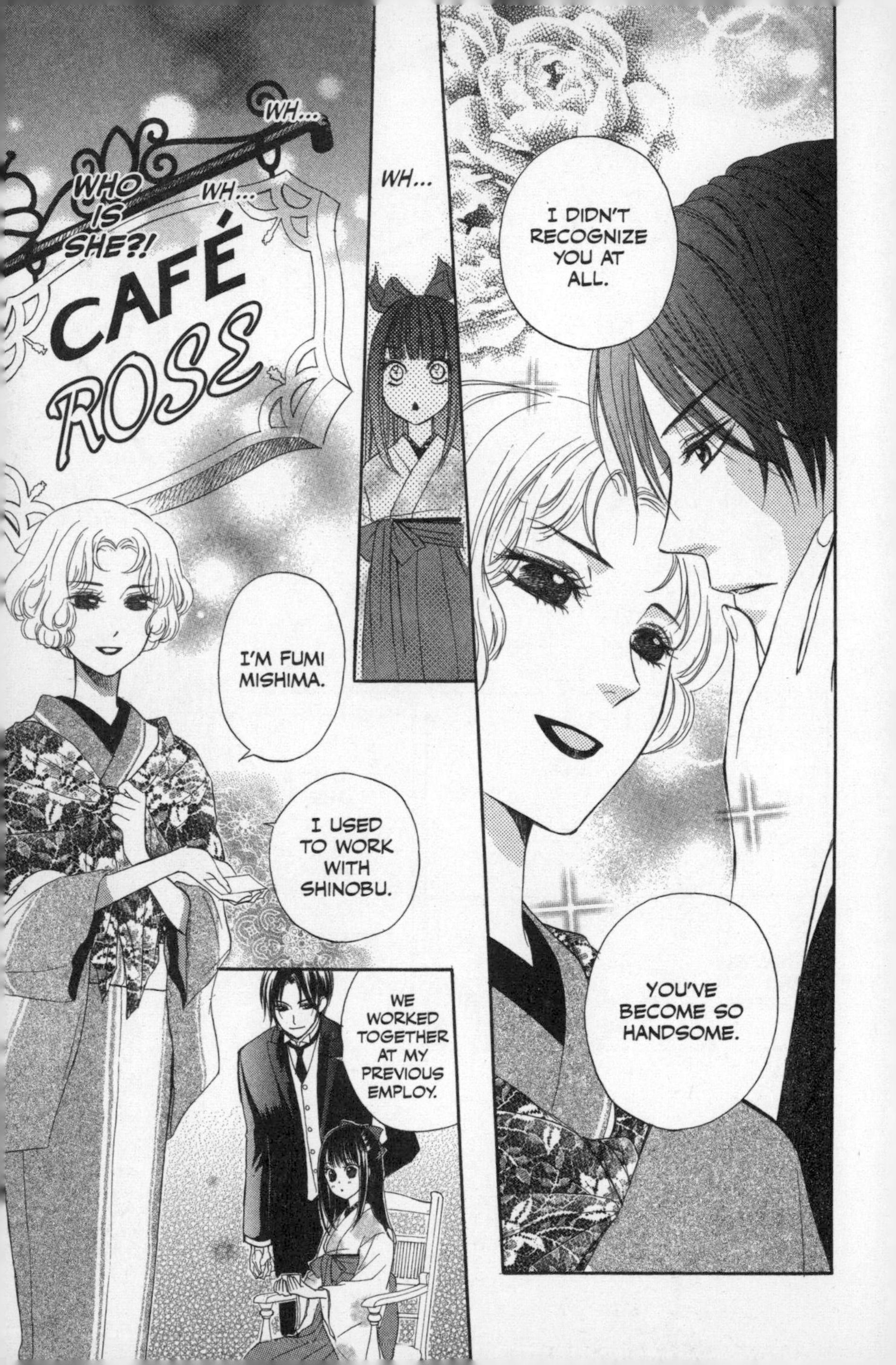
I DIDN'T RECOGNIZE YOU AT ALL.
YOU'VE BECOME SO HANDSOME.
WH...
WH...
WH...
WHO IS SHE?!
CAFÉ ROSE
I'M FUMI MISHIMA.
I USED TO WORK WITH SHINOBU.
WE WORKED TOGETHER AT MY PREVIOUS EMPLOY.

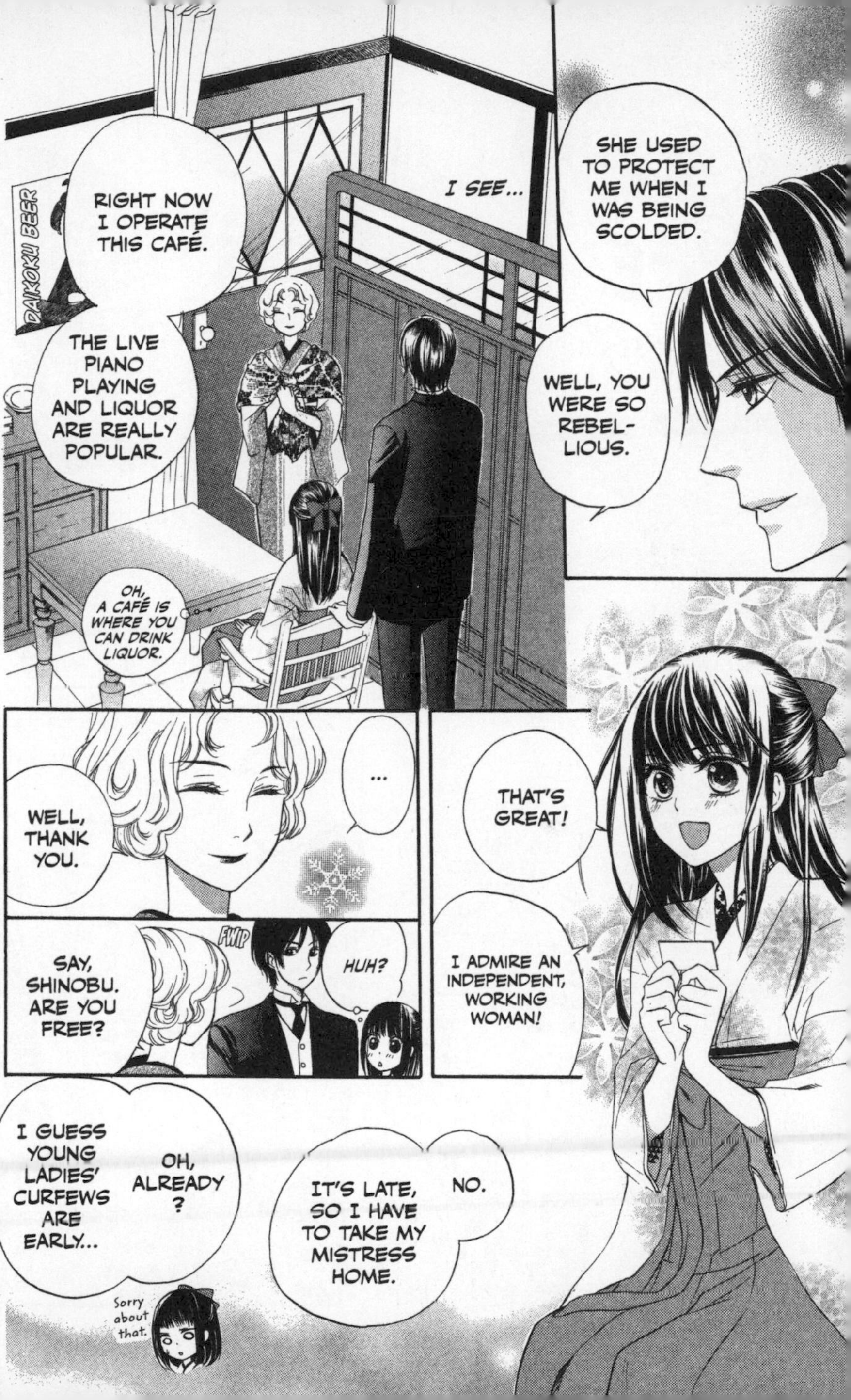
SHE USED TO PROTECT ME WHEN I WAS BEING SCOLDED.
WELL, YOU WERE SO REBELLIOUS.
I SEE...
RIGHT NOW I OPERATE THIS CAFÉ.
DAIKOKU BEER
THE LIVE PIANO PLAYING AND LIQUOR ARE REALLY POPULAR.
OH, A CAFÉ IS WHERE YOU CAN DRINK LIQUOR.
THAT'S GREAT!
I ADMIRE AN INDEPENDENT, WORKING WOMAN!
...
WELL, THANK YOU.
HUH?
FWIP
SAY, SHINOBU. ARE YOU FREE?
NO.
IT'S LATE, SO I HAVE TO TAKE MY MISTRESS HOME.
OH, ALREADY?
I GUESS YOUNG LADIES' CURFEWS ARE EARLY...
Sorry about that.

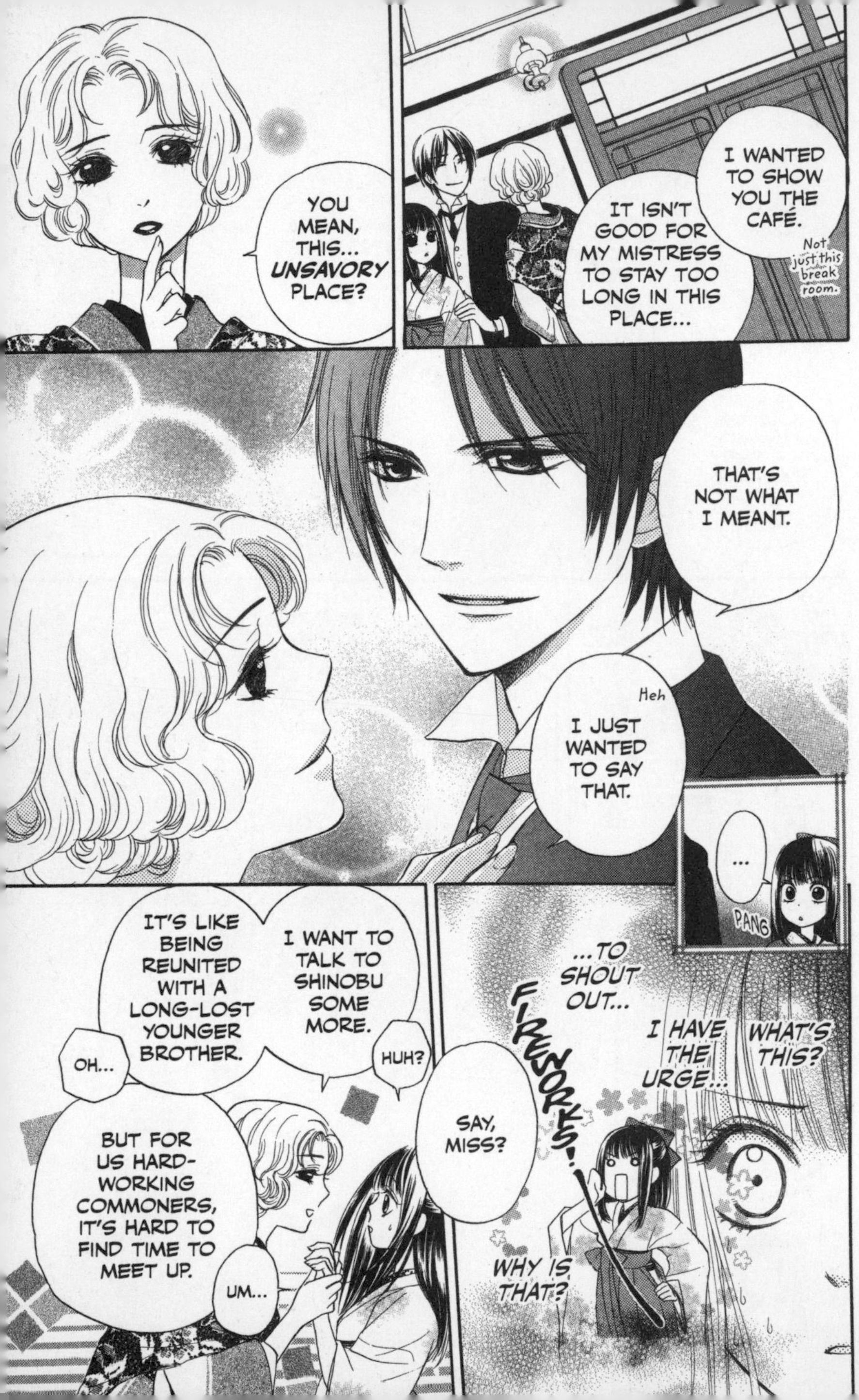
I WANTED TO SHOW YOU THE CAFÉ.
Not just this break room.
IT ISN'T GOOD FOR MY MISTRESS TO STAY TOO LONG IN THIS PLACE...
YOU MEAN, THIS... *UNSAVORY* PLACE?
THAT'S NOT WHAT I MEANT.
Heh
I JUST WANTED TO SAY THAT.
...
PANG
WHAT'S THIS?
I HAVE THE URGE...
...TO SHOUT OUT...
FIREWORKS!
WHY IS THAT?
I WANT TO TALK TO SHINOBU SOME MORE.
IT'S LIKE BEING REUNITED WITH A LONG-LOST YOUNGER BROTHER.
HUH?
OH...
SAY, MISS?
BUT FOR US HARD-WORKING COMMONERS, IT'S HARD TO FIND TIME TO MEET UP.
UM...

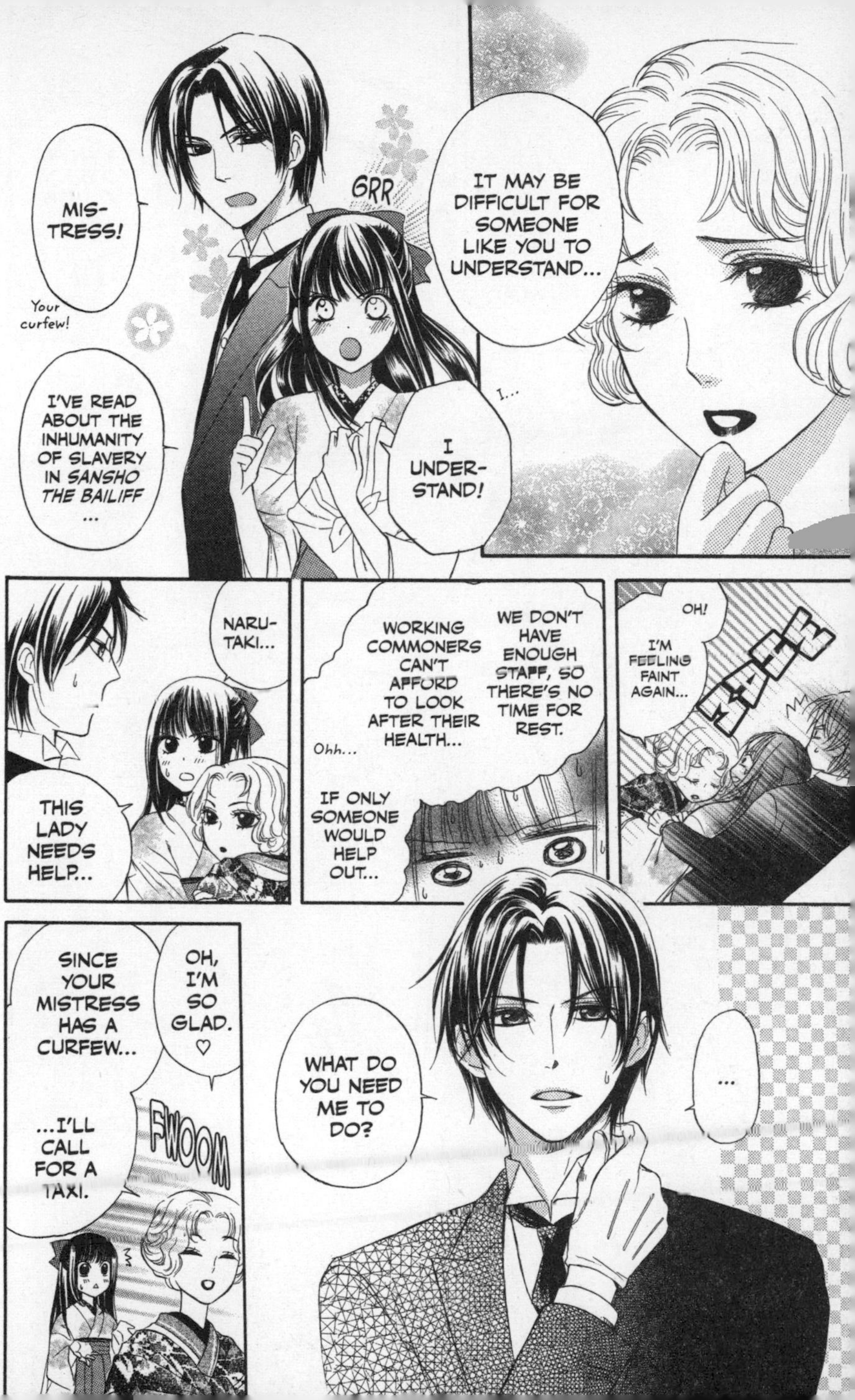
IT MAY BE DIFFICULT FOR SOMEONE LIKE YOU TO UNDERSTAND...
I...
I UNDER-STAND!
I'VE READ ABOUT THE INHUMANITY OF SLAVERY IN *SANSHO THE BAILIFF* ...
GRR
MIS-TRESS!
Your curfew!
OH!
I'M FEELING FAINT AGAIN...
WE DON'T HAVE ENOUGH STAFF, SO THERE'S NO TIME FOR REST.
WORKING COMMONERS CAN'T AFFORD TO LOOK AFTER THEIR HEALTH...
Ohh...
IF ONLY SOMEONE WOULD HELP OUT...
NARU-TAKI...
THIS LADY NEEDS HELP...
...
WHAT DO YOU NEED ME TO DO?
OH, I'M SO GLAD. ♡
SINCE YOUR MISTRESS HAS A CURFEW...
...I'LL CALL FOR A TAXI.
FWOOM

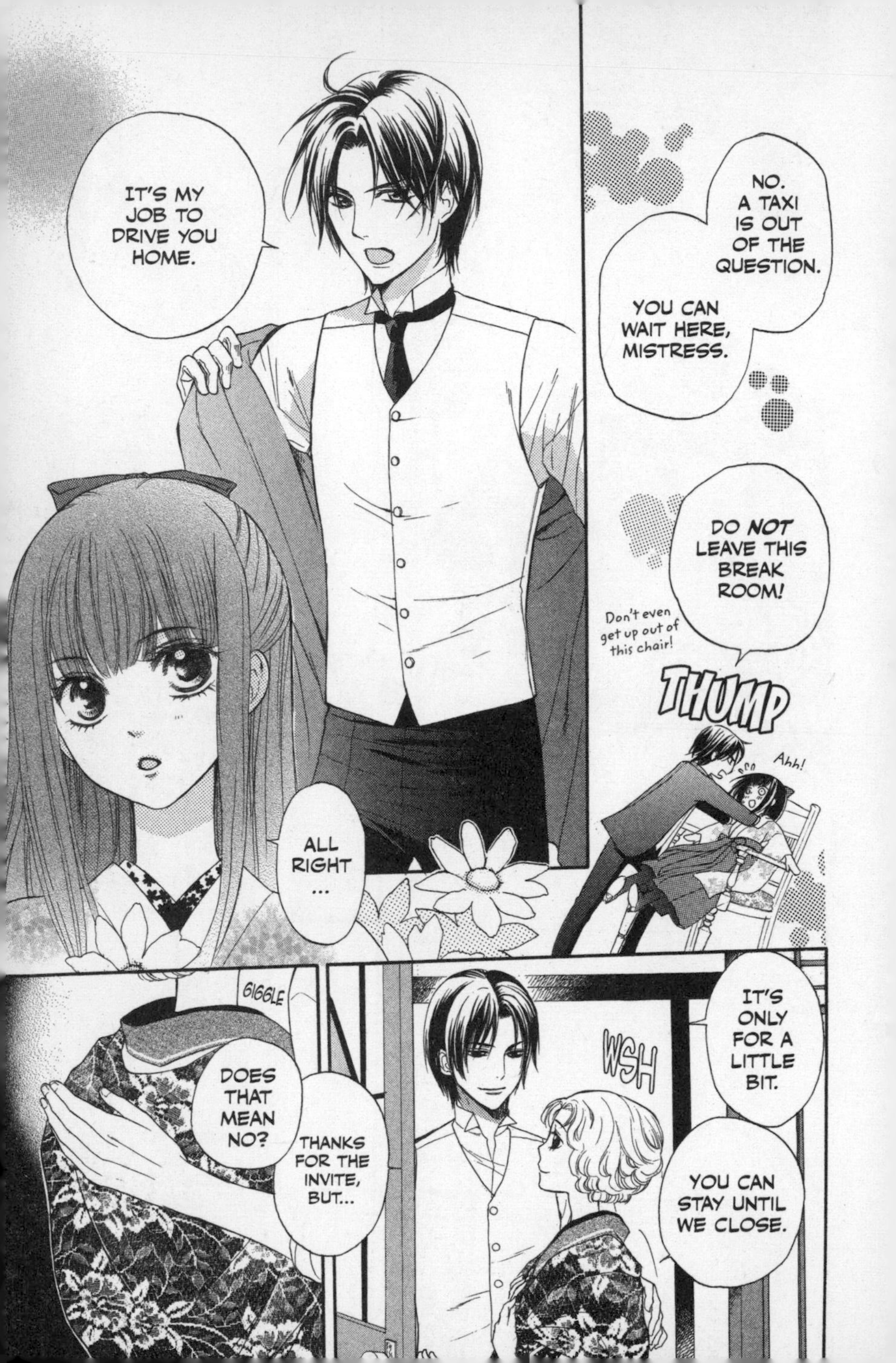
NO. A TAXI IS OUT OF THE QUESTION.
YOU CAN WAIT HERE, MISTRESS.
DO *NOT* LEAVE THIS BREAK ROOM!
Don't even get up out of this chair!
THUMP
Ahh!
IT'S MY JOB TO DRIVE YOU HOME.
ALL RIGHT...
WSH
IT'S ONLY FOR A LITTLE BIT.
YOU CAN STAY UNTIL WE CLOSE.
GIGGLE
THANKS FOR THE INVITE, BUT...
DOES THAT MEAN NO?

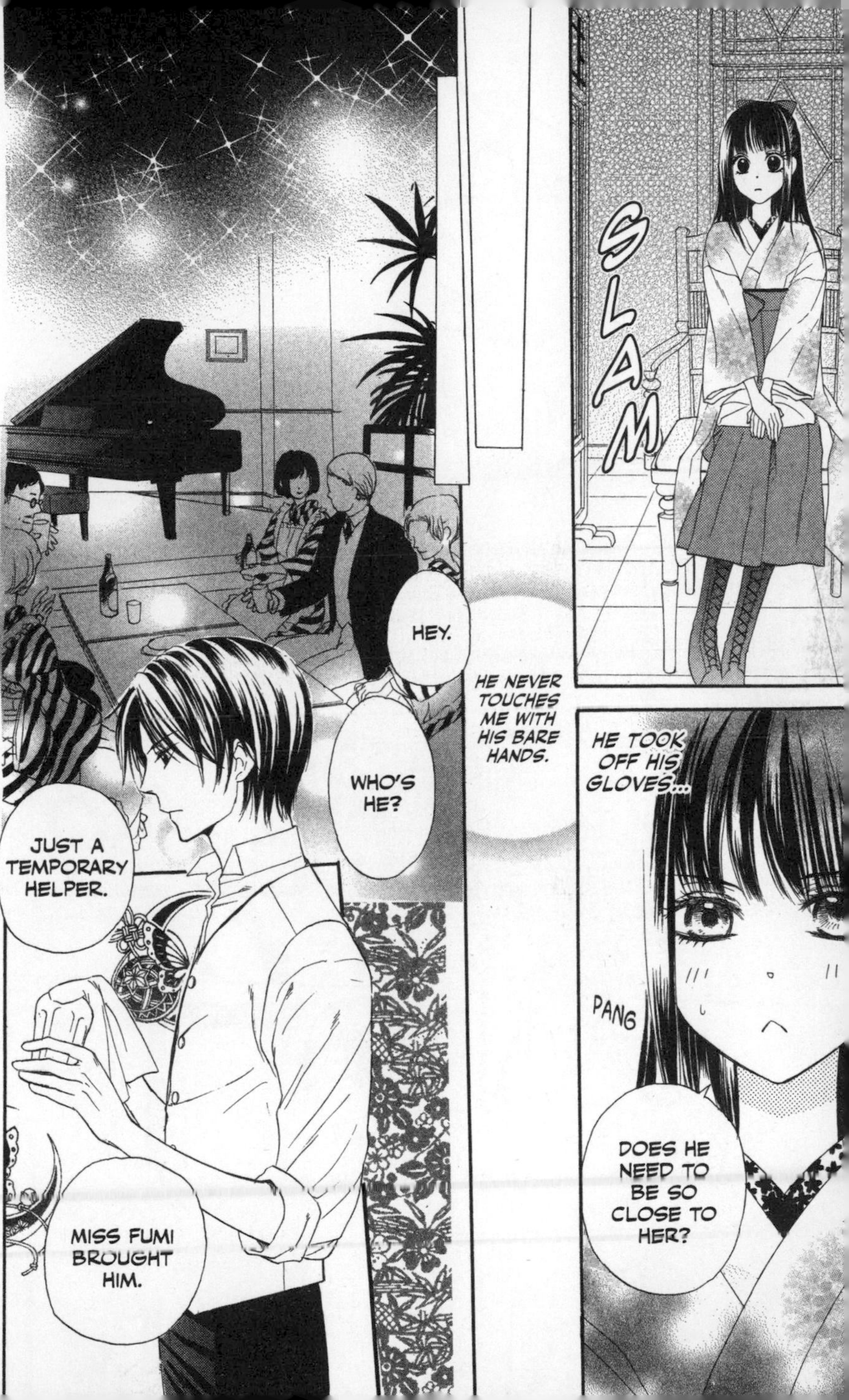
SLAM
HE TOOK OFF HIS GLOVES...
PANG
DOES HE NEED TO BE SO CLOSE TO HER?
HE NEVER TOUCHES ME WITH HIS BARE HANDS.
HEY.
WHO'S HE?
JUST A TEMPORARY HELPER.
MISS FUMI BROUGHT HIM.

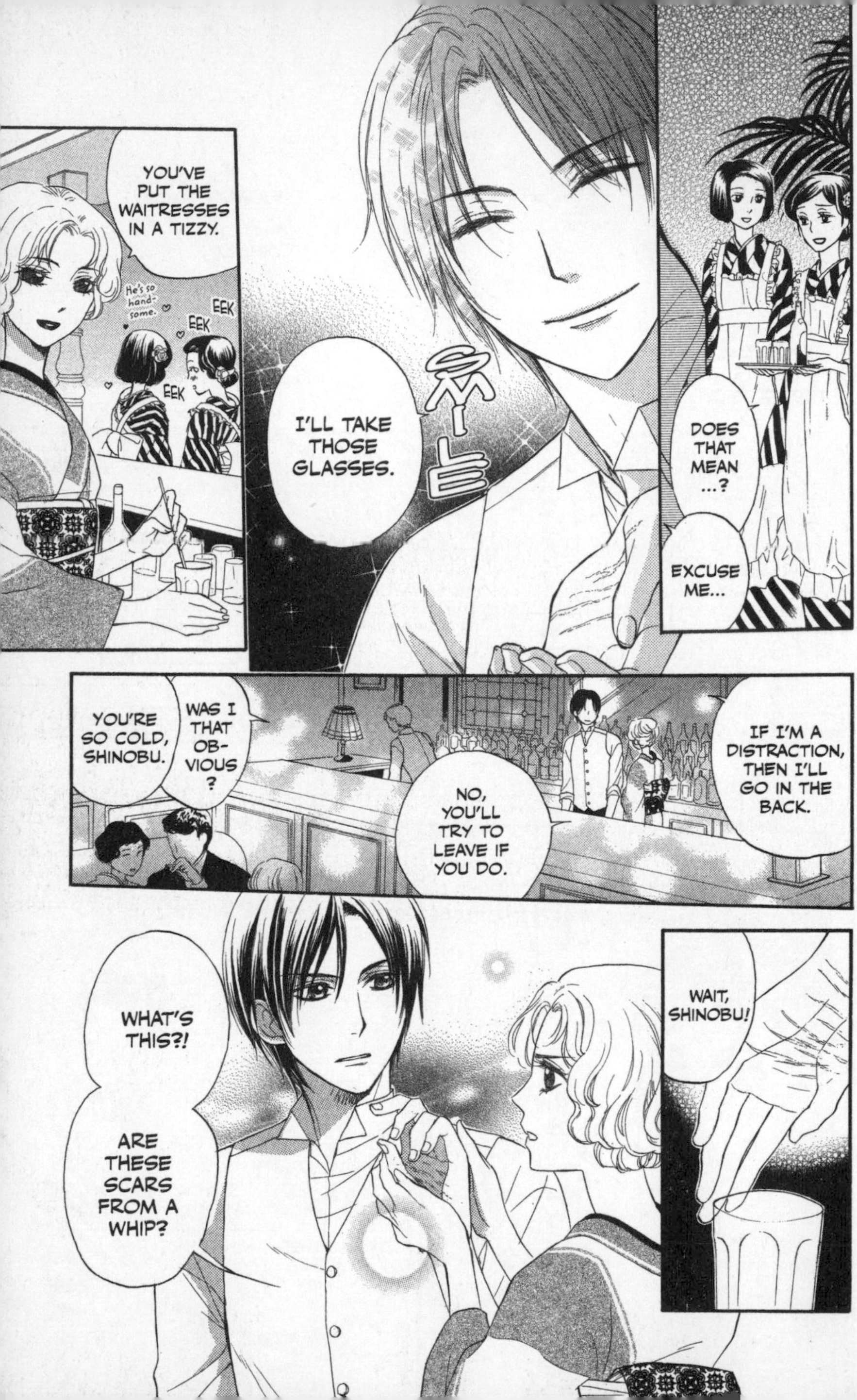
DOES THAT MEAN ...?
EXCUSE ME...
SMILE
I'LL TAKE THOSE GLASSES.
YOU'VE PUT THE WAITRESSES IN A TIZZY.
He's so hand-some.
EEK
EEK
EEK
IF I'M A DISTRACTION, THEN I'LL GO IN THE BACK.
NO, YOU'LL TRY TO LEAVE IF YOU DO.
WAS I THAT OB-VIOUS?
YOU'RE SO COLD, SHINOBU.
WAIT, SHINOBU!
WHAT'S THIS?!
ARE THESE SCARS FROM A WHIP?

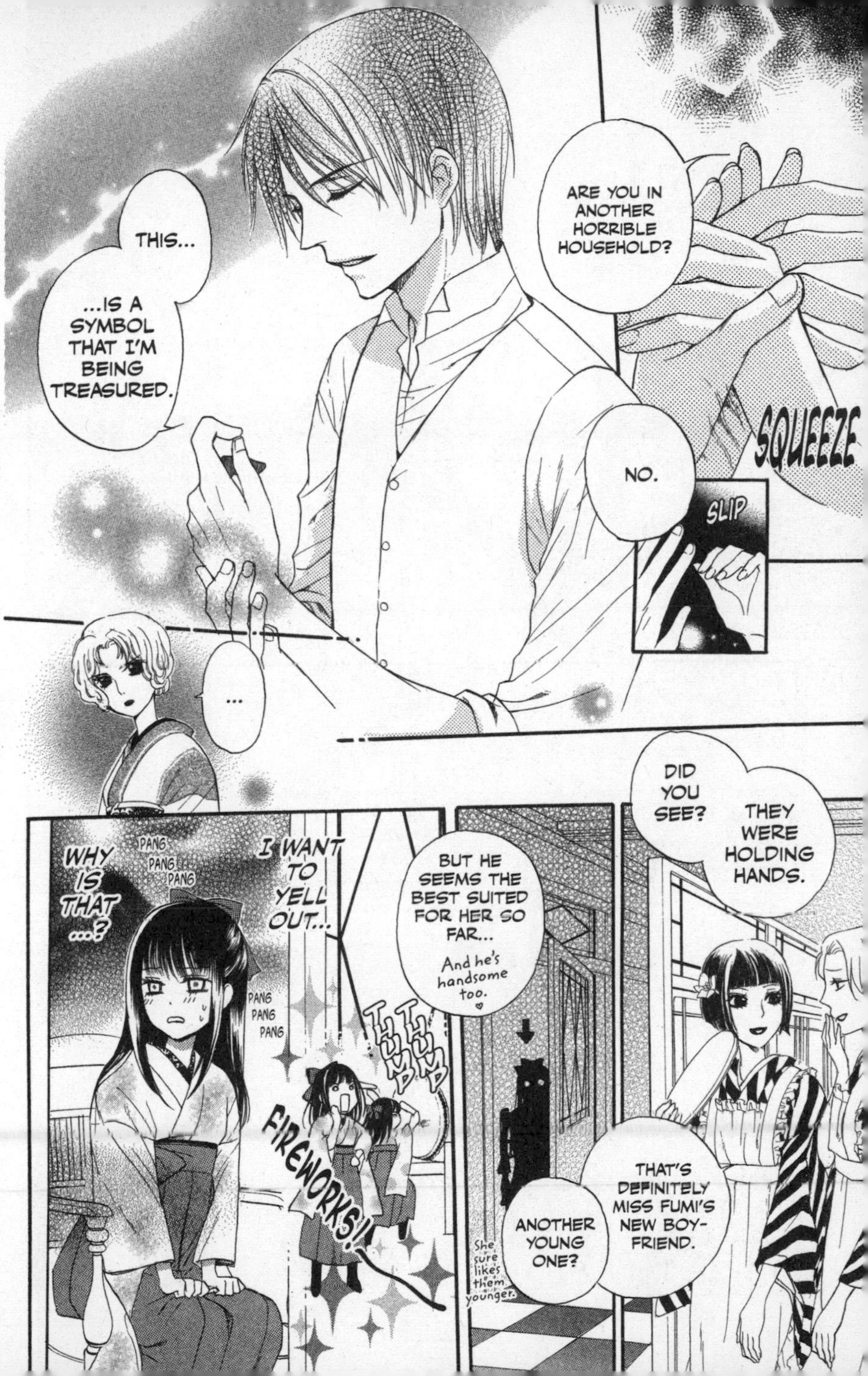
ARE YOU IN ANOTHER HORRIBLE HOUSEHOLD?
SQUEEZE
NO.
SLIP
THIS...
...IS A SYMBOL THAT I'M BEING TREASURED.
...
DID YOU SEE?
THEY WERE HOLDING HANDS.
THAT'S DEFINITELY MISS FUMI'S NEW BOY-FRIEND.
ANOTHER YOUNG ONE?
She sure likes them younger.
BUT HE SEEMS THE BEST SUITED FOR HER SO FAR...
And he's handsome too.
THUMP THUMP
FIREWORKS!!
I WANT TO YELL OUT...
PANG PANG PANG
WHY IS THAT...?
PANG PANG PANG

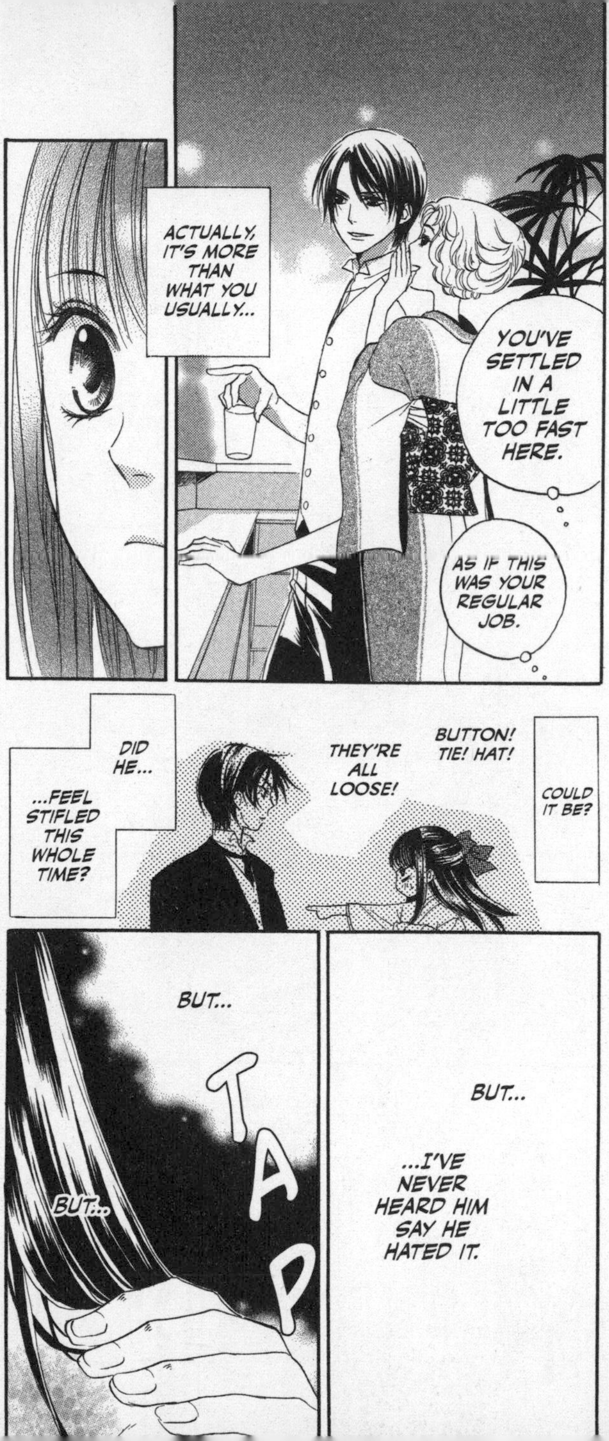
YOU'VE SETTLED IN A LITTLE TOO FAST HERE.
AS IF THIS WAS YOUR REGULAR JOB.
ACTUALLY, IT'S MORE THAN WHAT YOU USUALLY...
COULD IT BE?
BUTTON! TIE! HAT!
THEY'RE ALL LOOSE!
DID HE...
...FEEL STIFLED THIS WHOLE TIME?
BUT...
...I'VE NEVER HEARD HIM SAY HE HATED IT.
BUT...
TAP
BUT...

CHAPTER 4

*At first, this chapter was going to be all about Sayaka and Kazuko making up. But when I brought up this idea, I was asked to rethink it since **The Heiress** is about Sayaka and Narutaki.*

Also, I don't know if it's because there were fewer pages than usual, but I told my editor, "It seems like something's missing." "It's probably because Narutaki wasn't punished this time" is what came back. I think that's it.

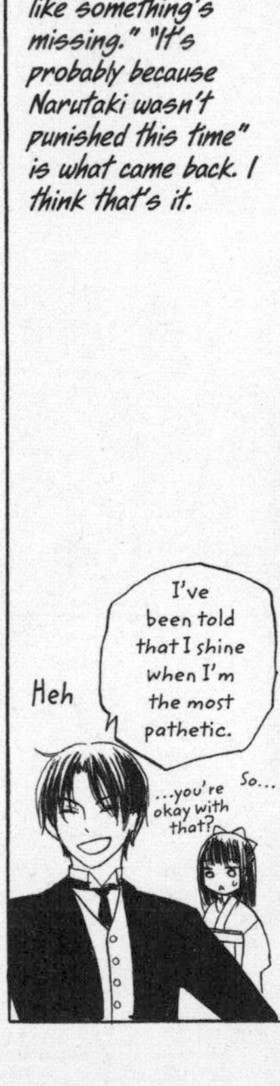
Heh
I've been told that I shine when I'm the most pathetic.
So...
...you're okay with that?

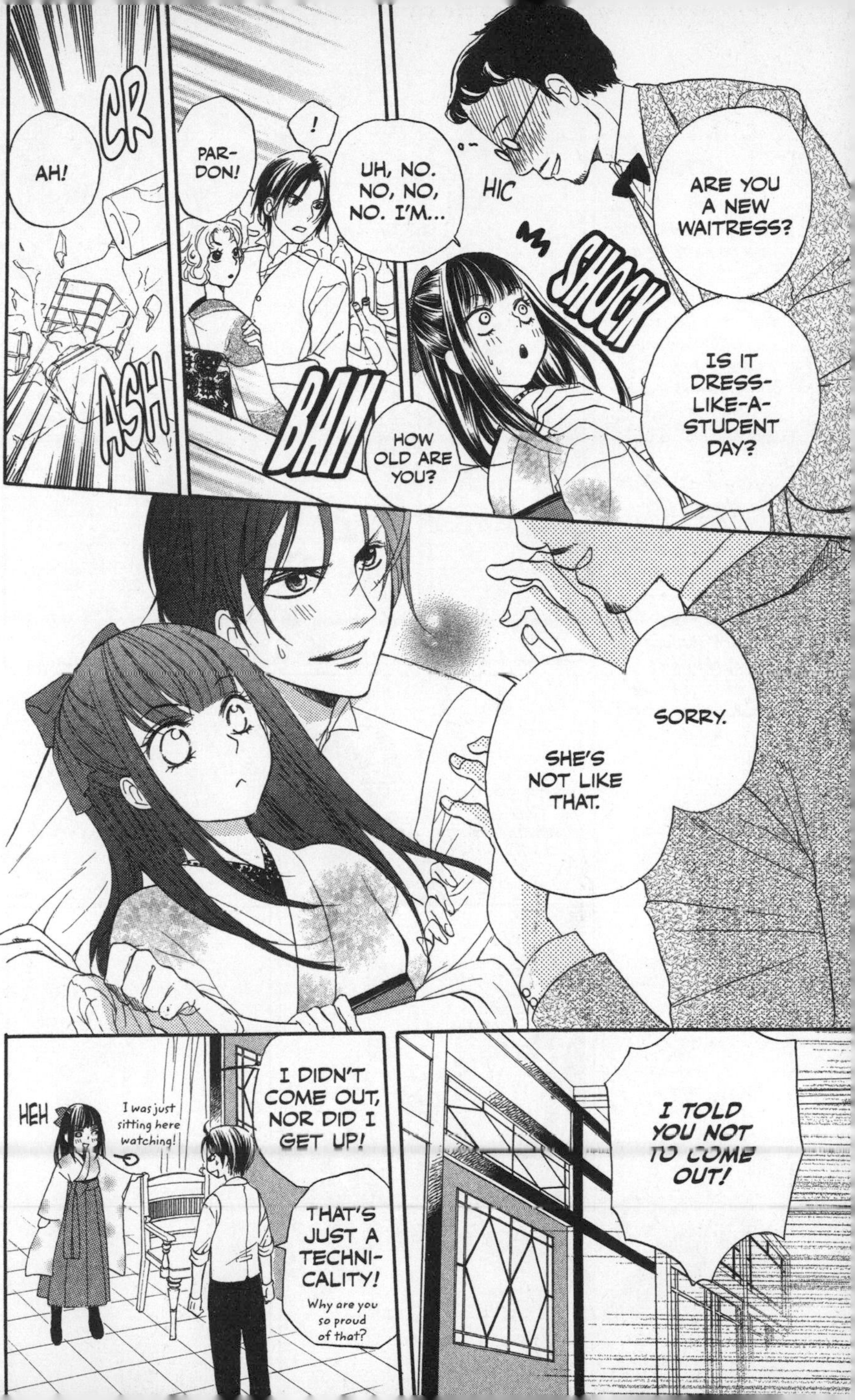
ARE YOU A NEW WAITRESS?
HIC
SHOCK
IS IT DRESS-LIKE-A-STUDENT DAY?
HOW OLD ARE YOU?
UH, NO. NO, NO, NO. I'M...
!
PARDON!
BAM
CR
AH!
ASH
SORRY.
SHE'S NOT LIKE THAT.
I TOLD YOU NOT TO COME OUT!
I DIDN'T COME OUT, NOR DID I GET UP!
I was just sitting here watching!
HEH
THAT'S JUST A TECHNICALITY!
Why are you so proud of that?

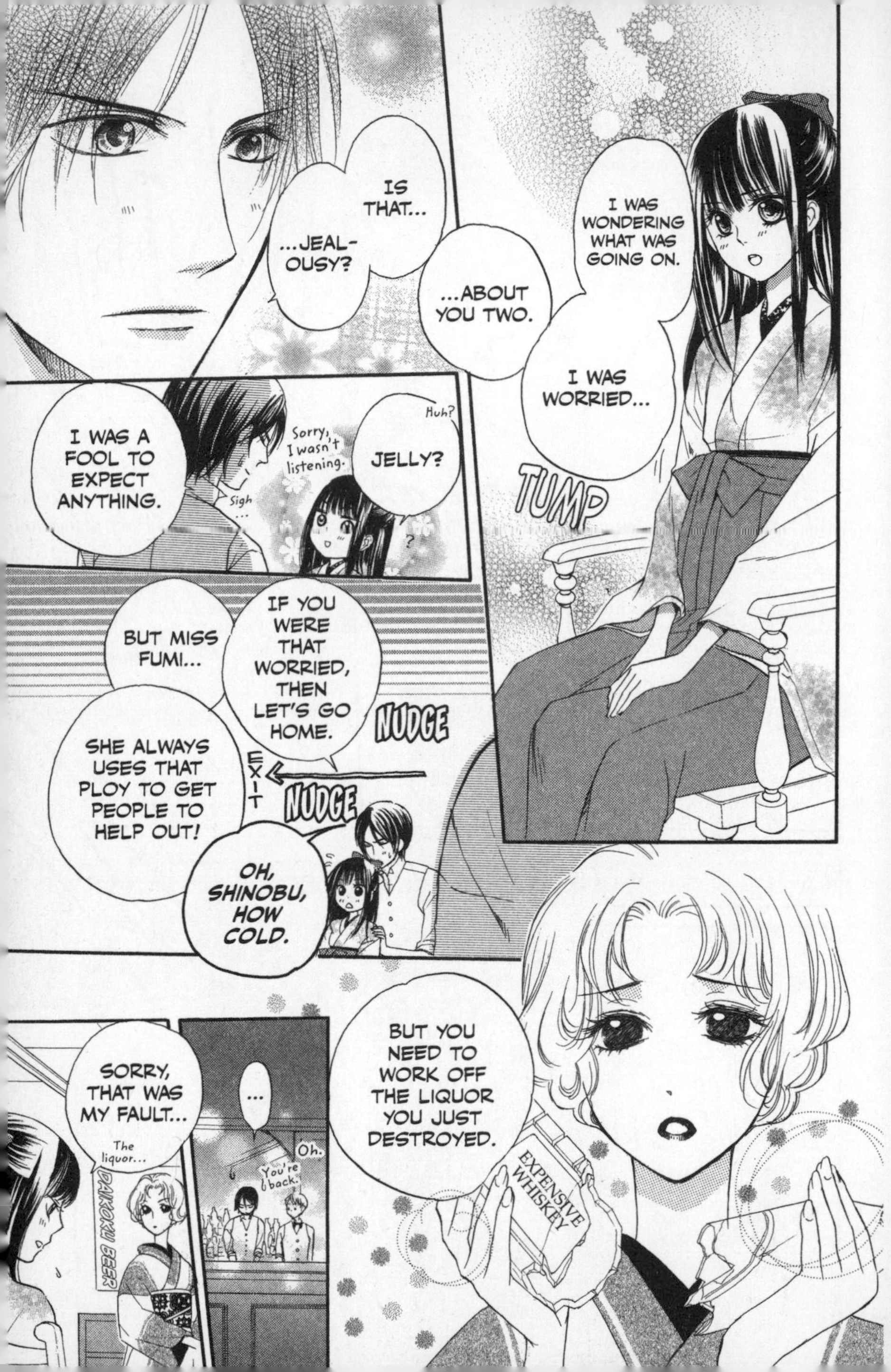
I WAS WONDERING WHAT WAS GOING ON.
...ABOUT YOU TWO.
I WAS WORRIED...
TUMP
IS THAT...
...JEAL-OUSY?
Huh?
JELLY?
Sorry, I wasn't listening.
?
I WAS A FOOL TO EXPECT ANYTHING.
Sigh...
IF YOU WERE THAT WORRIED, THEN LET'S GO HOME.
NUDGE
BUT MISS FUMI...
EXIT
NUDGE
SHE ALWAYS USES THAT PLOY TO GET PEOPLE TO HELP OUT!
OH, SHINOBU, HOW COLD.
BUT YOU NEED TO WORK OFF THE LIQUOR YOU JUST DESTROYED.
EXPENSIVE WHISKEY
...
Oh.
You're back.
SORRY, THAT WAS MY FAULT...
The liquor...
DAIKOKU BEER

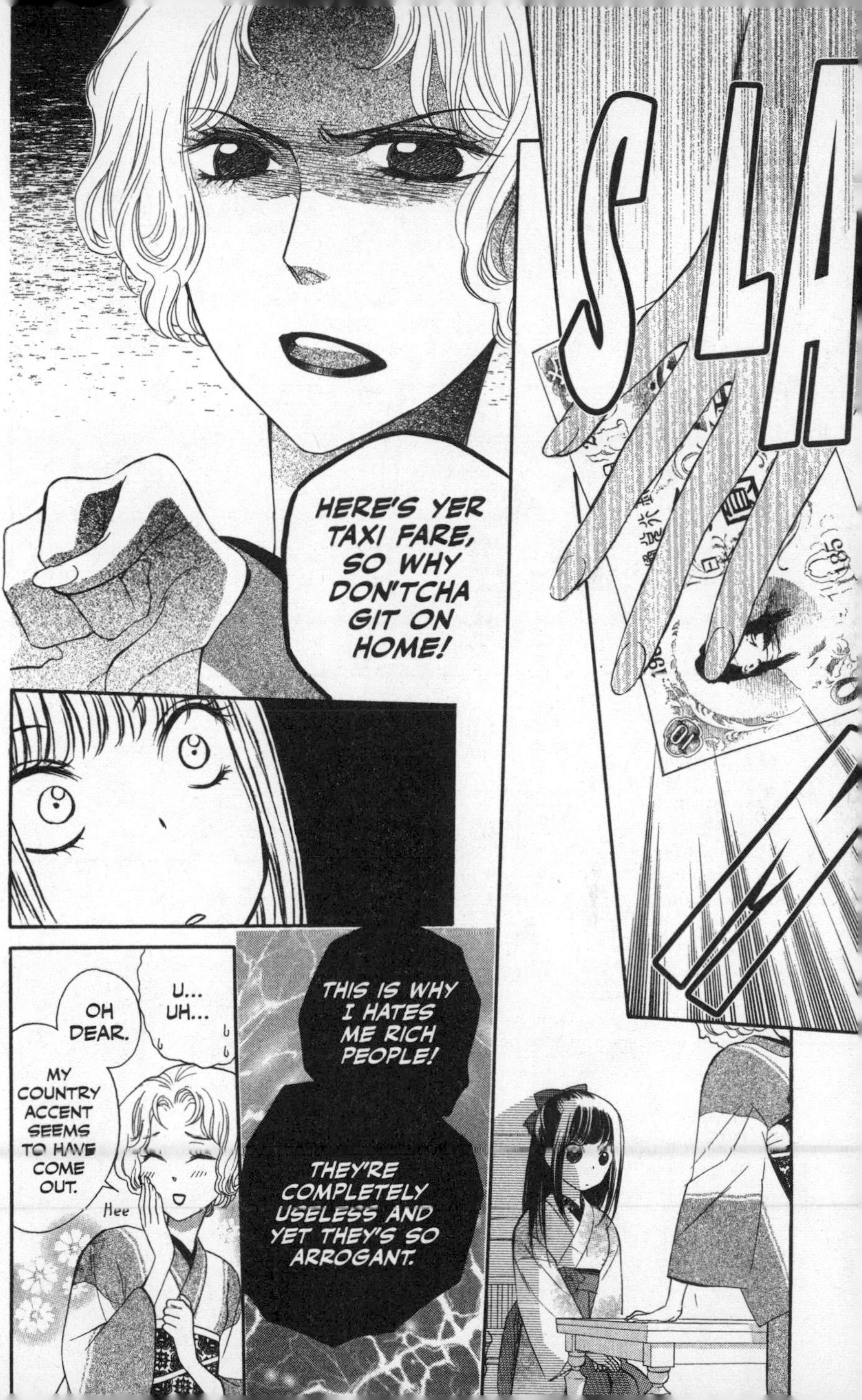
SLAM
HERE'S YER TAXI FARE, SO WHY DON'TCHA GIT ON HOME!
THIS IS WHY I HATES ME RICH PEOPLE!
THEY'RE COMPLETELY USELESS AND YET THEY'S SO ARROGANT.
U... UH...
OH DEAR.
MY COUNTRY ACCENT SEEMS TO HAVE COME OUT.
Hee

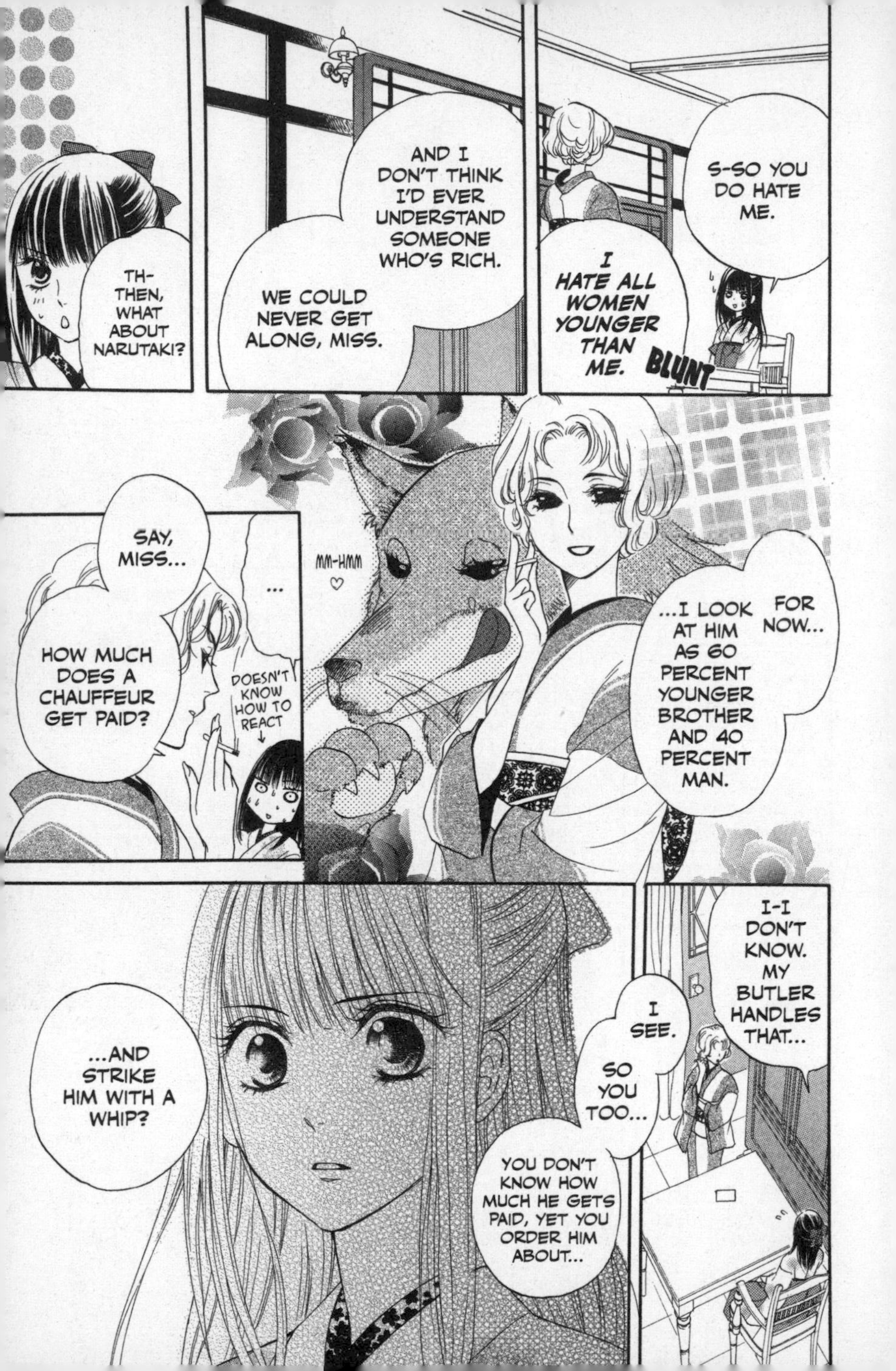
S-SO YOU DO HATE ME.
I HATE ALL WOMEN YOUNGER THAN ME.
BLUNT
AND I DON'T THINK I'D EVER UNDERSTAND SOMEONE WHO'S RICH.
WE COULD NEVER GET ALONG, MISS.
TH-THEN, WHAT ABOUT NARUTAKI?
FOR NOW...
...I LOOK AT HIM AS 60 PERCENT YOUNGER BROTHER AND 40 PERCENT MAN.
MM-HMM ♡
SAY, MISS...
...
HOW MUCH DOES A CHAUFFEUR GET PAID?
DOESN'T KNOW HOW TO REACT ↓
I-I DON'T KNOW. MY BUTLER HANDLES THAT...
I SEE.
SO YOU TOO...
YOU DON'T KNOW HOW MUCH HE GETS PAID, YET YOU ORDER HIM ABOUT...
...AND STRIKE HIM WITH A WHIP?

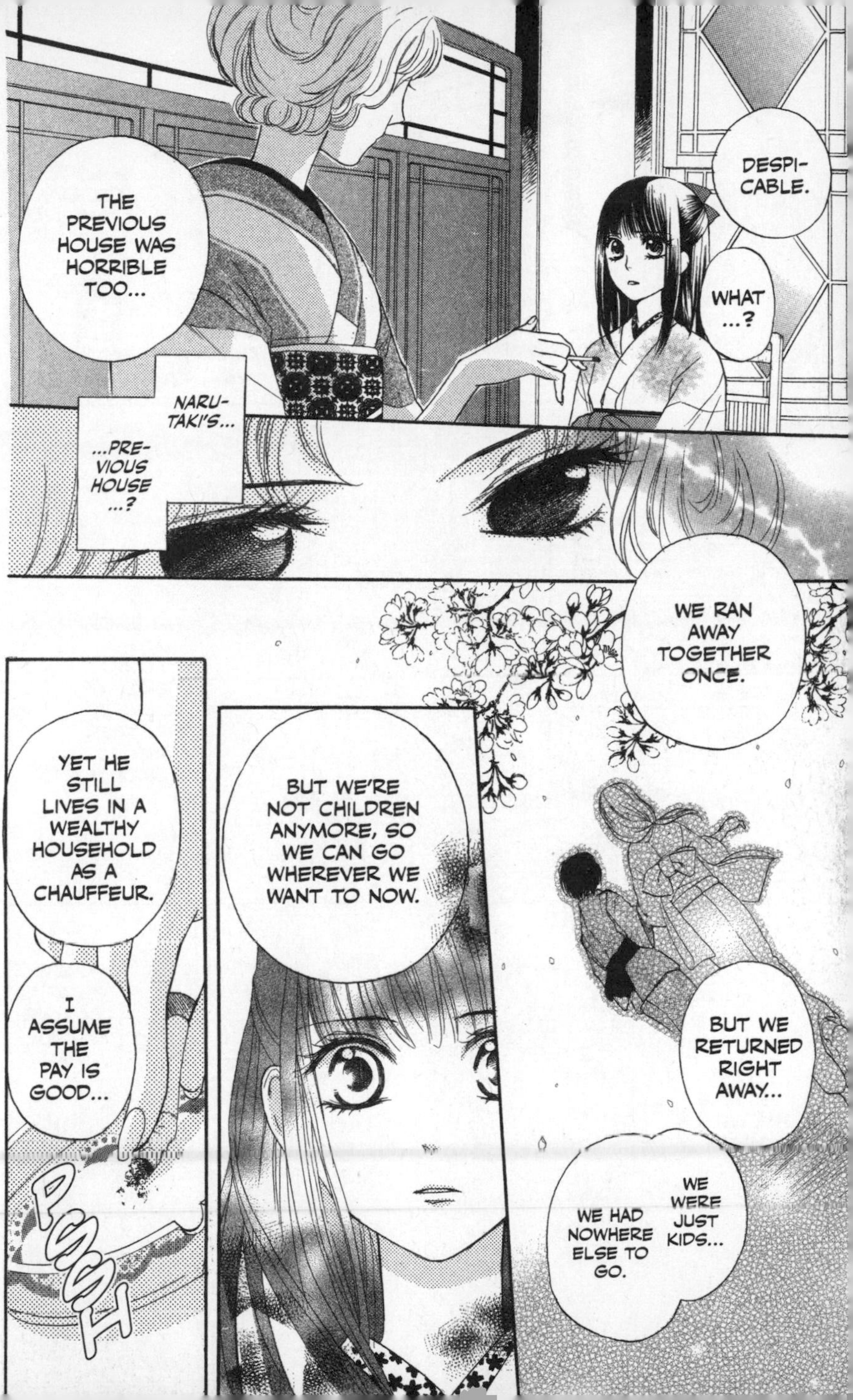
DESPI-CABLE.
WHAT...?
THE PREVIOUS HOUSE WAS HORRIBLE TOO...
NARU-TAKI'S...
...PRE-VIOUS HOUSE...?
WE RAN AWAY TOGETHER ONCE.
BUT WE RETURNED RIGHT AWAY...
WE WERE JUST KIDS...
WE HAD NOWHERE ELSE TO GO.
BUT WE'RE NOT CHILDREN ANYMORE, SO WE CAN GO WHEREVER WE WANT TO NOW.
YET HE STILL LIVES IN A WEALTHY HOUSEHOLD AS A CHAUFFEUR.
I ASSUME THE PAY IS GOOD...
PSSSH

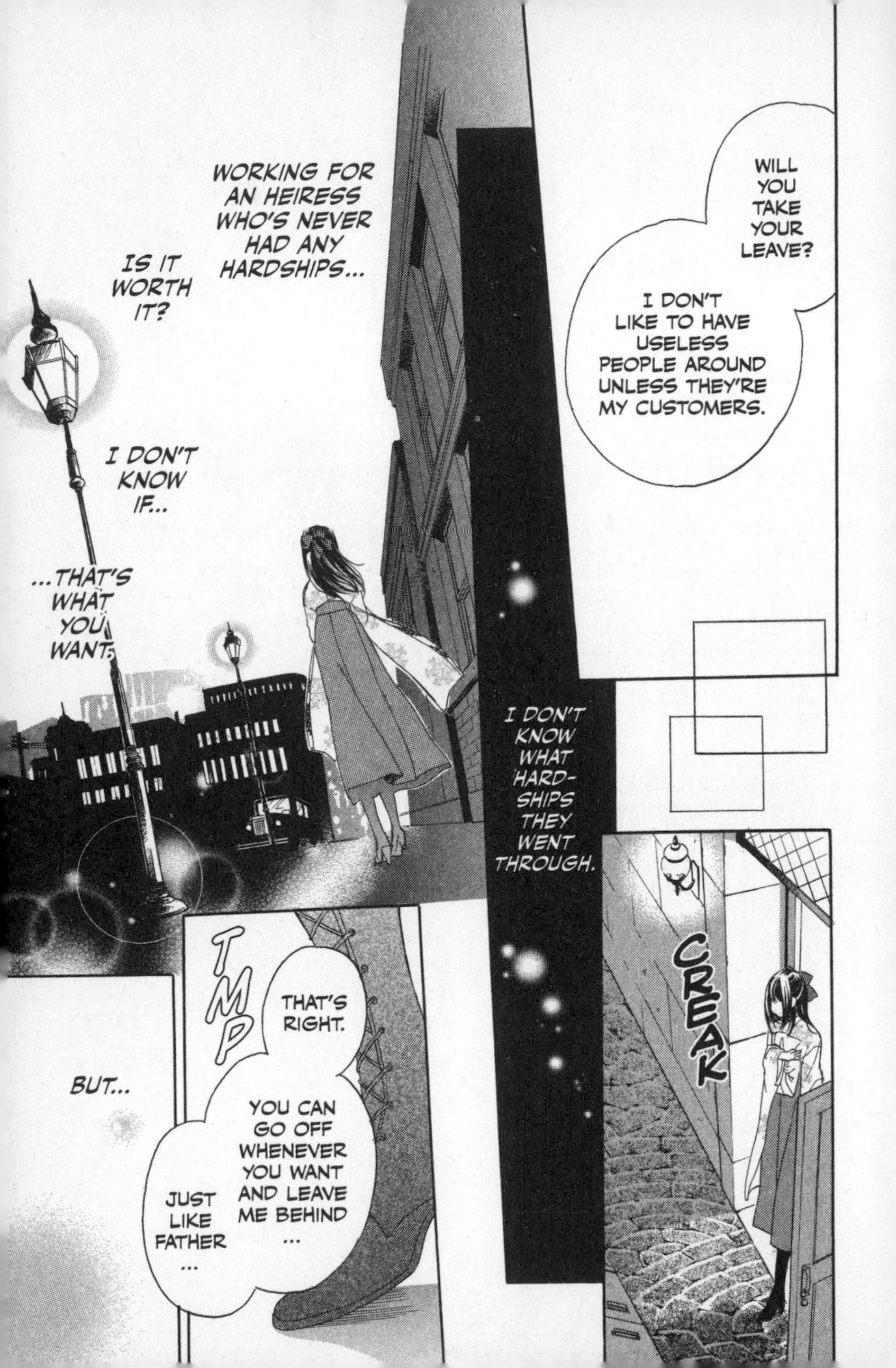
WILL YOU TAKE YOUR LEAVE?
I DON'T LIKE TO HAVE USELESS PEOPLE AROUND UNLESS THEY'RE MY CUSTOMERS.
WORKING FOR AN HEIRESS WHO'S NEVER HAD ANY HARDSHIPS...
IS IT WORTH IT?
I DON'T KNOW IF...
...THAT'S WHAT YOU WANT.
I DON'T KNOW WHAT HARD-SHIPS THEY WENT THROUGH.
CREAK
TMP
THAT'S RIGHT.
YOU CAN GO OFF WHENEVER YOU WANT AND LEAVE ME BEHIND ...
JUST LIKE FATHER ...
BUT...

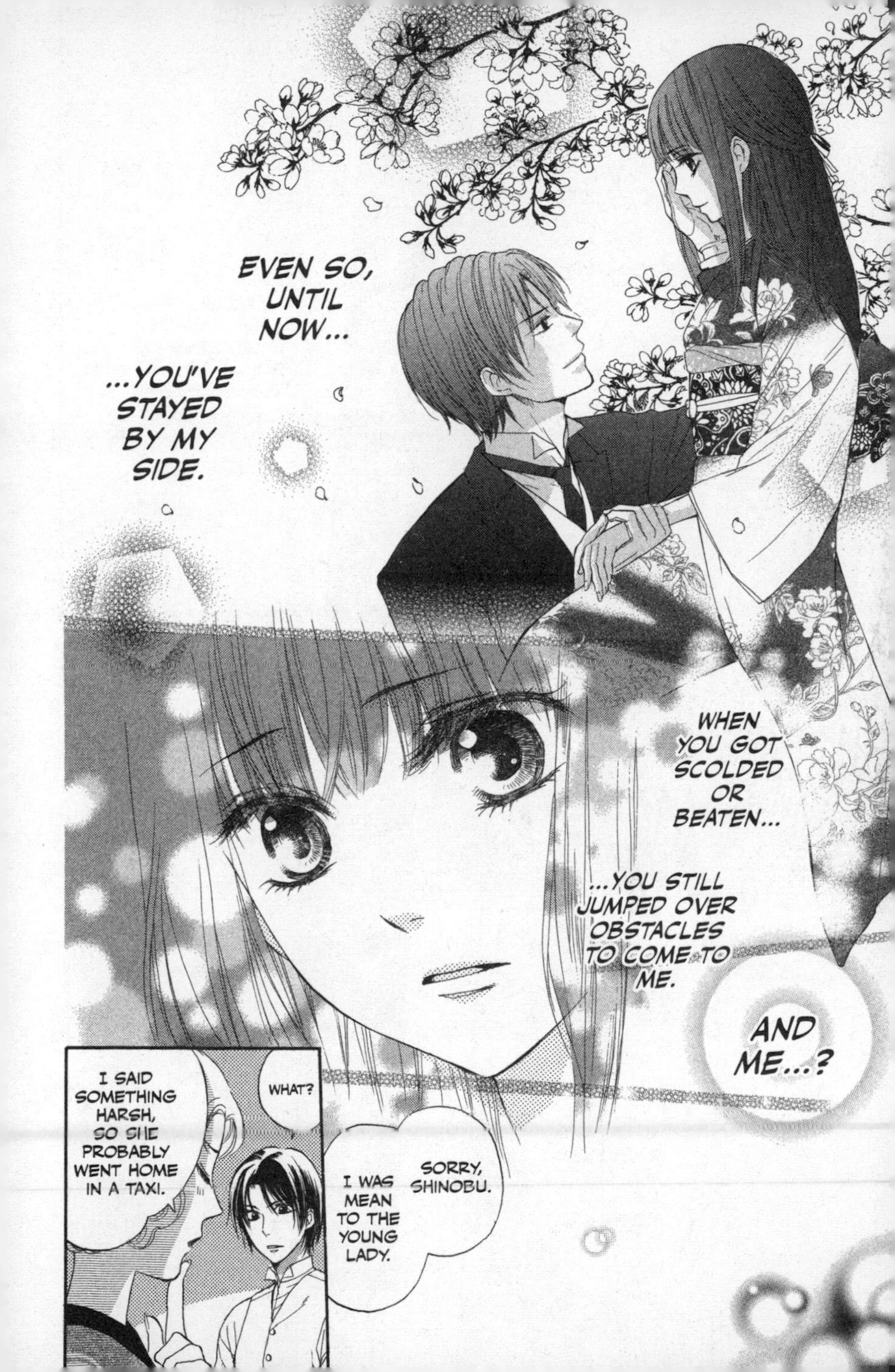
EVEN SO, UNTIL NOW...
...YOU'VE STAYED BY MY SIDE.
WHEN YOU GOT SCOLDED OR BEATEN...
...YOU STILL JUMPED OVER OBSTACLES TO COME TO ME.
AND ME...?
SORRY, SHINOBU. I WAS MEAN TO THE YOUNG LADY.
WHAT?
I SAID SOMETHING HARSH, SO SHE PROBABLY WENT HOME IN A TAXI.

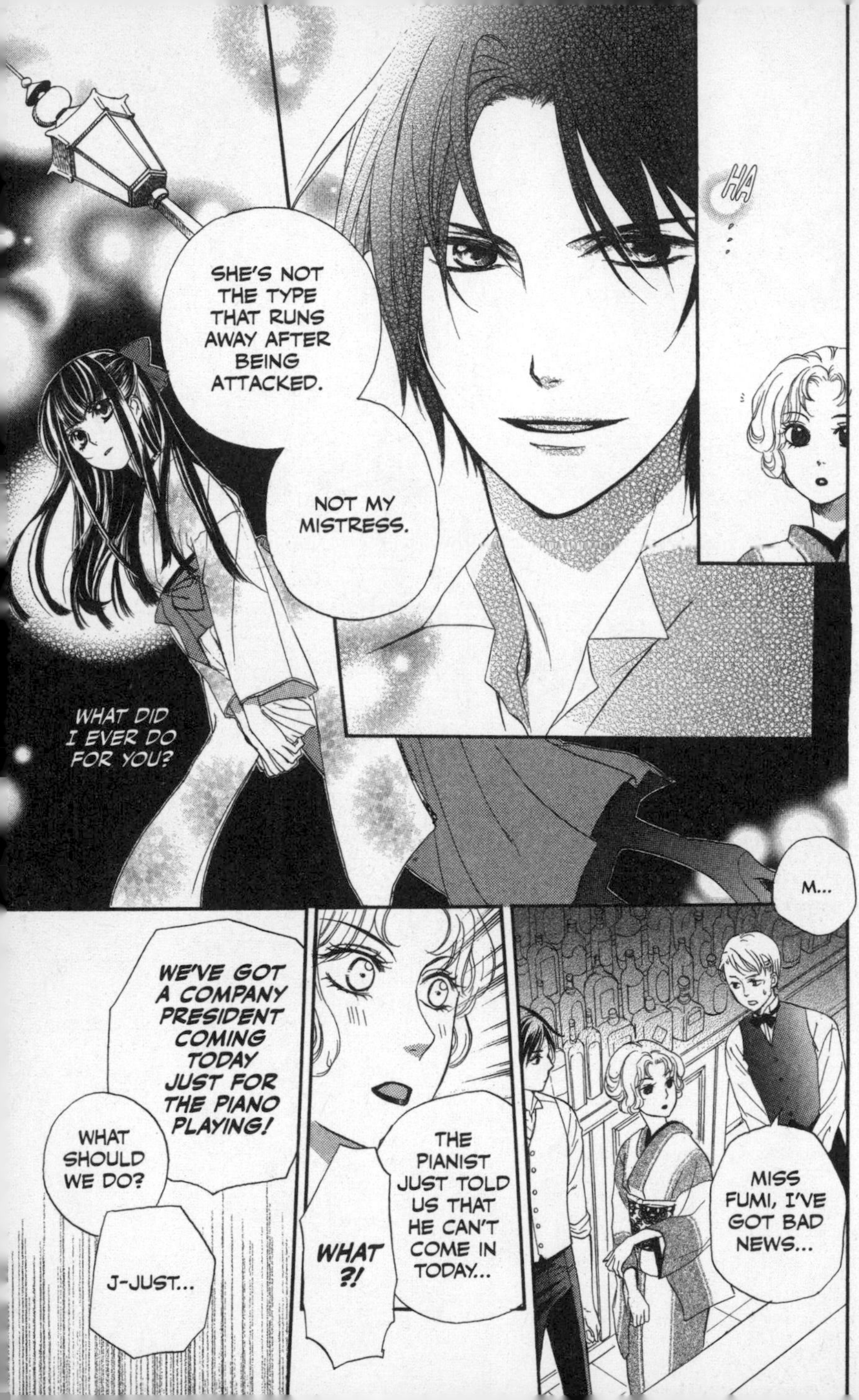
HA
SHE'S NOT THE TYPE THAT RUNS AWAY AFTER BEING ATTACKED.
NOT MY MISTRESS.
WHAT DID I EVER DO FOR YOU?
M...
MISS FUMI, I'VE GOT BAD NEWS...
THE PIANIST JUST TOLD US THAT HE CAN'T COME IN TODAY...
WHAT?!
WE'VE GOT A COMPANY PRESIDENT COMING TODAY JUST FOR THE PIANO PLAYING!
WHAT SHOULD WE DO?
J-JUST...

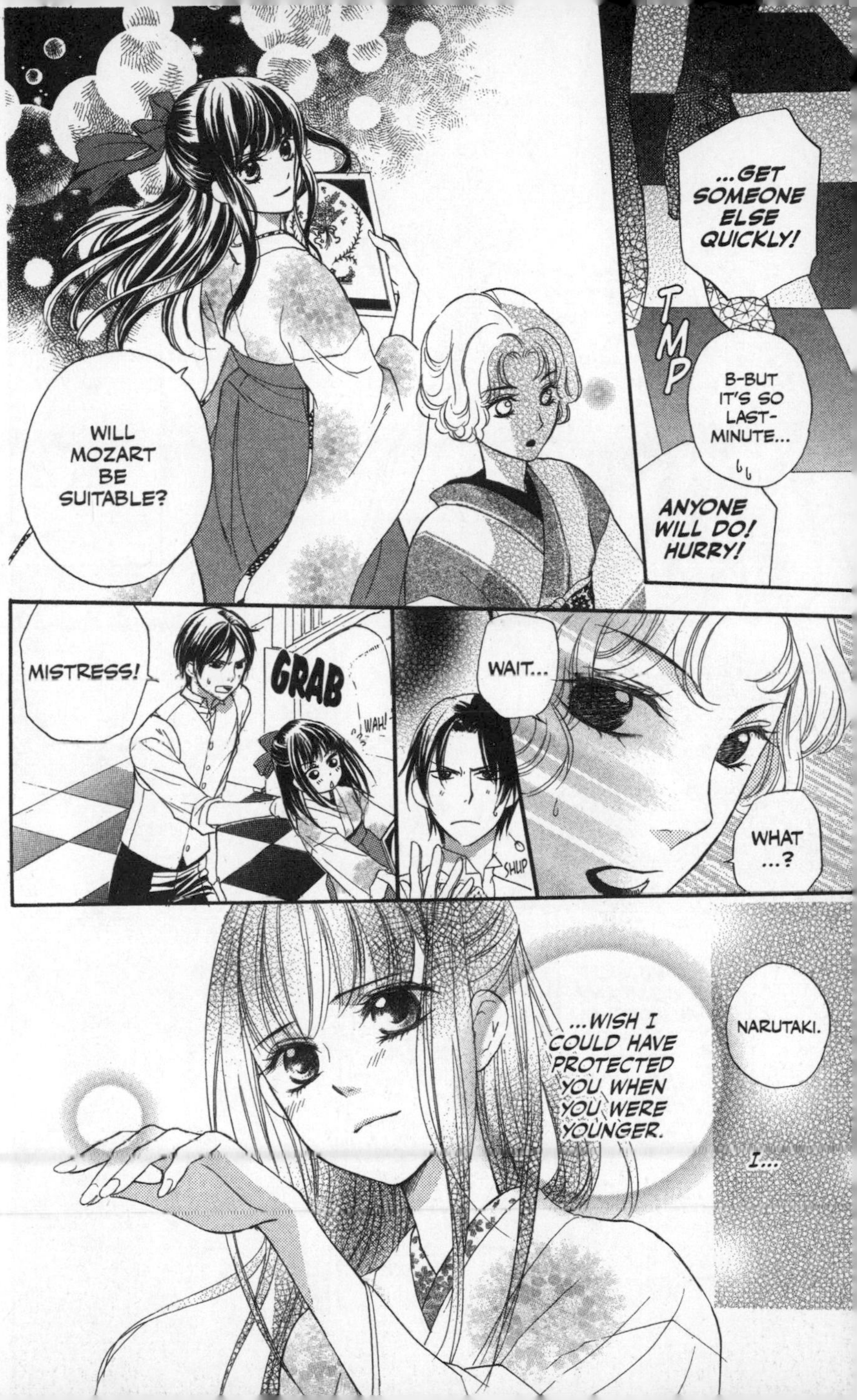
...GET SOMEONE ELSE QUICKLY!
TMP
B-BUT IT'S SO LAST-MINUTE...
ANYONE WILL DO! HURRY!
WILL MOZART BE SUITABLE?
WAIT...
WHAT ...?
SHUP
GRAB
MISTRESS!
WAH!
NARUTAKI.
I...
...WISH I COULD HAVE PROTECTED YOU WHEN YOU WERE YOUNGER.

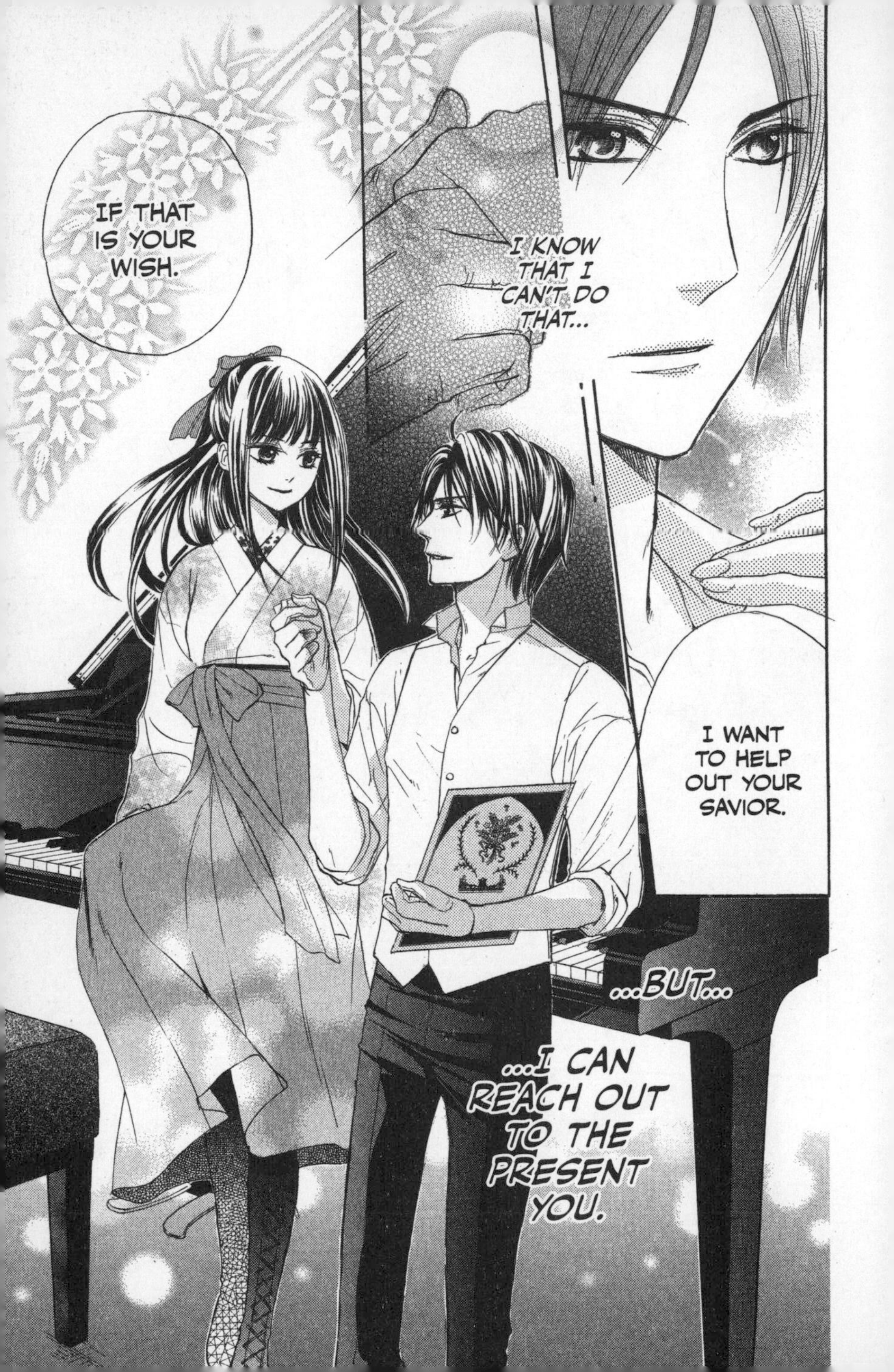
I WANT TO HELP OUT YOUR SAVIOR.
IF THAT IS YOUR WISH.
I KNOW THAT I CAN'T DO THAT...
...BUT...
...I CAN REACH OUT TO THE PRESENT YOU.

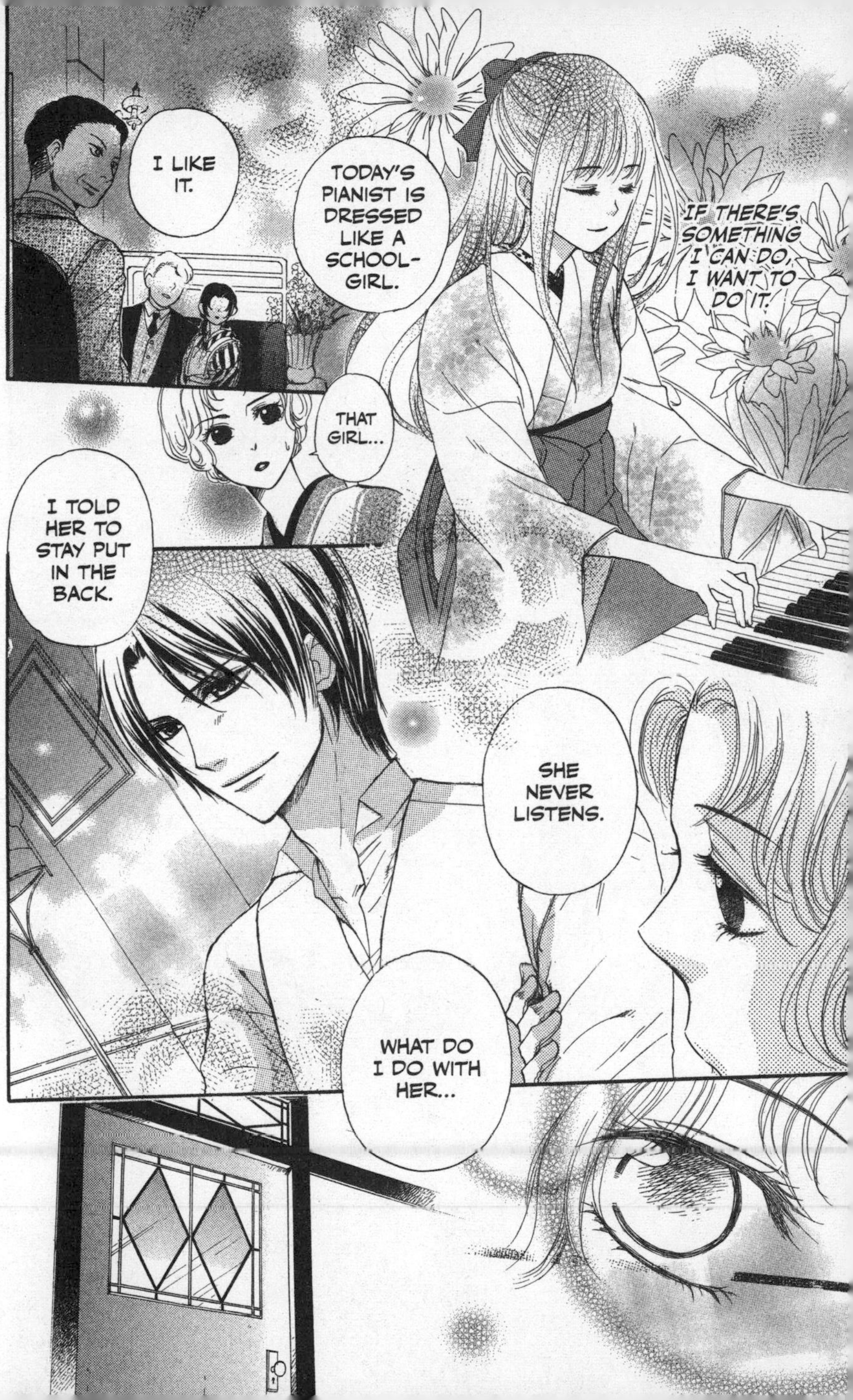
IF THERE'S SOMETHING I CAN DO, I WANT TO DO IT.
TODAY'S PIANIST IS DRESSED LIKE A SCHOOL-GIRL.
I LIKE IT.
THAT GIRL...
I TOLD HER TO STAY PUT IN THE BACK.
SHE NEVER LISTENS.
WHAT DO I DO WITH HER...

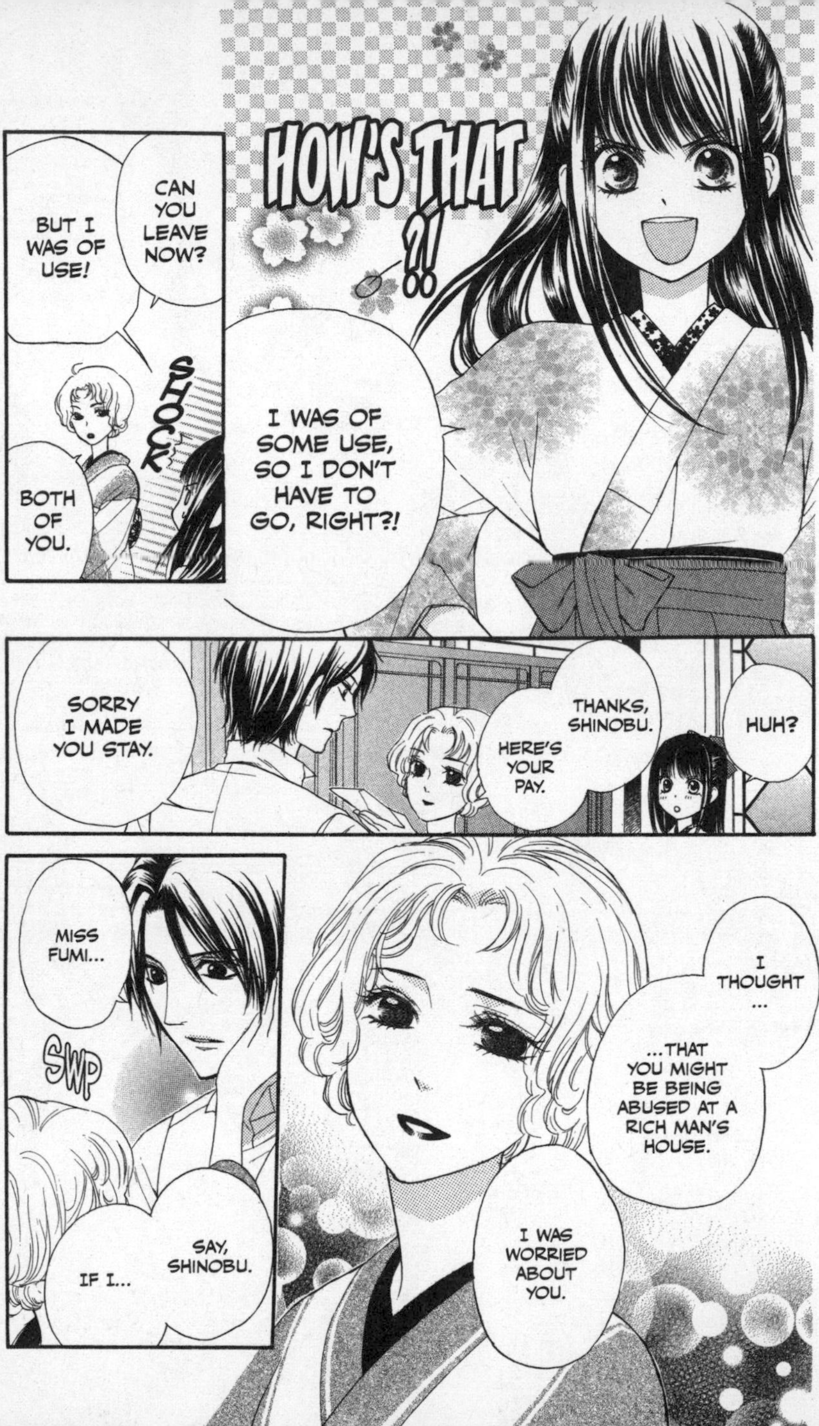

HOW'S THAT ?!
I WAS OF SOME USE, SO I DON'T HAVE TO GO, RIGHT?!
CAN YOU LEAVE NOW?
BUT I WAS OF USE!
SHOCK
BOTH OF YOU.
HUH?
THANKS, SHINOBU.
HERE'S YOUR PAY.
SORRY I MADE YOU STAY.
I THOUGHT...
...THAT YOU MIGHT BE BEING ABUSED AT A RICH MAN'S HOUSE.
I WAS WORRIED ABOUT YOU.
MISS FUMI...
SWP
SAY, SHINOBU.
IF I...

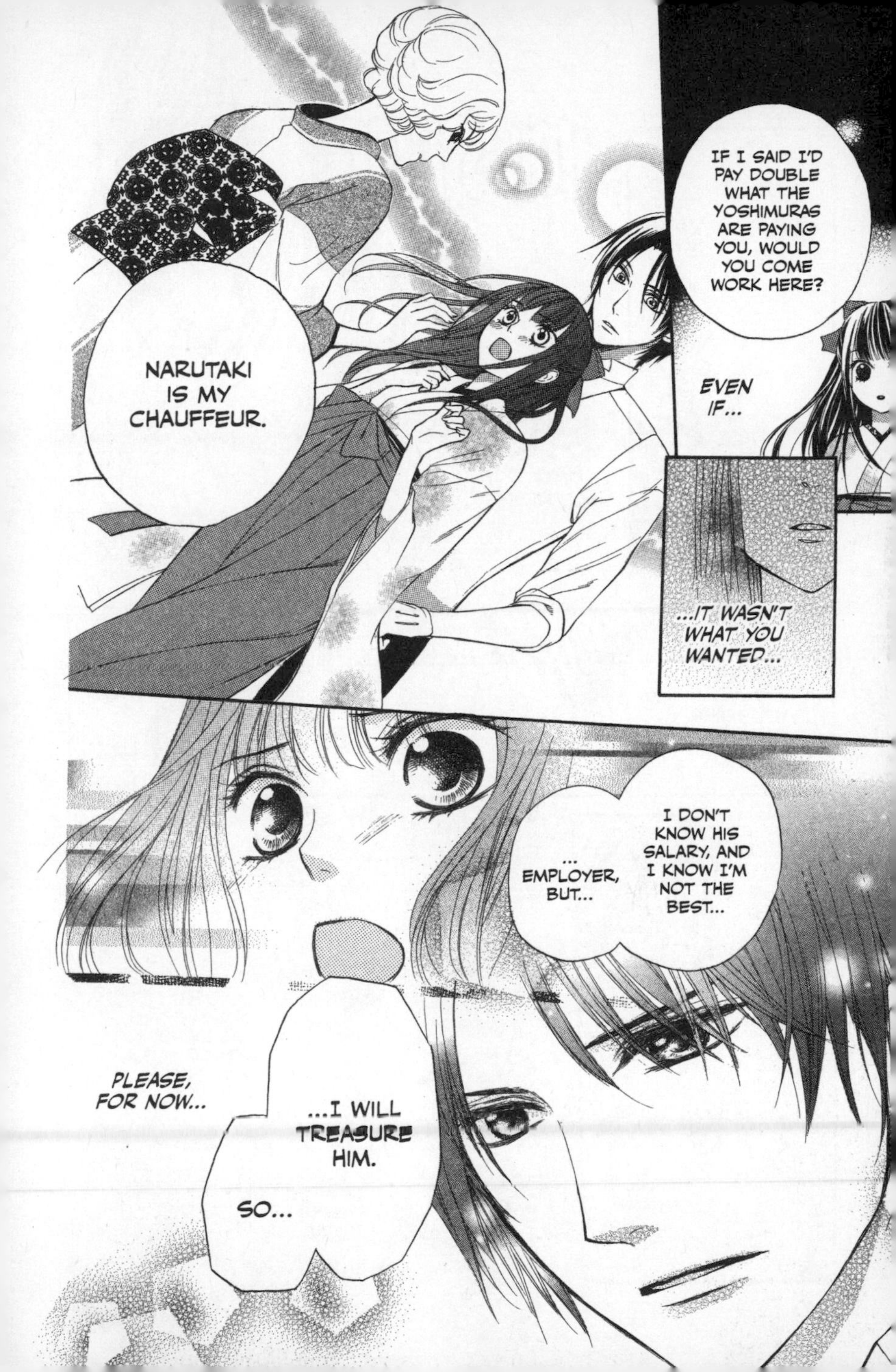

IF I SAID I'D PAY DOUBLE WHAT THE YOSHIMURAS ARE PAYING YOU, WOULD YOU COME WORK HERE?
EVEN IF...
...IT WASN'T WHAT YOU WANTED...
NARUTAKI IS MY CHAUFFEUR.
I DON'T KNOW HIS SALARY, AND I KNOW I'M NOT THE BEST...
... EMPLOYER, BUT...
...I WILL TREASURE HIM.
SO...
PLEASE, FOR NOW...

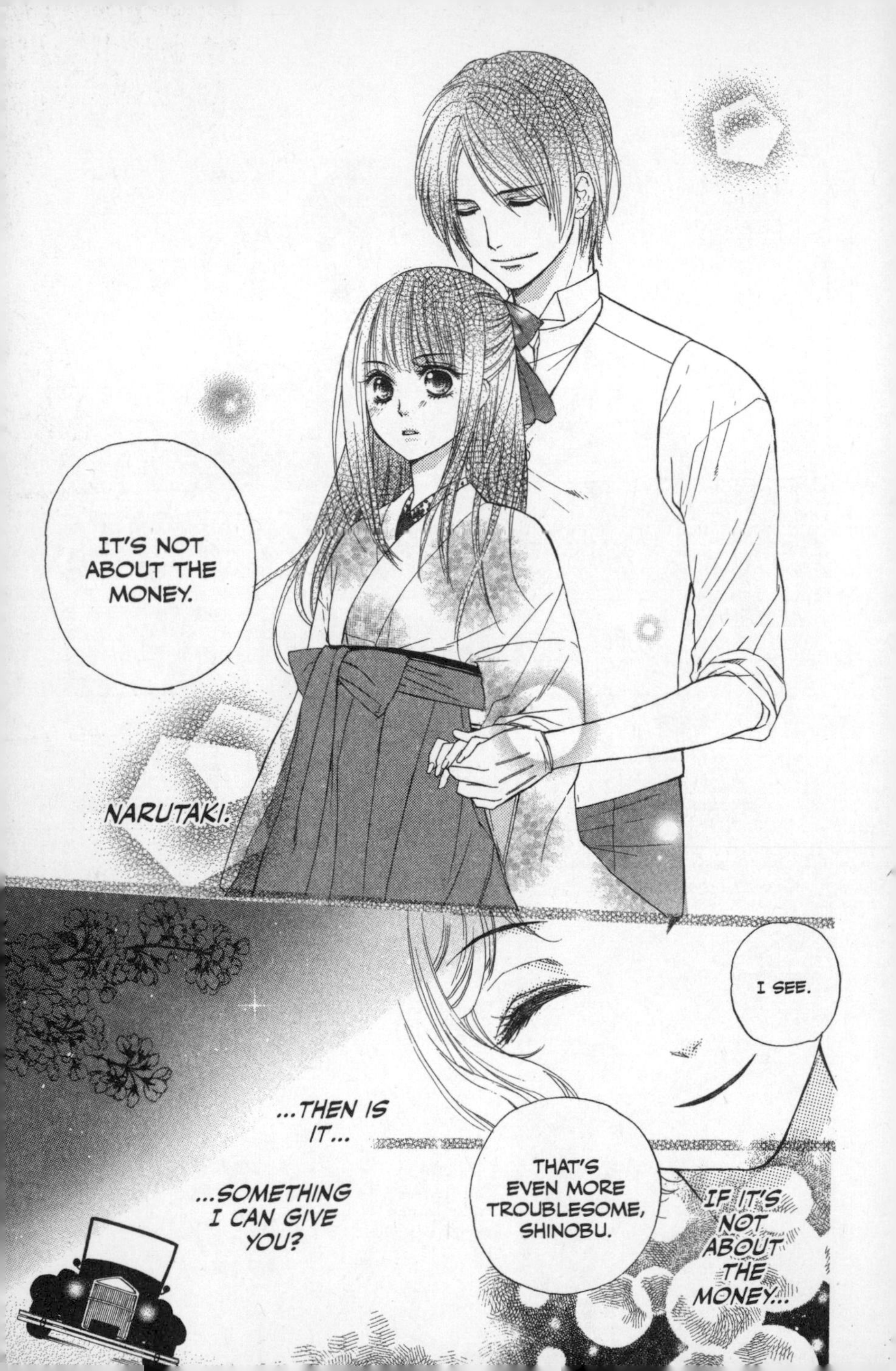
IT'S NOT ABOUT THE MONEY.
NARUTAKI.
I SEE.
IF IT'S NOT ABOUT THE MONEY...
THAT'S EVEN MORE TROUBLESOME, SHINOBU.
...THEN IS IT...
...SOMETHING I CAN GIVE YOU?

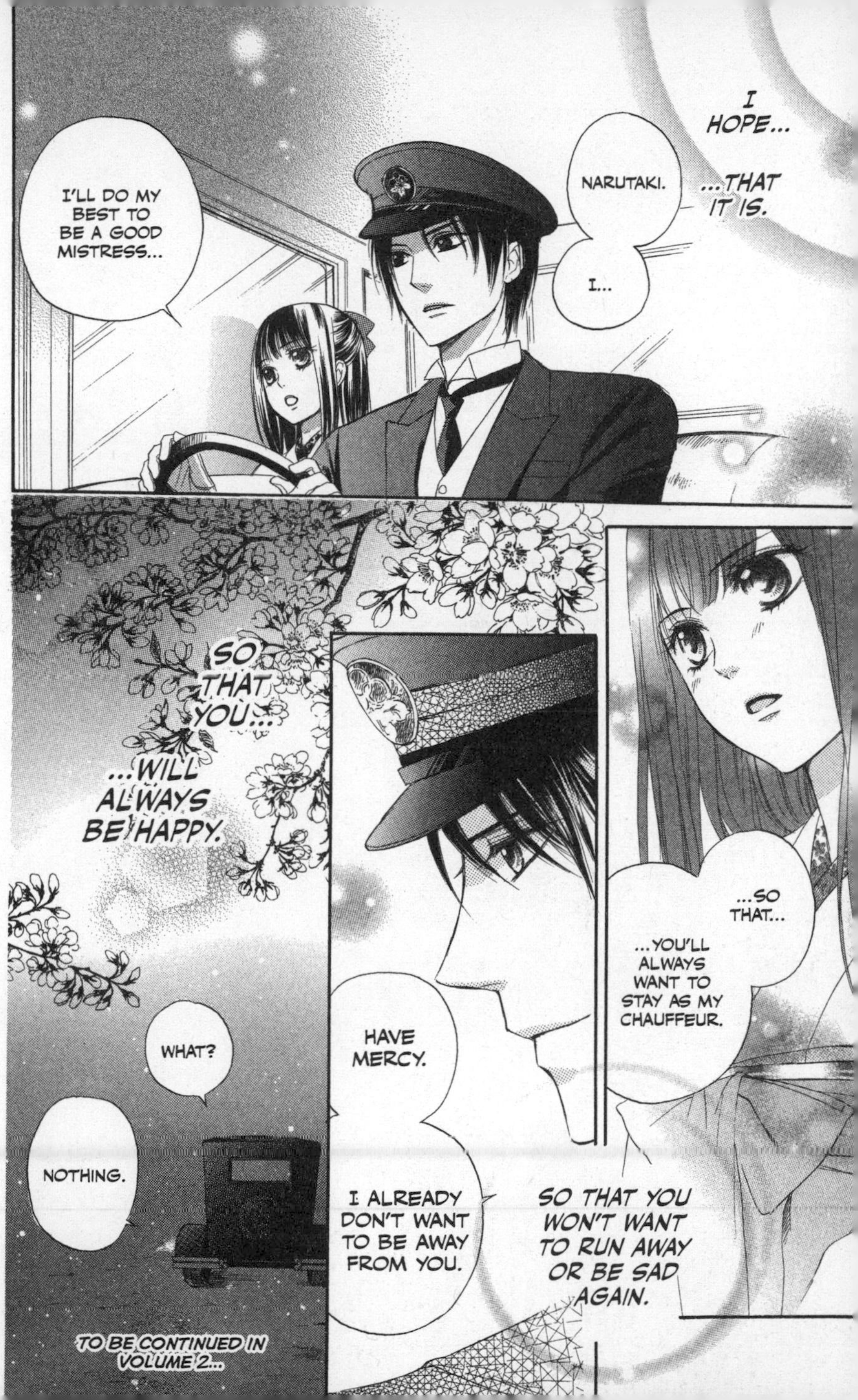
I HOPE...
...THAT IT IS.
NARUTAKI.
I...
I'LL DO MY BEST TO BE A GOOD MISTRESS...
...SO THAT...
...YOU'LL ALWAYS WANT TO STAY AS MY CHAUFFEUR.
SO THAT YOU WON'T WANT TO RUN AWAY OR BE SAD AGAIN.
HAVE MERCY.
I ALREADY DON'T WANT TO BE AWAY FROM YOU.
SO THAT YOU...
...WILL ALWAYS BE HAPPY.
WHAT?
NOTHING.
TO BE CONTINUED IN VOLUME 2...

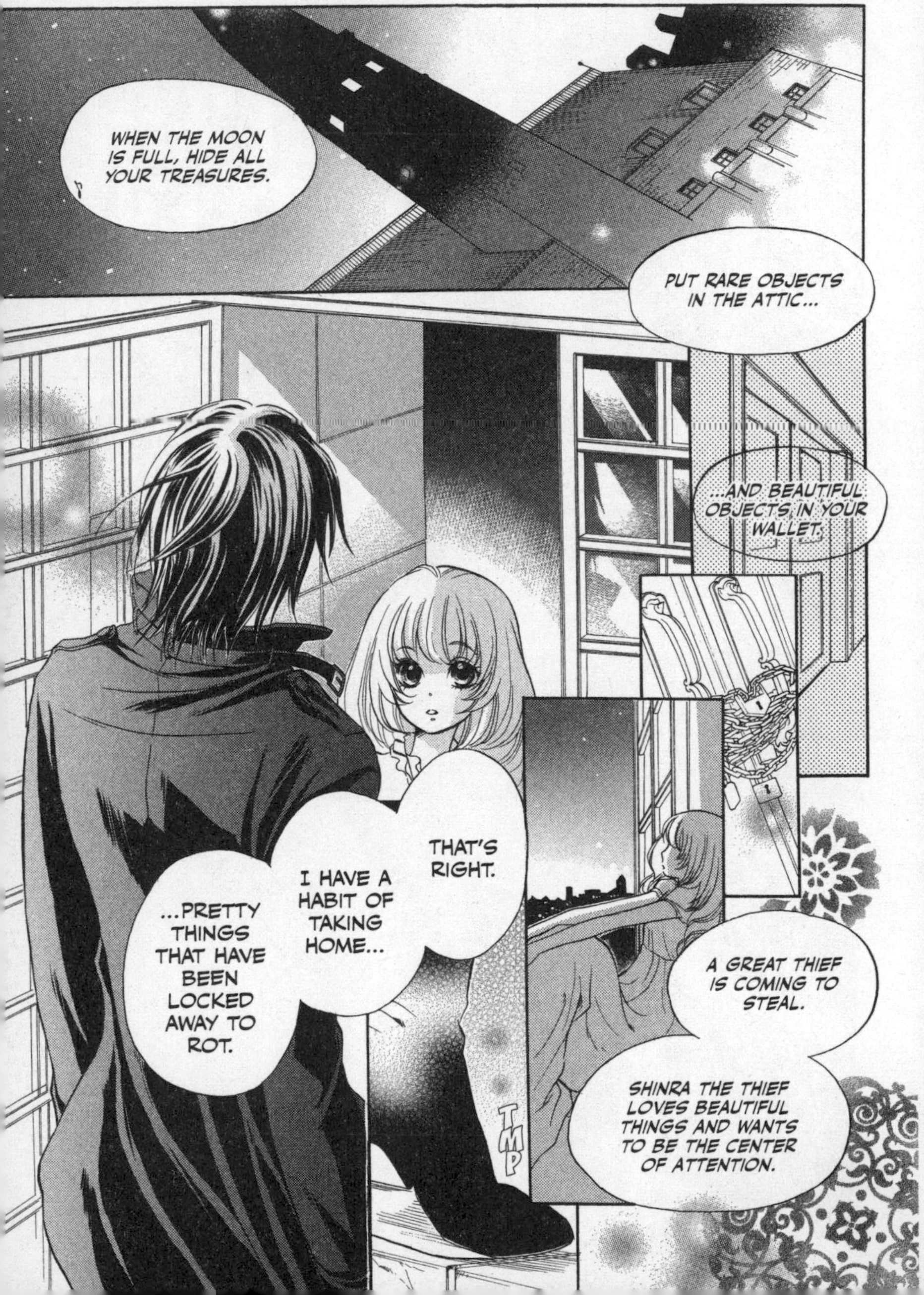
WHEN THE MOON IS FULL, HIDE ALL YOUR TREASURES.
PUT RARE OBJECTS IN THE ATTIC...
...AND BEAUTIFUL OBJECTS IN YOUR WALLET.
A GREAT THIEF IS COMING TO STEAL.
SHINRA THE THIEF LOVES BEAUTIFUL THINGS AND WANTS TO BE THE CENTER OF ATTENTION.
THAT'S RIGHT.
I HAVE A HABIT OF TAKING HOME...
...PRETTY THINGS THAT HAVE BEEN LOCKED AWAY TO ROT.
TMP

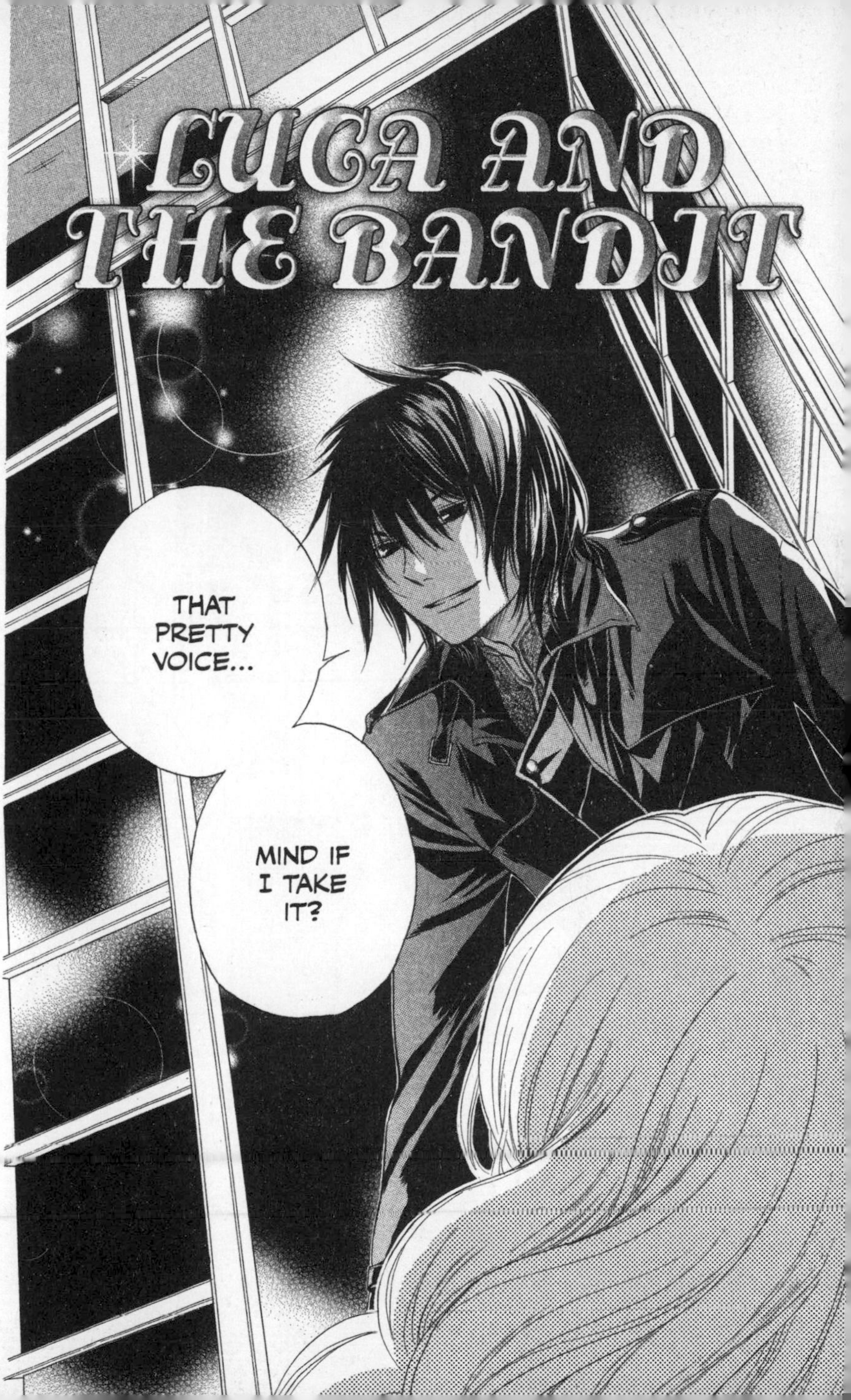
LUCA AND THE BANDIT
THAT PRETTY VOICE...
MIND IF I TAKE IT?

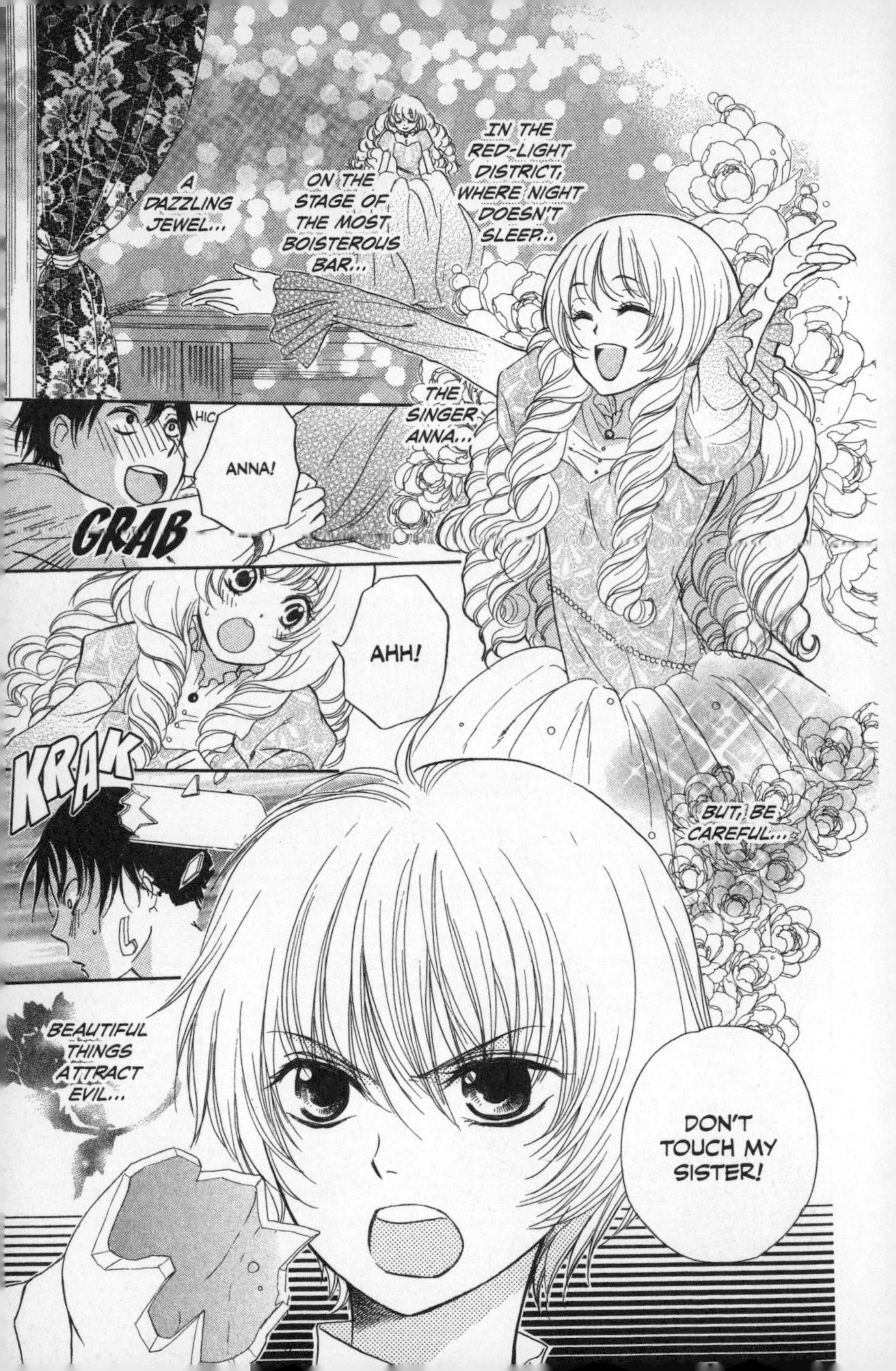
IN THE RED-LIGHT DISTRICT, WHERE NIGHT DOESN'T SLEEP...
ON THE STAGE OF THE MOST BOISTEROUS BAR...
A DAZZLING JEWEL...
THE SINGER ANNA...
HIC
ANNA!
GRAB
AHH!
KRAK
BUT, BE CAREFUL...
BEAUTIFUL THINGS ATTRACT EVIL...
DON'T TOUCH MY SISTER!

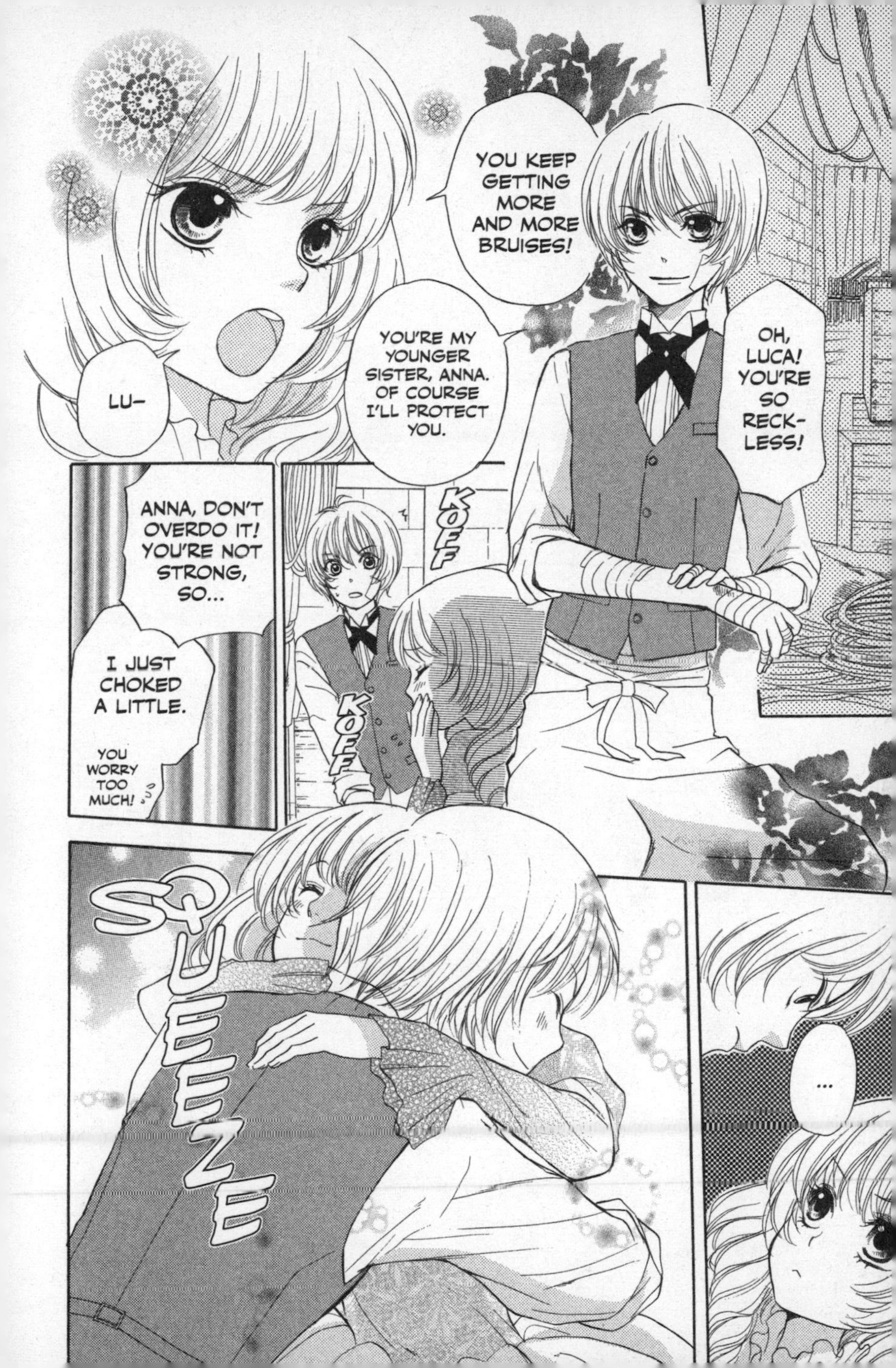

OH, LUCA! YOU'RE SO RECK-LESS!
YOU KEEP GETTING MORE AND MORE BRUISES!
YOU'RE MY YOUNGER SISTER, ANNA. OF COURSE I'LL PROTECT YOU.
LU-
KOFF
KOFF
ANNA, DON'T OVERDO IT! YOU'RE NOT STRONG, SO...
I JUST CHOKED A LITTLE.
YOU WORRY TOO MUCH!
...
SQUEEZE

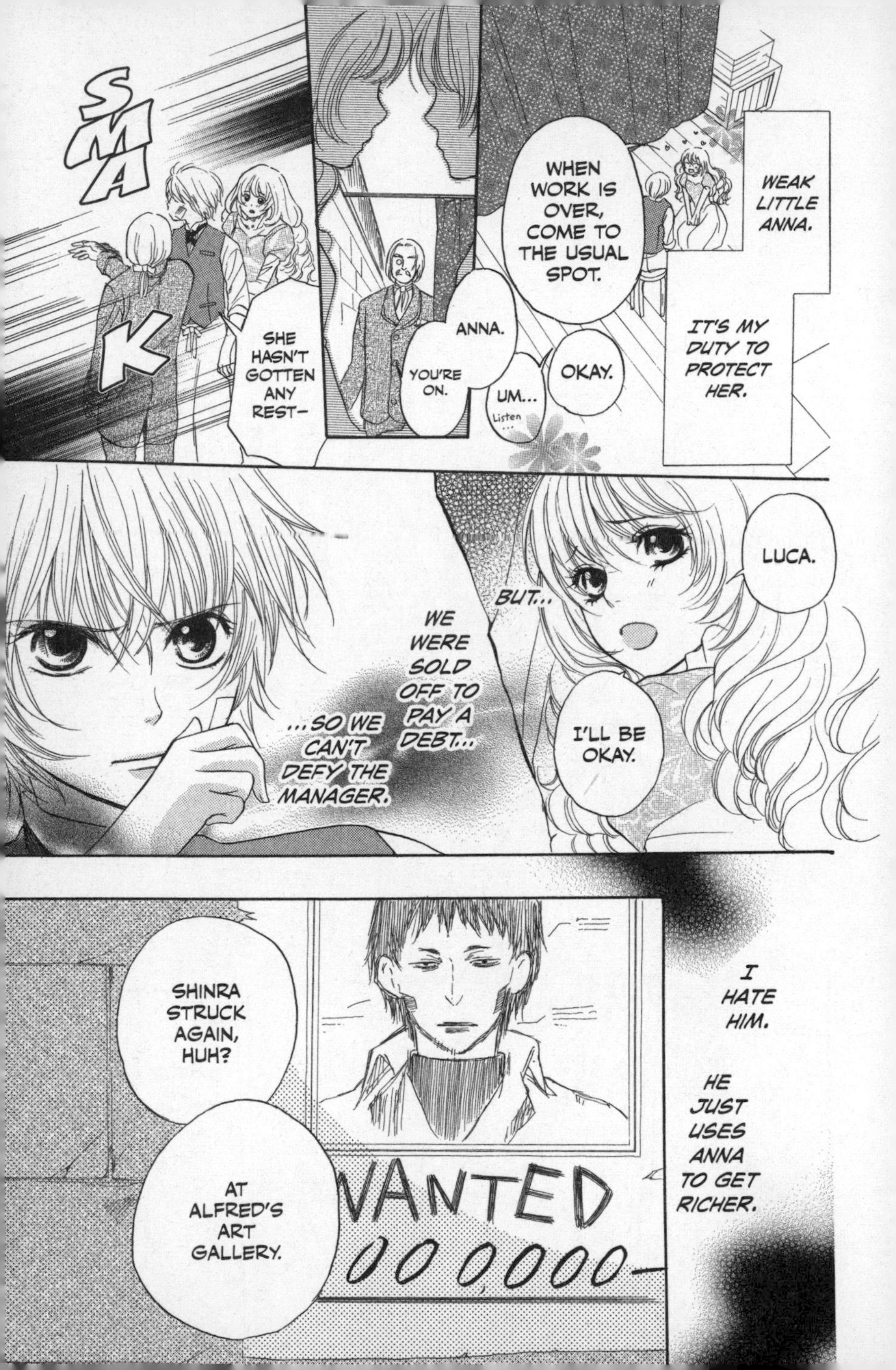
WEAK LITTLE ANNA.
WHEN WORK IS OVER, COME TO THE USUAL SPOT.
IT'S MY DUTY TO PROTECT HER.
OKAY.
UM... Listen...
ANNA.
YOU'RE ON.
SMACK
SHE HASN'T GOTTEN ANY REST—
LUCA.
BUT...
I'LL BE OKAY.
WE WERE SOLD OFF TO PAY A DEBT...
...SO WE CAN'T DEFY THE MANAGER.
I HATE HIM.
HE JUST USES ANNA TO GET RICHER.
SHINRA STRUCK AGAIN, HUH?
AT ALFRED'S ART GALLERY.

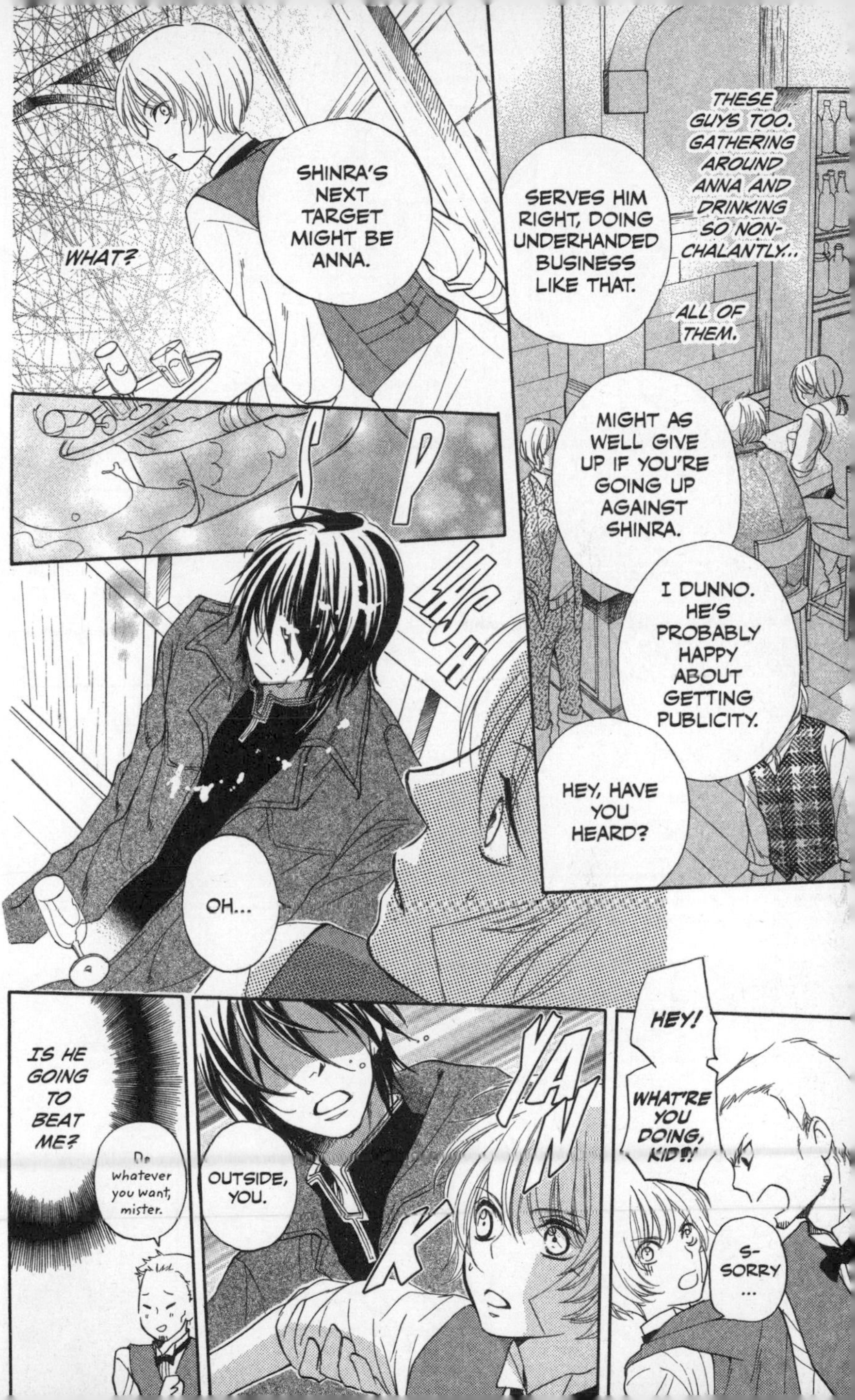
THESE GUYS TOO. GATHERING AROUND ANNA AND DRINKING SO NON-CHALANTLY...
ALL OF THEM.
SERVES HIM RIGHT, DOING UNDERHANDED BUSINESS LIKE THAT.
MIGHT AS WELL GIVE UP IF YOU'RE GOING UP AGAINST SHINRA.
I DUNNO. HE'S PROBABLY HAPPY ABOUT GETTING PUBLICITY.
HEY, HAVE YOU HEARD?
SHINRA'S NEXT TARGET MIGHT BE ANNA.
WHAT?
SPLASH
OH...
HEY!
WHAT'RE YOU DOING, KID?!
S-SORRY...
YANK
OUTSIDE, YOU.
Do whatever you want, mister.
IS HE GOING TO BEAT ME?

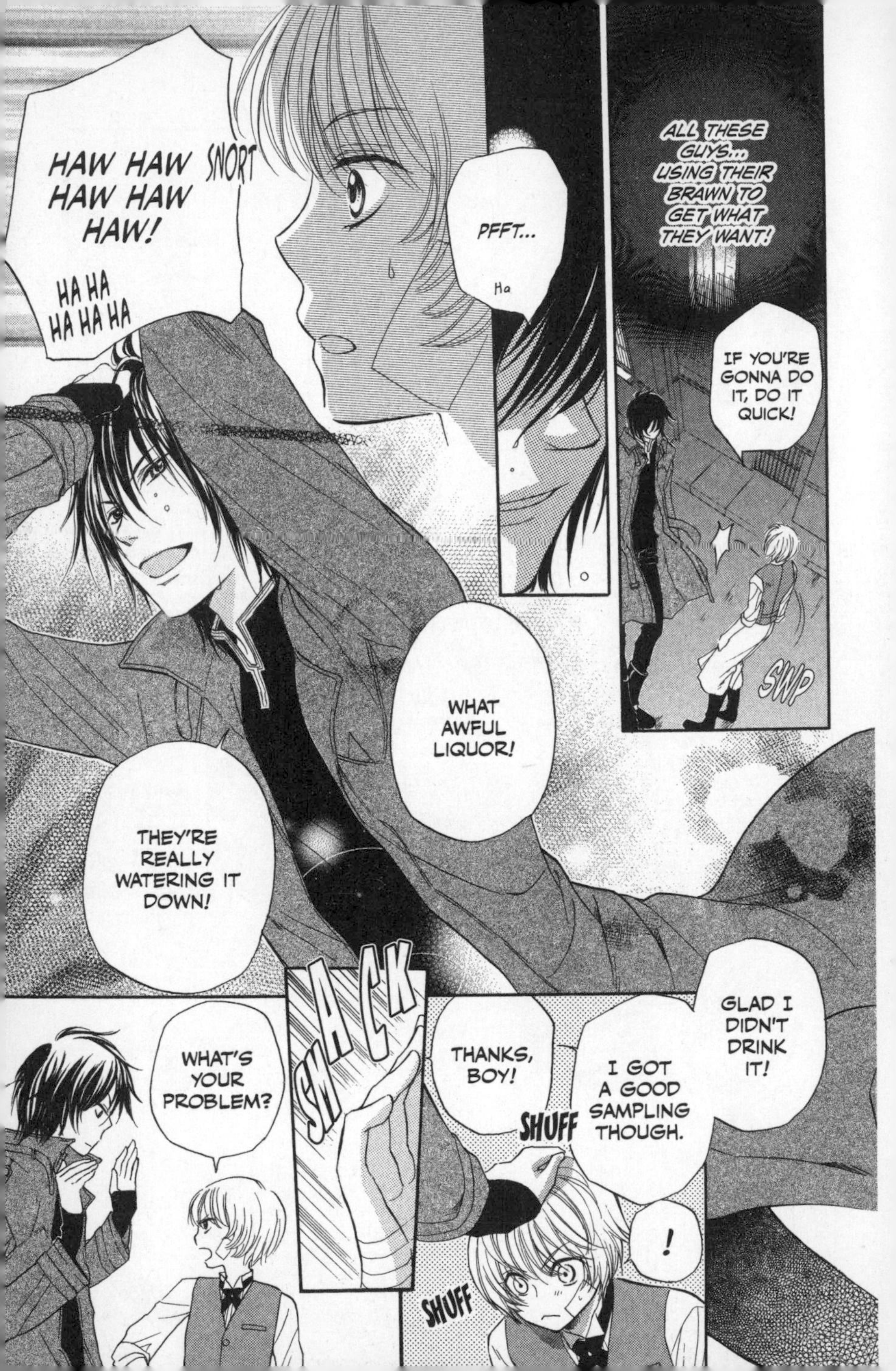
ALL THESE GUYS... USING THEIR BRAWN TO GET WHAT THEY WANT!
IF YOU'RE GONNA DO IT, DO IT QUICK!
SWP
PFFT...
Ha
HAW HAW SNORT HAW HAW HAW!
HA HA HA HA HA
WHAT AWFUL LIQUOR!
THEY'RE REALLY WATERING IT DOWN!
GLAD I DIDN'T DRINK IT!
I GOT A GOOD SAMPLING THOUGH.
THANKS, BOY!
SHUFF
!
SHUFF
SMACK
WHAT'S YOUR PROBLEM?

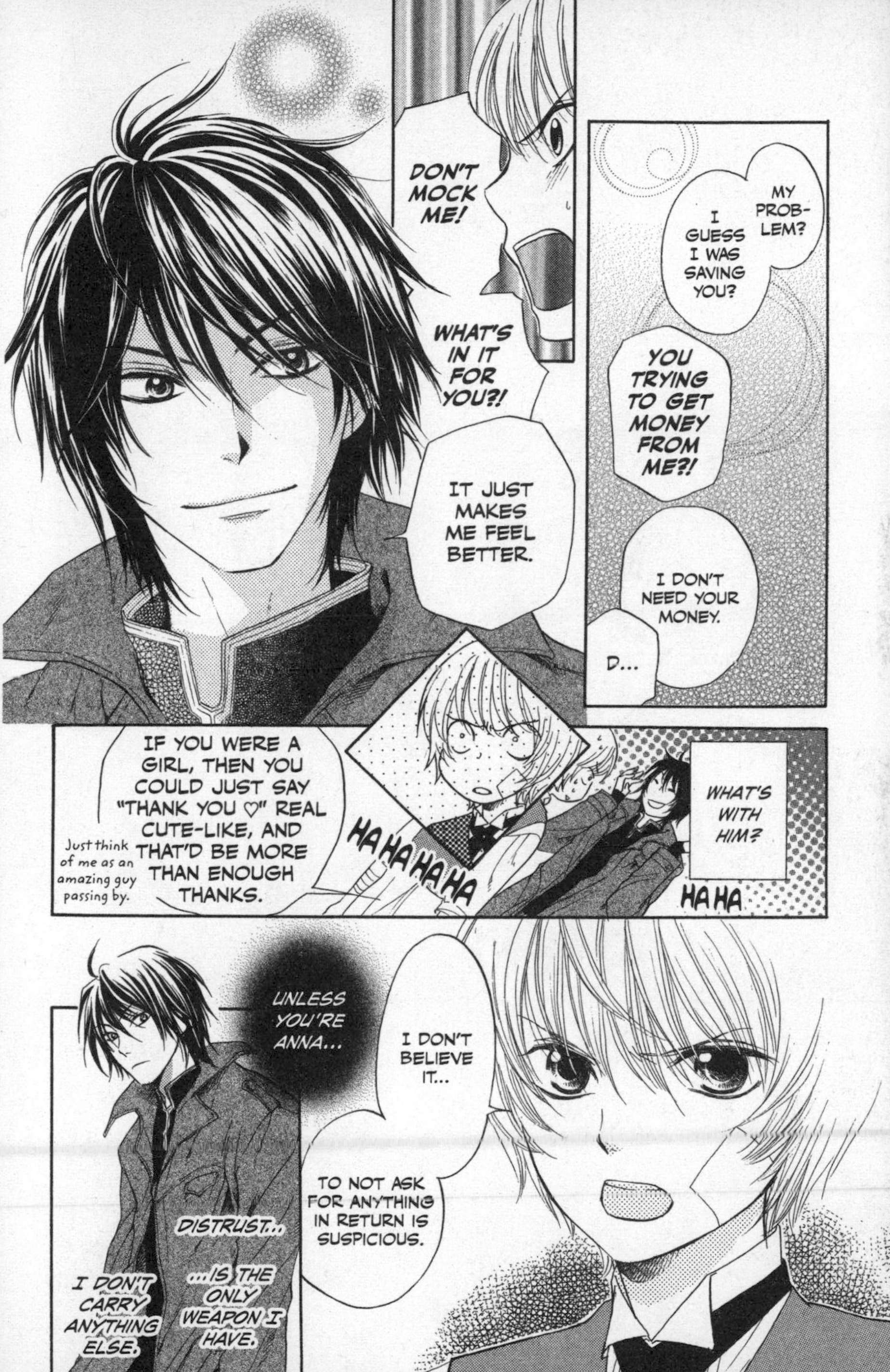
MY PROB-LEM?
I GUESS I WAS SAVING YOU?
YOU TRYING TO GET MONEY FROM ME?!
I DON'T NEED YOUR MONEY.
D...
DON'T MOCK ME!
WHAT'S IN IT FOR YOU?!
IT JUST MAKES ME FEEL BETTER.
WHAT'S WITH HIM?
HA HA
HA HA HA HA
IF YOU WERE A GIRL, THEN YOU COULD JUST SAY "THANK YOU ♡" REAL CUTE-LIKE, AND THAT'D BE MORE THAN ENOUGH THANKS.
Just think of me as an amazing guy passing by.
I DON'T BELIEVE IT...
TO NOT ASK FOR ANYTHING IN RETURN IS SUSPICIOUS.
UNLESS YOU'RE ANNA...
DISTRUST...
...IS THE ONLY WEAPON I HAVE.
I DON'T CARRY ANYTHING ELSE.

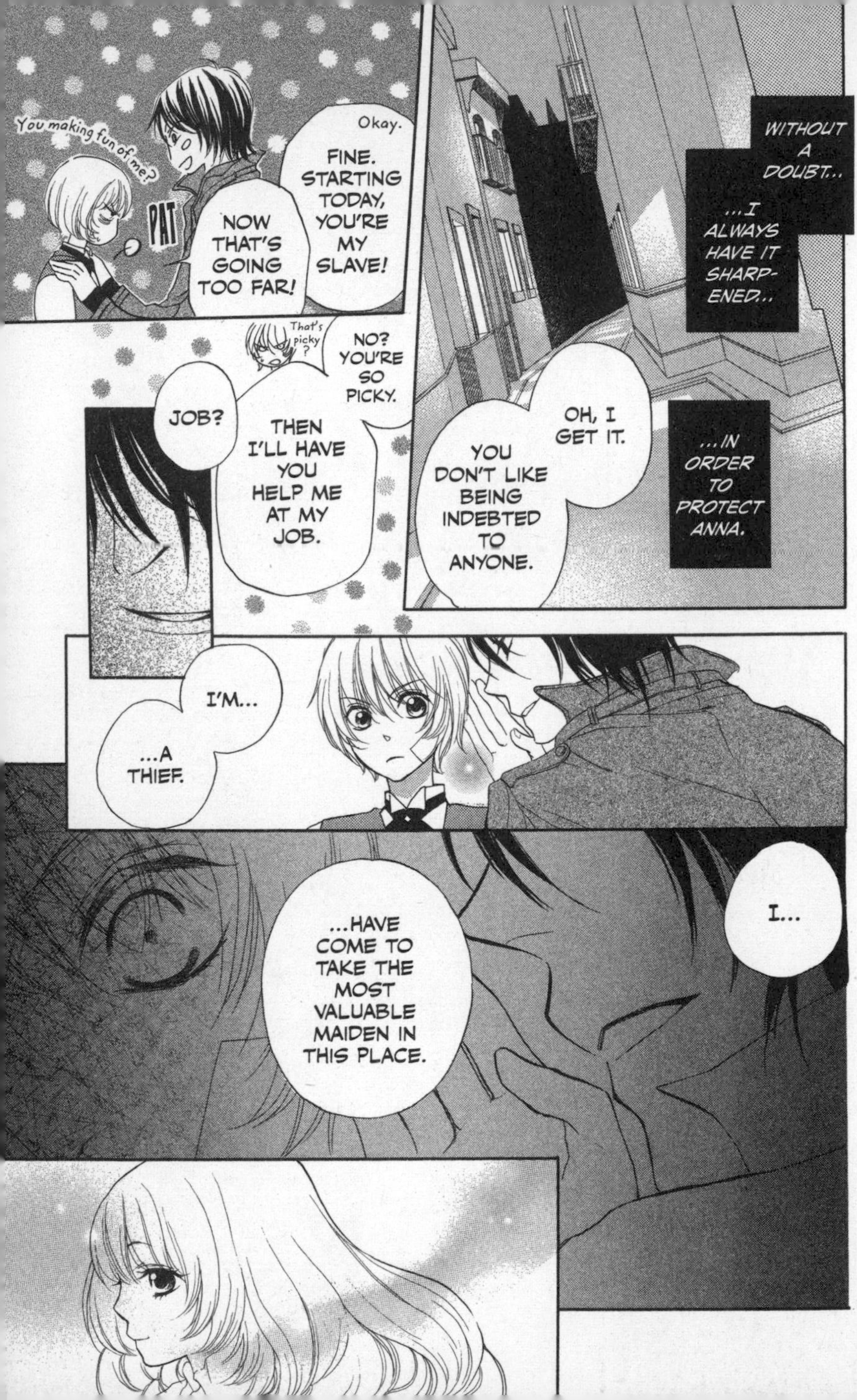
WITHOUT A DOUBT...
...I ALWAYS HAVE IT SHARPENED...
...IN ORDER TO PROTECT ANNA.
OH, I GET IT.
YOU DON'T LIKE BEING INDEBTED TO ANYONE.
Okay.
FINE. STARTING TODAY, YOU'RE MY SLAVE!
NOW THAT'S GOING TOO FAR!
PAT
You making fun of me?
NO? YOU'RE SO PICKY.
That's picky?
JOB?
THEN I'LL HAVE YOU HELP ME AT MY JOB.
I'M...
...A THIEF.
I...
...HAVE COME TO TAKE THE MOST VALUABLE MAIDEN IN THIS PLACE.

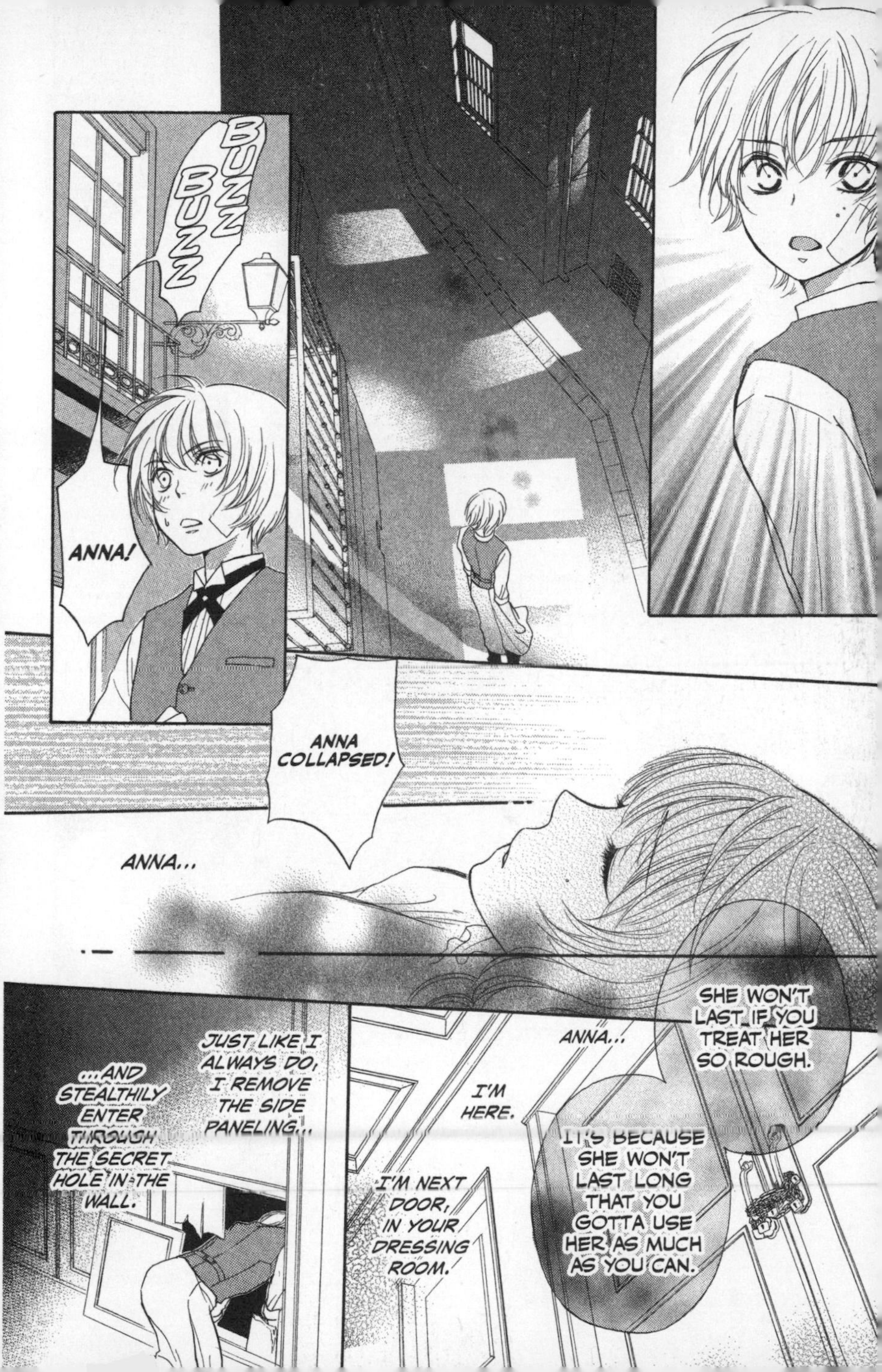
BUZZ BUZZ
BUZZ
ANNA!
ANNA COLLAPSED!
ANNA...
SHE WON'T LAST IF YOU TREAT HER SO ROUGH.
IT'S BECAUSE SHE WON'T LAST LONG THAT YOU GOTTA USE HER AS MUCH AS YOU CAN.
ANNA...
I'M HERE.
I'M NEXT DOOR, IN YOUR DRESSING ROOM.
JUST LIKE I ALWAYS DO, I REMOVE THE SIDE PANELING...
...AND STEALTHILY ENTER THROUGH THE SECRET HOLE IN THE WALL.

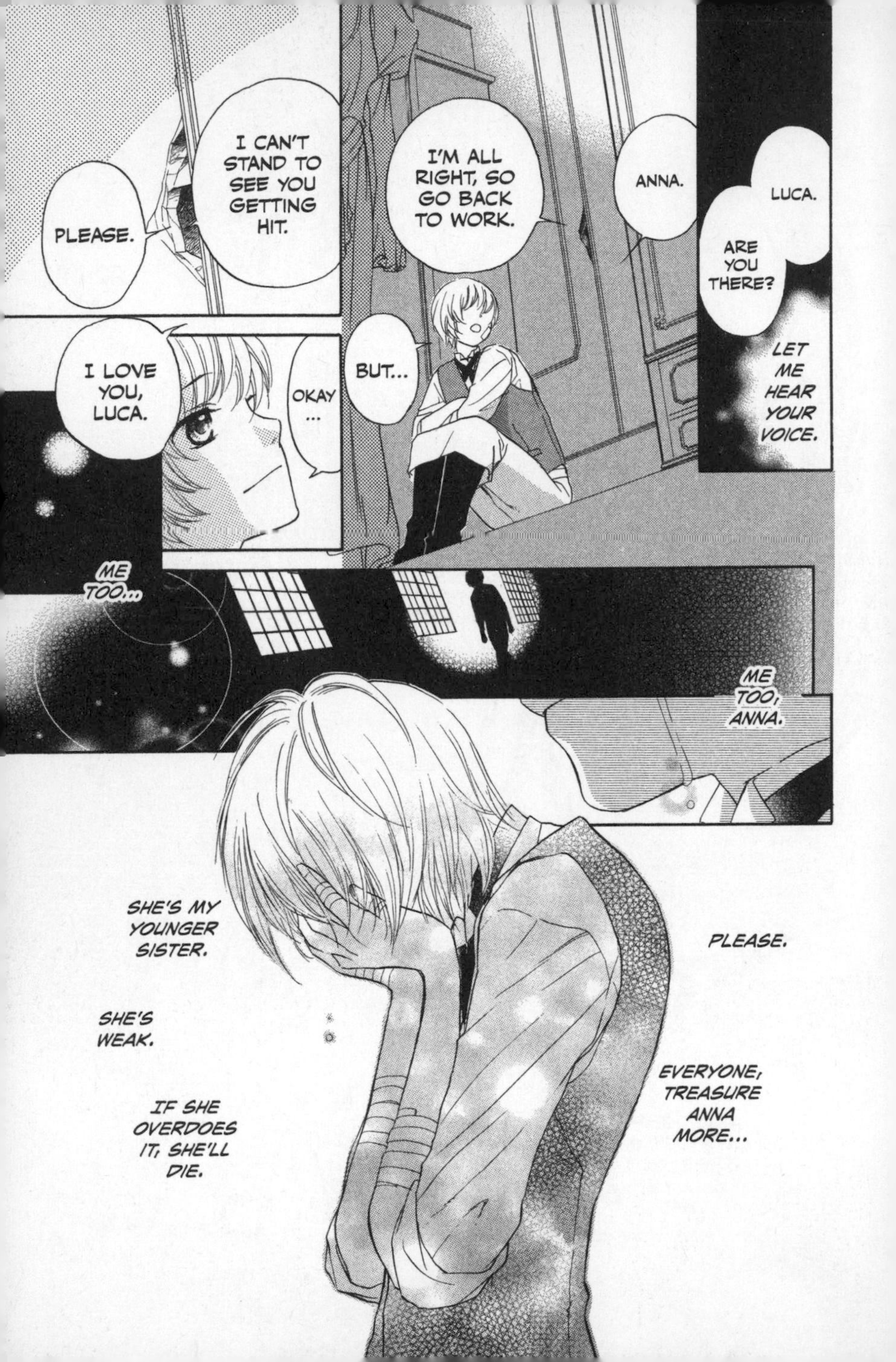
LUCA.
ARE YOU THERE?
LET ME HEAR YOUR VOICE.
ANNA.
I'M ALL RIGHT, SO GO BACK TO WORK.
BUT...
I CAN'T STAND TO SEE YOU GETTING HIT.
PLEASE.
OKAY...
I LOVE YOU, LUCA.
ME TOO...
ME TOO, ANNA.
PLEASE.
EVERYONE, TREASURE ANNA MORE...
SHE'S MY YOUNGER SISTER.
SHE'S WEAK.
IF SHE OVERDOES IT, SHE'LL DIE.

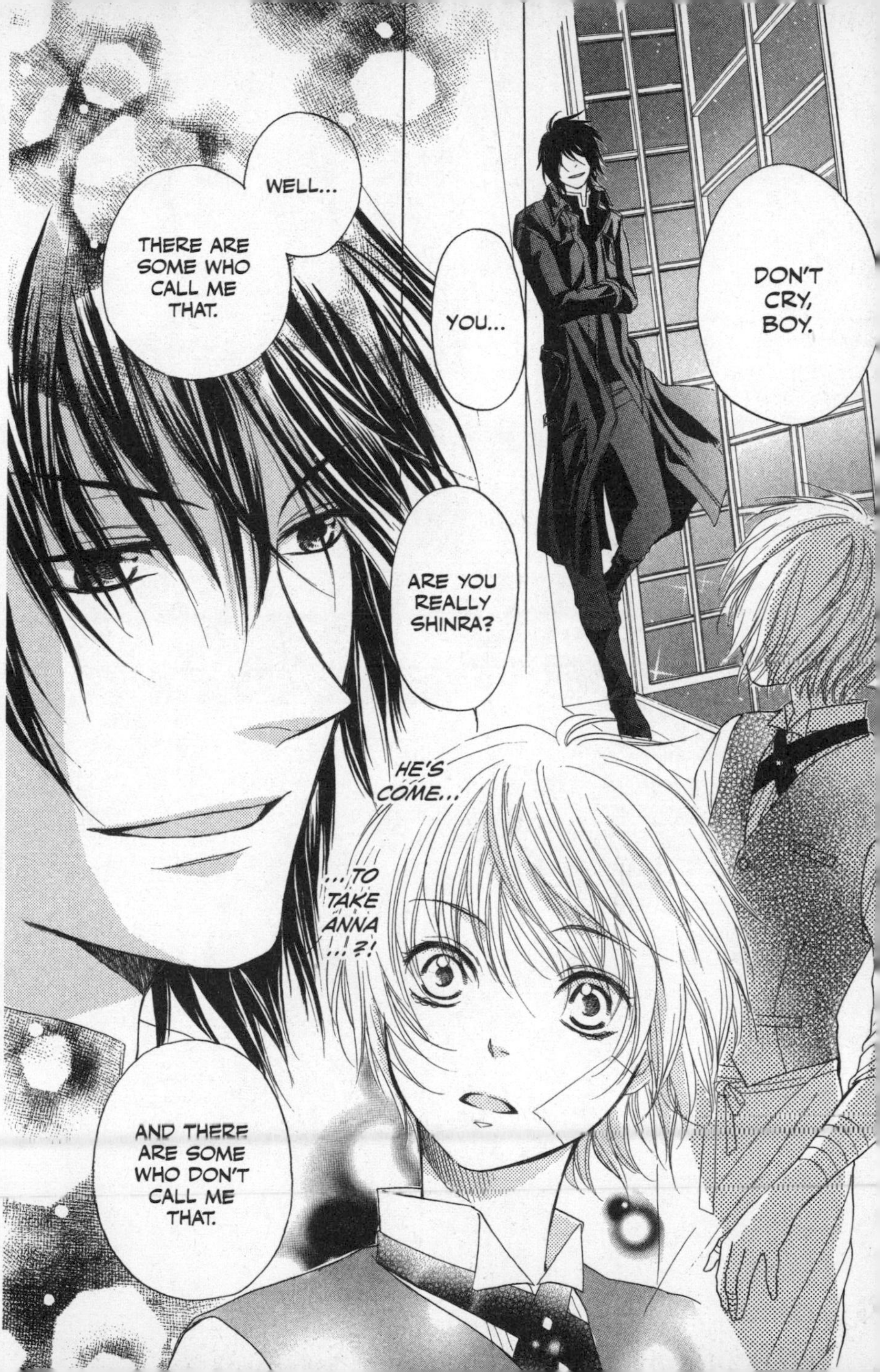
DON'T CRY, BOY.
YOU...
ARE YOU REALLY SHINRA?
WELL...
THERE ARE SOME WHO CALL ME THAT.
HE'S COME...
...TO TAKE ANNA...?!
AND THERE ARE SOME WHO DON'T CALL ME THAT.

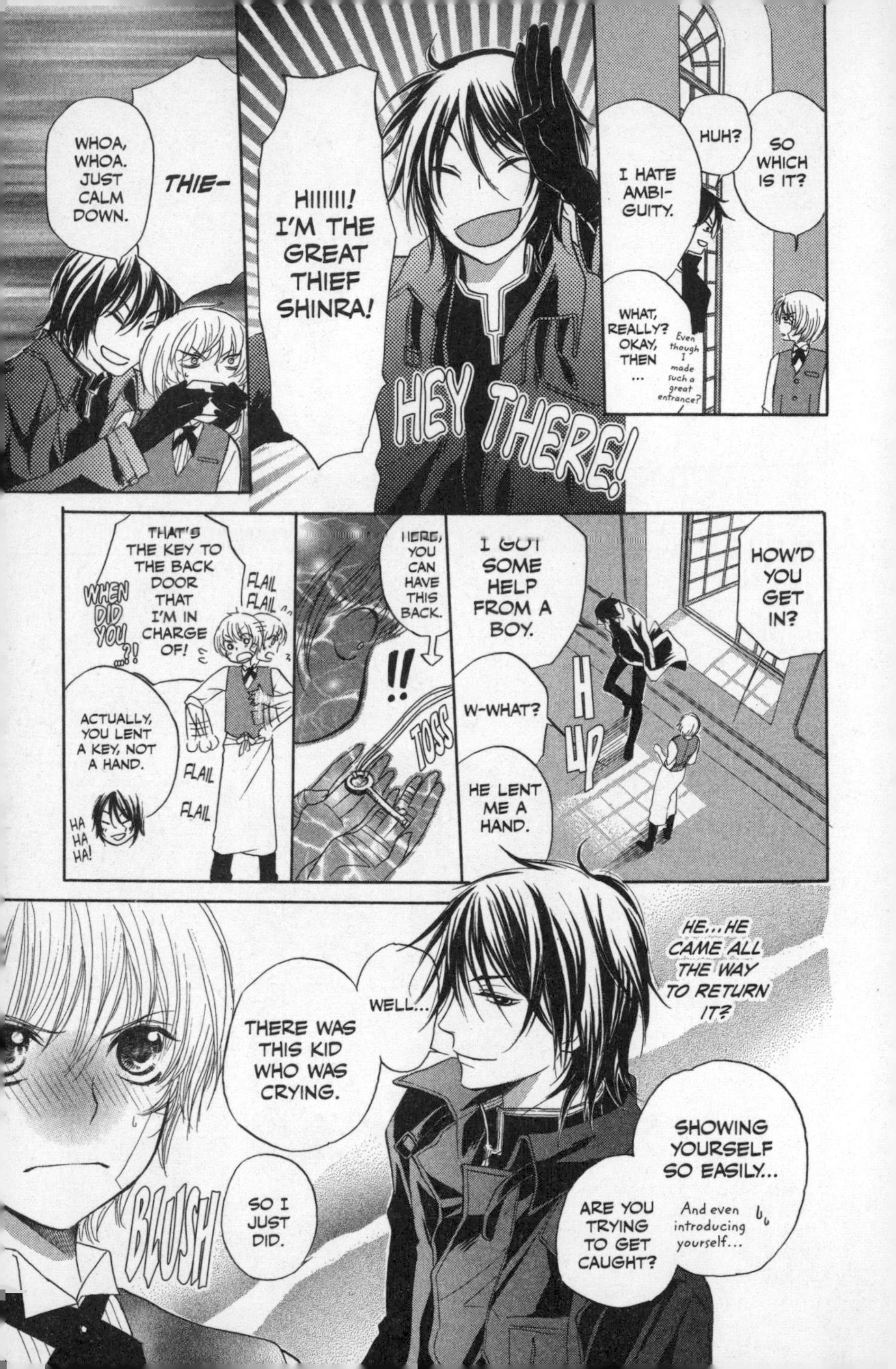

SO WHICH IS IT?
HUH?
I HATE AMBIGUITY.
WHAT, REALLY? OKAY, THEN ...
Even though I made such a great entrance?
HIIIIII! I'M THE GREAT THIEF SHINRA!
HEY THERE!
THIE-
WHOA, WHOA. JUST CALM DOWN.
HOW'D YOU GET IN?
I GOT SOME HELP FROM A BOY.
HUP
W-WHAT?
HE LENT ME A HAND.
HERE, YOU CAN HAVE THIS BACK.
!!
TOSS
THAT'S THE KEY TO THE BACK DOOR THAT I'M IN CHARGE OF!
FLAIL FLAIL
WHEN DID YOU ...?!
ACTUALLY, YOU LENT A KEY, NOT A HAND.
FLAIL
FLAIL
HA HA HA!
HE...HE CAME ALL THE WAY TO RETURN IT?
WELL...
THERE WAS THIS KID WHO WAS CRYING.
SHOWING YOURSELF SO EASILY...
ARE YOU TRYING TO GET CAUGHT?
And even introducing yourself...
SO I JUST DID.
BLUSH

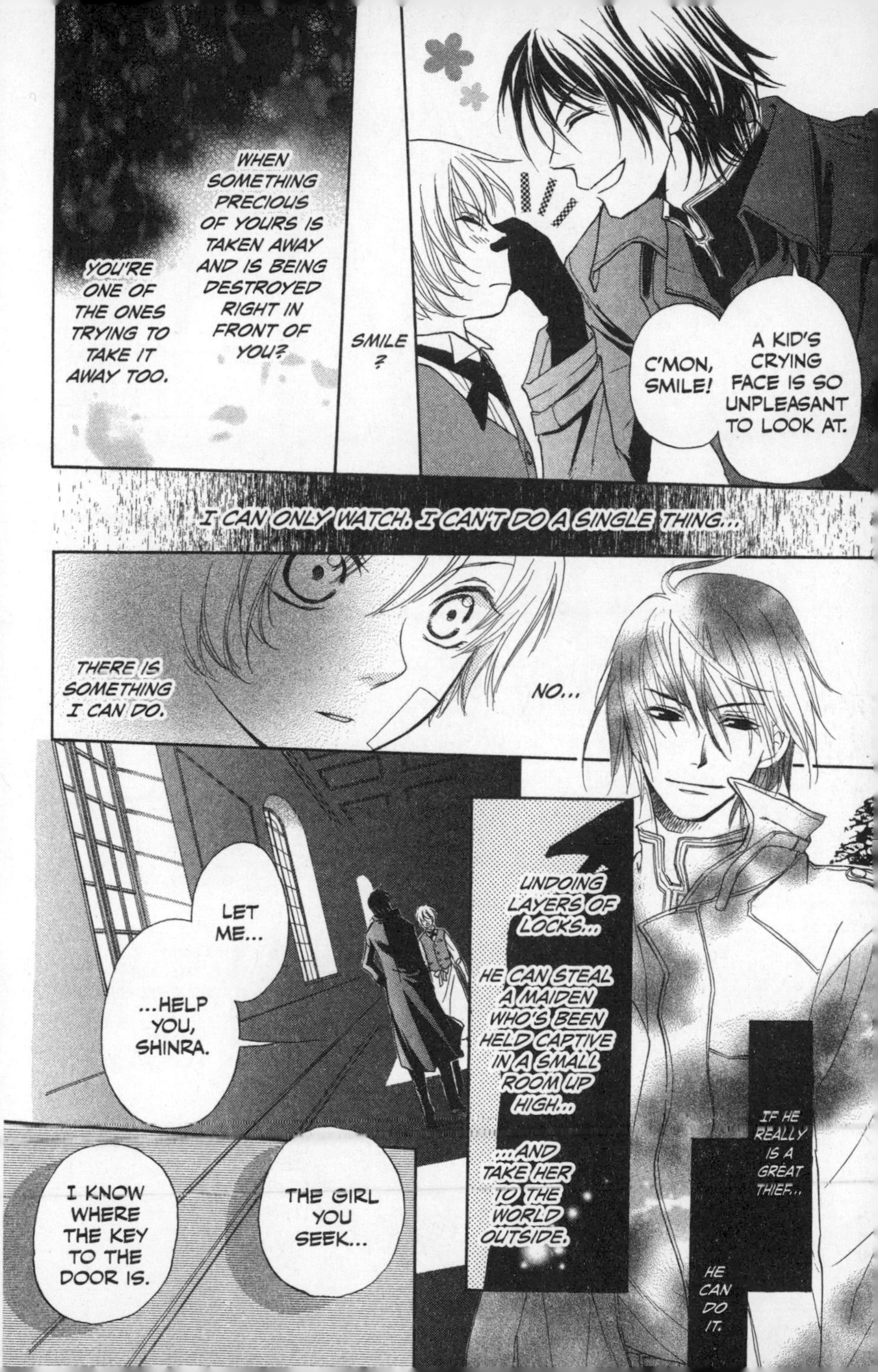
A KID'S CRYING FACE IS SO UNPLEASANT TO LOOK AT.
C'MON, SMILE!
SMILE?
WHEN SOMETHING PRECIOUS OF YOURS IS TAKEN AWAY AND IS BEING DESTROYED RIGHT IN FRONT OF YOU?
YOU'RE ONE OF THE ONES TRYING TO TAKE IT AWAY TOO.
I CAN ONLY WATCH. I CAN'T DO A SINGLE THING...
NO...
THERE IS SOMETHING I CAN DO.
UNDOING LAYERS OF LOCKS...
HE CAN STEAL A MAIDEN WHO'S BEEN HELD CAPTIVE IN A SMALL ROOM UP HIGH...
...AND TAKE HER TO THE WORLD OUTSIDE.
IF HE REALLY IS A GREAT THIEF...
HE CAN DO IT.
LET ME...
...HELP YOU, SHINRA.
THE GIRL YOU SEEK...
I KNOW WHERE THE KEY TO THE DOOR IS.

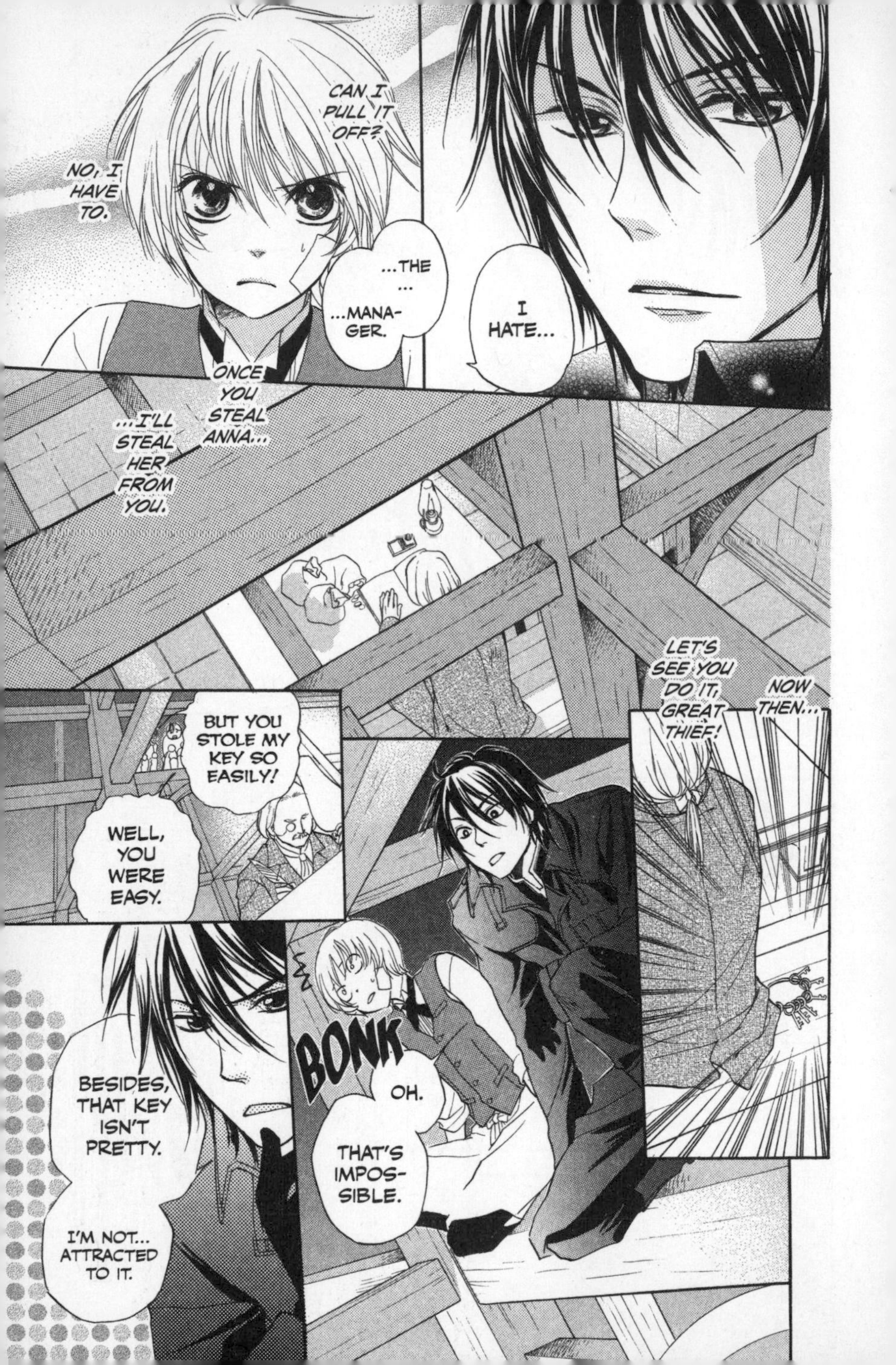
I HATE...
CAN I PULL IT OFF?
...THE ... ...MANA-GER.
NO, I HAVE TO.
ONCE YOU STEAL ANNA...
...I'LL STEAL HER FROM YOU.
NOW THEN...
LET'S SEE YOU DO IT, GREAT THIEF!
BUT YOU STOLE MY KEY SO EASILY!
WELL, YOU WERE EASY.
BONK
OH.
THAT'S IMPOS-SIBLE.
BESIDES, THAT KEY ISN'T PRETTY.
I'M NOT... ATTRACTED TO IT.

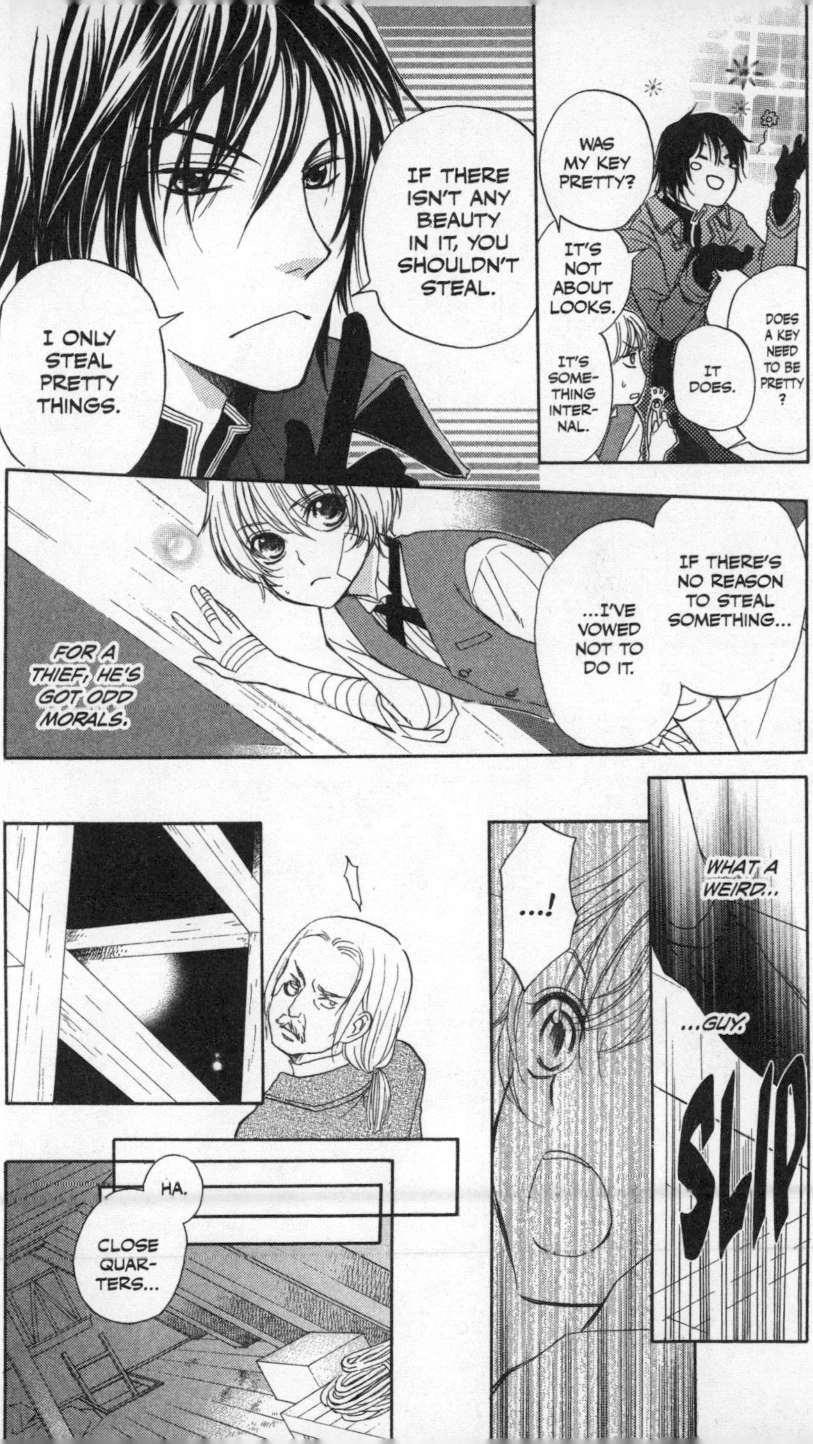

WAS MY KEY PRETTY?
DOES A KEY NEED TO BE PRETTY?
IT DOES.
IT'S NOT ABOUT LOOKS.
IT'S SOMETHING INTERNAL.
IF THERE ISN'T ANY BEAUTY IN IT, YOU SHOULDN'T STEAL.
I ONLY STEAL PRETTY THINGS.
IF THERE'S NO REASON TO STEAL SOMETHING...
...I'VE VOWED NOT TO DO IT.
FOR A THIEF, HE'S GOT ODD MORALS.
WHAT A WEIRD...
...GUY.
SLIP
...!
HA.
CLOSE QUARTERS...

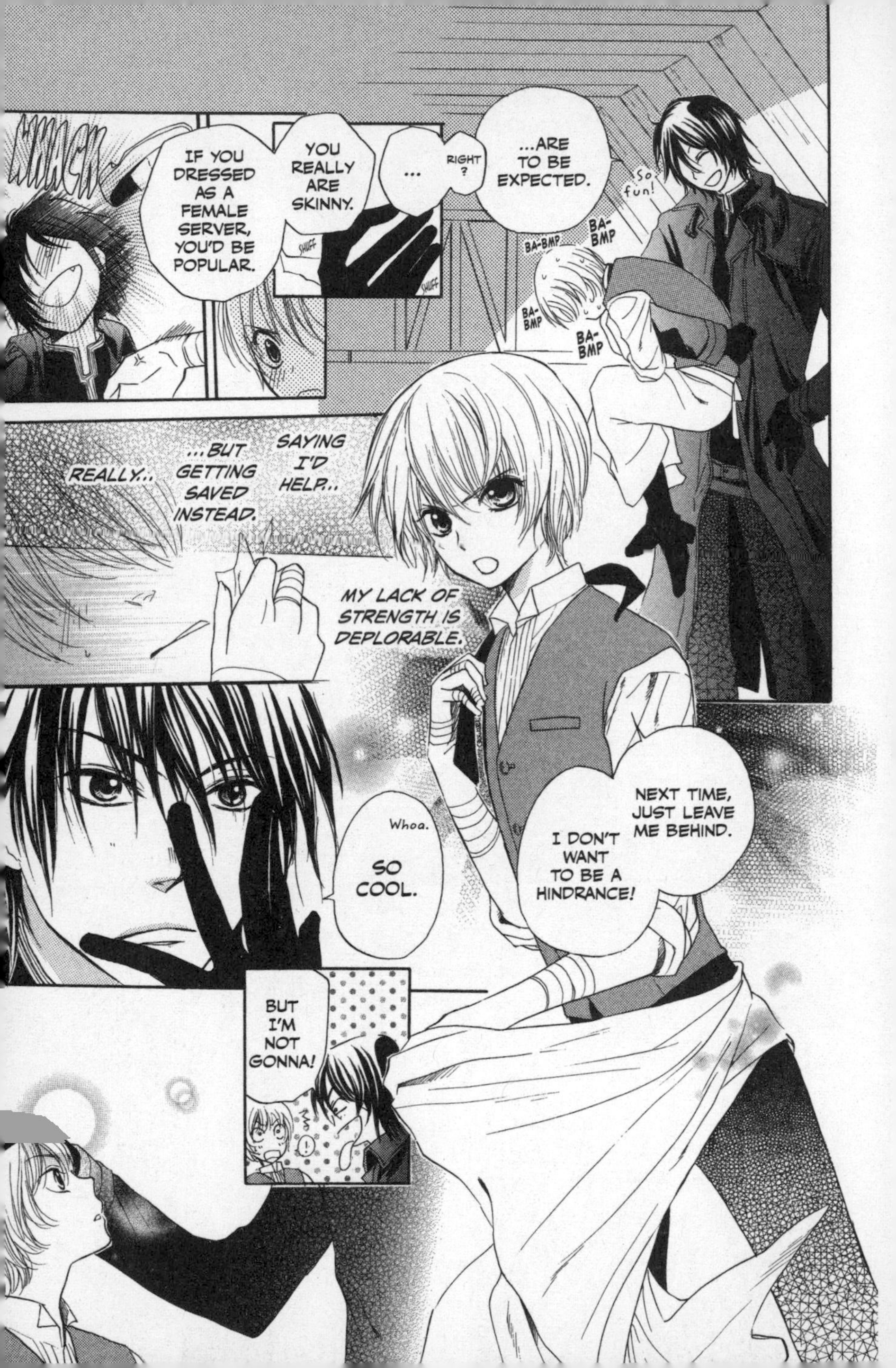

...ARE TO BE EXPECTED.
RIGHT?
So fun!
BA-BMP
BA-BMP
BA-BMP
BA-BMP
...
YOU REALLY ARE SKINNY.
SHUFF
SHUFF
IF YOU DRESSED AS A FEMALE SERVER, YOU'D BE POPULAR.
WHACK
MY LACK OF STRENGTH IS DEPLORABLE.
SAYING I'D HELP...
...BUT GETTING SAVED INSTEAD.
REALLY...
NEXT TIME, JUST LEAVE ME BEHIND.
I DON'T WANT TO BE A HINDRANCE!
Whoa.
SO COOL.
BUT I'M NOT GONNA!

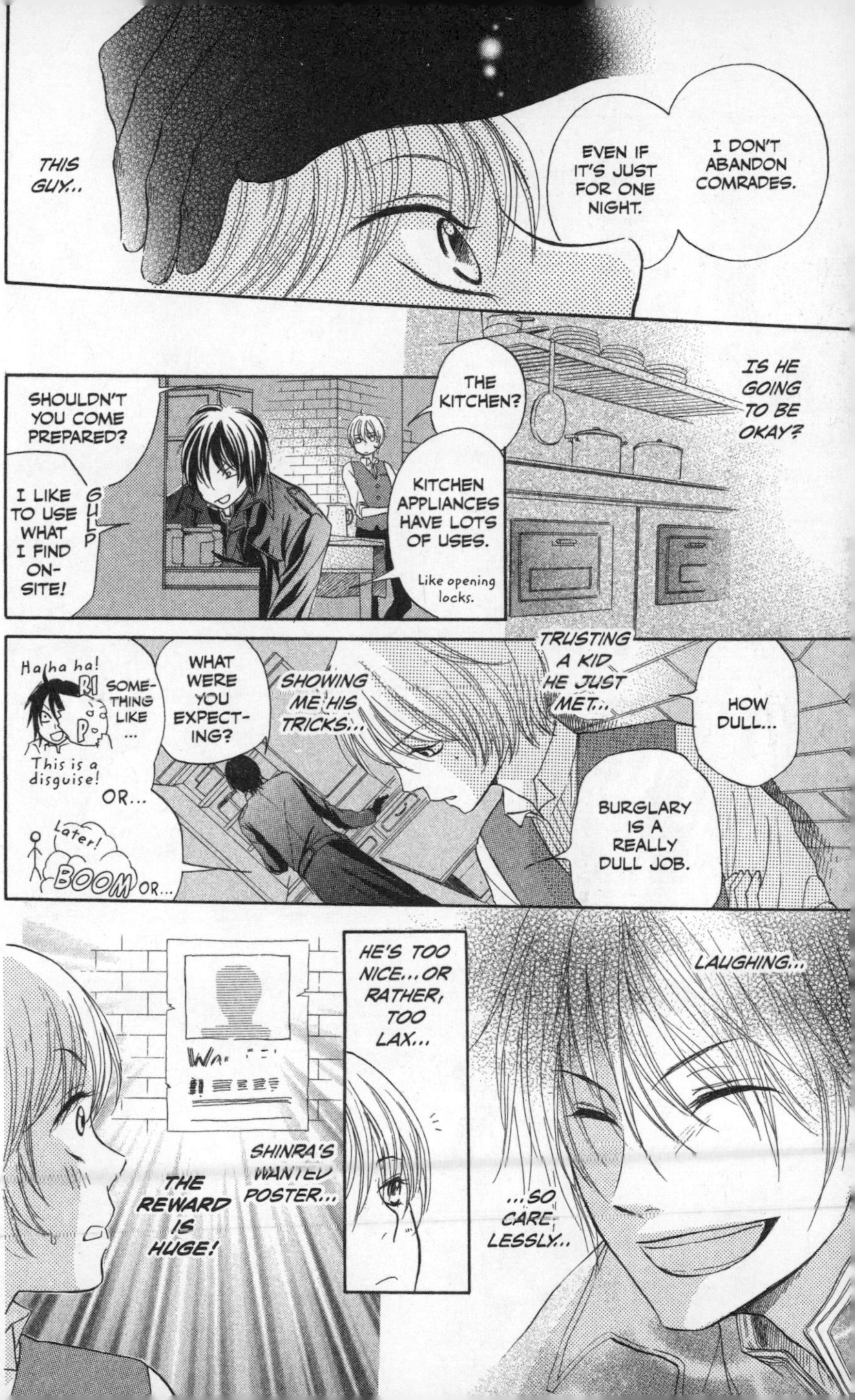
I DON'T ABANDON COMRADES.
EVEN IF IT'S JUST FOR ONE NIGHT.
THIS GUY...
IS HE GOING TO BE OKAY?
THE KITCHEN?
KITCHEN APPLIANCES HAVE LOTS OF USES.
Like opening locks.
SHOULDN'T YOU COME PREPARED?
GULP
I LIKE TO USE WHAT I FIND ON-SITE!
HOW DULL...
BURGLARY IS A REALLY DULL JOB.
TRUSTING A KID HE JUST MET...
SHOWING ME HIS TRICKS...
WHAT WERE YOU EXPECTING?
SOMETHING LIKE...
Ha ha ha!
RIP
This is a disguise!
OR...
Later!
BOOM
OR...
LAUGHING...
...SO CARELESSLY...
HE'S TOO NICE...OR RATHER, TOO LAX...
SHINRA'S WANTED POSTER...
THE REWARD IS HUGE!

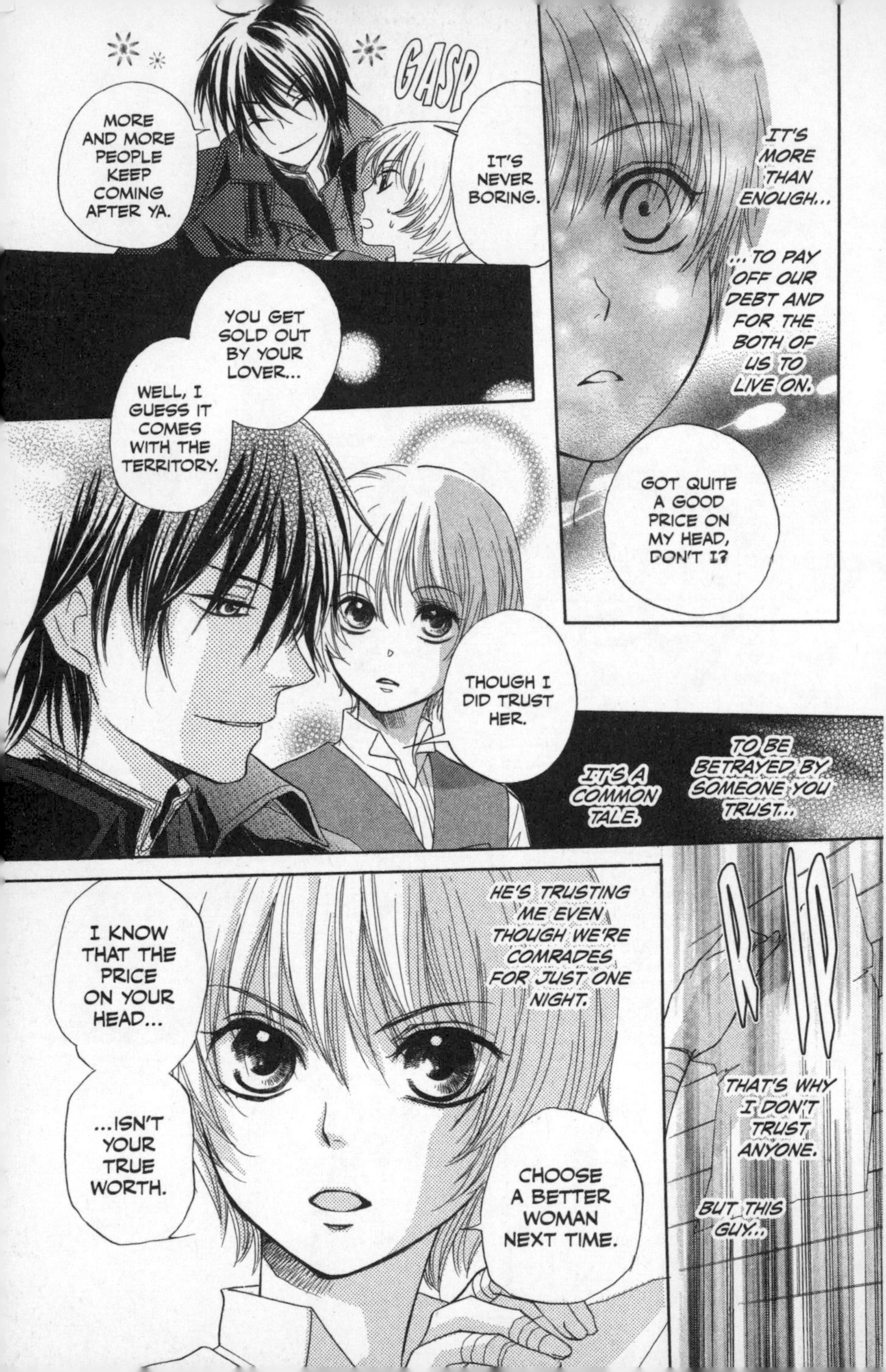
IT'S MORE THAN ENOUGH...
...TO PAY OFF OUR DEBT AND FOR THE BOTH OF US TO LIVE ON.
GOT QUITE A GOOD PRICE ON MY HEAD, DON'T I?
GASP
IT'S NEVER BORING.
MORE AND MORE PEOPLE KEEP COMING AFTER YA.
YOU GET SOLD OUT BY YOUR LOVER...
WELL, I GUESS IT COMES WITH THE TERRITORY.
THOUGH I DID TRUST HER.
TO BE BETRAYED BY SOMEONE YOU TRUST...
IT'S A COMMON TALE.
RIP
THAT'S WHY I DON'T TRUST ANYONE.
BUT THIS GUY...
HE'S TRUSTING ME EVEN THOUGH WE'RE COMRADES FOR JUST ONE NIGHT.
I KNOW THAT THE PRICE ON YOUR HEAD...
...ISN'T YOUR TRUE WORTH.
CHOOSE A BETTER WOMAN NEXT TIME.

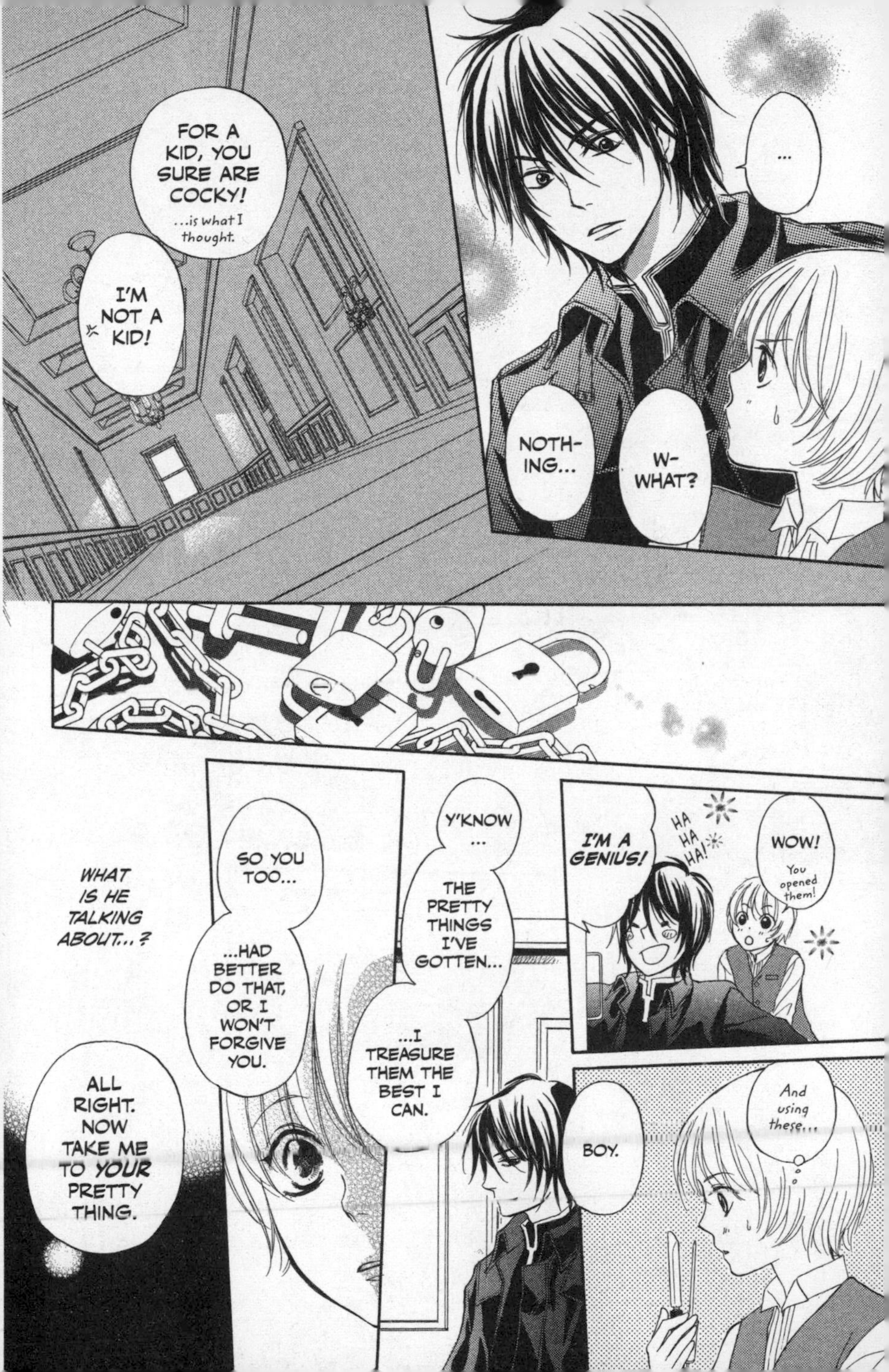
...
W-WHAT?
NOTHING...
FOR A KID, YOU SURE ARE COCKY!
...is what I thought.
I'M NOT A KID!
WOW!
You opened them!
HA HA HA!
I'M A GENIUS!
And using these...
BOY.
Y'KNOW ...
THE PRETTY THINGS I'VE GOTTEN...
...I TREASURE THEM THE BEST I CAN.
SO YOU TOO...
...HAD BETTER DO THAT, OR I WON'T FORGIVE YOU.
WHAT IS HE TALKING ABOUT...?
ALL RIGHT. NOW TAKE ME TO *YOUR* PRETTY THING.

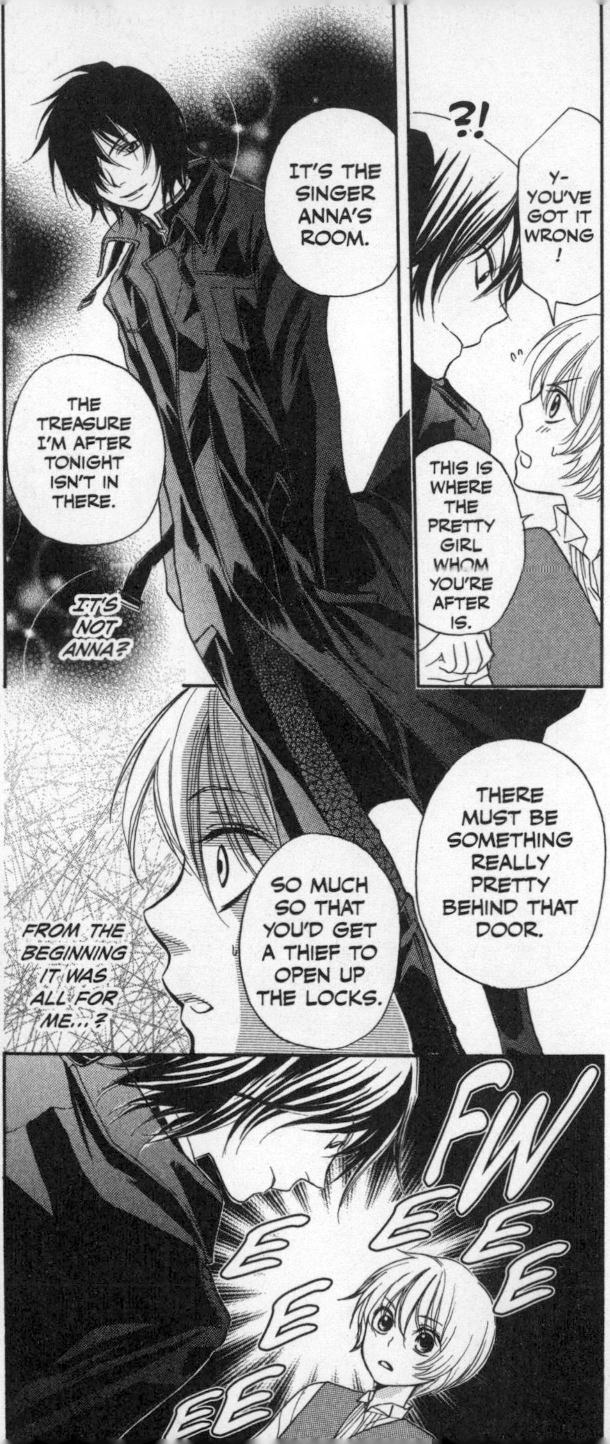
?!
Y-YOU'VE GOT IT WRONG!
THIS IS WHERE THE PRETTY GIRL WHOM YOU'RE AFTER IS.
IT'S THE SINGER ANNA'S ROOM.
THE TREASURE I'M AFTER TONIGHT ISN'T IN THERE.
IT'S NOT ANNA?
THERE MUST BE SOMETHING REALLY PRETTY BEHIND THAT DOOR.
SO MUCH SO THAT YOU'D GET A THIEF TO OPEN UP THE LOCKS.
FROM THE BEGINNING IT WAS ALL FOR ME...?
FWEEEEEEEEEEEE

LUCA AND THE BANDIT

I don't remember much from when I wrote this story.

I think I had a really hard schedule at the time, though that's entirely my own fault.

*I like pairing a carefree older guy with a serious type like Luca. The **Heiress and the Chauffeur** was probably born from this idea too.*

As I was drawing the story, I thought the ending was pretty obvious from the beginning, but it turns out that a lot of people didn't figure it out.

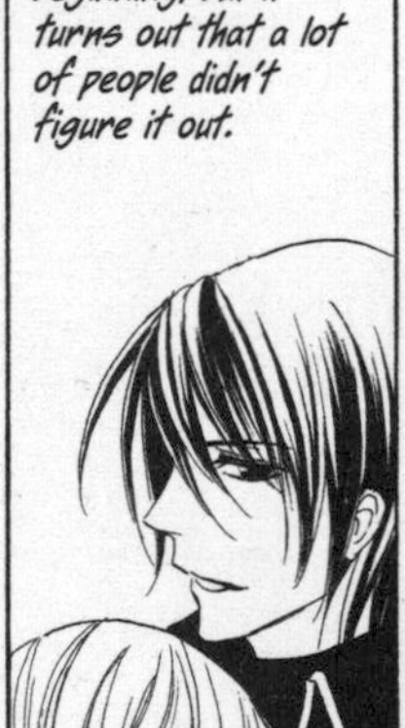

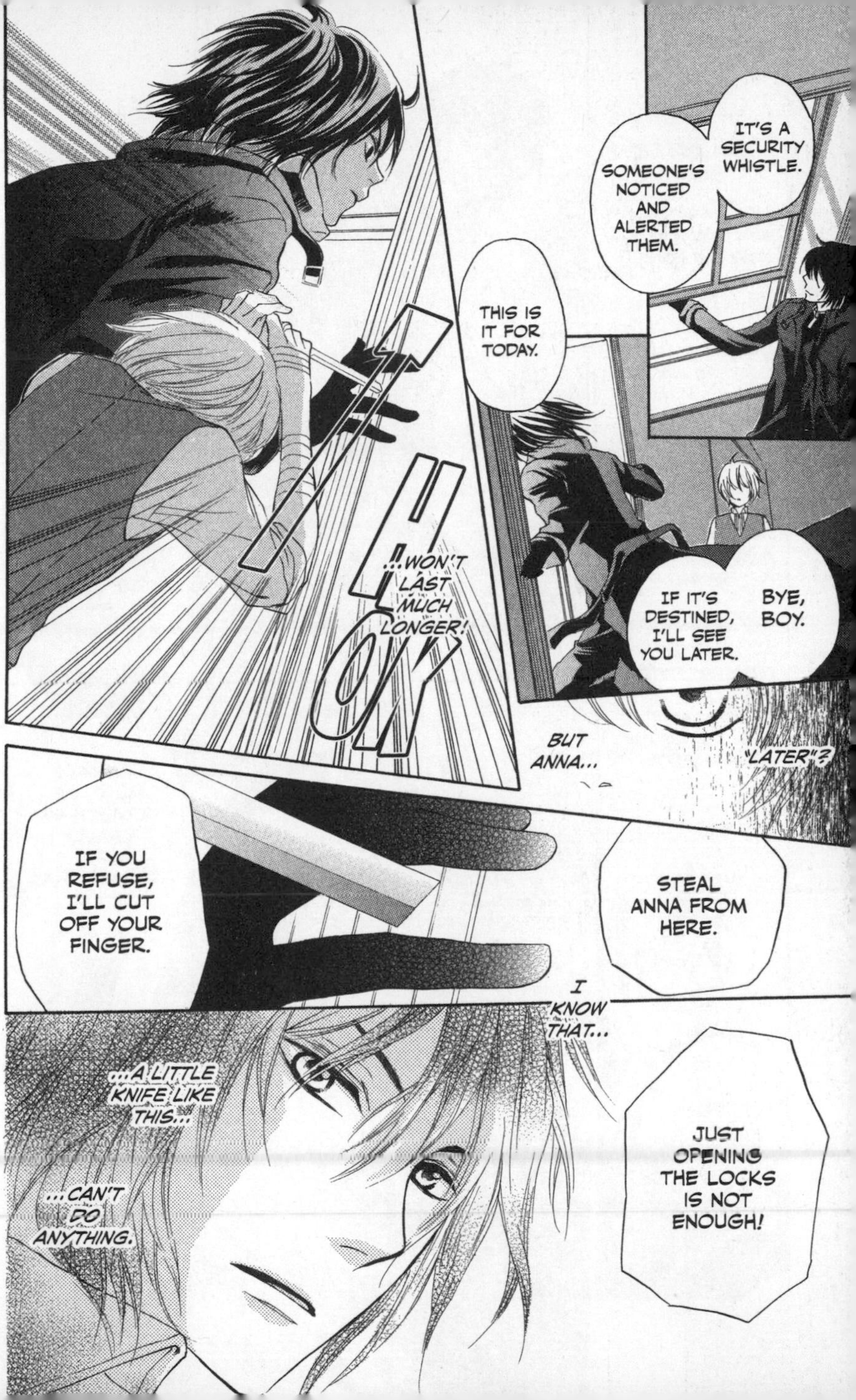
IT'S A SECURITY WHISTLE.
SOMEONE'S NOTICED AND ALERTED THEM.
THIS IS IT FOR TODAY.
BYE, BOY.
IF IT'S DESTINED, I'LL SEE YOU LATER.
...WON'T LAST MUCH LONGER!
"LATER"?
BUT ANNA...
STEAL ANNA FROM HERE.
IF YOU REFUSE, I'LL CUT OFF YOUR FINGER.
I KNOW THAT...
JUST OPENING THE LOCKS IS NOT ENOUGH!
...A LITTLE KNIFE LIKE THIS...
...CAN'T DO ANYTHING.

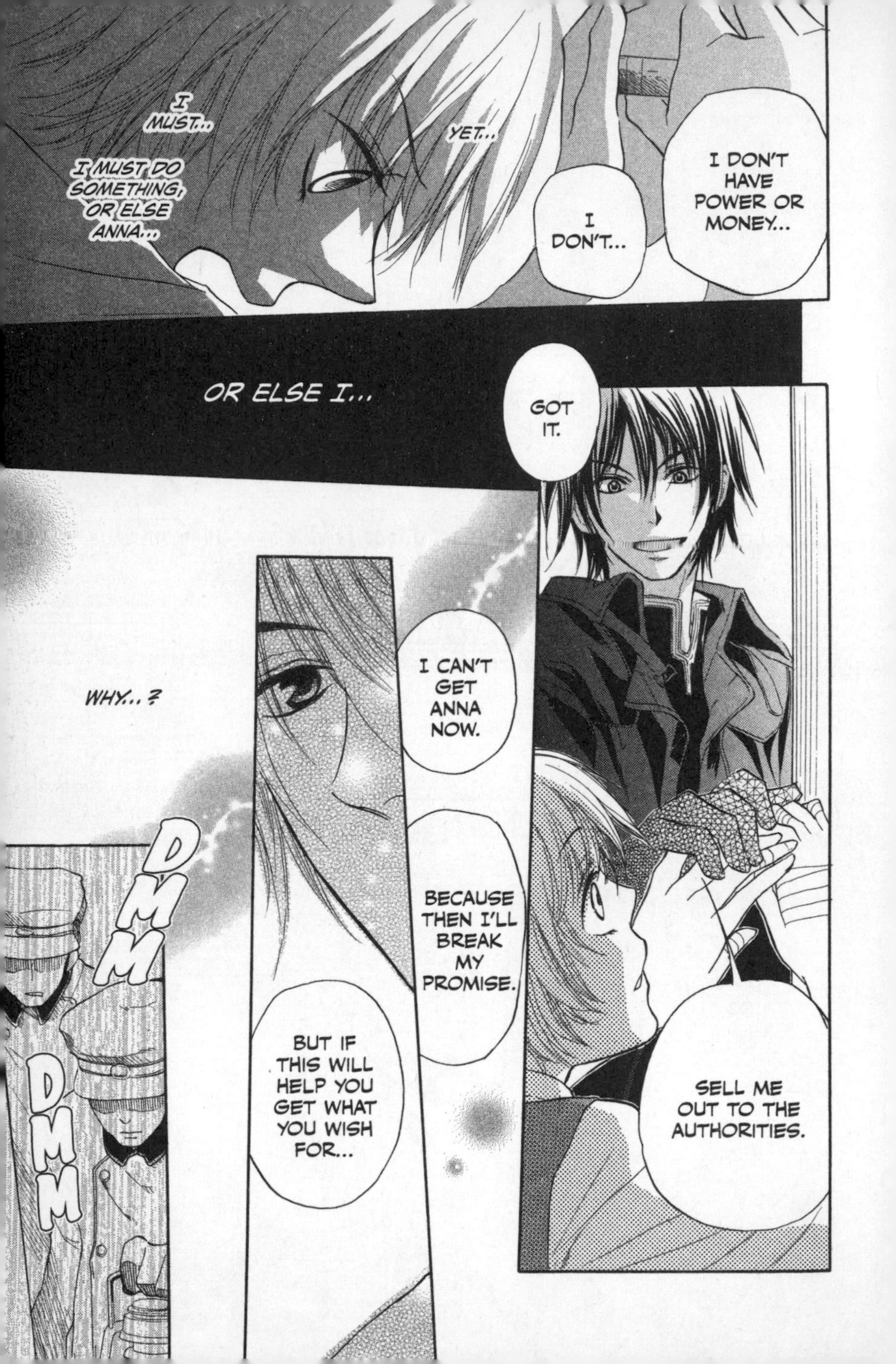
I DON'T HAVE POWER OR MONEY...
I DON'T...
YET...
I MUST...
I MUST DO SOMETHING, OR ELSE ANNA...
OR ELSE I...
GOT IT.
SELL ME OUT TO THE AUTHORITIES.
I CAN'T GET ANNA NOW.
BECAUSE THEN I'LL BREAK MY PROMISE.
BUT IF THIS WILL HELP YOU GET WHAT YOU WISH FOR...
WHY...?
DMMM
DMMM

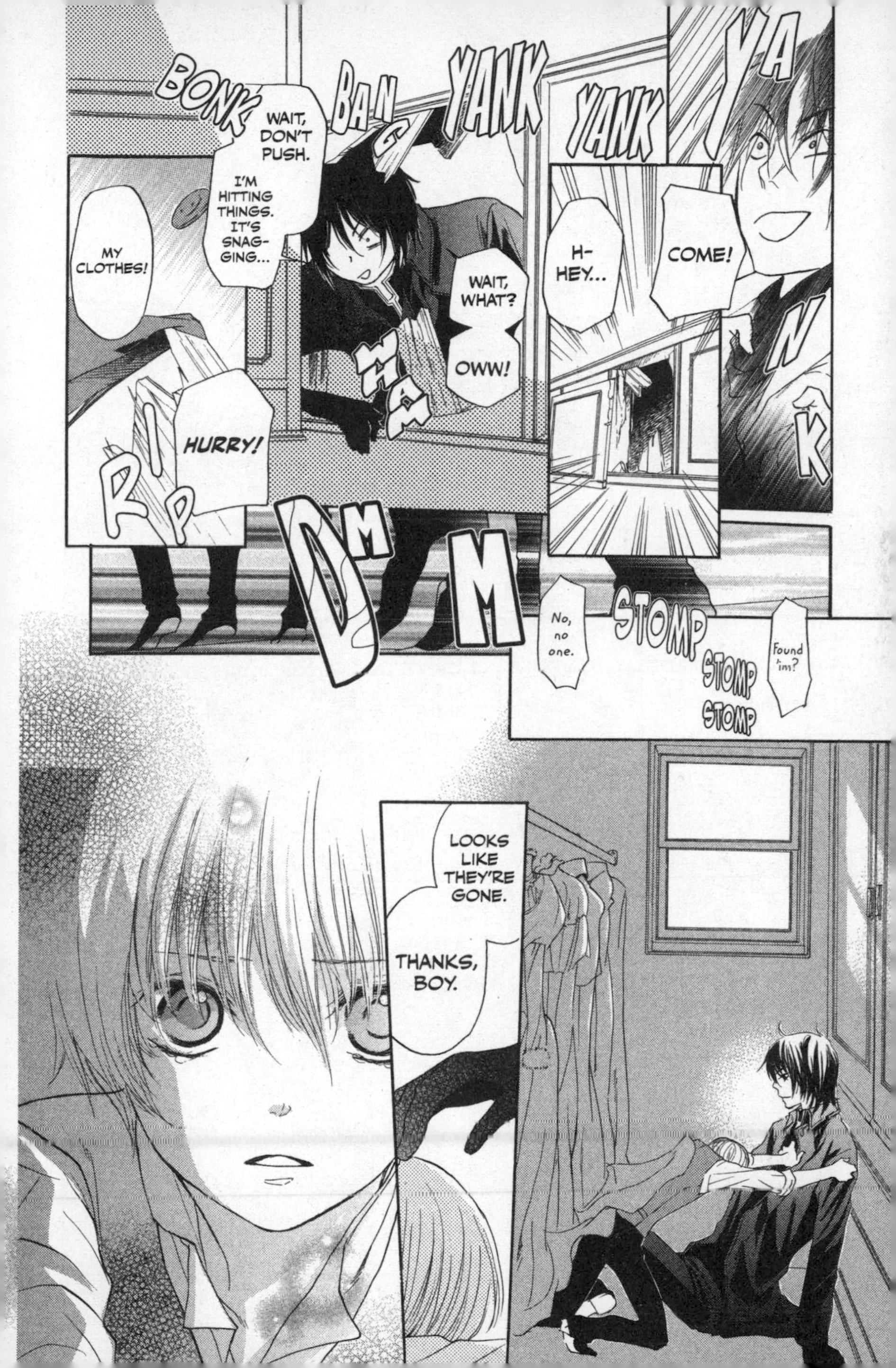
YANK
COME!
YANK
H-HEY...
YANK
BANG
BONK
WAIT, DON'T PUSH.
I'M HITTING THINGS. IT'S SNAG-GING...
MY CLOTHES!
WAIT, WHAT?
OWW!
WHAM
HURRY!
RIP
DMM
Found 'im?
STOMP
STOMP
STOMP
No, no one.
LOOKS LIKE THEY'RE GONE.
THANKS, BOY.

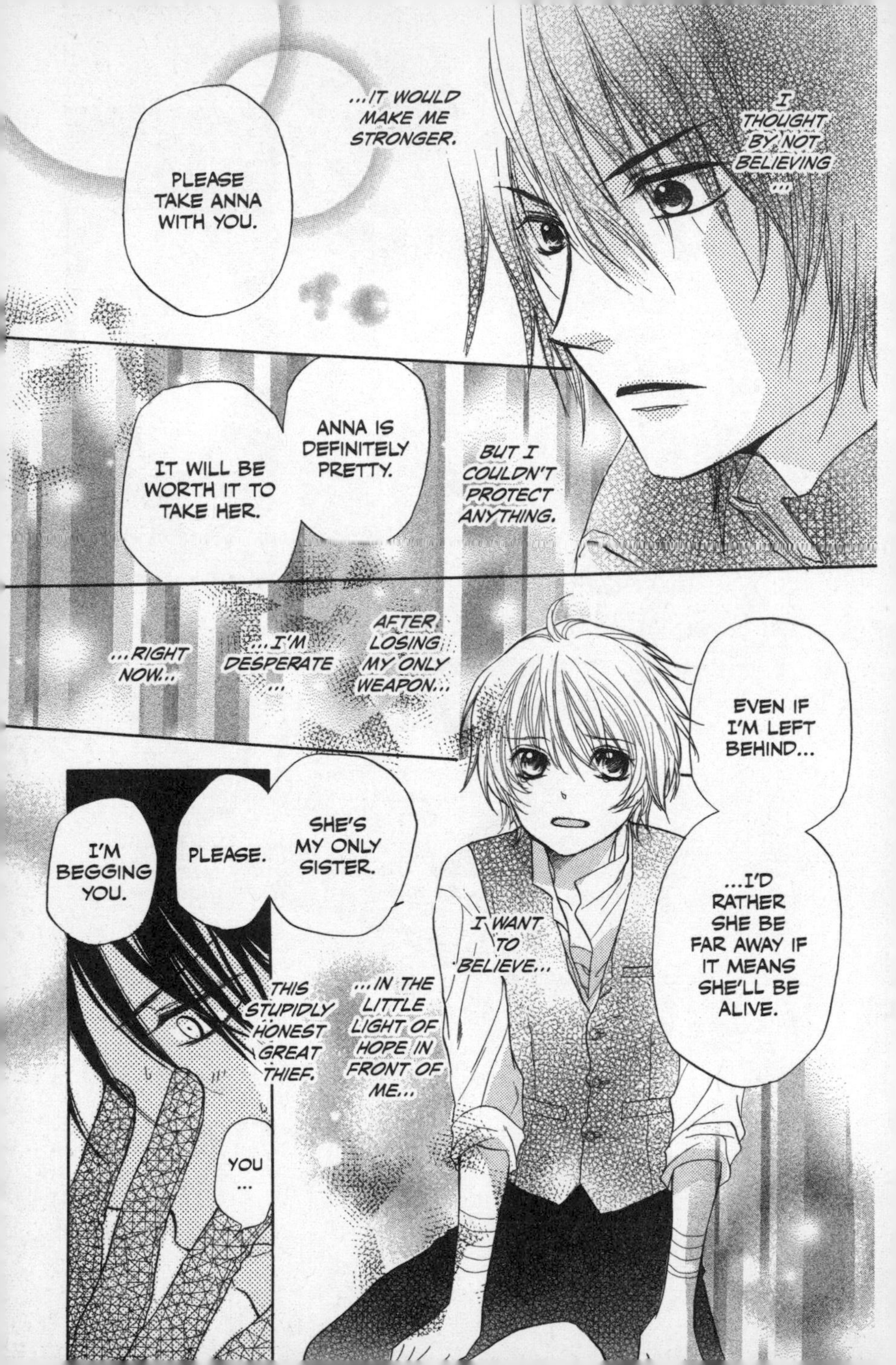
I THOUGHT BY NOT BELIEVING...
...IT WOULD MAKE ME STRONGER.
PLEASE TAKE ANNA WITH YOU.
BUT I COULDN'T PROTECT ANYTHING.
ANNA IS DEFINITELY PRETTY.
IT WILL BE WORTH IT TO TAKE HER.
AFTER LOSING MY ONLY WEAPON...
...I'M DESPERATE...
...RIGHT NOW...
EVEN IF I'M LEFT BEHIND...
...I'D RATHER SHE BE FAR AWAY IF IT MEANS SHE'LL BE ALIVE.
I WANT TO BELIEVE...
SHE'S MY ONLY SISTER.
PLEASE.
I'M BEGGING YOU.
...IN THE LITTLE LIGHT OF HOPE IN FRONT OF ME...
THIS STUPIDLY HONEST GREAT THIEF.
YOU...

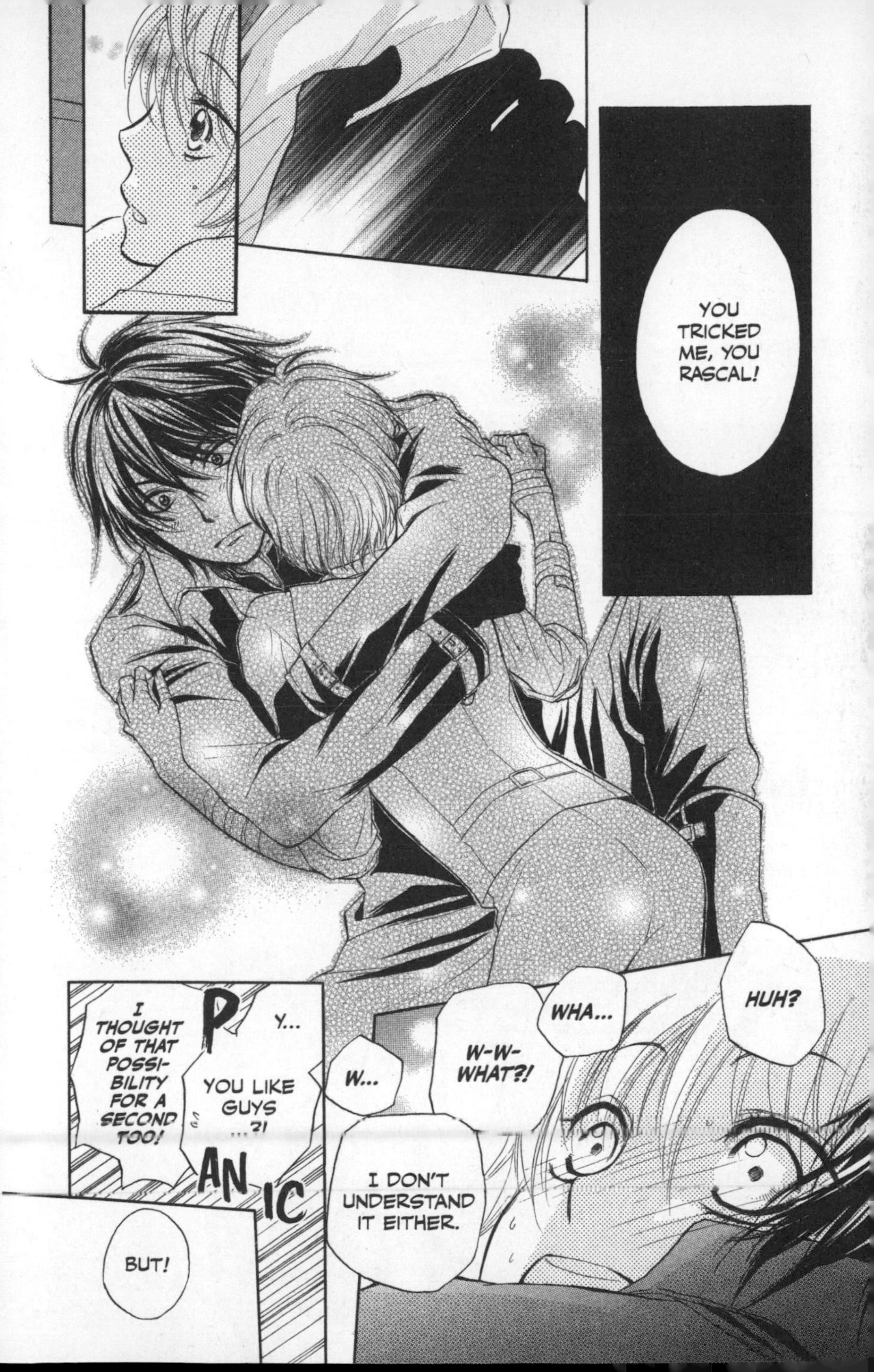
YOU TRICKED ME, YOU RASCAL!
HUH?
WHA...
W-W-WHAT?!
W...
I DON'T UNDERSTAND IT EITHER.
Y...
YOU LIKE GUYS ...?!
I THOUGHT OF THAT POSSIBILITY FOR A SECOND TOO!
PANIC
BUT!

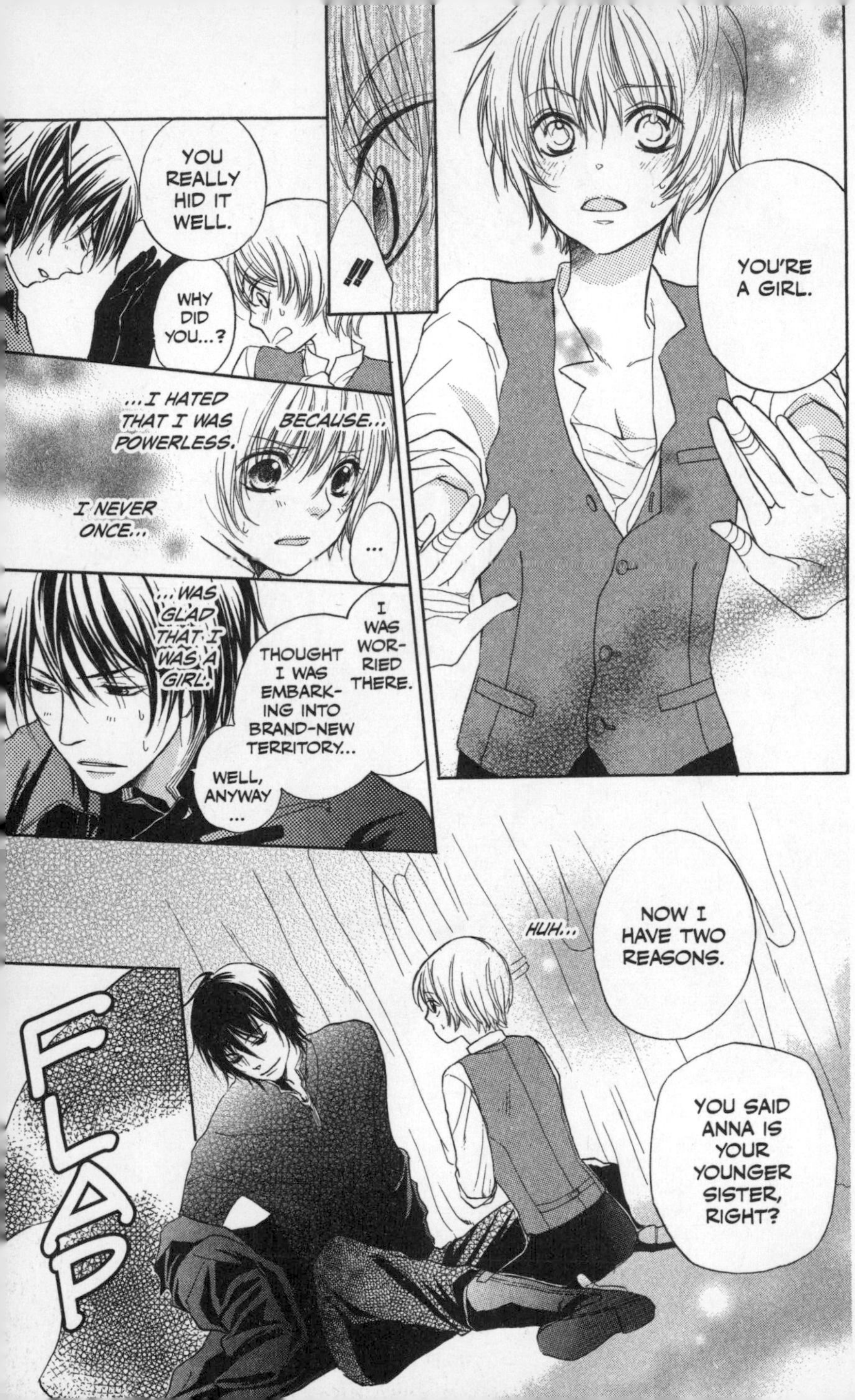
YOU'RE A GIRL.
!!
YOU REALLY HID IT WELL.
WHY DID YOU...?
BECAUSE...
...I HATED THAT I WAS POWERLESS.
I NEVER ONCE...
...
I WAS WORRIED THERE.
THOUGHT I WAS EMBARKING INTO BRAND-NEW TERRITORY...
...WAS GLAD THAT I WAS A GIRL.
WELL, ANYWAY ...
NOW I HAVE TWO REASONS.
HUH...
YOU SAID ANNA IS YOUR YOUNGER SISTER, RIGHT?
FLAP

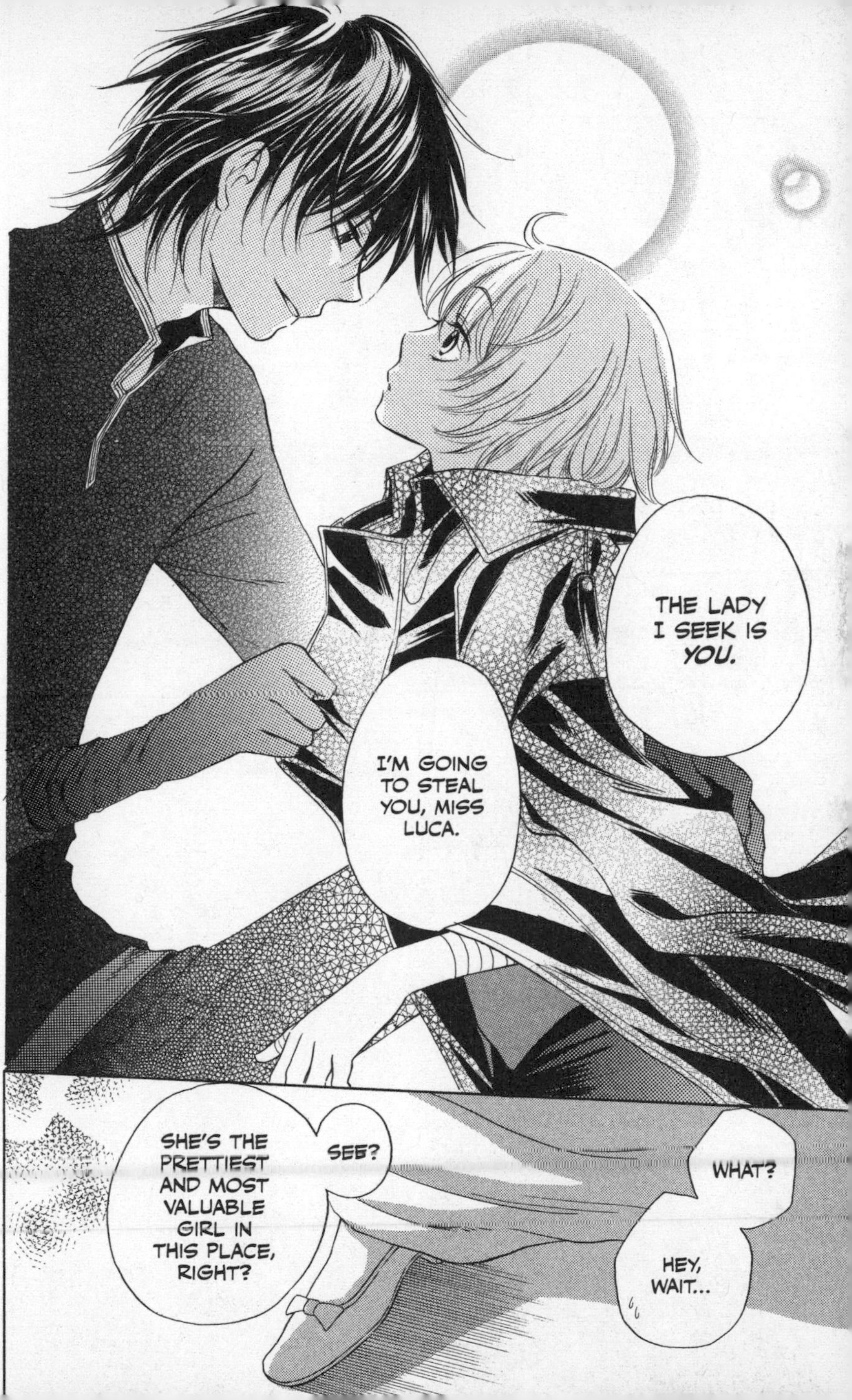
THE LADY I SEEK IS YOU.
I'M GOING TO STEAL YOU, MISS LUCA.
WHAT?
HEY, WAIT...
SEE?
SHE'S THE PRETTIEST AND MOST VALUABLE GIRL IN THIS PLACE, RIGHT?

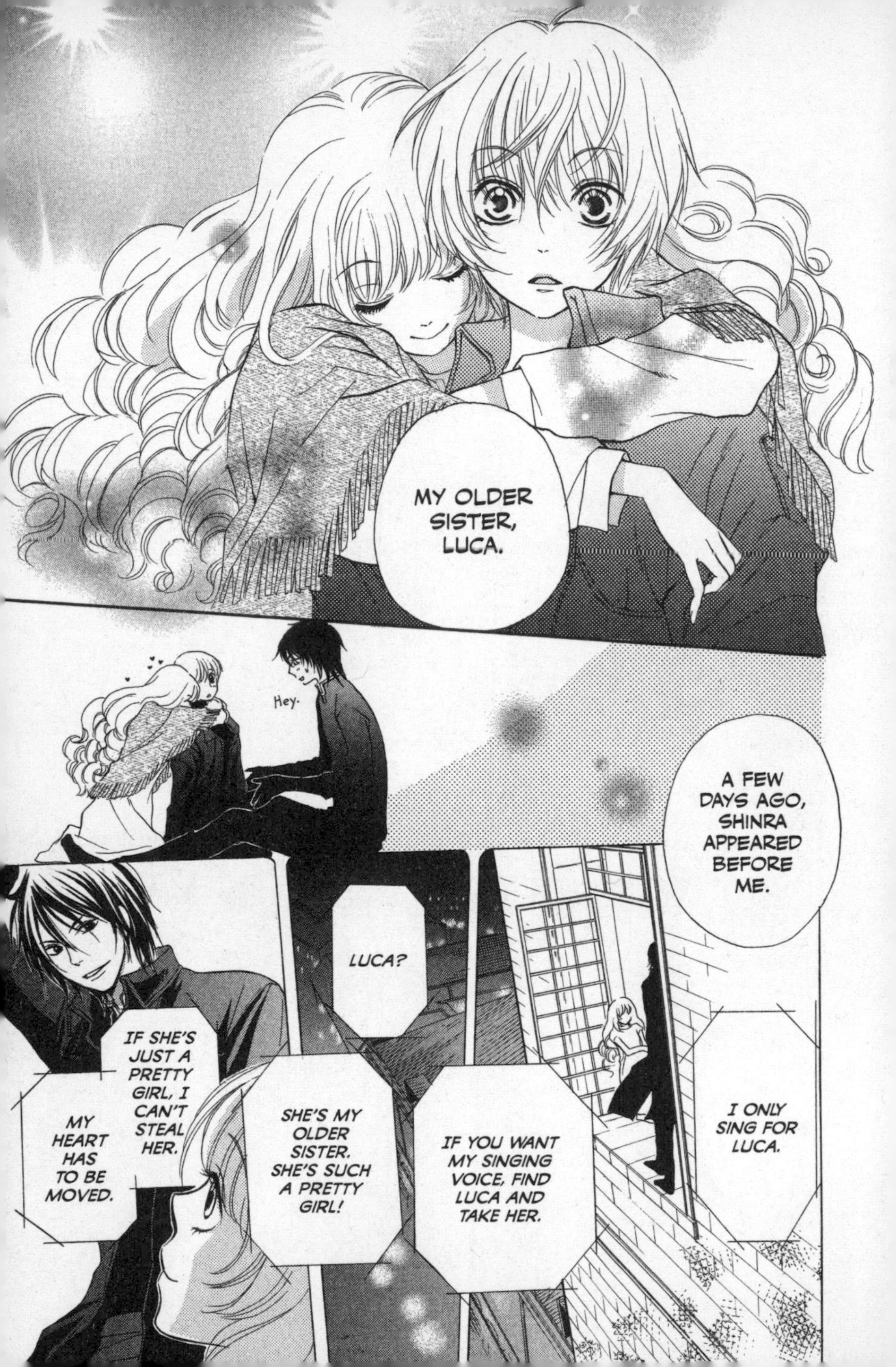
MY OLDER SISTER, LUCA.
A FEW DAYS AGO, SHINRA APPEARED BEFORE ME.
Hey.
I ONLY SING FOR LUCA.
IF YOU WANT MY SINGING VOICE, FIND LUCA AND TAKE HER.
LUCA?
SHE'S MY OLDER SISTER. SHE'S SUCH A PRETTY GIRL!
IF SHE'S JUST A PRETTY GIRL, I CAN'T STEAL HER.
MY HEART HAS TO BE MOVED.

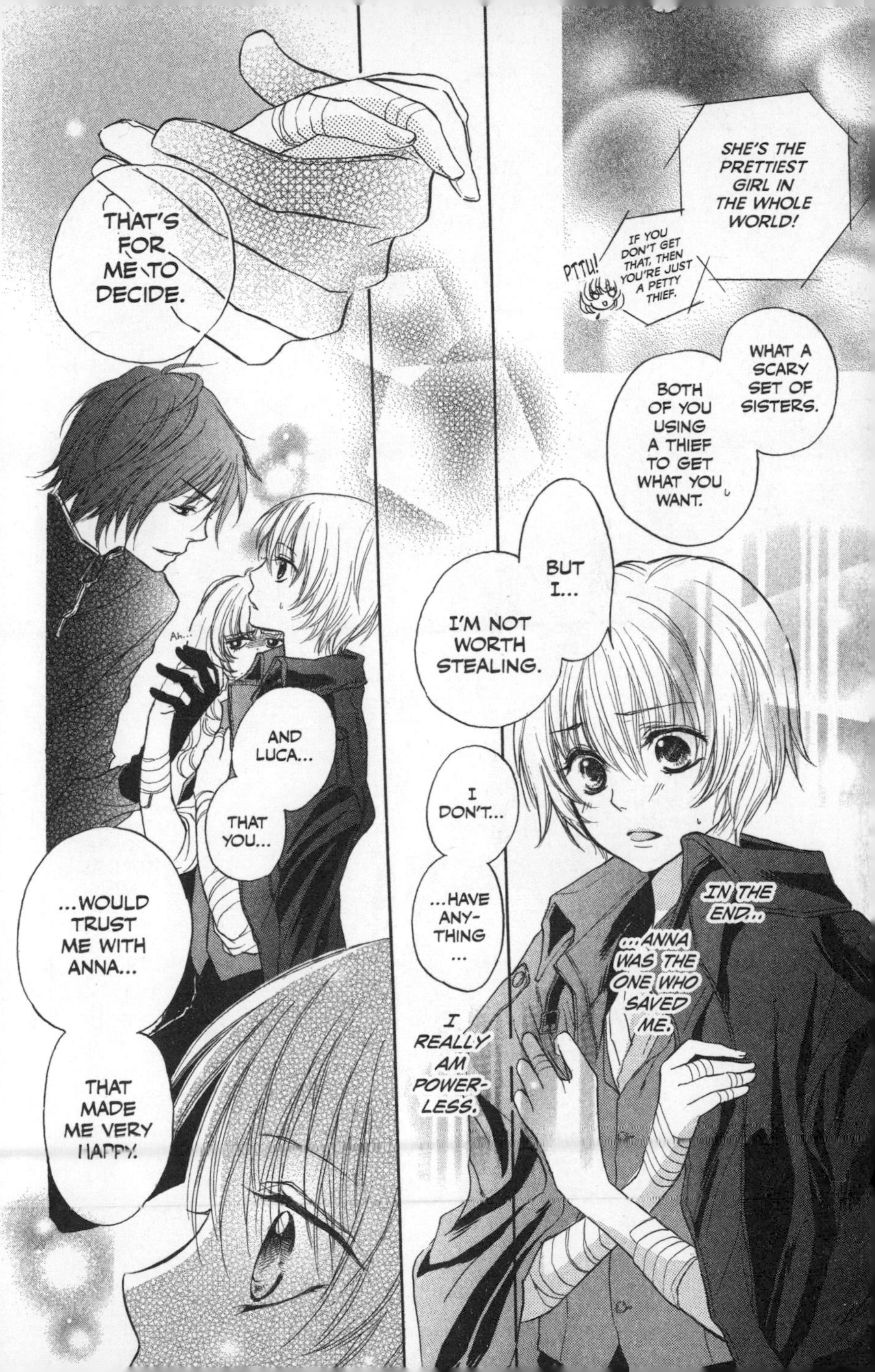
SHE'S THE PRETTIEST GIRL IN THE WHOLE WORLD!
PTTU!
IF YOU DON'T GET THAT, THEN YOU'RE JUST A PETTY THIEF.
WHAT A SCARY SET OF SISTERS.
BOTH OF YOU USING A THIEF TO GET WHAT YOU WANT.
BUT I...
I'M NOT WORTH STEALING.
IN THE END...
...ANNA WAS THE ONE WHO SAVED ME.
I DON'T...
...HAVE ANYTHING...
I REALLY AM POWERLESS.
THAT'S FOR ME TO DECIDE.
Ah...
AND LUCA...
THAT YOU...
...WOULD TRUST ME WITH ANNA...
THAT MADE ME VERY HAPPY.

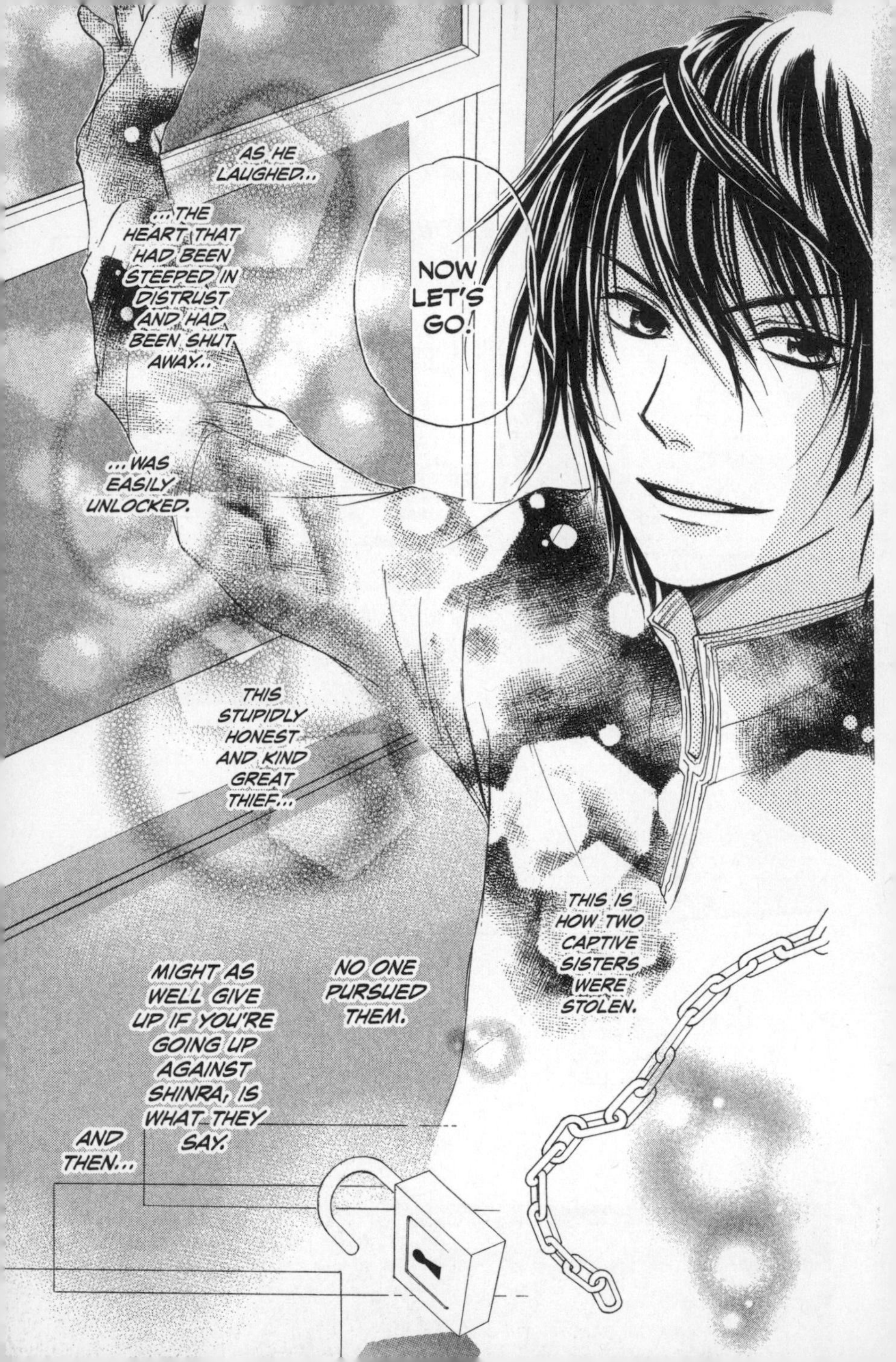
NOW LET'S GO!
AS HE LAUGHED...
...THE HEART THAT HAD BEEN STEEPED IN DISTRUST AND HAD BEEN SHUT AWAY...
...WAS EASILY UNLOCKED.
THIS STUPIDLY HONEST AND KIND GREAT THIEF...
THIS IS HOW TWO CAPTIVE SISTERS WERE STOLEN.
NO ONE PURSUED THEM.
MIGHT AS WELL GIVE UP IF YOU'RE GOING UP AGAINST SHINRA, IS WHAT THEY SAY.
AND THEN...

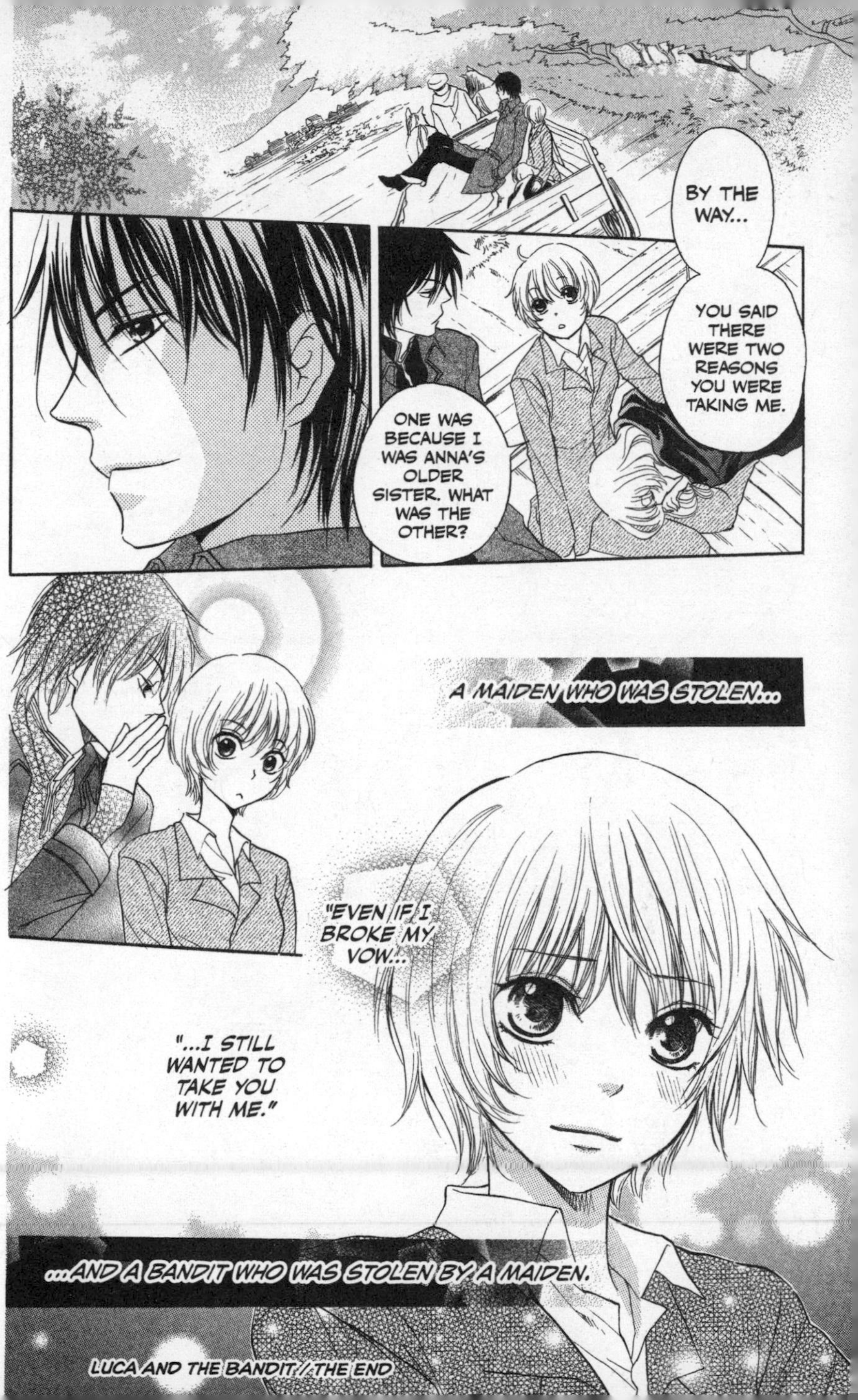
BY THE WAY...
YOU SAID THERE WERE TWO REASONS YOU WERE TAKING ME.
ONE WAS BECAUSE I WAS ANNA'S OLDER SISTER. WHAT WAS THE OTHER?
A MAIDEN WHO WAS STOLEN...
"EVEN IF I BROKE MY VOW...
"...I STILL WANTED TO TAKE YOU WITH ME."
...AND A BANDIT WHO WAS STOLEN BY A MAIDEN.
LUCA AND THE BANDIT / THE END

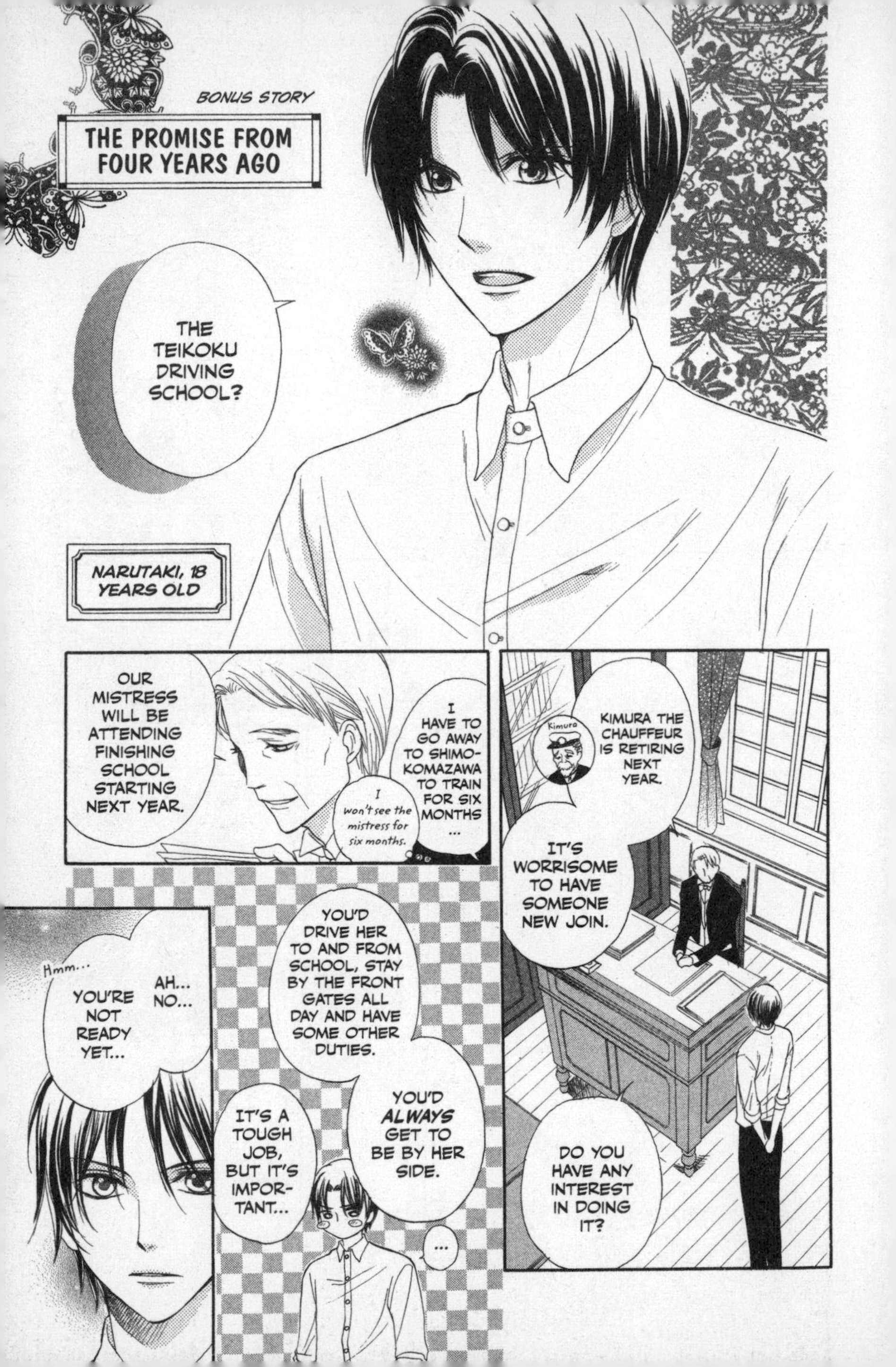

BONUS STORY
THE PROMISE FROM FOUR YEARS AGO
THE TEIKOKU DRIVING SCHOOL?
NARUTAKI, 18 YEARS OLD
KIMURA THE CHAUFFEUR IS RETIRING NEXT YEAR.
Kimura
IT'S WORRISOME TO HAVE SOMEONE NEW JOIN.
DO YOU HAVE ANY INTEREST IN DOING IT?
I HAVE TO GO AWAY TO SHIMO-KOMAZAWA TO TRAIN FOR SIX MONTHS ...
I won't see the mistress for six months.
OUR MISTRESS WILL BE ATTENDING FINISHING SCHOOL STARTING NEXT YEAR.
YOU'D DRIVE HER TO AND FROM SCHOOL, STAY BY THE FRONT GATES ALL DAY AND HAVE SOME OTHER DUTIES.
YOU'D *ALWAYS* GET TO BE BY HER SIDE.
IT'S A TOUGH JOB, BUT IT'S IMPOR-TANT...
...
AH... NO...
Hmm...
YOU'RE NOT READY YET...

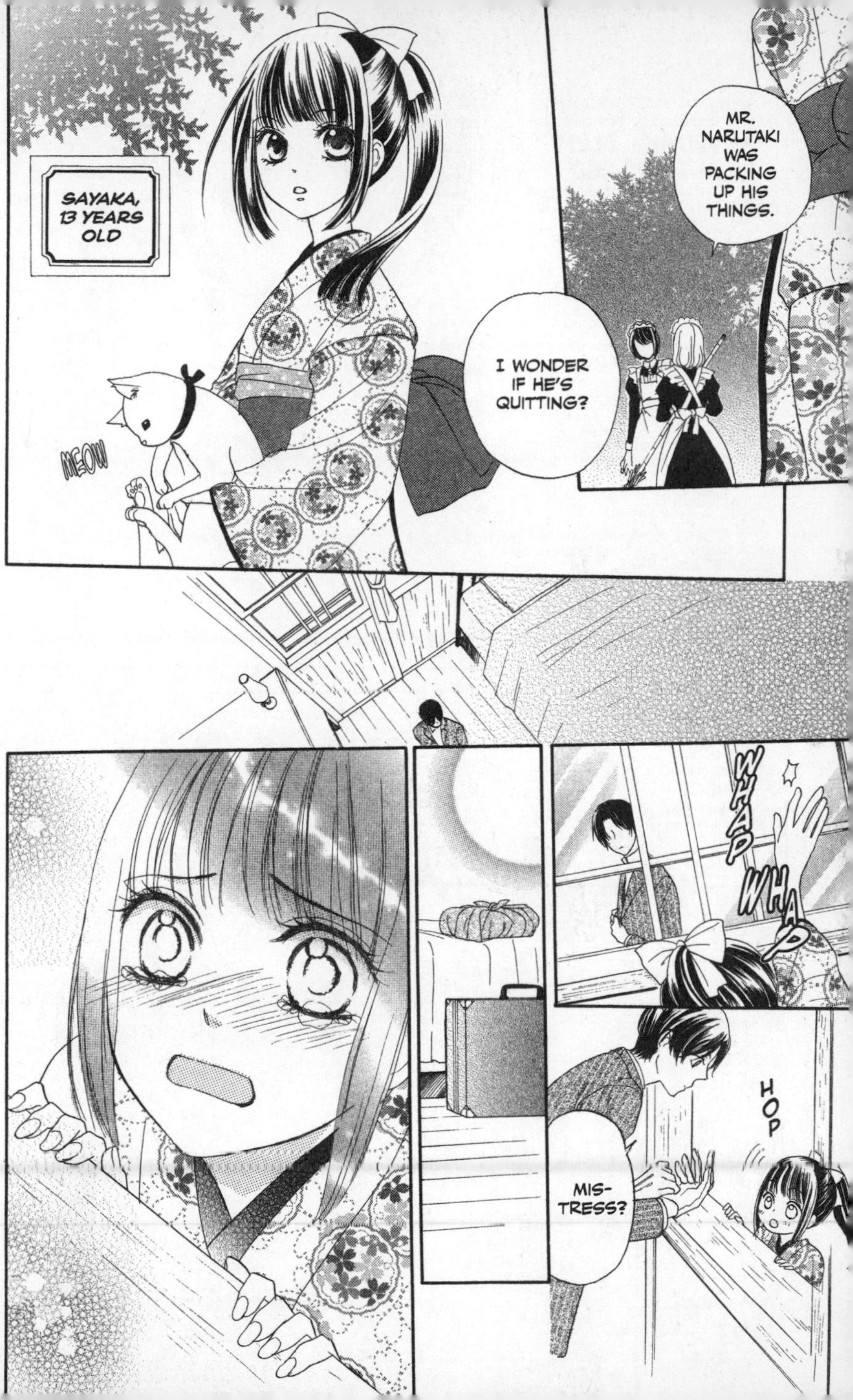
MR. NARUTAKI WAS PACKING UP HIS THINGS.
I WONDER IF HE'S QUITTING?
SAYAKA, 13 YEARS OLD
MEOW
WHAP WHAP
HOP
MIS-TRESS?

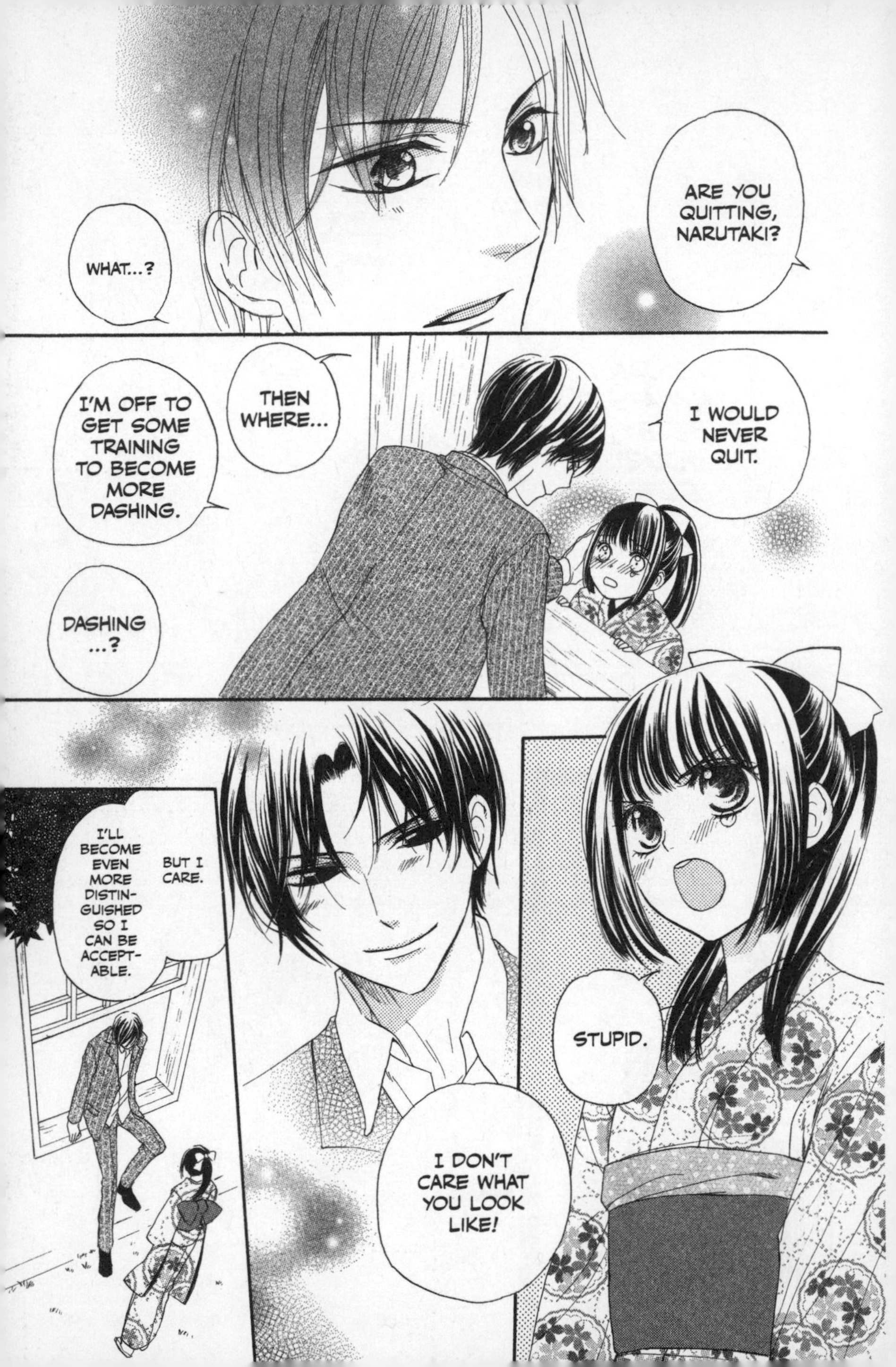
ARE YOU QUITTING, NARUTAKI?
WHAT...?
I WOULD NEVER QUIT.
THEN WHERE...
I'M OFF TO GET SOME TRAINING TO BECOME MORE DASHING.
DASHING ...?
STUPID.
I DON'T CARE WHAT YOU LOOK LIKE!
BUT I CARE.
I'LL BECOME EVEN MORE DISTIN-GUISHED SO I CAN BE ACCEPT-ABLE.

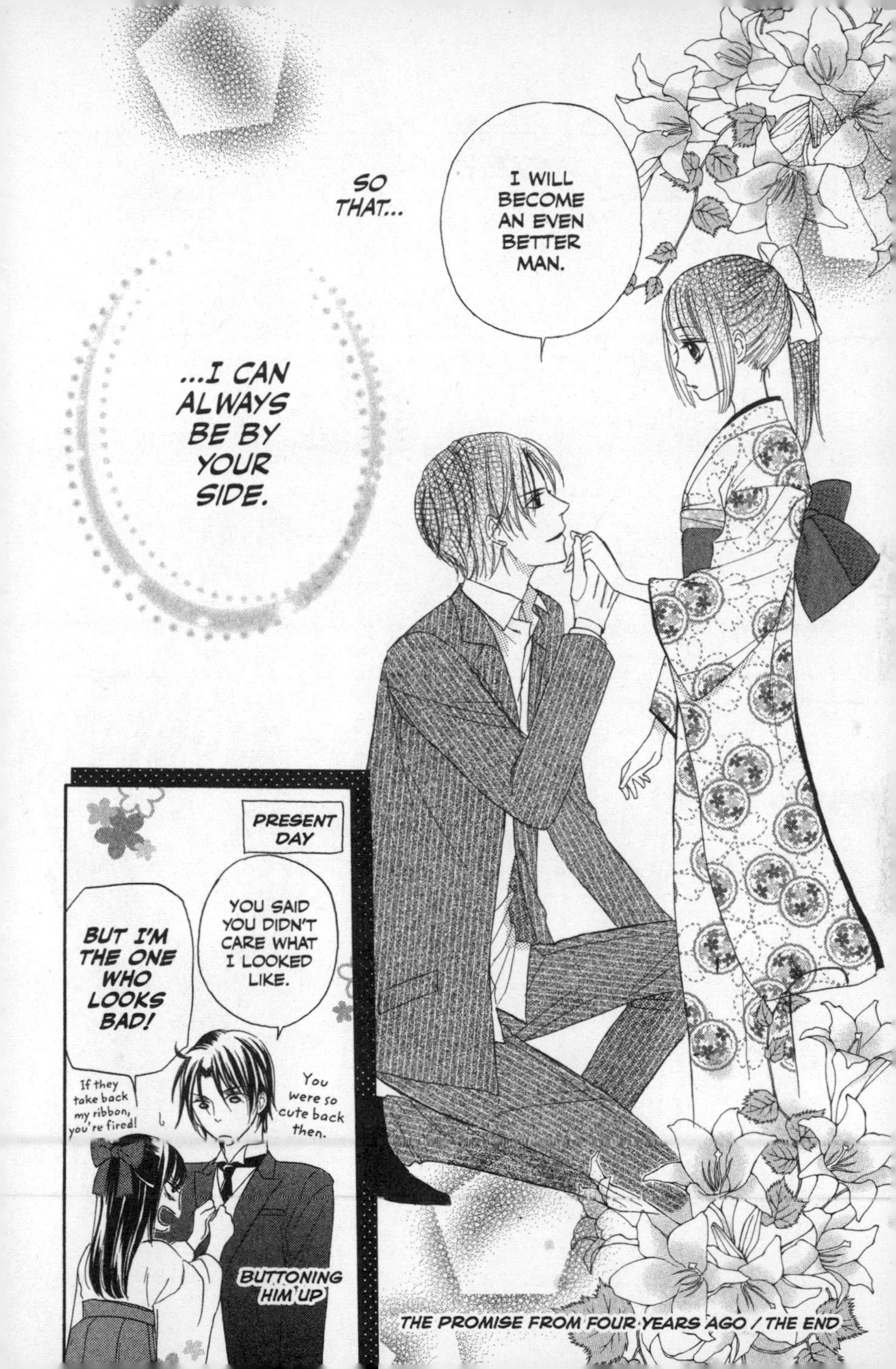
I WILL BECOME AN EVEN BETTER MAN.
SO THAT...
...I CAN ALWAYS BE BY YOUR SIDE.
PRESENT DAY
YOU SAID YOU DIDN'T CARE WHAT I LOOKED LIKE.
BUT I'M THE ONE WHO LOOKS BAD!
You were so cute back then.
If they take back my ribbon, you're fired!
BUTTONING HIM UP
THE PROMISE FROM FOUR YEARS AGO / THE END

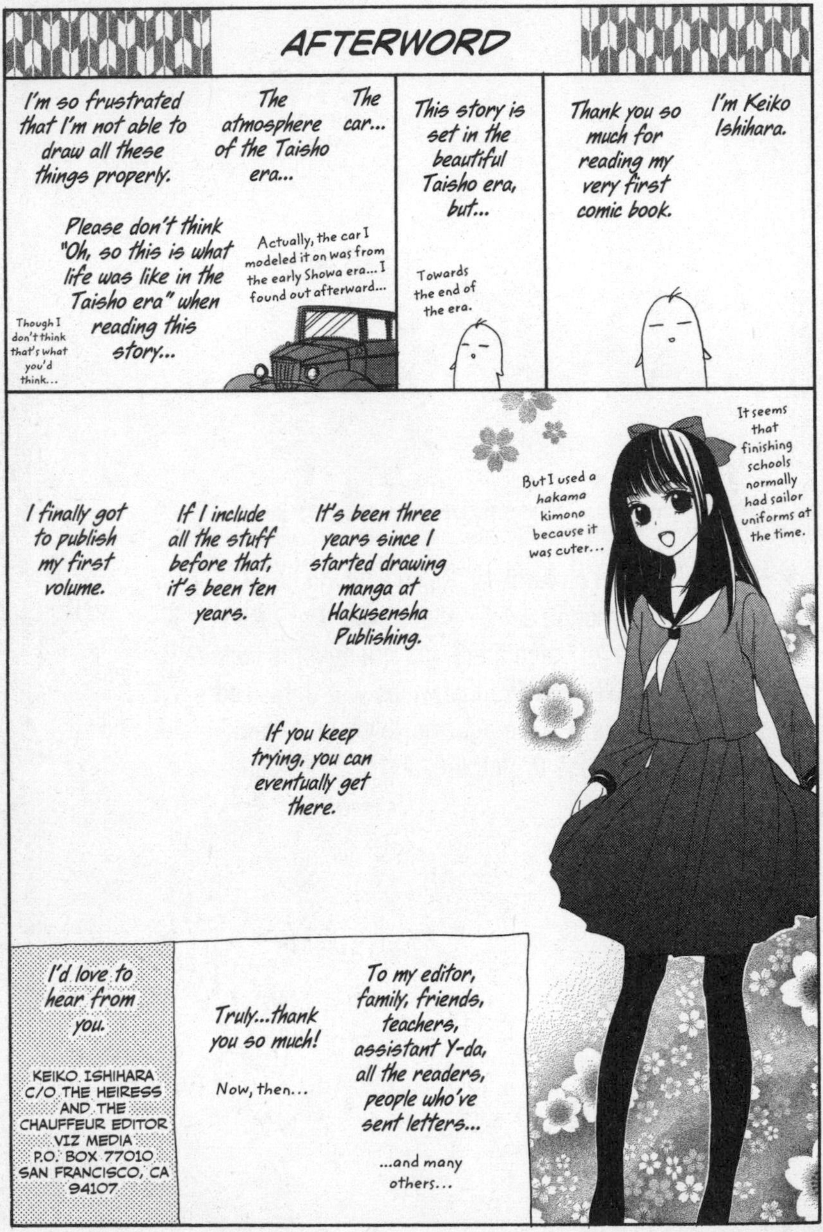
AFTERWORD
I'm Keiko Ishihara.
Thank you so much for reading my very first comic book.
This story is set in the beautiful Taisho era, but...
Towards the end of the era.
The car...
The atmosphere of the Taisho era...
I'm so frustrated that I'm not able to draw all these things properly.
Actually, the car I modeled it on was from the early Showa era... I found out afterward...
Please don't think "Oh, so this is what life was like in the Taisho era" when reading this story...
Though I don't think that's what you'd think...
It seems that finishing schools normally had sailor uniforms at the time.
But I used a hakama kimono because it was cuter...
It's been three years since I started drawing manga at Hakusensha Publishing.
If I include all the stuff before that, it's been ten years.
I finally got to publish my first volume.
If you keep trying, you can eventually get there.
To my editor, family, friends, teachers, assistant Y-da, all the readers, people who've sent letters...
...and many others...
Truly...thank you so much!
Now, then...
I'd love to hear from you.
KEIKO ISHIHARA
C/O THE HEIRESS AND THE CHAUFFEUR EDITOR
VIZ MEDIA
P.O. BOX 77010
SAN FRANCISCO, CA 94107

Born on April 14, Keiko Ishihara began her
manga career with *Keisan Desu Kara*
(It's All Calculated). Her other works include
Strange Dragon, which was serialized
in *LaLa* magazine. Ishihara is from
Hyogo Prefecture, and she loves cats.